Animal Ethics

There are many introductions to the animal ethics literature. There aren't many introductions to the practice of doing animal ethics. Bob Fischer's *Animal Ethics: A Contemporary Introduction* fills that gap, offering an accessible model of how animal ethics can be done today. The book takes up classic issues, such as the ethics of eating meat and experimenting on animals, but tackles them in an empirically informed and nuanced way. It also covers a range of relatively neglected issues in animal ethics, such as the possibility of insect sentience and the ethics of dealing with pests. Finally, the book doesn't assess every current practice using standard ethical theories, but tries to evaluate some of them using the moral frameworks endorsed by those involved. So, for instance, there is a chapter on the way that animal care and use committees try to justify some of the educational uses of animals, and the chapter on zoos considers the way that international zoological societies justify compromising animal welfare. The book wraps up with a discussion of the future of animal ethics. Each chapter opens with a helpful initial overview of the chapter and ends with a list of suggested readings to help students go further on their own.

Key Features

- Covers animal ethics from an empirically informed perspective, bringing philosophy into conversation with key issues in animal science, conservation biology, economics, ethology, and legal studies, among other fields
- Provides ample coverage of the most salient *current* topics, including, for example:
  ○ Debates about which animals are sentient
  ○ The suffering of wild animals
  ○ Research ethics
  ○ The boundaries of activism
- Avoids suggesting that animal ethics is simply the practice of applying the right general theory to a problem, instead allowing readers to first work out the specific costs and benefits of making ethical decisions
- Impresses upon the reader the need for her to work out for herself the best way forward with difficult ethical issues, suggesting that progress can indeed be made
- Includes summaries and recommended readings at the end of each chapter

Bob Fischer is Associate Professor of Philosophy at Texas State University. He's the editor of *The Routledge Handbook of Animal Ethics* (Routledge, 2020) and the author of *The Ethics of Eating Animals* (Routledge, 2020).

Routledge Contemporary Introductions to Philosophy
Series editor: *Paul K. Moser*, Loyola University of Chicago

This innovative, well-structured series is for students who have already done an introductory course in philosophy. Each book introduces a core general subject in contemporary philosophy and offers students an accessible but substantial transition from introductory to higher-level college work in that subject. The series is accessible to non-specialists and each book clearly motivates and expounds the problems and positions introduced. An orientating chapter briefly introduces its topic and reminds readers of any crucial material they need to have retained from a typical introductory course. Considerable attention is given to explaining the central philosophical problems of a subject and the main competing solutions and arguments for those solutions. The primary aim is to educate students in the main problems, positions and arguments of contemporary philosophy rather than to convince students of a single position.

Recently Published Volumes:

Phenomenology
Walter Hopp

Philosophical Logic
John MacFarlane

Philosophy of Action
Sarah K. Paul

Animal Ethics
Bob Fischer

Philosophy of Time
Sean Enda Power

For a full list of published *Routledge Contemporary Introductions to Philosophy*, please visit www.routledge.com/Routledge-Contemporary-Introductions-to-Philosophy /book-series/SE0111

Animal Ethics

A Contemporary Introduction

Bob Fischer

Routledge
Taylor & Francis Group

NEW YORK AND LONDON

First published 2021
by Routledge
52 Vanderbilt Avenue, New York, NY 10017

and by Routledge
2 Park Square, Milton Park, Abingdon, Oxon, OX14 4RN

Routledge is an imprint of the Taylor & Francis Group, an informa business

Library of Congress Cataloging-in-Publication Data
A catalog record for this book has been requested

ISBN: 978-1-138-48440-5 (hbk)
ISBN: 978-1-138-48443-6 (pbk)
ISBN: 978-1-351-05202-3 (ebk)

Typeset in Times New Roman
by Apex CoVantage, LLC

For Ms. Bettie—and for Jennifer, who loved her

Contents

Acknowledgments

If books were as good as their critics, then this one would be excellent. Cheryl Abbate told me everything was wrong with my views about cats. Heather Browning told me everything that was wrong with my claims about zoos. Candace Croney saved me from various errors in my survey of contemporary animal agriculture. Jim Davies pushed me to think much more carefully about animal consciousness. Trevor Hedberg brought some major structural issues to my attention. Jess du Toit improved the material on well-being and death. Carol Kline and Clare Palmer provided invaluable feedback on a chapter that, sadly, had to be cut for length. Steve McMullen helped me fine-tune my discussion of consumer ethics. Kian Mintz-Woo caught a number of problems in the moral theory chapter. Connor Kayhan Kianpour, Sean McMains, and two anonymous reviewers went through the whole manuscript with care, drawing my attention to more authorial failures than I care to admit. All around, I'm grateful.

Andy Beck, of course, deserves credit for letting me write the book in the first place. You couldn't ask for more understanding editor.

The production team made the book something you can hold. They did a lovely job.

Craig Hanks, my chair, gave me the time to write this book. For that, and much else, I'm in his debt.

Tori Cotton created the index and helped me check the proofs—two tasks that were onerous indeed. Thank you.

Finally, and with deep appreciation for her support and encouragement along the way: Alyse Spiehler. Of all the people with whom I've estimated urban rodent populations, you're my favorite.

1 Introduction

OVERVIEW

What's good for humans often conflicts with what's good for animals. How should we navigate those conflicts? When we think seriously and systematically about that question, we're on our way to doing animal ethics. This chapter introduces the idea of doing ethics, tackles some preliminaries about the language we use to discuss animals, and surveys the contents of the book. It also offers some insights into my approach to animal ethics. Ethics is hard, so it's difficult to be confident about our conclusions. At the same time, the stakes are high, both for people and animals, so we have to be willing to draw some tentative conclusions.

We eat animals. We wear their skins. We experiment on them, confine them in zoos, and regard them as nuisances who need to be managed. By and large, it isn't good for animals to be eaten, turned into belts, or serve as models in our research. Indeed, it seems pretty bad for them. But since it's good for us to use them in these ways, we do.

It may turn out, of course, that there's nothing wrong about the way that we use nonhuman animals. (I say "nonhuman" animals because we're animals too. More on language in a bit.) But even if there isn't, we shouldn't pretend that we're living in a world where animals are generally better off as a result of their interactions with us. Most the time, we aren't *trying* to be cruel. Most of us care, at least to some degree, about how things go for animals. But at the same time, we want to address more or less pressing human interests—economic, nutritional, aesthetic, medical, and so on—which happen to conflict in significant ways with what's good for nonhuman beings.

This book is about the ethical questions that these conflicts raise, and my goal is to help you think more clearly about them. Can we defend the way we treat animals? If so, how? If not, why not? Moreover, even if we *can* defend our practices, what should we strive for? That is, what would the ideal way of relating to animals be—even if we aren't morally required to do what's ideal? And if there's something wrong with what we're doing, what would it take to fix things—or at least to improve them?

You'll need a bit of background to grapple with these questions. However, this may be your first time thinking about animal ethics—or ethics generally—in a systematic way. So in the next few chapters, I'll give you an overview of the ideas, arguments, and major moral theories that have shaped the contemporary discussion. Then, we'll look at a range of specific ethical issues, including animal agriculture, zoos, pest control, the so-called "cat wars," and the ethics of activism. We'll conclude with some brief reflections on the future of animal ethics.

I should say at the outset that I'm trying to introduce you to animal ethics as a thing you might do, not as a literature about which you might learn. My goal isn't to survey as much as possible of what philosophers have said on the topic. There are excellent introductions to animal ethics that do have that goal, or something like it, and I encourage you to have a look at them. My favorite is Angus Taylor's *Animals and Ethics: An Overview of the Philosophical Debate*, which provides exactly what the title suggests and does it exceptionally well. Since there's no sense reinventing the wheel, I need to take a different tack.

My hope is to strike a balance between two goals: first, bringing you up to speed; second, modeling how animal ethics can be done. After all, animal ethics is a field of inquiry, and I want you to get a sense of how to do the inquiring. So while I often just map out theoretical options—especially in the first third of the book—I won't shy away from defending particular conclusions at various points along the way. I want you to see *how* I reason for this thesis or that; I want you to recognize me *doing* ethics, not just talking *about* ethics. That being said, I'm not expecting you to agree with me at every turn, or even most of the time. In fact, you'll get much more out of this book if you are highly critical of what I say. Where have I gotten the empirical details wrong? Where have I framed things poorly? Where have I relied on a mistaken moral assumption? When you start thinking through those questions, you'll be doing animal ethics.

In the rest of this chapter, we'll go over a few preliminaries. We'll begin with just a few thoughts about ethics as a field of study. Then, I want to explain some of the linguistic choices I make in this book. I'll wrap up with a preview of coming attractions.

Ethics

Ethics is one of the main subfields of philosophy, alongside epistemology, or the study of knowledge; metaphysics, or the study of reality; and logic, or the study of reasoning. We could give an equally simple characterization of ethics: say, the study of right and wrong. But that isn't so helpful, as ethics is about much more than right and wrong: it's also about what's valuable ("axiology") and broader questions about how we should live. Moreover, there's no good catchall expression for those topics. If I told you, for instance, that "ethics is the study of morality," I doubt you'd feel that you'd learned much.

Here's the upshot. It's really hard to give a good definition of "ethics" or "morality"—terms that I'm going to use interchangeably in this book. It's so hard, in fact, that I won't try. But we don't need a definition to get a sense of what it means to study ethics. There are essentially two ways into the discipline. You've already seen the first one: We look at something we do and ask, "Is this okay? Are there reasons *not* to act this way—reasons that should override whatever led us to act this way in the first place?" (The flipside: We look at something people condemn and ask, "Is this really wrong? Do people really have good reasons to be so critical of this behavior?")

So, for instance, we might notice that people breed brachycephalic dogs—dogs with extremely short snouts, like bulldogs and pugs—who consistently have respiratory problems as a result. Essentially, their nostrils are too small, their soft palate is too long, and their tracheas are too narrow. So, brachycephalic dogs are at risk of not getting enough oxygen when they exert themselves and can collapse as result; what's more, they're prone to heat stroke and heart disease. Nevertheless, many people think that these breeds are especially cute; they love the "squashed face" look. Is it okay to breed these dogs? If so, why? If not, why not? As soon as we start down this path, we're doing ethics. We identify the affected parties, we sort through the costs and benefits, we try to tease apart different motivations, we consider analogous cases, and so on. In other words, we try to think systematically about the reasons for and against what people do and reach a conclusion on that basis.

The first way into ethics starts with behavior—with things people do. The second way starts with principles—with moral generalizations. For instance, you shouldn't lie. But if you're in Germany in 1942, and you're hiding Jews in your attic, and the Nazis are at your door asking whether you've seen any Jews, then you'd better say that you haven't seen any. You also shouldn't steal. But if your friend is suicidal and you know where he keeps his pistol, then it's fine to take it without his permission. Obviously, you shouldn't kill people. But if someone attacks you with no provocation and your only means of self-defense is to use a deadly weapon, then use it you may. Once we recognize this, we quickly realize that these commonsense generalizations—don't lie, don't steal, don't kill people—aren't exceptionless principles. Instead, they are more like rules of thumb: very good guides to what you ought to do most of the time and very bad guides to what you should do all the time.

This invites us to ask: *Why* are these principles good rules of thumb? What are they getting right? Likewise, why are the exceptions, exceptions? What's special about those cases? There are lots of hypotheses to consider. Is the ultimate truth about morality that we ought to make the world the best place we can? Is it that we ought to do our best to respect others? Is it that we ought to cultivate character traits that allow us to live well with others? Perhaps instead, ethics is about pursuing an end to oppressive structures or about enabling people to live out their own visions of the good life. And again, we're doing ethics when we head down this path. We're investigating why we should do the things we ought to do; we're trying to figure out what explains why the right things are right and the wrong things are wrong (and the rest is the rest).

It isn't easy, and there's a real risk that our biases will lead us to endorse the conclusions that we want to be true, rather than those for which we can offer the best arguments, all things considered. But that's why ethics isn't something we do alone, in the privacy of our homes, cut off from the rest of the world. Instead, it's something we do together, in public, with as many different sorts of people as possible. We need to have our biases checked, and the best people to do that are the ones who aren't like us in various ways.

Ethics is the business of thinking hard about how to fit together all our ideas about what's good and bad, right and wrong, morally important and morally insignificant. It's an attempt to come up with principles that make sense of our moral judgments. Inevitably, our views won't fit together perfectly, and so we will have to do a lot of work, figuring out exactly which view should change and why. This is something we do in conversation with others, checking our biases and recognizing that the aim is rational persuasion: we are looking for conclusions that others can accept and take seriously, not just ones that we happen to like, given our own position in the world and its accompanying privileges.

With that basic picture in mind, there are two basic mistakes we should work to avoid when we launch into ethics. The first is being *overconfident*, being altogether too sure that we have things figured out. We shouldn't forget that history is littered with examples of moral error. What's more, we don't have to look into the distant past. There are still people who praise slavery as God's plan. And those who think that if a woman has sex before marriage, she should be killed for shaming her family. And those who think there's nothing wrong with blood sports, like dogfighting and cockfighting. If you were raised in different circumstances, you might well agree. Our moral views are shaped by all sorts of factors—when we were born, where we were born, to whom we were born, and much else. We all come from somewhere and bring that place's moral baggage along with us. So, we need to scrutinize ourselves; we need to question what feels obvious.

This requires humility. It isn't so hard to accept that people made some major moral mistakes *in the past*. It isn't so hard to accept that *other* people are making some major moral mistakes now. But it's uncomfortable to think that *we* might be making equally significant errors. Could it be true that we believe things that aren't simply incorrect, but are horrifically and terribly incorrect, causing untold amounts of suffering? Yes, it could, as it's been true of very many others. So let's be careful.

Overconfidence isn't our only problem. The other blunder is *under*confidence. When people contemplate all the moral disagreement in the world, they sometimes conclude that we just shouldn't make any ethical judgments about what other people do. On this view, ethics is a private matter. The thought often comes from a good place. It can be motivated by the very humility for which I've argued, by the idea that we shouldn't assume that we have a corner on the truth. Quite often, people are also trying to be respectful of difference, recognizing that there are many ways of putting a life together.

I have no objection to being humble and respecting difference. Three cheers for both. At the same time, though, we should remember two things. First of all, humility and respect for difference aren't barriers to *self*-assessment. Can we defend our own moral views from our own criticisms? Not always. It's often quite discouraging, in fact, to realize how far we are from our own ideals. So, we can do ethics to get our *own* houses in order: to improve the coherence and plausibility of our views, quite independently of whether we pass judgment on what anyone else does.

Second, let's not be too quick to concede to those who want to quarantine morality to the private realm. Moral principles are like social infrastructure: we use moral principles—moral norms—to guide our interactions with one another. For instance, we rightly criticize people for promoting racist ideologies, and it seems ridiculous to say that we shouldn't make judgments about the wrongness of promoting those perspectives. Indeed, it's because it's wrong to promote racist ideologies that it's appropriate to discourage people from promoting them, perhaps by creating hurdles so that it's harder for them to accomplish their goals. By contrast, we shouldn't criticize people for promoting the reduction of carbon emissions, as that definitely *isn't* wrong. As a result, it would be a mistake to make it harder for people to promote more climate-friendly policies. On the face of it, anyway, these kinds of moral judgments help us navigate the social world.

Moreover, as the world becomes more interconnected, it's increasingly difficult to avoid those interactions. We have to find ways of balancing the interests of diverse groups, and that requires finding norms that people can accept despite their many differences. They need to be designed to be compelling to anyone who's willing to think hard about how to live together. This isn't easy, and I'm not saying that we'll get there without an enormous number of false starts. But because we aren't islands, living fully independent lives, we have to try. Theorizing about ethical problems can be something we do in public, for the public, as members of the public. It can be a thing we do to help us live together better.

As you might imagine, there is much more to be said here. But for now, that will have to do. I'll say much more about practical problems in the second half of the book; I'll say a lot about moral principles and theories in the first half. The goal so far has just been to get us in the right frame of mind: appreciating the familiarity of ethical reasoning, being cautioned against being too sure that we have things figured out, and being encouraged not to give up too soon.

Before going any further, though, we need to talk about language.

Language

You might be surprised by the way I phrase things in this book. Consider, for instance, the term "companion animal." If you ask someone who works at an airline about companion animals, they might think you're talking about emotional support animals—the animals that people bring on board for mental health reasons.[1] In philosophical circles, though, people use the phrase "companion animals" to refer to many of those animals that everyone else calls "pets." What's so bad about the term "pets"? Why the terminological change?

This issue actually made it into the news several years ago. *The Journal of Animal Ethics* launched in 2011, and in its first issue, the editors included a note on the importance of language:

> we need to be mindful of our words. Language is the means by which we understand and conceptualize the world around us. . . . This obvious point has major implications for how we conceptualize and think about the many

worlds of animals. The words we use can help us to imagine other worlds, but more usually, they reflect and solidify our existing perceptions. . . . [Our] existing language about animals is the language of past thought—and crucially, that past is littered with derogatory terminology: "brutes," "beasts," "bestial," "critters," "subhuman," and the like. We will not be able to think clearly unless we discipline ourselves to use more impartial nouns and adjectives in our exploration of animals and our moral relations with them. . . . Specifically, we are inviting authors to use "companion animals" rather than "pets." Despite its prevalence, "pets" is surely a derogatory term with respect to both the animals concerned and their human caregivers. Again, the word "owners," though technically correct in law, harks back to a previous age when animals were regarded as just that: property, machines or things to use without moral constraint.

(Linzey and Cohn 2011, vii)

Commentators were quick to make fun of the editors for their remarks, but mixed in with the mocking, there was the occasional substantive response. Here's one example from Chuck Colson, a then-prominent evangelical Christian:

Of course, what we're seeing here is [the editors of *The Journal of Animal Ethics*] own prejudgment—that humans and animals are equals. . . . But we are not all equal. Humans alone bear the image of God. And animals cannot have "rights" in the way we humans do. Should we care for animals as part of God's creation? Of course. Christians have long recognized this. It was William Wilberforce, after all, who founded the Society for the Prevention of Cruelty to Animals. But to treat them as equals or even near-equals? Never.

(Colson 2011)

This isn't the place to assess the many claims on which this reply depends, including whether humans and animals are equals, whether anyone (human or nonhuman) bears the image of God, and whether animals can have rights.[2] For now, let's just note that Colson would agree with Linzey that we need to be mindful of our words, using language that reflects a defensible understanding of the beings in question. Whatever we make of Colson's response, he's right that the linguistic controversy isn't really about language, but about the way we understand both human and nonhuman animals. The disagreements here are deep.[3]

One of the basic ideas in this book is that we should think about many animals as *sentient individuals*. This is, each of these animals is a conscious being with a vantage point on the world, capable of feeling pain and pleasure, some*one* rather than some*thing*. To be clear: this alone doesn't imply that animals have rights, or that it's wrong to confine them in zoos, or that we shouldn't eat them. All it implies is that animals aren't robots: there's something it's like to be a bat, and it isn't always nice; bats feel, and they sometimes suffer. To signal that this assumption is in the background, I'll refer to most individual animals as "he" or "she," rather than "it."

Likewise, I'll talk about animals "who" have some feature, as opposed to animals "that" have it. And for the reason mentioned at the beginning of the chapter, I'll often talk about "nonhuman" animals to remind us that while we're different, we aren't *categorically* different from the individuals with whom this book is concerned.

I could go further. For instance, I could insist on talking about "fishes" rather than "fish," to remind us that a school of fish is, in fact, a collection of individuals rather than an undifferentiated mass. This could help us remember that there's a crucial difference between a pile of fishes on the deck of a boat and a heap of grain in a barn: each fish has a perspective; kernels of grain don't. But if we do this for fishes, then what about deer, moose, and sheep? "Deers," "mooses," and "sheeps"? I confess that, for aesthetic reasons, I'm unwilling to make that adjustment. I'm not exactly proud of it, but there it is. For the same reason, I'll often slide without commentary between terms like "human beings" and "people," even though there are philosophers who argue that animals are persons and so count as people. And to keep things interesting, I'll use terms like "critter" despite allegations that it's somehow demeaning. Variety is not just the spice of life, but of language, and I simply can't bring myself to write "human animal" and "nonhuman animal" every single time.

In some cases, however, my resistance isn't simply aesthetic. For instance, even if we have a very high view of nonhuman animals, we might not be sold on the view that we ought to talk in terms of "companion animals" rather than in terms of "pets." This is because even if the term "pets" signals that those animals are inferior to their owners, we might think it's important to use language that reflects the way people actually relate to those animals. Consider the way people often object to euphemisms like "enhanced interrogation techniques," which are used to avoid saying "torture," or the way that Southerners talked about "bonded labor" instead of "slave labor." When people criticize such euphemisms, they are essentially saying, "Don't pretend that you are doing something any less horrible than you actually are" or "Don't pretend that this system is anything other than what it is." And we might have a similar thought here: "Don't pretend that all dogs are 'companion animals.' Some of them live their lives in chains; some are beaten; many are neglected to some degree. Almost all live much shorter and poorer lives than they would if their owners were willing to pay for the best veterinary care available. Those are pets, not companions. Don't mask the problem by changing the language."

In other words, we don't need to limit ourselves to the phrase "companion animals" to communicate our respect for those animals. After all, the person who insists on saying "torture" rather than "enhanced interrogation techniques" respects the victims of torture at least as much as anyone else, if not more. Instead, if we just use "companion animals," we're making a strategic choice: we're saying we think we ought to use language that *doesn't* reflect many actual human–animal relationships in hopes of *improving* those relationships. And maybe it will. Or maybe it won't: perhaps that will just make us think we've made progress, while the ugly realities persist. It would take some work to show that this linguistic change is going to do what we might want it to do, and we can't do that work here. (I could make similar remarks about other expressions that have become popular among those who write in defense of animals, such as "farmed" animals as opposed to "farm animals," which is supposed to indicate more clearly that these are animals who are farmed rather than individuals whose purpose it is to be farmed.)

Here's the upshot. Language matters. Sometimes, I basically agree with arguments for revising our linguistic habits—for instance, I'll talk about "companion animals" as opposed to "pets." In other cases, I disagree with those arguments, and I'll use terms like "owners" instead of "guardians." (After all, even if animals shouldn't be treated like property, they so very often are.) And in other cases still, I'll let other values—such as aesthetic ones—guide my linguistic choices. I hope you recognize and reflect on these decisions and criticize me if you think I've made the wrong ones.

Coming Attractions

In what remains, I want to give you a quick overview of what's coming. The next chapter introduces you to some of the most foundational ideas in animal ethics: the idea of the moral community and the concept of speciesism. By the end of it, we'll see that we need to know a bit more about the minds of animals, so that's the subject of Chapter 3. After dipping our toes in those waters, we'll be ready to get back to moral theory, bring us to Chapters 4 and 5. They're a pair: the first tackles questions about what's good and bad for animals; the second looks at ways of theorizing about acting rightly and wrongly.

Next, you'll find a three-chapter block on animals as food. Unlike many introductions to animal ethics, I've decided to devote an entire chapter to the state of play in animal agriculture and aquaculture—that is, farming on land and farming in the sea. Following Peter Singer, who led the way in this respect, my overview is drawn almost entirely from industry rather than activist sources. The chapter following is devoted to assessing the industry, as well as the ethics of purchasing and consuming products from it. Immediately after that, you'll get a chapter on the fishing industry, which is importantly different from agriculture and aquaculture because the animals it kills are wild.

We then turn from food to research. The first of a pair of chapters focuses on the institutional context in which animal research and use occurs, with special attention to the committees that approve or disapprove those uses. Then, there's a more traditional investigation of whether and when animal research is justified.

The rest of the book is a tour through issues that I find interesting. We consider ways of improving zoos, the complexities of pest management, puzzles associated with having cats, and the ethics of activism. We wrap up with some brief reflections on the future of animal ethics.

As you'll see, I spend quite a lot of time on empirical and institutional issues—the entire chapter on agriculture and aquaculture, the legal loophole that allows for private zoos, and the difficulties of estimating rat populations. This is not a book about animal welfare or the challenges of conservation biology. It's a book about ethics. But insofar as our goal is to answer questions about what we ought to do and not simply wax eloquently about the rights of animals in the abstract, we had better know some things about what's feasible: about what we can actually get people to do and about what seems to be politically possible—even if, quite rightly, we also spend some time thinking about what we should hope for. Ethics, as I think of it, involves flitting back and forth between our ideals and our coldest, clear-eyed judgments about what's actually doable in the world in which we find ourselves. Those judgments may be tremendously far apart, or—in rare and hopeful cases—they may align perfectly. But it won't do any good to abandon either perspective. We have to keep both in mind. So if anything, I worry that there's too little empirical work in this book, not too much.

You'll see something else. Like all introductions, this one's opinionated: I have my views, and from time to time, I lay them on the table. As you might imagine, very few people write introductions to animal ethics who don't care at all about animals. It would be surprising if I didn't have any objections to the status quo.

Nevertheless, I think you'll see that I'm less opinionated than you might expect. Early in my college career, shortly after I decided to study philosophy, I found myself listening in on a conversation among some older students. A senior philosophy major was chatting with some of his friends who were studying other things, and they were asking him about his degree choice. He said that before he started studying philosophy, he would hear an argument, find it compelling, and then change his mind. A bit later, he would hear a different argument for the opposite conclusion, find it compelling, and change his mind again. And so he went, back and forth, influenced by whatever reasoning he had heard most recently. After studying philosophy, though, he wasn't so easily influenced. He was much better at seeing the flaws in arguments. Instead of constantly changing his mind, he now sticks to his guns.

My experience in philosophy has been both very similar and dramatically different. It's been similar in that philosophy has indeed improved my ability to assess the merits of arguments. I'm less easily taken in by bad reasoning than I once was—though perhaps still not as good as I should be! However, philosophy has in general lowered rather than raised my confidence about what to believe. When it comes to many of the biggest questions we face, I generally feel less sure about how to answer them than I once did.

I don't know how common this is. My impression, though, is that many philosophers have very strong views about all sorts of important moral questions. They are really confident about what we should do with respect to immigration or whether abortion is ever permissible. So, when they write introductory books like this one, their main challenge is to provide some semblance of neutrality. They are pretty confident that they know what we should do. They just recognize that, given that they are operating as teachers in this context, they shouldn't be too heavy-handed about their views. Instead, they should try to provide a range of perspectives and more or less even-handedly discuss the advantages and disadvantages of each.

The longer I study philosophy, though, the less confident I am about all sorts of things. So I don't find neutrality particularly challenging: I feel very well equipped to help you see the advantages and disadvantages of a wide range of views, as so many of them seem plausible to me in one way or another. Instead, my challenge is saying anything about how to decide among these views. When I do tip my hand, then, I'm not trying to convince you based on my say-so. Instead, I'm trying to model that I think animal ethics should get somewhere. I'm trying to show you that this isn't a game; we aren't just mapping out options for the fun of it. There is an enormous amount at stake, as a world reimagined for animals would be very different from the one we inhabit. This means, on the one hand, that we need to be very careful to get things right. On the other, though, it means that we need to be willing to draw some conclusions.

Further Reading

Armstrong, Susan J., and Richard G. Botzler. 2016. *The Animal Ethics Reader*. New York: Routledge.

DeGrazia, David. 2002. *Animal Rights: A Very Short Introduction*. New York: Oxford University Press.

Gruen, Lori. 2011. *Ethics and Animals: An Introduction*. New York: Cambridge University Press.

Nobis, Nathan. 2016. *Animals and Ethics 101: Thinking Critically About Animal Rights*. Open Philosophy Press.

Taylor, Angus. 2009. *Animals and Ethics: An Overview of the Philosophical Debate*. Peterborough, ON: Broadview Press.

Notes

1. According to the Air Carrier Access Act (ACAA), airlines must allow emotional support animals on board, assuming that certain requirements are satisfied. Some of them are related to species. For instance, airlines are "never required to accept snakes, reptiles, ferrets, rodents, sugar gliders, and spiders" (US DoT 2020). Legally, emotional support animals aren't service animals; instead, they are companion animals that provide therapeutic benefits to individuals with diagnosed mental or psychiatric conditions. According to the Americans with Disabilities Act (ADA), only dogs can be service animals, and they have to be trained to perform tasks for, or otherwise help, someone with a disability. In principle, animals of any species can be emotional support animals, and they don't need to be trained.
2. For a bit on the equality question, see the next chapter; for more on equality and some discussion of animal rights, see Chapter 5.
3. However, while they're deep, they're a bit less deep than you might think. One of the editors of *The Journal of Animal Ethics*, Andrew Linzey, is a Christian theologian too.

References

Colson, Chuck. 2011. "Pets vs. Companion Animals: Word Matter." *Christian Headlines*, May 17. www.christianheadlines.com/columnists/breakpoint/pets-vs-companion-animals-words-matter.html.

Linzey, Andrew, and Priscilla N. Cohn. 2011. "Terms of Discourse." *Journal of Animal Ethics* 1(1): vii–ix.

US DoT. 2020. "Service Animals (Including Emotional Support Animals)." *U.S. Department of Transportation*, April 17. www.transportation.gov/individuals/aviation-consumer-protection/service-animals-including-emotional-support-animals.

2 The Moral Community

OVERVIEW

Which beings matter morally? Why is it okay to step on a dried leaf just for the pleasure of the sound it makes but not okay to step on a toad for the same reason? This chapter introduces the concept of the moral community—the beings that matter morally—and explores hypotheses about what makes something a member of the moral community. It also grapples with speciesism, the idea that some beings are especially important (or unimportant, as the case may be) simply because of the biological category to which they belong. As we'll see, it's difficult to explain why species membership *itself* should matter.

In December 2007, in Camrose, Alberta, two 16-year-olds broke into the home of a family that was away for Christmas. On the first night, the teens ransacked the place. On the second night, the teens turned their attention to Princess, the family cat. They put her in the microwave and ran it for ten minutes, listening to her scream. Before they left, they spray-painted "It's in the microwave" on the wall. And next to that, "You had a nice cat."

I can't see any way to defend what those boys did. Set aside the breaking and entering; set aside the property damage. If we just focus on what they did to Princess, would *anything* make that okay? I can only come up with ridiculous things: for instance, *maybe* it would be okay if Princess were a robot, and the screams were just recordings. (Though even then it would be a bit disturbing for someone to enjoy the sound.) This simply isn't the kind of behavior that you can justify.

But why not, exactly? Why are we horrified by those teenagers? It feels too obvious to say, and yet we need to be explicit about it: they caused that cat excruciating pain, and they did it for fun. Those boys treated Princess like a thing; they didn't give her any consideration at all.

That brings us to the subject of this chapter. There are some things in the world—cats among them—deserving of our moral consideration. We make a mistake if we don't factor their interests into our deliberations. These are the beings that matter morally, the ones that, we'll say, are members of the moral community. (You'll sometimes hear "the beings that have *moral standing*" or "the beings that are *morally relevant*.") It's important, therefore, that we know what's in and what's out of the moral community, what matters and what doesn't.[1] In what follows, we'll try to get clear on this idea, consider theories about the boundaries of the moral community, and then look at a concept that's important for thinking about the structure of the moral community—namely, speciesism.

Understanding the Moral Community

Let's begin with a clarification. We are trying to figure out which beings count *at all*, morally speaking. That's what it means to ask about the scope of the moral community. At this juncture, we aren't saying anything about *how much* any particular being counts; we aren't saying anything about moral importance. (We'll talk about that later.) We're just after a better understanding of what makes something deserve *some* moral consideration, however slight. Obviously, Princess deserves more than the bare minimum in terms of moral consideration, so answering questions about the moral community won't tell us everything we want to know about her case. Still, it's a first step.

In our attempt to understand the idea of the moral community, it may help to begin with a legal analogy—though we'll quickly need to note some ways that the analogy breaks down. So, let's recall that the law recognizes a difference between *citizens* and *noncitizens*, and it assigns different rights to them accordingly. Citizens get some significant rights that noncitizens don't. (The former can vote, for instance.) Moreover, the citizen/noncitizen distinction isn't totally arbitrary: there's an explanation for any particular person's being a citizen (or not being one, as the case may be). The United States, for instance, has birthright citizenship: if you were born in the United States, then you're a citizen. This means that your being born here is what *explains* why you're a citizen (or your *not* being born here, and your not having been naturalized, etc., explains why you aren't one).

Membership in the moral community is a bit like citizenship. If you're a citizen of a country, then you have a certain privileged status in that country. If you're a member of the moral community, then others ought to factor your interests into their deliberations, their reasoning about what to do. If you *aren't* a citizen of a country, you still have some rights, although not as many. However, if a thing isn't a member of the moral community, it just doesn't matter *at all*. You, dear reader, definitely have moral value and so are a member of the moral community. By contrast, it seems very plausible that a bundle of hay—the stuff cattle eat—isn't a member of the moral community: it has no moral value in and of itself. (It has *financial* value, of course; you can exchange hay for money. But if you already own the hay, it's hard to believe that you'd be making a mistake if you were to burn some of it. If it isn't a mistake to ignore something in your moral deliberations—to destroy it simply because you want to—then it isn't a member of the moral community.) Finally, just as there is some explanation for your being or not being a citizen, there is an explanation for membership or nonmembership in the moral community. The fact that you matter morally isn't arbitrary; there's something about you that explains why you deserve moral consideration. Likewise, we should be able to explain why bundles of hay don't matter. Presumably, bundles of hay lack some important feature that's shared by beings who deserve moral consideration.[2]

In a bit, we'll consider some hypotheses about the features that chart the boundaries of the moral community. But before we get there, we need to set out an important distinction. We need to separate having obligations *to* something and having obligations *regarding* it. Here's the idea. If I own some firewood, then I can do whatever I want to it. For instance, if I want to burn it, I'm well within my rights to do so. But I could also paint pictures of owls on it, or carve wooden toys out of it, or sell it to someone in Missouri. But just because *I* can burn it, it doesn't follow that you can. There are constraints on how you relate to that firewood. Unless I give you permission, you can't burn it, or paint it, or carve wooden toys out of it, or truck it off to a different state. Obviously, there's nothing *intrinsically* wrong with any of these actions; they aren't wrong in and of themselves. Painting, carving, and moving firewood are all perfectly fine things to do in principle, assuming you own the firewood in question. So neither you nor I have any obligations *to* the firewood. It's the kind of thing that we can, in principle, treat in any way we like, up to and including destroying it. But you have some obligations *to me* that *regard* that firewood. You're obligated *to me* not to sell it to anyone in Missouri, since you don't own it. Your obligation *pertains* to the wood, but it isn't *to* the wood.

Questions about the scope of the moral community are questions about the list of beings *to whom* we have obligations—not the list of beings *regarding which* we have obligations. We can have obligations regarding all sorts of things that don't matter in and of themselves, instead mattering only because someone owns them, or cares about them, or has some interest in their protection.[3] (You could even have obligations regarding my grass clippings. If I say you can't touch them, then you can't.) But the members of the moral community? Those beings matter in and of themselves.[4]

People Matter; Animals Don't?

So which beings are those? Here's one perspective: you matter morally if you're a human being; otherwise, you don't. Call this the "Only Humans Count" theory. But this thought isn't terribly plausible. If it were correct, then it would be hard to explain why those boys acted so terribly when they cooked Princess in a microwave.

Granted, we could still say they acted wrongly, as they damaged someone else's property. But, of course, property damage isn't what makes that story horrifying. Someone might insist that *some* property damage is unusually important. After all, many people really care about cats, not to mention Princess's owners specifically. So maybe we can explain why those boys acted terribly by saying that they had especially significant obligations regarding Princess, albeit none to her. They had obligations to *other people* to respect the depth of their concern for Princess.

This theory seems overly complex. Why would we work so hard to avoid saying that we have obligations directly to nonhuman animals? But even if we can explain why we only have obligations to human beings, we're left with problems. If this theory works, it's only because people care so much about cats. So if we want to make trouble for the Only Humans Count theory, we just need to find cases where people don't care about the species in question.

Consider, for instance, that there aren't many people who care about rats. In general, people are very happy to have them killed. So imagine Bill, a guy who gets irritated with the TPS reports that he has to complete at work. To relieve the stress, he catches rats in live traps at the city junkyard. Then he brings them home, douses them with gasoline, and lights them on fire. He likes to watch them writhe as they burn; it just melts away the stress. (His, not theirs.) Is Bill doing anything wrong?

Yes indeed. But given the Only Humans Count theory, it isn't clear why. Almost no one cares about rats. It doesn't matter to most people whether rats live or die. So why shouldn't Bill set rats ablaze if it makes him feel better? Why shouldn't he take out his frustrations on them? For the sake of a handful of rat lovers who would be upset if they knew? Seems unlikely. After all, Bill's no fool: he won't let them know.

Someone might think: "Well, I certainly wouldn't want to hang out with someone like Bill. I wouldn't trust him with my children. He seems disturbed." This hints at a different sort of argument against Bill setting rats ablaze: perhaps he shouldn't light rats on fire because it will turn him into the sort of person who would mistreat human beings (who definitely do matter morally). The idea here is that Bill is acting wrongly *not* because he's hurting rats, but because he's doing something that would corrupt his character or would otherwise increase the odds of him harming beings who are morally important. On the assumption that he shouldn't do that, he shouldn't hurt the rats. This is generally known as the "indirect duty" view of our obligations to animals: we do have duties to them, in a sense, but only because those duties are, indirectly, to human beings.[5]

It's easy to come up with cases that make trouble for the indirect duty view. Just imagine a scenario where a person treats an animal in a truly horrific way and yet there is no chance that they'll ever harm another human being. So instead of having Bill burn rats at home, imagine that Bill is an eccentric billionaire. (Is there any other kind?) He buys a space shuttle and decides to leave the world behind, blasting off on a one-way mission to Pluto, never to return to Earth—or even to communicate with it. However, he brings some rats along for the ride, and you can fill in the gruesome details. In this scenario, it's very clear that nothing Bill does to the rats can have any impact on another human being, whether directly or indirectly. Hence, the indirect duty view can't condemn his cruelty. But it still seems wrong. So much for the indirect duty view.

Here's a much simpler and more plausible explanation for why Bill shouldn't torture rats: *it's very bad for the rats*. Let's go out on a limb and say that rats *suffer* when burnt alive.

If you agree, then you seem to be committed to saying that rats are members of the moral community. After all, you are saying that it doesn't matter whether anyone cares about rats: Bill has a good reason not to burn them simply because it would be bad for the animals were they to be aflame. He hasn't acted wrongly because he's violated his obligations *regarding* someone's rats, in the way it would be wrong if Bill were to steal and burn someone's firewood. Unlike the firewood, rats matter in and of themselves. And he hasn't acted wrongly because he's deforming his character. (Rather, he's deforming his character because he's torturing rats!) We have, then, a simple argument for expanding the moral community beyond the human. Are human beings the only members of the moral community? No: because if that were true, rats would be out. But rats are in, so the moral community is larger. Rats are the kinds of beings to whom we can have obligations.[6]

To be clear, this is a very weak claim. Nothing we've said so far commits us to the view that rats matter very much. Again, saying that rats are members of the moral community only implies that rats matter *some*. Moral *relevance*—that is, membership in the moral community—is one thing; moral *importance* is another. The members of the moral community are just the ones that you ought to think about, whether or not you care about them. Moral importance, by contrast, is a property that's had in varying degrees by the members of the moral community, they're the ones that are morally relevant to your deliberations. Some morally relevant beings are not very important at all: it doesn't take much to justify harming them. Others are extremely important, and it takes a great deal to justify harming them.

Obviously, we need to think about the factors that determine how morally important a being is, and we'll do that soon. For now, though, let's note this. You might be perfectly satisfied with the idea of recognizing a larger moral community, one including both human and nonhuman animals. But historically, many people have balked at it. They've thought that people matter in and of themselves, but animals matter only insofar as we invest them with importance. Are we just left with a battle of intuitions here? Is there anything more principled we can say?

The Argument From Species Overlap

There is at this juncture a classic argument that deserves some attention. For many years, it was known as "the argument from marginal cases," though that name is controversial now, as many of the "marginal cases" are human beings with severe cognitive disabilities. It seems patently wrong to refer to these individuals as "marginal," so we need a better name. Oscar Horta (2014) calls it the "argument from species overlap," which is more accurate anyway. So, that's the language we'll use in what follows.

The argument from species overlap is deceptively simple. Essentially, it goes like this. Let's suppose we want to say that all and only human beings are members of the moral community—that is, every human being is a member of the moral community, and no one else is. Then, we need to find some feature:

1. That we all share, since all humans are in
2. That no nonhuman animal possesses, since all animals are out
3. That *plausibly explains* why human beings matter, since this feature is supposed to be important; it's what distinguishes those beings who deserve moral consideration from those beings that don't

It isn't very hard to satisfy any two of these conditions, but it's very difficult to satisfy all three. Let's see why.

Suppose we start by looking for a trait that we all share. The most obvious one is *being human*. If we go for this option, then we are in the clear on the first and second conditions, since by definition, no nonhuman animal is human, whereas we all are. However, now we're going to struggle with the third condition. Having a certain kind of genome doesn't seem like a good explanation for being a member of the moral community. It seems that what matters are the characteristics that our genes produce—such as having the capacity to feel pain—rather than the specific kind of genome. To see this, just consider human beings' direct ancestor, *Homo erectus*—a species of hominid that was around for nearly 2 million years. Roughly 200,000 years ago, though, some members of *Homo erectus* became reproductively isolated and, as a result, speciation occurred; *Homo sapiens* came on the scene. But speciation doesn't mean that there were dramatic differences between *Homo erectus* and *Homo sapiens*; they were still very similar. There is some evidence that members of *Homo erectus* cooked with fire, made axes out of stone, carved designs into clamshells, and may even have made boats. Is it plausible that the members of *Homo sapiens* were morally important, while the members of *Homo erectus* were morally irrelevant? That's a hard pill to swallow. It seems far more plausible that mattering morally has to do with your capacities, not your species.

Of course, someone might reject evolutionary theory. I have nothing to say about that here, though it seems unwise. Alternatively, someone might insist that there is indeed a dramatic difference between *Homo erectus* and *Homo sapiens*: members of the latter have souls, while members of the former do not. Of course, it would be nice to have a good argument for this view that doesn't require us to accept an entire religious framework, which is obviously going to be controversial. I'm not sure that we're going to find one.[7] But even if we do get such an argument, it's unclear how much good it will do. We'll still be left with the question: What is it about souls that confers some special moral importance on those who have them? In other words, how do souls satisfy the third condition, explaining why certain individuals are members of the moral community? Presumably, a soul is just a different kind of thing out of which an individual can be made. Does it make you more important because it lasts longer? (Then why aren't rocks more valuable than puppies? Most rocks outlast dogs.) Is it more valuable because it ensures that individuals have certain capacities? That is, does having a soul enable ensouled beings to have, say, a more sophisticated mental life? Then why isn't that capacity—the capacity to have a more sophisticated mental life—what actually matters? In any case, without an answer to the explanatory question, the soul theory doesn't seem to have much to commend it as a criterion for membership in the moral community.

In any case, let's suppose instead that we focus on the second and third conditions: we look for a trait that no nonhuman animal possesses, since all animals are out of the moral community, and a trait that plausibly explains why human beings matter, since this feature is supposed to be what distinguishes those beings who deserve moral consideration from those beings who don't.

It's surprisingly difficult to find any trait that no nonhuman animals possess but that humans do. Humans aren't the only animals who reason or use tools; we aren't the only ones with linguistic abilities, complex social orders, and rituals for mourning the dead. For the sake of space, I won't review all the impressive things that animals can do, but a little searching on the Internet will turn up remarkable results. (For a few selective examples, though, see Chapter 3.) We should be very careful not to downplay the capacities of nonhuman beings.

But surely there are some important difference between human and nonhuman animals. We make skyscrapers and iPads and governments. Animals make burrows, and some of them can extract termites from termite mounds with a twig. We reflect on the significance of nonexistence and the deep structure of the universe; they think about getting food and avoiding predators. One way to get at the issue here is via a famous passage in *The Descent of Man* where Darwin says: "The difference in mind between man and the higher animals, great as it is, is certainly one of degree and not of kind" (1871, 105). This statement has three important parts. The first is, essentially, what we just said: human beings share with nonhuman animals many of the same cognitive and affective capacities; they may differ in degree, but not in kind. The second, however, is that these traits really *do* differ in degree: crows can count, but they can't do calculus; elephants mourn their dead, but they haven't developed the elaborate funeral practices that are common in human communities. The third part is that these differences of degree, when combined, create a "great" difference between human and nonhuman animals. Yes, animals have the cognitive capacities that allow them to use tools; no, they don't have the cognitive capacities that would allow them to build skyscrapers. Human beings have a suite of capacities that, while not unique, collectively enable a rich and complex way of life. And maybe it's this difference that matters: not one of kind, but one of sufficient degree to make us unique.

As soon as we recognize the differences between the capacities of humans and nonhumans, however, we should also realize that what we've just said isn't true of all human beings. Think about third-trimester fetuses, month-old infants, people with severe cognitive disabilities, dementia patients, and those in permanent vegetative states. If you are member of the moral community because you have certain sophisticated cognitive capacities, then these individuals *aren't* members of the moral community—that is, they don't matter morally *at all*.

Let's be clear here. I am *not* saying that we should deny any moral significance to third-trimester fetuses, month-old infants, people with severe cognitive disabilities, dementia patients, and those in permanent vegetative states. I am saying that *if* you need to have certain sophisticated cognitive capacities to be a member of the moral community, then these individuals are ruled out. And that's an unacceptable consequence.[8] Our theory of the moral community should recognize the moral worth of human lives; it shouldn't be inherently ableist or ageist, sexist or racist, or any other "-ist." It's starting to look like a good theory for all humans is also going to grant membership in the moral community to many nonhumans.

Someone might resist this. The thought might be: "All the individuals we've just considered are still human, and that's what makes them special." The problem with this claim is that once we abstract away from all the traits we seem to care about—the ability to feel pleasure and pain, sociality, language, self-awareness, empathy, and so on—being human is just one of many biological facts. Being human is a fact about our genetic codes, about our having a particular sequence of the bases that make up DNA. And strings of genetic material are very strange things to which to appeal to establish a being's moral importance. (Remember the discussion of *Homo erectus* and *Homo sapiens* from several paragraphs back.)

So, let's get back to basics. Remember Princess? We agreed that her pain matters. And likewise for the rats Bill killed. Being able to feel pain seems to be morally relevant: it gives you a really good reason not to do pain-inducing things to any individual with that ability. And, of course, an individual genome is relevant to whether an individual has the capacity to feel pain, so it can matter for that reason. But it seems like the capacity is what matters, not the genes per se.

Understandably, this isn't a welcome conclusion to those who want to defend the Only Humans Count theory of the moral community. After all, suppose that there *isn't* a connection between an individual's genome and a morally relevant capacity, such as being able to feel pain. Then, the earlier discussion implies that group membership doesn't matter. Even if the individual is a member of a group whose members typically have a capacity that grounds membership in the moral community, they can't "share" that membership with a being without that capacity; individuals don't "inherit" membership in the moral community from others. You get membership based on *your* capacities, not those of others.

This view is often called *moral individualism*, as opposed to relational approaches to membership in the moral community. Of course, "individualism" is a bad word these days; the cool kids are into things being "relational." But moral individualism has a lot going for it. Fundamentally, it's based on a commitment to fairness. We shouldn't think that men are generally more important than women because, historically, many important inventions were created by men rather than women. We shouldn't think that one culture is superior to another simply because, historically, it gave rise to lots of influential social and political ideas. Instead, we recognize that we need to have a more fine-grained analysis: Don't think about men or women generally or about something so vague as a "culture." Instead, look at particular individuals, see what they did, and then give credit (or blame!) where it's due.[9] Likewise, we shouldn't think that human beings are the only ones who matter just because many of them can do some very impressive things. Instead, we should look at the specific capacities of specific individuals, assessing membership in the moral community on that basis. And if we insist that all humans are members of the moral community—as we should— then we ought to adopt a theory of the moral community that acknowledges all human beings' moral significance. If that theory then includes nonhuman animals, so be it.[10]

What About Plants?

With all this in mind, suppose we abandon the idea of trying to draw the boundaries of the moral community so narrowly, granting that animals ought to be included in it. Once we start down this path, we have to ask why we shouldn't expand the moral community even further. Why, for instance, shouldn't we include all living things? The view that we should include all living things in the moral community is called *biocentrism*.

The first problem with biocentrism is that it has some counterintuitive implications. Imagine a weed growing up in the middle of an empty lot. (It's owned by the city, in case you are worried about trespassing.) You've had a long day, you're really frustrated, and you go for a walk. As you pass by the lot, you notice the weed and decide to pull it up, tossing it in the trash afterward. Did you do anything objectionable? I think most people would say: No, you didn't. But if that weed were a member of the moral community, you would have done something wrong indeed: you'd have harmed that plant. So, we shouldn't say that all living things are members of the moral community. Plants, we might say, are the kind of thing that you might have obligations *regarding*—if, for instance, someone had owned the lot, as opposed to it being vacant public property. However, you don't have any obligations *to* them.

Moreover, the view that life is sufficient for membership in the moral community faces another problem. What, exactly, makes something alive? Crystals, for instance, can grow, respond to stimuli, and achieve a kind of internal equilibrium. Do they have moral standing too? What about ecosystems or other ecological complexes? There are senses in which they, too, can act in these ways. Obviously, there are ways of restricting the definition of life, but then there will just be examples of things that *seem* to be alive—like viruses—that may not satisfy our more stringent criteria. Based on such problems, some biologists actually argue that it's a mistake to try to define "life." They think we should accept that there are simply different kinds of living things, with no features common to all. That may be good biology, but it makes for messy morals, as we're left without a clean way of determining which beings matter in and of themselves. Instead, we just have to look to see what biologists say for their own purposes—which almost certainly aren't the ethical purposes that drive our inquiry.

Despite these issues, we still haven't offered an explanation for why plants would be out of the moral community; we've just identified some challenges for the view. Perhaps the most famous hypothesis about the boundaries of the moral community is due to Jeremy Bentham, an English philosopher and social reformer, and it suggests an answer. In 1789, he wrote this:

> The day may come, when the rest of the animal creation may acquire those rights which never could have been withholden from them but by the hand of tyranny. The French have already discovered that the blackness of the skin is no reason why a human being should be abandoned without redress to the caprice of a tormentor. It may come one day to be recognized, that the number of the legs, the villosity of the skin, or the termination of the os sacrum, are reasons equally insufficient for abandoning a sensitive being to the same fate. What else is it that should trace the insuperable line? Is it the faculty of reason, or, perhaps, the faculty of discourse? But a full-grown horse or dog is beyond comparison a more rational, as well as a more conversable animal, than an infant of a day, or a week, or even a month, old.

> But suppose the case were otherwise, what would it avail? the question is not, Can they *reason*? nor, Can they *talk*? but, Can they *suffer*?
>
> (Bentham 1789, 143)

According to Bentham, what distinguishes the members of the moral community from all other beings? Answer: they are *sensitive* beings—that is, they're *sentient*, having the capacity to feel pain. In other words, when beings don't like being harmed, we ought to consider their interests before harming them; when beings don't care whether they are harmed or not—because they don't have cares at all—we may still have obligations *regarding* them, but we don't have any obligations *to* them.

Plants don't care what we do to them. Granted, they *react* to what we do to them, but they don't have minds; they don't get upset that they're being harmed, even if, as self-regulating systems, they respond to damage. By contrast, conscious beings can suffer; they care about how things go for them in a way that plants simply don't. Again, plants have interests—things go well for them when they have enough water and badly when they don't, and so forth—but they don't feel anything when these interests go unsatisfied. There isn't anything that it's like, from the first-person perspective, to be a plant that doesn't get enough water, whereas there is something that it's like to be a dog who doesn't get enough water. Dogs have a vantage point on the world; dandelions don't. That difference seems crucial, and it makes the presence or absence of consciousness seem exceptionally important.

For these reasons, many philosophers have concluded that sentience is indeed the line between those beings who are and aren't members of the moral community. If we go this route, then we are immediately faced with the difficult question of determining which beings, exactly, are sentient, and we'll explore that question in the next chapter. Before we get there, though, we need to say a bit about the notion of moral importance as opposed to membership in the moral community. And talking about that will require talking about speciesism.

Moral Importance and Speciesism

Picture a circle. The boundaries of it are the boundaries of the moral community. If you are inside the circle, you count morally; if you're outside, you don't. But now we want to know: Are all the beings in the moral community equally important? Do they all matter the same? Or is there a hierarchy? Is there a ranking from most to least morally significant? (If you like the visual, imagine taking that circle and turning it on its side. Does turning it reveal that you are dealing with a disk, perfectly flat across its surface, symbolizing that all individuals have the same moral importance? Or does turning the circle reveal a cone, with some individuals higher up than others?) And if so, what determines where you fall in the hierarchy?

Essentially, these questions are about whether the Principle of Equal Consideration of Interests is true. According to that principle, we ought to give equal weight in our moral deliberations to the like interests of all those affected by our actions. In other words, if we are equally hungry, and so have an equal interest in getting some food, then if someone is trying to decide how to distribute food, our hunger should get equal weight in their deliberations. That is, they shouldn't give any extra weight to my needs just because they happen to be mine or any extra weight to your needs just because they happen to be yours. Everyone's interests count the same.

What's really important about this principle is what it *doesn't* say. The Principle of Equal Consideration of Interests says nothing about your species. So if the principle is true, then it isn't just that my hunger counts the same as yours: it's also that my hunger counts the same as a dog's, or a beaver's, or a sparrow's. This is what leads Peter Singer—author of one of the classic texts in the animal movement, *Animal Liberation*—to make the following famous claim:

> Racists violate [the Principle of Equal Consideration of Interests] by giving greater weight to the interests of members of their own race when there is a clash between their interests and the interests of those of another race. Racists of European descent typically have not accepted that pain matters as much when it is felt by Africans, for example, as when it is felt by Europeans. Similarly those I would call "speciesists" give greater weight to the interests of members of their own species when there is a clash between their interests and the interests of those of other species. Human speciesists do not accept that pain is as bad when it is felt by pigs or mice as when it is felt by humans.
>
> (2016, 33)

If Singer is right, then the odds are good that almost everyone is speciesist, as almost all of us have a strong tendency to give extra weight to human interests.

To be clear, there's a sense in which Singer is *not* saying that your mother is no more important than a mouse. He grants that your mother may have various interests that mice lack, and so in practice, giving equal weight to the interests of both your mother and a mouse may look a lot like favoring your mother.[11] Crucially, though, it will look a lot less like favoring your mother than the status quo. Imagine how different things would be if we were to think that pain is pain, wherever it's found. If we suppose that one of the most important interests is the interest in not being in pain, then just imagine a case where a mouse has found his way into your mother's attic, and she would prefer that he not be there. Ordinarily, she might put out a sticky trap to kill him. (Google it.) But if the Principle of Equal Consideration of Interests is true, then that would probably be wrong: even if she has a range of interests that are set back by the presence of the mouse, the mouse has a very strong interest in not being in pain—one that probably outweighs your mother's less pressing interests.

Why believe that the Principle of Equal Consideration of Interests is true? One of the most basic ideas in ethics is that you should treat similar cases similarly. So suppose I come along and say that a student deserves an A on a paper because it's well-written and thoughtfully argued. And then I look at a different student's paper and say the same things about it—well-written, thoughtfully argued. However, instead of saying that it deserves an A, I say that it deserves a C. What do you think that second student is going to say? "That's not fair!" And that student would, of course, be entirely correct. It isn't fair. If being well-written and thoughtfully argued is enough for one student to earn an A, then it should be enough for another. Anything else would be arbitrary, and arbitrariness is unfair.

So let's assume that you should treat similar cases similarly. The obvious question is: When are cases similar? A plausible answer is: when there are no morally relevant differences between them. When we return to our two students, it's obvious that there are lots of differences between them. One of them might be male; the other female. One might have brown hair, the other blond. One might be a piano player; the other might play rugby. But imagine if I, as their professor, cited one of those differences as a justification for handing out different grades. "I gave Adam's paper an A and Clare's paper a C because Adam plays the piano and Clare doesn't." The right thing to say here is that whether you play piano shouldn't have anything to do with the grades that you received on a paper. What's relevant to grade assignments are the merits of the papers themselves, not any features of the individuals who wrote them. Those other features aren't morally relevant.

Recall that we're trying to think about the shape of the moral community. Is it fully egalitarian, with everyone's interests counting equally? Or do some individuals' interests matter more than others? Based on the reasoning in the last two paragraphs, we can say this: *if* there's any hierarchy, it should be based on *morally relevant features* of the individuals in question. I can't tell you in advance of considering a particular case those features that are and aren't morally relevant. Moral relevance depends on context. Is someone's height a morally relevant feature when it comes to promoting your employees? Well, not if we are trying to decide who deserves a promotion at a mid-sized paper company in Scranton, Pennsylvania. However, it might be morally relevant if we are selecting a center for a basketball team. (In other words, it wouldn't necessarily be discrimination to reject someone as a candidate for that position on a team because he happens to be eight inches shorter than someone else.) In basketball, height counts. In middle management, it doesn't.

This brings us back to animals. When is *species* a morally relevant property—the kind of property that could justify some hierarchy in the moral community? If we accept the idea that individuals' capacities are what matter and agree with the reasoning about fairness that we've just been considering, then the answer is probably: never. When species membership *seems* relevant, it will probably be because it's serving as a proxy for the capacities that are actually relevant. Why does species membership seem relevant when we are deciding who deserves the right to a basic education? Because chipmunks don't have an interest in a basic (human) education. But that isn't because they are chipmunks, per se: it's because they are beings who don't have the cognitive capacities to benefit from what we do in elementary and secondary schools (and are self-sufficient anyway).

Still, it may often seem to us that species membership *is* relevant. It may seem that when we are in various trade-off cases, where we have to balance the interests of human and nonhuman animals, the humans should generally win, even if the Principle of Equal Consideration of Interests suggests otherwise. What should we say about this?

I have a friend who grew up in San Antonio, Texas. She once told me that in her neighborhood, most people never unchained their dogs. The dogs were just left outside, rain or shine, summer and winter, on six-foot leashes. She used to get really upset about this, but every time she complained, one of her parents would say, "They're just dogs, Alicia."

Now, it isn't totally clear what Alicia's parents meant when they said that those dogs were just dogs. One thing they could have meant—though I don't think they did!—is that all dogs have some feature other than simply being dogs in virtue of which no one needs to worry about them being left outside in blistering heat and freezing cold, constantly chained to posts in people's backyards. For instance, perhaps they thought that dogs are excellent thermoregulators.

Probably not. Instead, they probably thought the interests of dogs just don't matter very much. (They probably didn't think, however, that dogs' interests were completely morally irrelevant; I'm sure these folks had their limits. They just didn't worry about chaining dogs outside.) For what it's worth, I don't think that being a dog—the simple fact of being a canine as opposed to something else—is relevant to the question of whether it's okay to treat dogs the way they did in Alicia's neighborhood. The people who say "They're just dogs" are guilty of speciesism. They are appealing to species as a morally relevant property when, in fact, it isn't morally relevant to the issue at hand. If your justification really does just boil down to species membership, then it seems like a pretty poor justification. Indeed, it seems arbitrary, and unfair to dogs, for precisely that reason.

You probably agree with me that species membership just isn't relevant to whether it's okay to treat dogs the way they did in Alicia's neighborhood. However, you are going to find yourself in situations throughout this book where you will be inclined to think that species *is* relevant, that it's okay to give special weight to human interests simply because they belong to humans. The challenge is to explain why you should trust that judgment any more than Alicia's old neighbors should trust theirs. After all, if you were to chat with them about all this, asking them why it's okay to ignore a dog's being uncomfortably hot or not having any freedom to roam, they would probably be confused. "We are talking about *dogs* here, right? Don't you get that? *Dogs*."

We are all a bit like Alicia's neighbors. We're all inclined to see species membership as the kind of thing that you can play as a trump card. "They are just *chickens*. They are just *rats*. They are just *shrimp*. Don't you get that?" But if we can play it, then so can Alicia's neighbors. And since they shouldn't, we probably shouldn't either.

So let's now go back to the question with which we began: When is species a morally relevant property? The answer that seems to be emerging is: maybe never. Instead, species membership is often a good proxy for properties that may matter morally—whether an individual is a chipmunk or a human being is relevant to whether it has an interest in elementary education—but all on its own, species doesn't seem to matter at all. And so when we are faced with a moral question, what we should do is focus on the features of the individuals who will be affected rather than the biological category into which they fall. Again, that biological category may be helpful for determining the features of the individuals, but it's going to be those features, and not the category, that matter in the end. And when people give individuals a moral boost simply because of species membership or downgrade them simply because of species membership, it seems fitting to charge them with speciesism.

It may turn out, of course, that individuals have very different interests, and some individuals may have greater interests than others. So it may be the case that if I die, I lose much more than, say, an iguana, because I am deeply invested in my future in a way that iguanas aren't—a fact explained by differences in our psychological capacities. And we can express that by saying that my life is more important than an iguana's. But if we accept the Principle of Equal Consideration of Interests, then this is always going to be a dangerous way of talking. It's going to make it easy to think that my interests just matter more than those of an iguana as opposed to the more complex truth. And what's that? Very roughly, it's that although my interests and an iguana's interests are equally important, I have certain interests that iguanas lack; so, when lives are at stake, giving our interests equal consideration in fact means favoring me over the iguana. It's a mouthful, but given our general tendency to privilege human interests over those of nonhuman animals, we should be careful with anything that makes that privileging easier.

Conclusion

Where are we? We started out by considering who is, and who isn't, a member of the moral community. We saw that it's difficult to defend a theory according to which humans are the sole members: a theory that doesn't include all humans is a nonstarter, and a theory that *does* include all humans will include many animals. While we didn't establish that sentience is the feature that grounds membership in the moral community, it does seem like a decent candidate. Having gotten that far, we then need to figure out whether the moral community is egalitarian, with everyone's interests counting equally, or whether the community is hierarchical, in that some individuals' interests count for extra. It seems, however, that there are some compelling arguments for saying that everyone's interests count equally, which means that species membership is no basis for downgrading the interests of porcupines, doves, and garter snakes. If those arguments carry the day, then there's an important sense in which everyone matters equally: there are no privileged members of the moral community. Granted, some individuals have interests that others don't, and that can be important to recognize when considering particular conflicts. Still, things look very different from this egalitarian point of view, as it requires us to take the interests of animals as seriously as we take our own.

We still haven't said anything about which animals are sentient (see Chapter 3). We haven't said anything about the specific interests that animals have (see Chapter 4). We haven't said anything about the nature of our *obligations, duties,* or *responsibilities* to animals (see Chapter 5). And we haven't said anything about the empirical issues that are relevant to determining how, exactly, we ought to act (see the rest of the book). All that's coming. Still, we've made some progress. We now have a way to talk about who matters morally. We've also identified some bad strategies for drawing the boundaries of the moral community, as well as a more promising one. Now if someone were to ask us whether and why it was wrong for those teens to put Princess in a microwave, it's clearer why the answer should focus on *her*, not her owners, and *her interests*, not anyone else's.

Further Reading

Bernstein, Mark. 2015. *The Moral Equality of Humans and Animals*. New York: Palgrave.

Kagan, Shelly. 2019. *How to Count Animals, More or Less*. New York: Oxford University Press.

Singer, Peter. 1975. *Animal Liberation*. New York: HarperCollins.

Taylor, Paul. 1986. *Respect for Nature: A Theory of Environmental Ethics*. Princeton: Princeton University Press.

Timmerman, Travis. 2018. "You're Probably Not Really A Speciesist." *Pacific Philosophical Quarterly* 99(4): 683–701.

Varner, Gary. 1998. *In Nature's Interests? Interests, Animal Rights and Environmental Ethics*. New York: Oxford University Press.

Williams, Bernard. 2006. "The Human Prejudice." In *Philosophy as a Humanistic Discipline*, edited by A. Moore, 135–152. Princeton, NJ: Princeton University Press.

Notes

1. At this stage in the conversation, I'm being careful to talk about beings "that" matter rather than beings "who" matter, so as not to prejudge the question of whether the moral community is composed entirely of sentient individuals.

2. Here's a meta-issue that I'm basically going to ignore here. We get to *decide* who's a member of our political community. We don't get to pick and choose on a case-by-case basis, but we do get to write the laws, and thereby determine who is and isn't a citizen. We might think that things are different in ethics: we *don't* get to decide who is and isn't a member of the moral community. Indeed, one standard view is that we discover, rather than stipulate, the criteria for membership, so we just have to see who's in and who's out. The worry, of course, is that if we reject this view, then we're left with arbitrariness. If we stipulate that beings matter if they can experience pain, and someone else stipulates that beings only matter if they happen to be members of their ethnic group, why is their stipulation any worse than ours?

3. Sometimes, of course, *we* are the people who care. I shouldn't use an American flag to clean a toilet, even if no one finds out about it, but not because I have any obligations to that piece of cloth. Instead, I'm committed to certain ideals in virtue of which I have obligations *regarding* that piece of cloth.

4. If you've encountered Kant's ethics, you may be inclined to hear me saying that members of the moral community are ends in themselves. But I'm not saying that. We're trying to think about the boundaries of the moral community prior to settling any questions about moral theory. This matters because we'll be leveraging claims about the scope of the moral community against a moral theory later on—namely, contractualism.

5. This view is usually associated with Immanuel Kant, who wrote in his *Lectures on Ethics*: "Our duties towards animals are merely indirect duties towards humanity. Animal nature has analogies to human nature, and by doing our duties to animals in respect of

manifestations of human nature, we indirectly do our duty towards humanity" (1930, 239). As Christine Korsgaard (2018) argues, however, there are ways of interpreting Kant in more animal-friendly ways.

6. This is a point to which we'll return in Chapter 13.

7. Suppose we accept some particular religious framework, one commitment of which is that we have souls, while *Homo erectus* did not. That isn't quite enough. That framework will also need to explain why it isn't objectionably arbitrary for God to give souls to human beings without giving them to *Homo erectus*, given the many similarities between the species and knowing full well the dramatic consequence of not having a soul—namely, not mattering morally at all. Someone might say: "It isn't objectionably arbitrary because humans are *created in God's image*, whereas nonhuman animals aren't." But first, the interpretation of this phrase is hotly contested among biblical scholars, and not all the interpretations provide a foundation for human uniqueness. (See Clough 2014.) Second, even if we opt for more traditional interpretations, they just push the question back, creating a certain version of the problem of evil. If God knows the dramatic consequences of not having a soul—namely, not deserving any moral protections—then why would God create beings who can feel pain without souls?

8. Not incidentally, this same problem is devastating for another common view about why human beings are the only members of the moral community: namely, because we are *moral* beings, having the capacity for moral reasoning. On top of this problem, there's also a kind of irony about that particular position, captured beautifully by Stephen Clark: "We are absolutely better than animals because we are able to give their interests some consideration: so we won't" (1984, 108).

9. Obviously, I'm not suggesting that men are better than women or that one culture is superior to another. Precisely the opposite! The point is that since we *shouldn't* accept those views, we shouldn't accept approaches that blur the distinctions between individuals and the groups of which they happen to be members.

10. A point of caution. Whenever we're doing ethics, we have to be really careful to check our tendency to defend self-serving moral hypotheses. Nobody wants to be wrong about whether animals matter. It would be massively inconvenient if we were wrong about that, as we would then have to question so much of what we currently take for granted about what is and isn't morally okay. So, when considering our inclination to defend human exceptionalism—the idea that human beings are, as a group, unique in being morally significant—we should at least pause to consider whether this inclination should be trusted. Sometimes, a hunch is worth following. Sometimes, a hunch says more about us than it does about the truth.

11. To return to the earlier visual metaphor, we actually need to turn two circles on their sides. One represents interests, and if the Principle of Equal Consideration of Interests is true, then placing that circle on its side reveals a flat disk. The other represents individuals who, for the purposes of this illustration, we can think of as bundles of interests. Because those bundles are different, laying that circle on its side reveals a cone, with larger bundles higher up than smaller ones.

References

Bentham, Jeremy. 1789. *The Works of Jeremy Bentham, Volume 1*. London: Sumpkin, Marshall, & Co., 1843.

Clark, Stephen R.L. 1984. *The Moral Status of Animals*. New York: Oxford University Press.

Clough, David L. 2014. *On Animals*. New York: Bloomsbury.

Darwin, Charles. 1871. *The Descent of Man and Selection in Relation to Sex*. Princeton: Princeton University Press, 1981.

Horta, Oscar. 2014. "The Scope of the Argument from Species Overlap." *Journal of Applied Philosophy* 31(2): 142–154. https://doi.org/10.1111/japp.12051.

Kant, Immanuel. 1930. *Lectures on Ethics*. Translated by Louis Infield. London: The Century Company.

Korsgaard, Christine M. 2018. *Fellow Creatures: Our Obligations to the Other Animals*. New York: Oxford University Press.

Singer, Peter. 2016. "Practical Ethics." In *The Animal Ethics Reader*, edited by Susan J. Armstrong and Richard G. Botzler, 32–41. New York: Routledge.

3   Animal Minds

OVERVIEW

In the last chapter, we considered arguments for the view that sentience grounds membership in the moral community. In other words, we ought to factor a being's interests into our moral deliberations just in case that being has the capacity to feel pleasure and pain. This invites us to ask some follow-up questions. The first is methodological: How do we determine which beings are sentient? The second applies that methodology: What does the evidence say about which beings are sentient? The third is about uncertainty: When the evidence is ambiguous, how should we proceed? This chapter tackles all three of these issues.

After years of living in New York City, the novelist Brad Kessler had had enough. So he and his partner, the photographer Dona Ann McAdams, bought an 18th-century farmhouse in Western Vermont. Not long thereafter, they decided to start raising dairy goats, and Kessler took up cheesemaking.

They named their goats: they had Hannah and Pie and Nisa, Penny, Eustace Tilley, and Lizzie. And to keep them producing milk, these does had to have kids. However, Kessler and McAdams only had so much room in their barn, so when Lizzie had two doelings, they needed to find a buyer.

In late August, a few months after the doelings had been born, a couple came for them. The goats were grazing up on the hill when the couple arrived, and most of them ran down out of curiosity. But not Lizzie. One of her kids called to her; she called back. The kid scampered up the hill, they spent a moment together, and the doeling scampered down again. Kessler writes:

> Did Lizzie sense her kid was leaving? Was the doeling saying goodbye? The questions about animal cognition are endless—what do they know and how much and are they conscious or even self-conscious? We might never fully know, yet the longer I spent with our goats, the more complex and wondrous

their emotional life seemed: their moods, desires, sensitivity, intelligence, attachments to place in one another, and us. But also the way they communicate messages with their bodies, voices, and eyes in ways I can't even try to translate: their goat song. Lizzie and her kid were having a conversation—if only I had ears to understand.

"We need another and a wiser and perhaps more mystical concept of animals," the naturalist Henry Benston wrote. "In a world older and more complete than ours they moved finished and complete, gifted with extensions of the sense we have lost or never attained, living by voices we shall never hear. They are not brethren, they are not underlings; they are other nations, caught with ourselves in the net of life and time."

Lizzie's kids were bundled into the blue pickup. The humans exchanged money and papers. Lizzie at last came down the hill and called to her twins. The other kids pressed their faces to the fence and called too. After the pickup left, Lola lay flat in the grass. Lisa and Pie and Hannah cuddled under the bright sun, while Penny and Eustace Tilley grazed on the hill. Lizzie alone remained by the fence for another full hour. She stared down the driveway, high wind in her hair, looking at the place where her daughters last had been.

(2009, 154–155)

When I read this, it seems to me that we know the answers to Kessler's questions. Lizzie did sense that her kid was leaving; her doeling was indeed saying goodbye. And what's more, we know that Lizzie was, in some way, mourning her loss. She wasn't merely confused in the way she might have been had someone played a trick on her with mirrors, where she could see her kids one moment and couldn't the next. That's why she was rooted by the fence, her eyes fixed down the driveway.

Someone might worry, though, that in saying all this, I'm *anthropomorphizing* Lizzie: I'm assuming that she is much more like a human being than she actually is. To avoid making this mistake, ethologists—those who study animal behavior—often cite a principle called Morgan's Canon. This principle was named after the famous 19th-century ethologist, C. Lloyd Morgan, who first expressed the idea:

In no case may we interpret an action at the outcome of the exercise of a higher psychical faculty, if it can be interpreted as the outcome of the exercise of one which stands lower in the psychological scale.

(1894, 53)

The basic thought is that when we are trying to explain animal behavior, we should appeal to the simplest mechanisms possible. So, if there is any way to explain Lizzie's behavior *without* appealing to her having certain beliefs and emotional capacities, that's the explanation we should adopt. And while this might sound perfectly reasonable, it actually stands in tension with another highly plausible principle. In Sir Isaac Newton's *Principia*, he developed a series of rules for the study of the natural world, the second of which says:

The causes assigned to natural effects of the same kind must be, as far as possible, the same.

(1999, 441)

If we apply this rule to Lizzie's case, we get something like: if a human organism were to behave the way Lizzie did, and the best explanation of the human's behavior appealed to certain beliefs and emotions, then we should explain Lizzie's behavior the same way.

Morgan's Canon and Newton's Second Rule have a lot going for them. Just consider someone who's definitely *not* obeying Morgan's Canon. In response to the question, "How can I know my dog's religion?," Antony Van Der Mude, a data analyst (!), wrote this about his now-deceased miniature Schnauzer:

> [Emma] was a believer in Animism. . . . One evening, I rolled [her tennis ball into] the metal panel underneath the dishwasher. The ball made a deep "boom" when it hit and stayed underneath the dishwasher door. This scared the heck out of Emma. She was also now presented with the problem of how to retrieve her ball. She very quietly and carefully snuck up to the gap beneath the dishwasher and when she got close enough, grabbed the ball and ran away. It was pretty obvious to me that she believed that there was some animate spirit underneath the dishwasher door that spoke when the ball rolled under there. She stole her ball back carefully so as not to disturb or get caught by this spirit. Observations of animals have shown that they share many of the traits we once thought to be exclusively human. . . . Religion is such a basic part of most people's inner lives, I find it reasonable that my dog would have a simple religion too.
>
> (2015)

As charming as this hypothesis is, it attributes a *much* more complicated mental life to our canine companions than is necessary to explain the behavior. And as a check on this kind of excess, Morgan's Canon is valuable indeed.

At the same time, though, there's much to be said for Newton's Second Rule. In the 17th and 18th centuries, there were scientists who were skeptical about animals feeling anything at all: they thought that without a soul, an organism was just a robot, an automaton. This view is usually associated with Rene Descartes, though there's some controversy about whether he actually held it.[1] In any case, it's generally agreed that some people did and that they acted quite awfully as a result. Here's the way Nicholas Fontaine, one of Descartes's contemporaries, describes the behavior of those convinced of the automaton view:

> The [Cartesian] scientists administered beatings to dogs with perfect indifference and made fun of those who pitied the creatures as if they felt pain. They said the animals were clocks: that the cries they emitted when struck were only the noise of a little spring that had been touched, but that the whole body was without feeling. They nailed the poor animals up on boards

by their four paws to vivisect them to see the circulation of the blood which was a subject of great controversy.

(Quoted in Rosenfield 1968, 54)

Attributing religious beliefs to a Schnauzer is one kind of a failure. This, of course, is a remarkable failure in the other direction: it may even require willful ignorance to explain cries of suffering without any appeal to suffering. If we are going to explain human beings' responses to injury by saying that they are in pain, then we should say the same of nonhuman animals.

So we can see the value of both Morgan's Canon and Newton's Second Rule. At the same time, we can see their limits. Morgan's Canon is not just the (relatively) benign principle that we ought to default to the simplest explanation of the data. Instead, it says that we ought to prefer a particular kind of simplicity—simplicity of cognitive mechanism—even if that seems to be in tension with other relevant considerations. After all, if we always explain behavior via the simplest possible cognitive mechanism, then we may actually create unnecessary complexity elsewhere in our overall theory.

Here's the idea. Suppose that we could, in principle, explain why a dog is nursing her wounded paw by saying that it's a reflexive behavior rather than a conscious response to pain. In a sense, that would be simpler: we wouldn't have to appeal to a more sophisticated mechanism (conscious experience and choice), but could make do with a simpler one (a reflex). We don't have to say that the dog *felt* or *decided* anything. But that kind of simplicity—simplicity of cognitive mechanism—isn't the only kind that matters. We should also value simplicity when it comes to theorizing about the *evolutionary origins* of cognitive capacities. All else equal, a theory is simpler if it says that neural structures produce roughly the same effects in different organisms over time. That is, if a neural structure in *humans* seems to be associated with pain, then the simplest theory is that similar structures in *dogs* produce pain. The alternative would be to say that the mechanism for producing pain changed dramatically at some late point in the story of life—after the last common ancestor between humans and dogs—which makes our theory about evolutionary history more complex.

Likewise, Newton's Second Rule can get us into trouble. It's very easy to think that we're observing the same kind of natural effects when, in fact, we aren't. If, for instance, a human were to create a fairly elaborate structure, we might assume that she'd learned how to do it through trial and error or that she'd been taught by someone else. However, a study by Weber et al. (2013) showed that this probably isn't the right explanation for mice, at least when it comes to their burrows. They looked at two different species: deer mice and Oldfield mice. Deer mice make a fairly simple home: they dig a short tunnel that leads to a nest. Oldfield mice, by contrast, make something more complex: they dig a longer tunnel to the nest, plus an additional escape tunnel out the back, just in case a predator comes in via the usual route. We might think that word got around in the Oldfield mouse community that it's better to be safe than sorry. However, this doesn't seem to be the case. The researchers raised baby mice from each species in cages where they couldn't create burrows and then when they were mature let them loose into pens that were filled with sandy soil. Right away, the deer mice dug burrows like the ones that wild deer mice dig, and likewise for the Oldfield mice. The researchers also bred hybrid mice and were able to show on that basis that the behavior is genetic: they were able to modify the kinds of burrows that the mice created simply by breeding different kinds of hybrids. So, "same effect, same cause" isn't a perfectly reliable rule.

What we need, then, is a kind of middle way between Morgan's Canon and Newton's Second Rule. And while it would be wonderful to have something more precise, perhaps the best we can say, following the philosopher David Hume, is that we ought to proportion our beliefs to the evidence. In other words, we should consider all the information available to us, of whatever kind, and then see what it collectively supports. In some cases, this body of information will make it reasonable for us to believe a particular conclusion about the cognitive capacities of the members of a certain species. ("The members of species X can feel pain." "The members of species X can't remember events that occurred more than six months ago.") In other cases, however, our evidence just won't be good enough to settle the question we care about. In the case of unsettled questions, we might take on certain working hypotheses for the sake of motivating further research. ("Let's assume that members of this species can, in fact, have thoughts about future events, and then consider just how far into the future these animals can plan.") Alternatively, we might accept certain hypotheses for the purposes of settling policy. ("Let's treat these animals as sentient, even if we aren't sure that they are.") But either way, we won't actually believe these hypotheses; we'll remain agnostic. That's what it means to proportion our beliefs to the evidence.

If we proceed in this Hume-inspired way, then the next question is: What kind of evidence should we consider when trying to make judgments about the mental lives of nonhuman animals? It matters, of course, what we want to learn. If we're interested in investigating the emotional lives of animals, we will need to study animals differently than if we're trying to learn about, say, whether animals can count. In the rest of this chapter, though, let's think about how we might assess the most pressing question for our purposes: namely, whether an animal is sentient, whether she has the capacity for positive and negative affective states, whether she can feel pleasure and pain. As we've already seen, sentience is often taken to be the feature that grounds membership in the moral community. So, while it's hardly the only thing that matters morally, it may well be foundational.

Assessing Sentience

Remember Lizzie, the mother goat? We might doubt that she understands all that much about the loss of her doelings. However, I assume we agree that she's sentient. Maybe she and her daughter weren't saying goodbye when the little one scampered up the hill, but we don't doubt that she's conscious. Maybe Lizzie wasn't mourning, but if she were to be attacked by a fox, she would feel pain. The relevant question, then, is *which* nonhuman animals are sentient rather than *whether* any are. How should we go about answering this question?

Unfortunately, there is no simple or straightforward test you can employ. It would be very nice if, when you looked at neurons through a microscope, you could see fine print on each one that declared, "I, in tandem with others, produce consciousness!" or "I'm just here to process inflexible responses to stimuli!" This would really simplify things. Our task would just be to open up skulls and peer inside. Sadly, though, neurons are much more coy, and we will have to employ more indirect methods.

The first of these indirect methods is to look for behavioral evidence. For instance, does this organism behave in ways that would be difficult to explain without consciousness? Is there evidence that the organism is forming representations of the world around it—perhaps using them to navigate or catch prey or what have you? Likewise, does this organism behave in ways that seem to indicate the presence of pain?[2] Does the organism recoil when exposed to extreme heat? Does it nurse damaged limbs?

However, behavioral evidence alone can be misleading. We know, for instance, that there is a difference between nociception and pain. Pain is a mental event of some kind, and it's what seems to matter morally. But nociception is a very primitive capacity to detect noxious stimuli, and nociceptors—the neurons that do the detecting—can cause animals to behave as though they were in pain, to flinch or withdraw limbs all on their own, with no brain involvement whatsoever. (Researchers have demonstrated this in different ways, but the most compelling evidence involves studies on decapitated animals.) So, we can't just look at the way nonhuman animals respond to chemical irritants, or heat, or pinpricks, or anything else; we have to have some evidence that information from their nociceptors are being processed by their nervous system in some more complex way.

So, second, it makes sense to look for morphological similarities between human beings—critters that, presumably, we know to be conscious—and various nonhuman animals. For instance, do they have brains that are organized more or less like ours? Or, failing that, do they have structures that seem to perform the same functions, integrating and processing information from different sensory modalities? If the answer is "yes," then it becomes much more plausible that nociception is being processed as pain. It becomes more plausible still if animals produce their own opioids, such as enkephalins and endorphins, that, in humans, function a bit like the body's own morphine supply, providing relief from pain. Likewise, it helps the case if you can inject an analgesic like morphine and thereby change behavior. In one study on trout, for instance, the researchers injected acid and an analgesic into the lips of some fish and just the acid into the lips of others. All showed signs of stress, but the latter group showed a greater number of behavioral correlates of pain, and for longer, than the former. This suggests that the morphine was doing the same thing in the fish that it does in us: namely, reducing pain (Mettam et al. 2011).

Third, we can think about evolutionary considerations. On one level, this is a different spin on the previous point about morphological similarity. For instance, we can consider our evolutionary relationship to the organism in question. If we are fairly closely related, then we would expect their (similarly structured) brains to produce sensations similar to the ones that ours generate. Of course, if our last common ancestor was much further back, that's no evidence that their brains *don't* produce sensations like ours; it's just that we can't appeal to evolutionary closeness as an argument *for* similarity. Moreover, it's important to remember that some traits have evolved more than once—winged flight, for example. If a trait is valuable enough, solving a problem that's faced by many organisms in many contexts, then it very well may arise multiple times in different evolutionary lineages. As a result, it's important to consider the selection pressures on a given type of organism. Things brings us to the deeper evolutionary question: namely, the value of the trait. How would consciousness benefit the members of the species, and what would the cost be of having it? Would organisms benefit from using simpler cognitive mechanisms to navigate their environments, perhaps because they're faster or less energy intensive?

This kind of reasoning invites us to think more generally about what consciousness does for the individuals who have it. Presumably, consciousness is somehow adaptive—that is, it's fitness enhancing—but it isn't clear why. Its main function could be to help organisms integrate information across various sensory modalities. Or it could enable more flexible behavior. Or it could enhance social learning and coordination. Or it might provide organisms with richer motivational states—pain, fear, empathy, and so on—that allow them to navigate their environments more skillfully. And, of course, it could do all these things. From an evolutionary perspective, consciousness—like gills, opposable thumbs, and antennae—is just one more trait. Hence, it's important to know what it does for the organisms who have it. If we can answer that question, then we can think about when and where it may have evolved.

When we put all this together, we get a basic method for assessing whether particular animals are sentient. First, consider their behavior. Second, consider their bodies. Third, consider whether consciousness would have been adaptive for organisms of their kind. When scientists do all this, most of them attribute consciousness to a great many species. Essentially, while there are lots of debates about the specific mental capacities of rats and pigs, there's almost no debate about whether mammals are conscious. Likewise, while there are significant disagreements about the specific mental capacities of chickens and hawks, there is almost no disagreement about whether birds have conscious experiences. This is, essentially, the conclusion of the Cambridge Declaration on Consciousness, signed in 2012 by a number of prominent scientists at the first annual Francis Crick Memorial Conference:

> Convergent evidence indicates that non-human animals have the neuroanatomical, neurochemical, and neurophysiological substrates of conscious states along with the capacity to exhibit intentional behaviors. Consequently, the weight of evidence indicates that humans are not unique in possessing the neurological substrates that generate consciousness. Nonhuman animals, including all mammals and birds, and many other creatures, including octopuses, also possess these neurological substrates.
>
> (Low 2012)

The upshot, for our purposes, is that it's safe to work from the assumption that the animals on whom we'll focus here—the chickens, pigs, and cattle on our farms; the mice in our labs; the cats and dogs in our homes—are conscious. And since much of the evidence for consciousness is also evidence for the capacity to experience pleasures and pains, we can assume that these animals are sentient.

Still, we aren't only concerned with pigs, mice, and dogs. What about salmon? What about crickets? While we can't answer these questions in any definitive way here, we can lay out some of the considerations that are relevant. As we'll see, the case for fish being sentient is reasonably strong. Insects are more complicated, and I'm not sure what to say there. But that's to be expected. The science of animal minds is complicated, and some animals are especially difficult to research. Our goal here isn't to settle all the questions worth asking. Instead, it's to get a sense of what we know and what we still need to learn. As I've already said, we do know quite a lot. And where we aren't sure what to conclude, we can think about how to respond to our uncertainty—which is exactly what we'll do at the end of this chapter.

Fish

It's important to recognize that fish are, in fact, an enormously diverse group of organisms, with nearly 35,000 species identified, and some of them are more closely related to human beings than they are to one another. (For that reason, among others, biologists sometimes say that the term "fish" expresses a folk concept—that is, a concept that ordinary people use but that doesn't map onto the taxonomy that biologists actually use.) In any case, fish are typically divided into four main subgroups: hagfish, lampreys, cartilaginous fish, and bony fish. Hagfish and lampreys are different types of jawless fish that are often mistaken for eels (which are bony fish), hagfish being unique as the only known creatures with a skull but without a spinal column. Cartilaginous fish include sharks, rays, sawfish, and skates. Bony fish, however, represent the vast majority of fish species, and they make up the varied and large remainder. (From a phylogenetic perspective, every tetrapod is a bony fish, including you!) Because there are so many kinds of fish, there's no way to establish, in the limited space available, that the capacities of any one species are shared by others. So, all we can do here is consider some suggestive facts, and while we need to be cautious about generalizing from them, they paint a surprisingly rich picture of these aquatic beings.

Fish can do some impressive and surprising things. They can, for instance, use tools. In captivity, pinktail triggerfish have been known to grab pebbles in their mouths and tap them on the tank wall at feeding time, as if to remind people that they're hungry. And in the wild, orange-spotted tusk fish have been filmed smashing clams against rocks to break them open. Moreover, they seem to engage in play as well, tossing objects around, mock fighting with one another—and not just with their own kind. There are videos of fish repeatedly returning to a person to be picked up, caressed, and tossed back in the water.

Fish can also keep track of a lot of information. Guppies can tell the difference between new and familiar members of the school, keeping track of about 15 individuals. For some species, such as guppies, that capacity seems to be limited to members of their own kind. But cleaner fish, by contrast, seem to remember who their clients are, devoting their energy to several dozen specific individuals of various species over a period of weeks or months. Fish can also remember and respond appropriately to information that's unfamiliar in their native habitats. Archerfishes, which can squirt jets of water from their mouths, have been presented with pictures of human faces, and they've learned to shoot the one that rewards them with food.

Finally, they have impressive memories. One researcher, Culum Brown, did a study where he placed rainbowfish in a tank to test their ability to solve a navigation task. He set up a mechanism that dragged a net across the tank, stopping about an inch from the end, with just one hole in it large enough for the fish to pass through. Initially, the fish panicked, couldn't find the opening, and were trapped against the glass. However, within five trials, most of them learned the escape route and darted through the hole when the net swept across. Strikingly, Brown did the same study with these fish almost a year later, with no intervening practice. They did just as well on the first try, displaying less panic and navigating the task admirably. Rainbowfish only live three years, so this demonstrated they have the ability to retain such information for a full third of their lifespan (Brown 2001).

The physiology of fish is also revealing. Fish have nociceptors, and their bodies produce opioids that reduce the aversiveness of negative stimuli. Moreover, their brain activity when injured is similar to what we find in the vertebrates who live on land. If you were to jab a goldfish just behind her gills, you'd be stimulating her nociceptors. The electrical activity that results doesn't simply occur in the hindbrain and brainstem—responsible for reflexive behavior—but the cerebellum, tectum, and telencephalon, which, in other vertebrates, appear to be essential to conscious experiences. And crucially, fish don't simply react reflexively to pain: they seem to be able to reason about it, making trade-offs between the goal of avoiding pain and getting food, or staying close to their school. As the intensity of the threat increases, fish are more wary; as their hunger increases, they're more bold.

Finally, there are some evolutionary arguments for fish being conscious. First, there's an argument from theoretical parsimony (or simplicity), which Culum Brown summarizes neatly:

> the fundamental argument for fish feeling pain . . . is founded in part on the conservative nature of vertebrate evolution. If the rest of the vertebrates feel pain, then the most parsimonious hypothesis is that they do so because pain evolved deep in the evolutionary history of vertebrates (perhaps even before teleosts). Rather than to suppose that pain spontaneously arose somewhere else in the vertebrate lineage (e.g., between amphibians and reptiles), it is more parsimonious to infer that fish feel pain for the same reasons the rest of the vertebrates do.
>
> (2016, 2)

Second, there's an argument based on a plausible theory about the function of consciousness that's due to Bjorn Merker (2005). He points out that if you're a mobile animal with multiple sensory modalities, then you're taking in different kinds of information from those modalities—visual, auditory, tactile, and so on. And as you move, the information coming in from each sensory modality is constantly changing.

What's more, some of that information is about you—hearing your own footfalls or seeing your own hands—and some of it is about other entities in the world. You need some way to integrate all that information so that you can actually use it to make decisions. This, Merker thinks, is what consciousness is for: it allows you to distinguish yourself from all the things you aren't, as well as integrate and resolve the tensions between the steady stream of information from your senses. If this is right, then we would expect consciousness to be widely distributed in the animal kingdom: if the members of a species are highly mobile and have multiple sensory modalities, then they are probably conscious.

If we're sympathetic to Merker's theory about the function of consciousness, then fish are the kinds of beings we'd expect to have it: fish are highly mobile creatures with multiple sensory modalities. They navigate complex environments; they have to avoid various threats, including predators and disease vectors; they need to find mates and food. What's more, they have a range of sensory capacities, including, in some species, ones we lack, such as the ability to detect electrical fields. For these reasons, it's important that they have the ability to form representations of that environment and understand their place in it. This enables them to make decisions that are sensitive to a range of factors, weighing and balancing risks and benefits in a rapid way.

Nevertheless, it's worth pointing out that there are theories that say the cortex is required for consciousness—which mammals have, but fish lack, and which is associated with many of the capacities that we associate with consciousness in human beings (including pain perception, memory, speech, and so on). And there are reasons to doubt Merker's information integration theory, since we've made robots that integrate information across sensory modalities, and we assume that they aren't conscious.

Still, we might think that the evidence for fish sentience is good enough that we ought to be cautious. This is the position of the American Veterinary Medical Association (AVMA) on fish—which, in turn, has become the position of many people involved in animal research involving fish, as they generally follow the AVMA's recommendations. According to the AVMA Guidelines for the Euthanasia of Animals, "the preponderance of accumulated evidence supports the position that finfish should be accorded the same considerations as terrestrial vertebrates in regard to relief from pain" (Leary et al. 2020, 12). In other words, though the AVMA isn't quite ready to come out and say that fish feel pain, they think the evidence is strong enough that we should be as careful with them as we are with mammals and birds. And if we can agree on that much, then for our purposes here, that may be all we need.

Insects

What about insects, though? Like fish, insects demonstrate surprisingly complex behavior. Consider, for instance, this impressive review of what bees can do:

> There is evidence that honeybees can learn abstract concepts including same/different, larger/smaller, and above/below. They can also transfer these concepts

across sensory modalities (e.g., from vision to olfaction). Honeybees can be taught addition and subtraction procedures, appear to have the concept of "zero", and can learn to attend to global or local features of objects. Bumble-bees can not only learn complex and highly non-instinctive tasks, such as rolling a tiny ball or pulling a string to reel in a reward: they can transmit this information culturally. They can also recognize objects and patterns through one modality (e.g., touch, olfaction) that they previously encountered only in another modality (e.g., vision). . . . Bees have been taught to distinguish between human painting styles (such as impressionism and cubism) using techniques and controls that were used to demonstrate the same ability in pigeons. Bees and wasps can learn to recognize [human] faces and patterns holistically, with performance that approximates that of vertebrates trained to make the same sorts of discriminations.

(Mikhalevich and Powell 2020, 6)

Bees are particularly well-researched, so we know a lot about them. However, other insects have impressive capacities as well. Dung beetles use patterns in the stars to be able to roll balls of dung in a straight line. Some types of ants coordinate their efforts to search for things by touching their antennae together, and they can learn from other ants as to whether they should go searching for food. There are insects who make tools: ants use stones and soil as projectiles, and crickets build instruments that help to amplify their mating calls. Kissing bugs can remember the features of their environment, systematically avoiding places where they previously experienced aversive stimuli. Paper wasps can recognize individual members of other species members by learning the patterns of markings on their bodies.

Moreover, we can appeal to Merker again. Klein and Barron (2016) make the case that we find systems that seem to fulfill the same functions, such as movement coordination, in both vertebrates and invertebrates. When it comes to vertebrates, those systems seem to support conscious awareness. Consciousness seems to be valuable to mobile organisms that find themselves having to integrate various sources of information—visual, auditory, and so forth. And that's a reason to think that invertebrates, including insects, are conscious too.

What about feeling pain? The evidence is difficult to interpret. Insects have nociceptors, and some insects react to analgesics in ways that suggest these negative signals can be blocked. Cockroaches leave a heated box more slowly after being injected with morphine, and bees who receive morphine sting less aggressively after having a round of electrical shocks. What's more, it doesn't look like morphine is simply decreasing behavioral responsiveness generally. For instance, fruit flies tend to move toward light, but if they're placed in a glass tube and the center of that tube is heated, they won't pass through the hot portion. However, if given an analgesic, they're willing to pass through that otherwise-uncomfortable spot, again reaching the light source. Fruit flies also act in ways that suggest they can learn to avoid painful stimuli: they can come to associate electric shock with an odor, and then will avoid that odor for up to 24 hours afterward.

However, insects often don't respond to damage in the way we might expect. A team of entomologists, for instance, once wrote this:

> [O]ur experience has been that insects will continue with normal activities even after severe injury or removal of body parts. An insect walking with a crushed tarsus, for example, will continue applying it to the substrate with undiminished force. Among our other observations are those on a locust which continued to feed whilst itself being eaten by a mantis; aphids continuing to feed whilst being eaten by coccinellids; a tsetse fly which flew in to feed although half-dissected; caterpillars which continue to feed whilst tachinid larvae bore into them; many insects which go about their normal life whilst being eaten by large internal parasitoids; and male mantids which continue to mate as they are eaten by their partners. Insects show no immobilisation equivalent to the mammalian reaction to painful body damage, nor have our preliminary observations of the response of locusts to bee stings revealed anything analogous to a mammalian response.
>
> (Eisemann et al. 1984, 166)

Of course, opioids may be allowing insects to stay the course despite extensive bodily damage. And in any case, we would expect some important differences between the behaviors of insects and other animals just due to the differences in their composition. The exoskeletons of insects are made of chitin, which doesn't grow back. So, insects don't have the same incentive to protect damaged parts of their bodies that many other animals have. A dog's leg can heal, so it makes sense to try to save a damaged limb; however, an ant's leg won't, so it may as well be abandoned.

Still, there is some evidence that insects just aren't as cognitively integrated as vertebrates are. Insects have relatively small, distributed nervous systems that generally don't exceed 1 million neurons (humans have around 100 billion). If we assume that cognitive sophistication varies with the number and organization of neurons and that consciousness is a fairly sophisticated way of processing information, then we shouldn't assign a high probability to the hypothesis that insects are conscious. Moreover, Shelley Adamo (2019) points out that relative to the number of neurons in the insect brain, insects have very few output neurons, creating chokepoints that limit the information that can be transmitted between the brain's main parts. Indeed, these parts aren't even directly connected, and there's some evidence that they work in parallel rather than together as insects try to navigate the world—a fact that isn't surprising, given the energy demands of a highly interconnected brain.

These points alone wouldn't be very compelling if we needed consciousness and pain perception to explain what insects can do. However, it's unclear whether that's true. We can now make robots that can reproduce many of the behaviors that we see in insects. For instance, robots have been programmed to respond to "painful" (damaging) stimuli and become "fearful" of potential sources of pain. If we assume that we haven't yet created conscious robots, then it's safe to say that many sophisticated behaviors don't require consciousness. Morgan's Canon, let's recall, essentially tells us not to appeal to something like consciousness if we can explain insect behavior without it. When we combine observations about behavioral responses to damage, the degree of neural connectivity in insects (the number of connections between neurons relative to the total number of neurons), and the capacities of robots, it's reasonable to doubt whether insects can experience pain.

But what about that first evolutionary argument that we discussed regarding fish? That argument, you'll recall, said that evolution is conservative: if other vertebrates (besides fish) feel pain, then the simplest hypothesis is that the capacity for pain evolved very early in vertebrate history. Someone might think: Why not generalize this argument? We could say that if other highly mobile, multisensoried organisms feel pain, then the simplest hypothesis is that the capacity for pain evolved very early in the history of highly mobile, multisensoried organisms. And while this argument may be right, it isn't the trump card that it was in the case of fish. When it comes to insects, the behavioral evidence isn't straightforward: the neurological differences between fish and other vertebrates are much smaller than the differences between vertebrates and insects, and we can explain at least some of the things that insects can do without appealing to consciousness. Things are messier here.

To be clear: I'm not saying that insects *aren't* conscious. Instead, I'm trying to give you a glimpse into the complexities here. To some degree, we have to get comfortable with a fair amount of uncertainty when it comes to the study of animal minds. Some things are clear: for instance, there shouldn't be any debate about whether Lizzie is sentient. Some things are clear enough: the evidence for fish sentience, for example, seems to warrant giving them the benefit of the doubt. Some things, though, are as clear as mud, and we can only muddle through.

Uncertainty

But what does it mean to muddle through? How should we proceed when we just aren't sure what to say about the cognitive capacities of some animal or other?

It matters how we answer these questions. Suppose we said: we should always give animals the benefit of the doubt. If that were right, then we should assume that insects are both conscious and can feel pain—they're fully sentient—and that they matter morally. What would follow? Well, consider the number of bugs killed by cars. Arnold van Vliet, a Dutch entomologist, came up with an estimate:

> In 2007, over 7 million cars [in the Netherlands] traveled about 200 billion kilometers. If we assume for simplicity that every month the average is the same for all cars, then 16.7 billion kilometers are traveled a month. In just the license plates, 3.3 billion bugs are killed per month. The front of the car is at least forty times as large as the surface of the plate. This means that cars hit around 133 billion insects every month.
>
> (Messenger 2018)

If the Dutch kill 133 billion insects every month *just by driving*, then the mind boggles at the number across the globe. If insects matter as much as other sentient beings, then driving isn't just a moral issue because of greenhouse gas emissions: it's a moral issue because it involves killing an incredible number of morally significant creatures. And, of course, driving is hardly the worst thing that we do to insects. We probably kill orders of magnitude more with the pesticides that we spray on our crops.

In and of itself, this isn't much of a reason to deny that insects are conscious. Sometimes, uncomfortable conclusions are true! However, it's also the case that there are huge opportunity costs associated with giving insects the benefit of the doubt: if they aren't conscious, then due to their enormous numbers, treating them *as though* they were conscious would mean redirecting a huge number of resources away from beings who are clearly conscious (like mammals). We shouldn't do that lightly.

So maybe we shouldn't always go the benefit of the doubt route. However, it seems like a mistake to ignore animals entirely in our deliberations. A middle way is to go the expected utility route. This is essentially a kind of actuarial ethics. Let's suppose that an actuary is trying to price car insurance for a teenager. How does she do it? Very, very roughly, she looks at the odds that someone in that group is going to have an accident, the possible cost of such an accident, and multiplies: if 1 of every 100 teenage drivers gets into an accident each month, and on average, those accidents cost the insurance company $15,000, then just to break even, the company needs to charge $150 per month. The expected utility approach to moral risk works the same way: we look at the odds of the relevant state of affairs, consider the value at stake if that state of affairs is realized, and multiply. If it works for risk assessment elsewhere, perhaps it works in ethics too.

In the present case, this means considering two things: first, the odds that insects are sentient; second, the kind of mental life that insects would have *if* they were sentient. To give a toy example, we might say that while we're totally confident that pigs are sentient, we could go either way on insects: we think it's 50–50. Moreover, we could say that even if insects are sentient, we think that their mental lives are probably much simpler, with dramatically less capacity for pleasure and pain than pigs possess—maybe only 10%. Then, we would get the result that the pleasures and pains of an insect are worth 5% of the pleasures and pains of a given pig. Or, to put it differently, if you had a choice between harming 20 insects and harming one pig in roughly comparable ways, it would be a toss-up. Essentially, this process gives us the discount rate for insects: the moral significance of insects based on the odds we assign to their sentience and the odds of their having a rich mental life.

As soon as we say that, we might think that our estimates were way too high. However, given the sheer number of insects, even very low estimates leave us with dramatic implications. Let's suppose there are 10 quintillion insects in the world. Now consider an observation that Jeff Sebo (2018) makes. Suppose there's just a 5% chance that insects are sentient and that insects, on average, have only a tenth of a percent the capacity for pleasure and pain as human beings do. Then, given the 10 quintillion population estimate, we should say that the pleasure and pain experienced by these insects is *morally equivalent* to the pleasure and pain of 500 trillion humans.

Of course, this radical result isn't quite as disconcerting as the result we would get if we were to go with the benefit of the doubt approach. Then, even if we discounted at the same rate (a tenth of a percent) based on relative capacity for conscious pleasure and pain, we would get the result that the total amount of conscious pleasure and pain experienced by insects is equal to that of *1 quadrillion* humans. Somehow, though, that's not much consolation.

The upshot: whether we tackle moral risk via the benefit of the doubt approach or the expected utility approach, we end up with an uncomfortable conclusion: given their sheer numbers, the (possible) suffering of insects is a massive moral issue, potentially greater than all others. What to do?

There are a few options. First, we could just bite the bullet and say that we've massively underestimated how important insects are. We thought that it was morally okay to kill extraordinary numbers of insects to grow food, but perhaps that's just wrong and we should be minimizing the number we kill. I don't feel particularly comfortable with that conclusion, but who cares about my comfort? Maybe we should just follow the numbers.

Second, we could argue about the numbers. Maybe we've been too generous to insects—though that's a bit hard to believe, as Sebo used pretty low probabilities, which make for a rather aggressive discount rate. Even if the discount rate wasn't aggressive enough, though, our revised results probably aren't going to be much more palatable. Would you feel better if it were to turn out that the insects on Earth are as important, morally speaking, as 500 billion humans? We could get that equivalence if we were to say that the odds of insect sentience are 1,000 times lower than Sebo supposes—though *surely* the odds are higher than that. And still, the result is hard to swallow.

A third option is to take all this as a reason to rethink our account of the moral community. For instance, maybe we should adopt an approach according to which you only matter morally if you have certain sophisticated cognitive capacities (or if you stand in the right sort of relationship to beings with those capacities). As we saw in Chapter 2, though (and will see in more detail in Chapter 5), such proposals face some fairly serious objections.

I'm not sure which of these options is best or whether there's a better option waiting in the wings. Insects are a tough problem in animal ethics, and I don't think anyone has a completely satisfying story right now. As far as I can see, all the options come with significant costs.

That being said, the problem here isn't really about particular methodologies for handling moral risk: the benefit of the doubt approach and the expected utility approach. Instead, the problem is that lots of methodologies are going to deliver weird results when we consider, first, extremely numerous beings (insects) and, second, the trait that's often seen as relevant to moral status (sentience). After all, just consider the wild result we might get if we were to apply the same reasoning to plants. There are even more of them, and we are constantly interfering with their lives—mowing lawns, spraying pesticides, and imposing an untold number of other harms on them. Even if we assign an extraordinarily low probability to plant sentience, the consequences are likely to be dramatic. And if we go with the benefit of the doubt approach, those consequences will be more dramatic still.

So, we might want to be cautious about how we use these frameworks. Perhaps they need to be improved, or perhaps there are special reasons not to employ them in cases either involving extremely numerous beings or that focus on the property that confers membership in the moral community.

Still, however surprising it was to find ourselves suddenly thinking so highly of insects, let's note that these frameworks for handling risk seem perfectly sensible when we get away from insects and questions about who matters. When we turn our attention to other animals and other capacities, both the benefit of the doubt and expected utility approaches strike me as pretty reasonable.

Think of Lizzie again. When I consider her story, I still find myself thinking that she was, on some level, mourning the loss of her daughters. Admittedly, I can't demonstrate that. I can't point to the empirical research that establishes, beyond a reasonable doubt, that goats *mourn*. But it seems sensible—and perhaps as importantly, humane—to give Lizzie the benefit of the doubt. Likewise, it seems sensible to think about the probability that she can mourn, and the gravity of that harm if she can suffer it, and to let that guide our decision-making. And either way, we can take a harder and more critical look at the choices that her owners, Kessler and McAdams, made. Whichever framework we invoke, we can say this much. If there's a chance that your actions are going to cause an animal to suffer an abiding sadness, then even if you aren't sure about the details of her mental life, you'd better have a good, not-purely-self-interested reason to take that risk. Animals deserve that much.

Further Reading

Ackerman, Jennifer. 2017. *The Genius of Birds*. New York: Penguin Books.

Andrews, Kristin. 2020. *The Animal Mind: An Introduction to the Philosophy of Animal Cognition*. New York: Routledge.

Andrews, Kristin, and Jacob Beck. 2018. *The Routledge Handbook of Philosophy of Animal Minds*. New York: Routledge.

Balcomb, Jonathan. 2016. *What a Fish Knows: The Inner Lives of Our Underwater Cousins*. New York: Farrar, Straus and Giroux.

de Waal, Frans. 2017. *Are We Smart Enough to Know How Smart Animals Are?* New York: W. W. Norton & Company.

Godfrey-Smith, Peter. 2016. *Other Minds: The Octopus, the Sea, and the Deep Origins of Consciousness*. New York: Farrar, Straus and Giroux.

King, Barbara. 2017. *Personalities on the Plate: The Lives and Minds of Animals We Eat*. Chicago: University of Chicago Press.

Schukraft, Jason. 2020. "Invertebrate Sentience." *Effective Altruism Forum*. https://forum.effectivealtruism.org/s/sHWwN8XydhXyAnxFs.

Tye, Michael. 2017. *Tense Bees and Shell-Shocked Crabs: Are Animals Conscious?* New York: Oxford University Press.

Notes

1. See Cottingham (1978) for arguments that Descartes had more plausible views.
2. *Technically*, what matters is the suffering that's usually, but not always, associated with pain. Just as you can have nociception without pain (for evidence, see plants), you can have pain without suffering. But we're going to ignore that wrinkle here. For a detailed philosophical discussion of the relationship between pain and suffering, see Klein (2015).

References

2015. "How Can I Know My Dog's Religion?" *Quora*, June 1. www.quora.com/How-can-I-know-my-dogs-religion.

Adamo, Shelley. 2019. "Is It Pain If It Does Not Hurt? On the Unlikelihood of Insect Pain." *The Canadian Entomologist* 151(6): 685–695. https://doi.org/10.4039/tce.2019.49.

Brown, Culum. 2001. "Familiarity with the Test Environment Improves Escape Responses in the Crimson Spotted Rainbowfish, *Melanotaenia duboulayi*." *Animal Cognition* 4: 109–113. https://doi.org/10.1007/s100710100105.

Brown, Culum. 2016. "Comparative Evolutionary Approach to Pain Perception in Fishes." *Animal Sentience* 11: 1–7. https://animalstudiesrepository.org/cgi/viewcontent.cgi?article=1029&context=animsent.

Cottingham, John. 1978. "'A Brute to the Brutes?': Descartes' Treatment of Animals." *Philosophy* 53(206): 551–559.

Eisemann, C.H., W.K. Jorgensen, D.J. Merritt, M.J. Rice, B.W. Cribb, P.D. Webb, and M.P. Zalucki. 1984. "Do Insects Feel Pain? A Biological View." *Experientia* 40(2): 164–167.

Kessler, Brad. 2009. *Goat Song: A Seasonal Life, Short History of Herding, and the Art of Making Cheese*. New York: Scribner.

Klein, Colin. 2015. *What the Body Commands: The Imperative Theory of Pain*. Cambridge, MA: MIT Press.

Klein, Colin, and Andrew B. Barron. 2016. "Insects Have the Capacity for Subjective Experience." *Animal Sentience* 9(1): 1–52.

Leary, Steven, Wendy Underwood, Raymond Anthony, Samuel Cartner, Temple Grandin, Cheryl Greenacre, Sharon Gwaltney-Brant, Mary Ann McCrackin, Robert Meyer, David Miller, Jan Shearer, Tracy Turner, and Roy Yanong. 2020. *AVMA Guidelines for the Euthanasia of Animals: 2020 Edition*. Schaumburg, IL: American Veterinary Medical Association.

Low, Phillip. 2012. "The Cambridge Declaration on Consciousness." *Francis Crick Memorial Conference*, July 7. http://fcmconference.org/img/CambridgeDeclarationOnConsciousness.pdf.

Merker, Bjorn. 2005. "The Liabilities of Mobility: A Selection Pressure for the Transition to Consciousness in Animal Evolution." *Consciousness and Cognition* 14(1): 89–114. https://doi.org/10.1016/S1053-8100(03)00002-3.

Messenger, Stephen. 2018. "Trillions of Insects Killed by Cars Every Year, Says Study." *Treehugger*, October 11. www.treehugger.com/cars/trillions-of-insects-killed-by-cars-every-year-says-study.html.

Mettam, Jessica J., Lois J. Oulton, Catherine R. McCrohan, and Lynne U. Sneddon. 2011. "The Efficacy of Three Types of Analgesic Drugs in Reducing Pain in the Rainbow Trout, *Oncorhynchus mykiss*." *Applied Animal Behavior Science* 133(3–4): 265–274. https://doi.org/10.1016/j.applanim.2011.06.009.

Mikhalevich, Irina, and Russell Powell. 2020. "Minds without Spines: Evolutionarily Inclusive Animal Ethics." *Animal Sentience* 29(1): 1–25.

Morgan, C.L. 1894. *An Introduction to Comparative Psychology*. London: The Walter Scott Publishing Co.

Newton, Isaac. 1999. *The Principia: The Authoritative Translation: Mathematical Principles of Natural Philosophy*. Translated by I. Bernard Cohen, Anne Whitman, and Julia Budenz. Oakland, CA: University of California Press.

Rosenfield, Leonora. 1968. *From Animal Machine to Beast Machine*. New York: Octagon Books.

Sebo, Jeff. 2018. "The Moral Problem of Other Minds." *The Harvard Review of Philosophy* 25: 51–70. https://doi.org/10.5840/harvardreview20185913.

Weber, J., B. Peterson, and H. Hoekstra. 2013. "Discrete Genetic Modules are Responsible for Complex Burrow Evolution in Peromyscus Mice." *Nature* 493: 402–405. https://doi.org/10.1038/nature11816.

4 Welfare and Death

OVERVIEW

What makes an animal's life go well? What makes it go poorly? And when an animal dies, is her death itself—the mere fact of her ceasing to be alive—bad for her? After providing some historical context for thinking about animal welfare, this chapter maps out the three most prominent philosophical accounts. Then, it shows that these theories have very different implications when we consider the plight of wild animals, who suffer a great deal in their natural habitats. Finally, the chapter considers the question of the badness of death for animals, including some of the challenges associated with determining whether death is worse for humans or nonhumans.

Porphyry was a 3rd-century Neoplatonic philosopher. He was fond of Chrysippus's work—who lived half a millennium earlier—and he provides the following account of one of Chrysippus's views:

> The Gods made us for the sake of themselves, and for the sake of each other, and that they made animals for the sake of us; horses, indeed, in order that they might assist us in battle, dogs, that they might hunt with us, and leopards, bears, and lions, for the sake of exercising our fortitude. But the hog (for here the pleasantry of Chrysippus is most delightful) was not made for any other purpose than to be sacrificed; and God mingled soul, as if it were salt, with the flesh of this animal, that he might procure for us excellent food.
>
> (1823, Bk 3, §20)

Porphyry runs with Chrysippus's idea. He goes on to quote Carneades—a member, and later the head, of Plato's Academy during the 2nd century BCE—who thought that "everything which is produced by nature, is benefitted when it obtains the end to which it is adapted, and for which it was generated" (1823, Bk 3, §20). With Carneades's theory in hand, Porphyry can say not just that hogs are designed to be killed for human consumption, but that they are *benefitted* by being slaughtered. According to Porphyry, it's actually good *for hogs*—not just for people—that hogs are killed and eaten. After all, that's the end to which they're adapted and for which they were generated. In other words, it's why they were created.

I'm not recommending Porphyry's view. I bring it up, however, to highlight that it matters what we say about animal welfare or well-being—two terms that I'll use interchangeably, which just refer to how an animal is doing, how she's faring, how her life is going.[1] If Porphyry is right, then the members of at least one species aren't living their best lives if left to their own devices, rooting and foraging as they please. Instead, they're living their best lives when turned into a meal. And while contemporary theories of animal welfare tend not to have such radical implications, they do bear in significant ways on the questions that we'll be considering later in the book. These theories give different answers to questions like:

- Is it good for animals to be in the wild, free from human intervention?
- How much does it matter whether they can engage in "natural" behaviors?
- Is pain as bad for animals as it is for human beings?
- How bad is it for animals to die?

In this chapter, then, we'll consider theories about what makes animals' lives go well and poorly, as well as theories about whether and when death is bad for them. To begin, though, let's briefly consider a watershed moment in discussions of animal welfare, at least in animal agriculture.

Scientists on Welfare

In 1964, Ruth Harrison—a British writer and activist—published a book called *Animal Machines*, detailing the plight of animals in poultry and livestock farming in England. The book prompted the British government to appoint a commission to investigate the welfare of animals in intensive farms. This commission, chaired by F. W. Rogers Brambell, presented its findings in 1965: "Report of the Technical Committee to Inquire into the Welfare of Animals Kept under Intensive Livestock Husbandry Systems," now generally known as the Brambell Report. The Brambell Report was important for several reasons, not the least being its specific practical recommendations. Among other things, it specified minimum sizes for the cages of laying hens, a certain amount of floor space for broiler chickens (chickens raised for meat), adequate lighting conditions for inspection, and the end of debeaking (the removal of part of a chick's beak). The report made analogous space recommendations for pigs and cattle, specifically mentioning the importance of freedom of movement. It also discouraged removing the tails of pigs, as well as keeping cattle perpetually tethered, and discussed the importance of providing adequate bedding for all species. (For more on all these practices, see Chapter 6.)

However, quite apart from these guidelines, there are two reasons why the Brambell Report is seen as a watershed moment in conversations about animal welfare. First, the report actually defines "welfare," claiming that "welfare is a wide term that embraces both the physical and mental well-being of the animal" (Brambell 1965, 9). This might not seem so significant, but the emphasis before the report had been squarely on *physical* health, often understood in terms of productivity. So, a fast-growing chicken was seen as healthy chicken, even if that rapid growth was causing suffering. (To this day, many broiler chickens grow at rates that lead to cardiovascular, respiratory, skeletal, and muscular problems. Again, see Chapter 6.) The report made it clear that the mental states of the animal are important and goes to some length to argue that animals have mental lives, that they can experience pain and suffering, and that it matters whether their desires are frustrated.

This brings us to the second reason why the Brambell Report matters. The report makes the case that it's important to protect animals' ability to do certain basic things:

> In principle, we disapprove of a degree of confinement of an animal which necessarily frustrates most of the major activities which make up its natural behaviour and we do not consider such confinement or restraint permissible over a long period unless the other advantages thereby conferred upon the animal are likely to be very substantial. An animal should at least have sufficient freedom of movement to be able without difficulty, turn around, groom itself, get up, lie down and stretch its limbs.
>
> (1965, 13)

These five abilities—to turn, groom, get up, lie down, and stretch out—became known as "the five freedoms" and later took on a life of their own. The British government created the Farm Animal Welfare Advisory Committee in response to the Brambell Report, and when, in the late 1970s, the committee was asked to revise the Welfare Codes that were currently in place, they offered a more expansive vision of what should be included: "freedom from hunger, thirst or malnutrition; appropriate comfort and shelter; prevention, or rapid diagnosis and treatment, of injury and disease; freedom to display most normal patterns of behaviour; and freedom from fear" ("Farm Animal Welfare" 2009, 2). Now, the five freedoms are usually codified as follows:

1.   Freedom from hunger and thirst: by ready access to fresh water and a diet to maintain full health and vigor
2.   Freedom from discomfort: by providing an appropriate environment, including shelter and a comfortable resting area
3.   Freedom from pain, injury, or disease: by prevention or rapid diagnosis and treatment
4.   Freedom to express normal behavior: by providing sufficient space, proper facilities, and company of the animal's own kind
5.   Freedom from fear and distress: by ensuring conditions and treatment that avoid mental suffering

Of course, most farmed animals don't enjoy the kinds of environments that we might picture based on these freedoms, but that's a story for another chapter (yet again, Chapter 6).

These two developments—a definition of "welfare" that includes the mental states of animals and the emphasis on protecting animals' ability to engage in certain behaviors—are crucial to understanding the legacy of the Brambell Report. In essence, it marked an important philosophical development in animal science and agricultural policy. The five freedoms represent the idea that many things that were formerly seen as *constitutive* of animal welfare—such as rapid growth or high milk production—are, at best, *proxies* for animal welfare. While there is some sense in which it's good to be "healthy," where farmers interpret that as meaning that the animal is laying eggs, providing milk, or gaining weight at the desired pace—that doesn't necessarily tell us what we want to know about how an animal is doing.

However, the Brambell Report doesn't offer us a coherent theory of animal welfare. To see this, let's note that the report doesn't specify the relationship between animals' mental states, natural behaviors, and welfare. Everything it says is compatible with the view that animal's welfare levels are determined by their mental states, and natural behaviors only matter insofar as they affect animals' mental states. It's obvious how the negative freedoms are linked to mental states, such as not being hungry and thirsty, not being in pain, and so on: they are just listing experiences that animals shouldn't have. But we can also read this idea into the positive freedoms, such as the freedom to move in certain ways. For instance, it's *stressful* for chickens not to be able to stretch their wings, so making that freedom of movement possible brings them some psychological comfort. On this view, the problem with a proxy for welfare like weight gain is that while it *might* give you some indication of what's going on in animals' minds, it might not. There may be circumstances where weight gain just doesn't tell you anything about whether animals are suffering. This view says: when you want to understand how animals are doing, you need to focus on their mental states.

But the Brambell Report doesn't force this interpretation. There is another way of thinking about the relationship between animals' mental states, natural behaviors, and welfare. For all the report says, you could maintain that the fourth freedom— that animals should be free to express "normal," "natural," or "species-specific" behavior—represents a separate dimension of animal welfare. On this reading, the idea is *not* that it's good to be able to express natural behaviors because it feels good to express them (or it's stressful not to express them). Instead, the idea is that it's *intrinsically good* for animals to be able to express natural behavior—that is, good in itself—even if exhibiting natural behaviors doesn't serve their mental well-being. On this view, weight gain is also a poor proxy for welfare, though for an entirely different reason. Weight gain just isn't correlated with whether animals can do the things that are good for them.[2] This view says: when you want to understand how animals are doing, you need to look, at least in part, at what they're able to do.

We'll return to this theory of welfare, and the mental state–focused one, in just a moment. At this juncture, though, the big picture is this: if your thinking about animal welfare has largely been shaped by interacting with cats and dogs, then it might seem obvious that their mental lives matter, as well as that certain species-specific behaviors are good for them. But historically, this is an enormous development. However, it's also a development that leaves some important philosophical questions unanswered. So, let's now be more precise. What are the main theories of well-being out there? How do they relate to the ideas that we've been exploring so far?

Philosophers on Welfare

When we turn our attention to the philosophical literature, we find three main theories of well-being: hedonism, the desire satisfaction theory, and perfectionism. They are all general theories of well-being, meant to apply to human and nonhuman animals. For simplicity's sake, then, I'll sometimes talk about their advantages and disadvantages using human examples, even though our main concern here is their application to nonhuman animals. In any case, the most prominent versions of all three theories agree that we ought to attend to the mental states of nonhuman animals, though they disagree about the mental states that matter, and they disagree about whether mental states are all that matter. Let's see how each theory works.

Hedonism

If you hear someone being described as a hedonist, you would probably take that to mean that he's all about the next high. And although that's not the way philosophers use the term, you'll be able to see the connection. According to the hedonist's account of well-being, pleasures make your life go well; pains make it go poorly. Everything else is good for you only insofar as it provides pleasures or spares you from pains; everything else is bad for you only insofar as it causes pain or prevents you from securing pleasures.

Hedonism can sound hedonistic—in the "all about the next high" sense—because it's easy to interpret "pleasures" too narrowly. The idea is *not* that the only things that contribute to well-being are lollipops and orgasms. Instead, the idea is that *whatever sorts of pleasures there are*, those are the things that make you better off. For a sow, for instance, the pleasure of feeding may be very different from the pleasure of being close to her young, which may be very different from the pleasure of the sun on her back. But if they are all pleasures, they all advance her well-being.

There's a straightforward argument for hedonism that goes as follows. Just consider anything that we would normally think of as good for you—for instance, having your favorite meal. But now suppose that instead of making you happy, you find it bland and boring, and you're left feeling disappointed. Was it good for you to have that meal? Arguably not: that meal *would* have been good for you had it made you happy, but since it didn't, it wasn't. Likewise, consider cases where people work really hard to achieve things that ultimately leave them feeling empty. Think of the athlete who strives to win, finally defeats all her competitors, but then just feels cold when holding the trophy, wondering why she sacrificed so much for a piece of metal. Was it good for her to win? Arguably not: it would have been good for her had she enjoyed it, but to put in all that effort and be deeply dissatisfied? That's tragic. So, although it might *seem* as though there are many things that are good for you beyond pleasure, once we remove the pleasure, we also seem to remove the goodness. And if nothing is good or bad for you except insofar as it produces pleasures and pains, then hedonism is true.

Hedonism has a lot going for it as an account of animal welfare. It's hard to see why we would think that something is good for nonhuman animals if it doesn't ultimately make them happier—or, even worse, if it ultimately leads to more pain. Think of the perfectly ordinary, but extraordinarily difficult, choices that so many people have to make as their companion animals get older. Is it worth putting my dog through this painful procedure to extend her life a bit longer? Will her life be good enough afterward? Will she have enough good moments to justify what I would have to put her through? These questions make a lot of sense if we are hedonists: they sound like ways of asking whether, on balance, a dog is going to have enough plea-sure to outweigh the pain that the veterinarian is going to cause, as well as whatever pain comes along with the remaining conditions from which the dog suffers. And if the answer to that question is negative—if there won't be enough pleasure—then it's hard to see why we would say that having more life would be good for her. At least for animals, it seems plausible that life is valuable (when it *is* valuable) because of the good experiences it contains. Those experiences are what make things go well for the animal, and bad ones are what make things go badly.

However, hedonism faces some difficult objections. Consider people who really enjoy experiencing pain in certain contexts—extreme athletes or people who are into BDSM. The hedonist has to say that either these people are getting enough pleasure from pain that they are winning on balance, or that they are mistaken about their experiences and are actually experiencing pleasure that only appears to be pain. I'm not sure that either of these stories is very plausible.

To see why not, let's consider the case of extreme athletes. Some people attempt to run 100-mile races, aren't able to complete them, and suffer enormously in the process. Nevertheless, they still think that the experience was good for them; they report being glad that they did the race. Is that because they are just so *happy* after the race? Not necessarily: they are often in an enormous amount of pain. Is it because they get enough happiness *later on*, perhaps over months or years later, that offsets the pain of the race? Again, not necessarily: they can be glad they ran the race while still shuddering at the memory; they can be glad to have faced that challenge, to have learned something about themselves, even if it concerns their limits. Are they reporting that they are glad because they are just mistaken about their experiences? Maybe they weren't really in pain? Clearly not. So, the hedonist has to say that these people are just wrong: the hedonist has to say that it wasn't good for them to run these races. However, there should be a very strong presumption in favor of taking people at their word when it comes to what's good for them. We want a democratic theory of well-being, which means that we should do our best to avoid rejecting sin-cere and thoughtful self-reports about what's good and bad for a person.

Desire Satisfaction Theory

And we *can* avoid it: we can be desire satisfaction theorists. According to this view, something is good for you if it satisfies your desires, and it's bad for you if you desire not to have it. So, a difficult race can be good for a person because it can satisfy their desires. And more generally, because we generally want pleasures and prefer to avoid pains, a desire satisfaction theory can account for all the cases we mentioned earlier that seemed to favor hedonism.

Of course, desire satisfaction theories have their own challenges. One of the classic problems is the suicidal teen. Consider the broken-hearted 16-year-old, recently dumped by his significant other, and now determined to end it all. It seems clear that he shouldn't—that it isn't in his best interests to kill himself—and yet it's exactly what he desires. Someone might object that it isn't what he *really* desires. Deep down, this person might say, he really wants to live. But while we might want to believe that, the dark reality is that many people who contemplate suicide really do want to die; that's their considered wish. If we are still convinced that it would be bad for the broken-hearted 16-year-old to take his own life—not just bad because his family and others would be traumatized, but bad for *him* specifically—then we need to give a different account of well-being.

Before we consider one last alternative, though, let's note that while this issue is a serious one for the desire satisfaction theory as a general theory of well-being, applying to both human and nonhuman animals, someone might not think that it's much of a problem when we narrow the scope to nonhuman animals specifically. The desire satisfaction theory struggles with the suicidal teen case because it's one where our considered judgment about what's good for the teenager conflicts with his desires. However, perhaps there aren't any such cases when we turn to nonhuman animals; we might think that nonhuman animals don't have the kinds of desires that would create these kinds of puzzles. So, maybe we can defend a more limited desire satisfaction theory, applying only to nonhuman animals.[3]

Or maybe not. First, and squarely on the issue at hand, consider a fox with a broken leg. While he's in enormous pain, he's absolutely determined not to allow the wildlife veterinarian to get near him. If this fox has any desires at all, one of them is not to be touched by the vet. However, it's obviously true that what's best for the fox is that the vet be able to care for him; it's indeed good for the fox to be touched by the vet, though, sadly, the fox isn't in a position to appreciate that. Moreover, it isn't as though the fox is necessarily going to realize, after the procedure, that the vet *isn't* a threat. His desires aren't going to be updated after the fact. So, we can't appeal to his future desires to get out of this problem. The desire satisfaction theory seems committed to saying that it's good for him not to be touched by the vet, even though we agree that this is false.

The second problem for even a limited desire satisfaction theory, however, is at least as serious, if not more. Consider what a desire satisfaction theory says about cases where you have no desires at all. There are lots of things, of course, that you've never thought about, and so you don't have explicit preferences regarding those things. However, the desire satisfaction theory can say what's good and bad for you is determined either by the desires you've actually got or by the desires you would have if you were to consider the thing in question. That is, even unthought-of counterfactual desires can determine what's good for you. To make this concrete, let me just report that until I wrote this paragraph, I'd never thought about whether

I'd like to take a trip to Mumbai. Now that I'm considering it, I think I would: it sounds like a totally fascinating place to explore, and I'm sure I'd learn a ton. So, the desire satisfaction theorist can say that when I was still working on the *previous* paragraph—that is, before I'd ever thought about taking a trip to Mumbai—taking that trip still would have been good for me based on the desires I'd have if I were to think about it.

But what can the desire satisfaction theorist say about cases where I can't think about the thing in question? What if I'm unable to form the relevant thought? This is a real problem when it comes to nonhuman animals, some of whom lack the cognitive sophistication to think about the costs and benefits of different courses of action. Consider, for instance, a perfectly ordinary decision that many people make regarding their cats—namely, whether to spay or neuter them. All things considered, would a particular tom prefer to be neutered and let out much more frequently (because his owners aren't worried about him impregnating local female cats) but then miss out on sexual experiences when he's let out? Or would he prefer *not* to be neutered and to be let out much less frequently but have the opportunity for sexual satisfaction when he's able to roam? Lots of cat owners would like an answer to this question. However, while they might make reasonable judgments on behalf of their cats, they can't know what any individual cat really prefers, as cats simply can't consider the question. And because they can't consider it, we can't appeal to what they would desire if we were to put the question to them. So is there no fact of the matter when it comes to whether or not it's good for cats to neuter them? That doesn't seem right, but it isn't clear how the desire satisfaction theorist can resolve this problem.

Perfectionism

These problems with hedonism and desire satisfaction theory may lead us to wonder about our third option: perfectionism. How does that view work? The other name for perfectionism is "the objective list theory," which gives you some sense of the approach. Essentially, the perfectionist says that there are some things that are objectively good for you, others that are objectively bad for you, and you can simply be mistaken about what's on each list. Of course, most perfectionists will say that pleasure is one of the things that's objectively good for you; it just isn't the only thing. What's on each list (of things that are good for you and of things that are bad for you) probably depends on the kind of being you are, so we should expect differences between species. For humans, though, the positive list might include pleasure, knowledge, friendship, and achievement; the negative list might include suffering, ignorance, loneliness, and meaninglessness.

Perfectionism can easily navigate all the problem cases that we've considered so far. The race was good for our extreme athlete because even failure was a kind of achievement, as evidenced by the grit it took to make it through some significant portion of the race. The suicidal teen is wrong that dying would be good for him, as he would be missing out on the good things that more life would enable him to have, no matter what he currently desires. The fox with a broken leg is just mistaken about what's in his interest: his health is best served by the compassionate wildlife vet.

And it doesn't matter whether cats can consider their preferences regarding freedom to roam relative to sexual autonomy; the objective list theorists can just say that one of them is more important, and that determines what's good for our tom. Moreover, perfectionism fits neatly with some common judgments. We often think it's good for people to know certain uncomfortable truths, even if they'd rather not, and even if it makes them unhappy to have that knowledge. While hedonism can't explain this, perfectionism can: if knowledge *in itself* is good for you, then it's good for you even when it doesn't bring you pleasure. That's what it means for knowledge to be good for you in itself; its goodness isn't derived from its ability to give you something else (such as happiness).

Hedonism and the desire satisfaction theory are different ways of developing the idea that when it comes to welfare, mental states are what matter. Perfectionism is the way to go if you want to say that there is at least one dimension of welfare that *doesn't* reduce to either pleasures and pains or satisfied and unsatisfied desires. If some things are good for animals independently of whether those things make animals happy or satisfy their desires, then perfectionism is true.

Of course, the hard work for the perfectionist is to explain why specific things are on these lists, as well as how we might know that they are. Sure, if there are objective lists that specify what's good for each individual (or each kind of individual), and if we can figure out what those lists say, then we can address all sorts of puzzle cases. But this is where hedonism and the desire satisfaction theory really shine. We like pleasures, and in general, anyway, getting what you want certainly seems to be good for you. As a result, those seem like very plausible foundations for accounts of well-being. There is no real mystery about why pleasure would be good; it seems like if anything is good for you, pleasure is. But when we ask why we should think that knowledge is good for you, that question does seem like it needs an answer. Consider the fact that a surprising number of deer, elk, and moose suffer from chronic wasting disease, which steadily turns their brains into sponges. As a result, they become emaciated, lose control of their bodily functions, and then die. Are *you* really better off for knowing that? (The animals might be, at least if you can help them. But we're focused on you here.) If you *are* better off, why?

Even if perfectionists can handle this explanatory problem—that is, provide a plausible story about why whatever's on the list is, in fact, objectively good for you—we face a difficult epistemological problem when it comes to animals (that is, a problem relating to how we know). This epistemological issue looms large because we are theorizing about other beings, not about ourselves. When theorizing about human beings, we have access to our own mental lives and can discuss them with others. But in the case of nonhuman animals, we are trying to figure out what's good for them without being able to communicate with them in the way we'd like. We have to give an account of what's in their interests based on complex inferences from their behavior to their preferences, at the same time recognizing that their understanding of their own situations may be impoverished relative to our understanding. How do you figure out what's good for someone when she can't tell you, and you couldn't completely trust her even if she could?

Welfare in the Wild

It's clear, then, that all these theories have virtues and vices, advantages and dis-advantages. However, rather than try to sort out which is best—a task that's beyond the scope of this book—let's try to make the choice between them more stark. We can see the choice between these theories particularly clearly when we consider the suffering of wild animals. In recent years, it's become increasingly common to see philosophers arguing for the view that most wild animals don't live lives that are good on balance. They reach this view by arguing that suffering predomi-nates in nature—that is, there's more suffering than pleasure. But the inference from "suffering predominates" to "life isn't good on balance" requires a theory of well-being. For instance, the inference goes through if hedonism is true, since if hedonism is true, then there is nothing more to well-being than pleasures and pains. So, a life that's mostly painful experiences is a life that's bad on balance. But the inference doesn't go through on versions of perfectionism that give enough weight to the goodness of living freely in the wild. On those views, suffering could pre-dominate, and yet most animals' lives could be worth living.

Before we investigate theories of well-being any further, though, let's say some-thing quickly about the claim that gets this conversation off the ground—namely, that suffering predominates in nature. That might seem completely crazy. Why believe it?

I'm going to say a lot about this issue in Chapter 8, so I won't go into much detail here. The short version, however, is that as strange as the hypothesis may sound, it fits neatly with what we know about the causes and scope of suffering in the natural world. Richard Dawkins puts it well:

If Nature were kind, She would at least make the minor concession of anes-thetizing caterpillars before they were eaten alive from within. But Nature is neither kind nor unkind. She is neither against suffering nor for it. Nature is not interested in suffering one way or the other unless it affects the survival of DNA. It is easy to imagine a gene that, say, tranquilizes gazelles when they are about to suffer a killing bite. Would such a gene be favored by natural selection? Not unless the act of tranquilizing a gazelle improved that gene's chances of being propagated into future generations. It is hard to see why this should be so, and we may therefore guess that gazelles suffer hor-rible pain and fear when they are pursued to the death—as many of them eventually are. The total amount of suffering per year in the natural world is beyond all decent contemplation. During the minute it takes me to compose this sentence, thousands of animals are being eaten alive; others are running for their lives, whimpering with fear; others are being slowly devoured from within by rasping parasites; thousands of all kinds are dying of starvation, thirst and disease. It must be so. If there is ever a time of plenty, this very fact will automatically lead to an increase in population until the natural state of starvation and misery is restored.

(1996, 132)

The upshot: suffering is pervasive in nature, and given how natural selection works, *that's exactly what we should expect.*

Nevertheless, this dark view isn't widely held, and many have thought precisely the opposite. Henry Thoreau, for instance, wrote that "[e]very creature is better alive than dead, men and moose and pine-trees, and he who understands it aright will rather preserve its life than destroy it" (2009, 112). And perhaps both of Thoreau's ideas are correct: the first about all lives being worthwhile, the second about it being fitting to preserve those lives. In any case, the goal here isn't to settle any questions about whether suffering predominates in nature. Instead, the goal is to think about the implications *if* that's true. So for now, let's just consider whether Thoreau could appeal to any of the theories we've considered—hedonism, the desire satisfaction view, and perfectionism—to defend his position that very unpleasant lives are still worth living.

Hedonists, of course, will just say that Thoreau is wrong: if the lives of most wild animals contain more suffering than pleasure, then their lives *aren't* worth living.[4] If we are going to save Thoreau's view, we will need to look elsewhere.

The desire satisfaction theory allows that if someone would rather stay alive despite the suffering he's experiencing, then he's better off alive. In principle, then, a desire satisfaction theorist could say that while suffering might predominate in nature, as long as animals still strive to survive, we have some evidence that they prefer survival all things considered. So, that's a reason to think that their lives are worth living, difficult though they may be.

Desire satisfaction theorists can go further. In addition to being able to explain how it could be good for an animal to continue living despite the suffering he's experiencing, it can explain how it could be good for an animal to live in the wild specifically despite the suffering it causes. Some have contested exactly that point. Consider this comment from Mark Sagoff:

> The ways in which creatures in nature die are typically violent: predation, starvation, disease, parasitism, cold. The dying animal in the wild does not understand the vast ocean of misery into which it and billions of other animals are born only to drown. If the wild animal understood the conditions into which it is born, what would it think? It might reasonably prefer to be raised on a farm, where the chances of survival for a year or more would be good, and to escape from the wild, where they are negligible.
>
> (1984, 303)

In other words, Sagoff thinks that if animals could choose between living in the wild and living on a farm, they'd choose a farm, given how bad the wild is. Sagoff's main goal here is to challenge a kind of rosy optimism about the wild, and that's fair enough. But a desire satisfaction theorist can say that even if suffering predominates in nature, as long as animals would choose freedom over captivity, we have some evidence that they prefer the wild, all things considered. And that's a reason to think that they are better off in the wild, even with all its horrors.

However, there is an important clause in Sagoff's claim: his observation is based on something he takes to be impossible, namely, that "the wild animal [understands] the conditions into which it is born." This brings us back to the question, considered earlier, about whether uninformed desires can determine what's good for an individual. If uninformed desires *do* play a role in determining an individual's welfare, then the desire satisfaction theorist is in the clear. But if not, then perhaps the desire satisfaction theorist has to disagree with Thoreau and concede to Sagoff. Maybe we should only take animals' desire to avoid pain as determining what's bad for them, in which case the wild looks bad indeed.

By now, it might not be surprising that the perfectionist is the one who can definitely agree with Thoreau. The perfectionist can say that it's indeed good for wild animals (or perhaps for all animals) to be free to live their lives as they see fit, even at the cost of extensive pain. Moreover, the perfectionist can say that simply being alive is so good for you that, unless suffering is all-consuming and excruciating, it's best for you to go on. Again, Thoreau claimed: "Every creature is better alive than dead, men and moose and pine-trees, and he who understands it aright will rather preserve its life than destroy it." At least some perfectionists will agree with the first part of that statement based on a judgment about the contribution of being alive to well-being. And *if* they agree with that, then they are a long way toward an argument for the second part of Thoreau's view. If, in fact, every creature is better off alive than dead, and we ought to do what's best for these creatures, then we ought to try to preserve their lives.

Here's the upshot. Let's suppose that suffering predominates in nature. If we are hedonists, then that means we have good reason to worry that most animals are living lives that are bad on balance. If we are desire satisfaction theorists, by contrast, it's more complicated: it depends on whether we think uninformed desires determine what's good for animals. If so, then given the way so many animals fight to survive, their lives may be worth living despite dramatic suffering. If not, then not. Finally, if we are perfectionists, we can certainly say that life in the wild is worth its costs and so that most animals have lives that are good on balance. But as you might guess, based on the discussion in the last section, it may be difficult for perfectionists to explain why life in the wild is so valuable.

Throughout this book, we'll consider questions about how the suffering of wild animals ought to be factored into various moral problems. For now, though, what matters is just that we become a bit more thoughtful about the relationship between suffering, well-being, and the idea of a life worth living. According to hedonism, the relationship is straightforward: suffering sets back well-being, and if you experience more of it than not, your life isn't worth living. According to the desire satisfaction theory, suffering sets back well-being when we don't want it—which is, of course, most of the time. Still, even if we experience more suffering than we want—and even more suffering than not—that doesn't necessarily imply that our lives aren't worth living. We might value other things enough to make it worth continuing, and if so, our lives can be good enough (at least in one sense of that phrase). Finally, while there are lots of versions of perfectionism, some of them agree with the desire satisfaction theory: while suffering is indeed bad for us, it can predominate without making our lives not worth living. The desire satisfaction theory and perfectionism have different virtues and vices, and the choice between them is complex. The main point here, however, is just that it matters which of these theories is true. Major questions—such as whether we ought to intervene in nature to relieve the suffering we find there—depend on what we say.

Welfare and Death

Let's close by thinking about the relationship between welfare and death. Is death bad for you? If so, why? If not, why not?

Some people think that this issue is actually pretty easy to resolve. Donald Broom, a prominent animal scientist, says that "the animal welfare issue is what happens *before* death, including how [animals] are treated during the last part of their lives, often the pre-slaughter period and then the method by which they are killed" (2011, 126 emphasis added). On Broom's view, death can't be bad for you, as you aren't alive when it happens! By contrast, veterinarian James Yeates claims that "death is contrary to an animal's interests, i.e., death is a welfare issue" (2010, 239). Who's right?

To answer this question, we need to get a bit clearer about the issue at hand. Crucially, we need to be careful to distinguish questions about *dying* from questions about *death*. Dying is a process that ends in death. And dying, of course, is often very bad for animals. Dying can be immensely painful, a prolonged process of suffering as a result of injury or disease. In other cases, thankfully, dying isn't painful at all. When researchers euthanize animals, they aim to cause no more pain than a needle prick, and surely even some deaths in the wild are basically pain-free—as, for instance, when a small animal is almost instantly killed by a larger predator, never even aware of the presence of a threat. So if we want to know whether *dying* is bad for an animal, we know what to investigate. If, however, we want to know whether *death* is bad for animals, things are more complicated. In this case, we're asking whether death *itself* is bad for animals. Perhaps equivalently (or perhaps not): Is an animal harmed by having died? Would it have been better for that animal to have continued living?

In some cases, it seems fairly clear that an animal isn't worse off for not having had more life; it would not have been better for the animal to have continued living. Some parasites, for instance, appear to make life so unbearable for their hosts that their hosts would be better off dead. It's also easy to imagine cases where a feral hog has been shot badly by an aerial gunner, with no possibility of survival, but with a long process of dying ahead. Surely, it would be better for that hog to die than to continue suffering. In lots of other cases, though, it seems plausible that it would be better for animals to continue living. Consider a lion basking in the sun, full after a good meal. It's hard to deny that it would be good for that cat to have more such experiences, implying that were a poacher to shoot him, he would be worse off than he otherwise would have been.

How should we think about these mundane observations about the relative goodness and badness of death and life? The answer matters a great deal, since many questions in animal ethics turn on what we say here. Is humane agriculture morally okay, where animals live excellent—if abbreviated—lives? When, if ever, is it morally okay to cull some animals to save others? Is it okay to euthanize some animals for research purposes, assuming that the research promises significant benefits for human beings? The answers are going to depend, at least in part, on whether it's actually bad for the relevant animals to die. If animals lose nothing in death, then it's going to be much easier to defend all sorts of practices. Of course, it will still matter whether the deaths can be made painless (or sufficiently close to it). But if death itself is bad for animals, then ensuring a painless death doesn't address all the issues that need to be addressed. There is, in addition, the simple fact that an animal's life is lost.

There are, essentially, two ways to think about the badness of death: there are *comparative* and *noncomparative* accounts. According to comparative accounts, death is bad for someone because it deprives that individual of the good things she would have had if she'd survived. There are as many comparative accounts as there are things to compare when making this assessment. So, for instance, we might think we should assess whether death is bad for an individual based on whether, had she survived, she would have had more positive than negative affective states, whether she would have had more pleasures than pains. This is a way that hedonists might approach things. Alternatively, we might assess whether death is bad for an individual based on whether, had she survived, she would have had the majority of her preferences satisfied. This is the standard route for desire satisfaction theorists. Alternatively again, we might consider whether her welfare is positive overall—where we understand her welfare partly in terms of her ability to engage in natural or species-specific behaviors. This is one option that the perfectionist can take.

By contrast, noncomparative accounts say that what makes death bad has nothing to do with how things would have gone for an individual had she survived. Some argue, for instance, that death is bad for an individual simply because death destroys something valuable—namely, the individual herself. Others argue that death is bad for an individual because of the way that it restricts her autonomy, limiting her options in the most drastic way. Perhaps the most radical account of the badness of death says that it's only bad for an individual if it causes the individual pain—and while dying can, of course, cause considerable pain, being dead never does. (You can't be hurt if you can't feel at all, and you can't feel at all when you're dead.) On this view, usually associated with the ancient philosopher Epicurus, death isn't bad for anyone, human or nonhuman. But as we saw, it's a view that still has some currency: as we saw at the beginning of this section, at least one animal scientist, Donald Broom, appears to believe it.

Comparative accounts fit very well with the illustrations we used earlier. When we frame the issue in terms of whether an animal would suffer extensively if she were to survive—as when we consider the impacts of parasites on their hosts or the feral hog who's been shot—the goal is to assess whether one state of affairs (nonexistence) is better than another (extensive suffering). That seems to be the idea behind asking whether a particular animal would be better off dead.

So, if we accept a comparative account, then if we think that the life of an animal is bad on balance (and can't be improved), we'll conclude that she would be better off dead, and so death wouldn't be a harm to her; if, by contrast, we think that the life of an animal is good on balance (it is likely to stay that way, at least for some period of time), then we'll conclude that she's better off alive, and so death *would* be a harm.

However, comparative accounts (and some noncomparative accounts) leave us with a puzzling question: How *could* death be bad for an individual? She isn't there to experience it, or even to be the subject of harm. (In other words, who, exactly, is there to be harmed when the individual is dead? She no longer exists!) These kinds of considerations lead us back toward the radical position that death isn't actually bad for anyone. While it might be hard to believe that this view is true, given how hard we all work to avoid death, it takes some work to explain what's wrong with it. And if we accept an account according to which death isn't bad for anyone, then killing will be much easier to defend, since the most important issues are going to relate to the animal's experiences when dying, not the fact of death itself. As a result, it will be much easier to make the case for humane animal agriculture, noninvasive animal research, and much else.

Wrinkles for Comparative Theories

In what remains, let's set aside the view that death isn't bad for anyone. Instead, let's consider just a few of the wrinkles for comparative theories.

Here's one of them. Let's suppose, for simplicity, that we're hedonists. Then, if we want to know whether death is bad for a squirrel, we look at the expected distribution of pleasures and pains in that individual's life. However, we might think that not all pleasures and pains should count equally. Maybe the experiences that the squirrel would have next week are more important than the ones she'd have next year. This idea—that we ought to discount future pleasures and pains for many nonhuman animals—is the upshot of a prominent theory according to which the badness of death depends, at least in large part, on the degree to which an individual is *psychologically connected* to her future.[5] That is, individuals with the capacity to anticipate and contemplate their futures—making long-term plans and strategizing about the way they want their lives to go—are psychologically connected to their futures in a way that simpler minds are not. At the limit, we might imagine individuals who live entirely in the moment, driven to act in an inflexible manner by desires to have certain needs satisfied, but without any conscious thought about the future state of affairs that would result in those needs being satisfied. In a sense, those individuals don't have any "claim" to future experiences; there is some important sense in which those future experiences aren't really theirs. By contrast, individuals with rich psychological connections to their futures do, in a sense, have a claim to those future states—those future states are relevant to who they are now, in the present, insofar as they anticipate them, desire them, and so on.

If we accept this approach, then given a spectrum of psychological complexity, the closer the individual is toward the simple end, the less death takes from her; she doesn't seem to have a stake in her own future in the way that the highly psychologically connected individual does. And the closer the individual is toward the complex end, the more death takes from her. Given the many different kinds of minds in the animal kingdom, it follows from this view that death probably isn't as bad for some species as it is for others. Even if insects are sentient, and so we should be worried about their welfare, we might not have to worry about killing them—as long as we do it painlessly. But when it comes to chimps, the story is likely very different. So the first wrinkle for comparative views has to do with what, exactly, we ought to compare within a life: the entire future that an individual would have or just part of it? And if just part of it, why that part?

The second wrinkle has to do with comparisons across individuals. Suppose we are trying to decide whether my death would be worse for me than a toad's death would be for her. (As we saw in the last chapter, this issue is relevant to foundational questions about the shape of the moral community.) If we are comparativists, then we answer this question by looking to see what I stand to lose versus what the toad stands to lose. It might seem obvious that I stand to lose more, as I am—if I may say so—a being with greater cognitive sophistication than the average toad. However obvious it may seem that I have more to lose, there are considerations that point the other direction. Consider these brilliant lines from Marge Piercy:

> The dream of toads: we rarely
> credit what we consider lesser
> life with emotions big as ours,
> but we are easily distracted,
> abstracted. People sit nibbling
> before television's flicker watching
> ghosts chase balls and each other
> while the skunk is out risking grisly
> death to cross the highway to mate;
> while the fox scales the wire fence
> where it knows the shotgun lurks
> to taste the sweet blood of a hen.
> Birds are greedy little bombs
> bursting to give voice to appetite.
> I had a cat who died of love.
> Dogs trail their masters across con-
> tinents. We are far too busy
> to be starkly simple in passion.
> We will never dream the intense
> wet spring lust of the toads.
> ("Toad Dreams" 1983)

If Piercy is right, then while I may be (marginally) smarter than a toad, I may experience the world less intensely. Indeed, I may experience the world less intensely precisely *because* of differences in our cognitive capacities. This, it seems, is the view that Judith Jarvis Thomson proposes:

> It seems to me . . . that other things being equal it is worse to cause an animal pain than to cause an adult human being pain. An adult human being can, as it were, think his or her way around the pain to what lies beyond it

in the future; an animal—like a human baby—cannot do this, so that there is nothing for the animal but the pain itself.

(1990, 292–293)

Bernard Rollin puts the point even more vividly, saying that if animals are in pain, "their whole universe is pain; there is no horizon; they *are* their pain" (1998, 144). We might interpret what Piercy says along these lines: perhaps *all* the experiences of animals—not just the experience of pain—consume them in a way that our experiences don't. This could be because we can always stand back from our experiences and contemplate them, or contemplate something else and distract ourselves. On this view, animals are absorbed by their experiences in a way that we rarely, if ever, are.

Quite apart from everything we've just said, it's true that depending on our theory of well-being, we can construct cases where an animal has more to lose by dying than a human being. Consider a case involving a young healthy elephant and a very elderly human being, body wracked in pain due to cancer, suffering from dementia on top of that, with days left to live. It seems plausible that on many accounts of well-being, the elephant has more to lose here. But if we accept Piercy's view, it could turn out that it's fairly common for animals to have more to lose in death than we do, at least for animals whose lives are going well. If animals are generally enjoying their lives and they get much more enjoyment out of their experiences than we get from ours, then if hedonism is true, those animals may actually have more to lose than many human beings. (But, of course, if animals' lives aren't going well—as may be the case, of course, for most wild animals—then the case for their lives being bad on balance is even stronger. If, as Rollin suggests, animals *are* their pain when they're in pain, then given the ample evidence of suffering in nature, a pessimistic view about wild animal welfare is all the more likely to be correct.)

We can't explore Piercy's view in any detail here. So, I simply raise this possibility as a check against any tendency to assume that humans have a greater capacity for well-being *simply* because humans have certain rich cognitive capacities. That could be true, but it would take some argumentation to establish it.

Conclusion

Porphyry had a remarkable theory of animal well-being, albeit mostly because of how self-serving it was. He thought that it was good for animals to be killed for human consumption. And granted, it may be true that it's morally permissible to slaughter animals for food. If so, though, that probably isn't because the animals are better off for it. But while it's clear that we ought to replace Porphyry's view, it isn't entirely clear what the replacement should be. There are many difficult theoretical choices when we start thinking about animal welfare and the badness of death. Most obviously, there are choices between the main theories of animal well-being—hedonism, desire satisfaction theory, and perfectionism—but also between various ways of developing those views. And when we turn our attention to death in particular, we see that things are no simpler.

I have no axe to grind here; I don't have a view that I'm keen to defend. So all I'll say is that the answers to the questions raised here are important ones, as they have implications for every question in animal ethics where the welfare and lives of animals are at stake—which is to say, almost all of them. Either we need answers or we need to get comfortable doing ethics with a lot of uncertainty.

Further Reading

Akhtar, Sahar. 2011. "Animal Pain and Welfare: Can Pain Sometimes Be Worse for Them than for Us?" In *The Oxford Handbook of Animal Ethics*, edited by Tom L. Beauchamp and R. G. Frey, 495–518. New York: Oxford University Press.

Browning, Heather. 2020. "The Natural Behavior Debate: Two Conceptions of Animal Welfare." *Journal of Applied Animal Welfare Science* 23(3): 325–337.

Bruckner, Donald. 2019. "Philosophy and Animal Welfare Science." *Philosophy Compass*. https://doi.org/10.1111/phc3.12626.

Fletcher, Guy. 2017. *The Philosophy of Well-Being*. New York: Routledge.

Fraser, David. 2008. *Understanding Animal Welfare: The Science in its Cultural Context*. New York: Wiley-Blackwell.

Monsó, Susana. Forthcoming. "How to Tell If Animals Can Understand Death." *Erkenntnis*.

Purves, Duncan, and Nicolas Delon. 2018. "Meaning in the Lives of Humans and Other Animals." *Philosophical Studies* 175(2): 317–338.

Rice, Christopher. 2016. "Well-Being and Animals." In *The Routledge Handbook of Philosophy of Well-Being*, edited by Guy Fletcher, 378–388. New York: Routledge.

Višak, Tatjana, and Robert Garner. 2015. *The Ethics of Killing Animals*. New York: Oxford University Press.

Notes

1. Hence, talk about well-being is talk about what's good for an individual, as opposed to what's good in general or good for others. When a weary nurse does a double shift to cover for a sick co-worker, she's doing something that's good in general (the world is a better place for the sacrifices of people like her) and good for the patients. However, it isn't necessarily good for her: we can imagine cases where her well-being would be best served by some more sleep. Of course, that doesn't mean she shouldn't cover the shift. Quite often, we shouldn't do what's in our interests, what best advances our well-being. The point is just that we can distinguish—and should distinguish—what's good for each individual from what's good generally, as well as questions about individuals' well-being and what individuals ought to do.
2. In fact, it's negatively correlated with freedom of movement. If you want to make animals gain weight rapidly, you don't let them run around, as they burn calories that way.
3. I haven't yet said anything about a restricted version of hedonism, but I will!
4. In principle, of course, a hedonist could say that pleasures contribute more to well-being than pains take away from it, and then the story would get more complicated. However, it's difficult to see what would motivate a view like this. Also, remember when I considered a version of the desire satisfaction theory that was restricted to nonhuman animals? Now you can see one counterintuitive implication of a version of hedonism that's restricted to nonhuman animals—namely, this radical implication regarding the lives of wild animals. Granted, we can always bite the bullet; the point here is just that there's a bullet to bite.

5. Many people hold some version of this theory, but Jeff McMahan (2002) is usually given credit for its canonical statement. He calls it the "time-relative interest account" of the badness of death.

References

2009. "Farm Animal Welfare in Great Britain: Past, Present and Future." *Farm Animal Welfare Council*, October. https://assets.publishing.service.gov.uk/government/uploads/system/uploads/attachment_data/file/319292/Farm_Animal_Welfare_in_Great_Britain_-_Past__Present_and_Future.pdf.

Brambell, Rogers F.W. 1965. "Report of the Technical Committee to Enquire into the Welfare of Animals kept under Intensive Livestock Husbandry Systems." *Her Majesty's Stationery Office*, December. https://edepot.wur.nl/134379.

Broom, Donald M. 2011. "A History of Animal Welfare Science." *Acta Biotheoretica* 59: 121–137.

Dawkins, Richard. 1996. *River Out of Eden: A Darwinian View of Life*. New York: Harper Collins.

McMahan, Jeff. 2002. *The Ethics of Killing: Problems at the Margins of Life*. New York: Oxford University Press.

Piercy, Marge. 1983. "Toad Dreams." *Poetry Foundation*. www.poetryfoundation.org/poems/44883/toad-dreams.

Porphyry. 1823. *Select Works of Porphyry*. Translated by Thomas Taylor. London: J. Moyes, Greville Street.

Rollin, Bernard E. 1998. *The Unheeded Cry*. Ames: Iowa State University Press.

Sagoff, Mark. 1984. "Animal Liberation and Environmental Ethics: Bad Marriage, Quick Divorce." *Osgoode Hall Law Journal* 22(2): 297–307.

Thomson, Judith Jarvis. 1990. *The Realm of Rights*. Cambridge, MA: Harvard University Press.

Thoreau, Henry D. 2009. *The Maine Woods: A Fully Annotated Edition*. Edited by Jeffrey S. Cramer. New Haven: Yale University Press.

Yeates, James W. 2010. "Death is a Welfare Issue." *Journal of Agricultural and Environmental Ethics* 23: 229–241.

5 Moral Theory

OVERVIEW

Why should we do what we ought to do? What is it about the right actions that makes them right? Likewise, why shouldn't we do what we ought not to do? What is it about the wrong actions that makes them wrong? Moral theories propose answers to these questions. This chapter surveys the moral theories that have been most influential in recent animal ethics, including utilitarianism, the rights view, virtue ethics, and care ethics. It also offers a brief glimpse into the "critical turn" in moral theorizing, which sets aside standard questions about right-making and wrong-making features of individual actions, focusing instead on diagnosing what's wrong with the social structures within which those actions occur.

Suppose we agree that sentience is the dividing line between those beings who are and aren't members of the moral community. Suppose we agree, at least in the majority of cases, about those beings who are, and that aren't, sentient. Suppose we even agree about a theory of well-being. Still, we haven't said much about how we ought to act. In other words, even after we settle the issues just mentioned, we're left with some difficult questions: Is it okay to kill some animals to benefit others (as when wildlife managers cull members of one species to help members of a different one)? Is it fine to use chickens for our purposes, as long as they live nice lives (as promised, if not necessarily delivered, by "humane" farms)? And what should guide us in the all-too-familiar cases we've already discussed, such as making decisions about when to euthanize elderly companion animals?

There are many proposals that we could discuss here, far more than I can fit into the space available. What's more, I can only sketch the ones I can mention. As a result, we're going to move quickly here. Our aim is to identify the ways we *could* reason about our obligations to nonhuman animals, not to decide how we *should* reason about them. (For much more, see the Further Reading section.)

Moral Theory and Methodology

To begin, though, we need to say just a few words about moral theory and methodology. One standard goal for a moral theory is to explain when actions are *obligatory* (when they are morally required, or they are what you ought to do), when actions are *wrong* (when they are morally forbidden, or they're what you ought not to do), and when actions are *permissible* (neither obligatory nor wrong; okay to do). Moral theories often try to do much more—including, for instance, provide accounts of the virtues, the moral community, well-being, praise and blame, and much else. But traditionally, the package includes a story about the obligatory, the wrong, and the permissible.

How do we argue for one theory or another? What's the method we're supposed to employ? The short answer: *reflective equilibrium*. And while this idea might sound complicated, it's actually fairly familiar. Essentially, we start with some ordinary observations about what seems true, morally speaking. It seems pretty clear, for instance, that we shouldn't lie, steal, or kill people. It also seems pretty clear that there are some exceptions to these general principles. As we discussed in the introduction, we shouldn't lie. But if we're in 1942 Germany, and we're hiding Jews in our attic, and the Nazis are at our door asking whether we've seen any Jews, then we should lie. And so we gather examples like this, noting both the general principles and the features of the exceptions, and start generating hypotheses about what's going on. What's the underlying moral principle that would, if true, explain why we shouldn't lie, steal, or kill—except when we should?

After we get a proposal on the table, we apply it to some new cases. Suppose we are trying to figure out when it's wrong to lie, and our hypothesis in the wake of the "Nazi at the door" case is "don't lie unless someone's life is at stake." Good start. But now we need to think about some other examples to see whether our hypothesis holds up. What about a case where you are being asked to testify in a murder trial? Someone's life is at stake—they will give this person the death penalty if he's convicted—but it doesn't seem like it's okay to lie on the stand. So, we need to revise our hypothesis again.

Eventually, our hypotheses will become far more nuanced, and we'll turn away from simple examples, focusing on more complex issues. (What does our hypothesis imply about the rights of marginalized populations in democratic societies, our duties to the global poor, and the limits of state power during wartime?) But whether the hypothesis and the cases are simple or intricate, the process is the same. We face the choice of whether (a) to revise our hypothesis about the underlying moral principle, whether by refining it or generating an entirely new one, or (b) to revise the moral judgments with which our hypothesis conflicts. Sometimes, we'll decide that our moral judgment about a case is nonnegotiable: we shouldn't endorse any theory that, for instance, implies that it's fine to torture nonhuman animals for fun. Sometimes, we'll decide that our principle is more plausible than a moral judgment: we may have thought that it was okay to spend money on luxury goods while poor people starve, but our moral principle says it isn't, and we end up agreeing with the principle.

This isn't a quick process, nor is it guaranteed to produce agreement. We might spend a lot of time thinking very hard about moral theory and find ourselves divided at the end. There is no reason to think that we're all going to agree about which judgments are nonnegotiable, or which principles are so plausible that it's worth changing our minds about anything with which they conflict. But as far as I can tell, this is the only game in town; there is no alternative moral methodology that's guaranteed to leave us holding hands and singing in unison. So, we just have to do our best with the method of reflective equilibrium, being as transparent as possible with one another about our reasons for our theoretical choices.

With that said, let's consider a handful of prominent moral theories, touching on their pros and cons as we go.

Consequentialism

Perhaps the most famous and familiar moral theory is *consequentialism*. According to this moral theory, an action is morally right—it's morally mandatory or morally obligatory; it's what you must do, morally speaking—just in case it produces the most good. It's wrong otherwise. On this view, then, the right course of action is the one that produces the best results. But which results count? Consequentialists don't agree about this, but the most famous answer is *utility*, and *utilitarians* are consequentialists who say that an action is morally required if it produces the most utility overall. We can think of utility as representing a unit of happiness, a way of measuring the amount of happiness that an action produces. To be clear, as with the last chapter's discussion of "pleasure," "happiness" doesn't simply refer to the feeling you get when you taste good chocolate; it's supposed to be a much broader notion, encompassing all the ways that you can be psychologically better off. So there is a kind of happiness associated with eating chocolate, but there are also the various kinds associated with playing with your child, finishing a particularly complex math problem, and taking a quiet walk in the woods. These are all very different forms of happiness, but they are no less real for that. (Also, and as you might imagine, there are lots of philosophical complexities associated with measuring happiness, but we aren't going to worry about them here. There is an entire field of research—animal welfare science—that tries, among other things, to address such puzzles when it comes to what animals like and dislike.)

For present purposes, what matters is that utilitarianism says we shouldn't care about anything *other* than maximizing utility. Notice that there is no mention here about *whose* utility we ought to maximize: it's just utility, period, impartially considered. On this sort of view, your utility is no more important than a mouse's utility, which is no more important than an elephant's utility. The theory is thoroughly egalitarian in this respect.

Utilitarianism has many attractive features:

1. As just mentioned, the theory is thoroughly egalitarian. Everyone's interests are considered equally. This, of course, leads to some radical consequences, but in a world full of deeply partial beings, an impartial moral view might be

particularly attractive: it corrects our tendency to favor the near and dear, insisting that no one matters more than anyone else. (Recalling the discussion from Chapter 2 about whether we should accept the Principle of Equal Consideration of Interests, utilitarianism rejects any hierarchy in the moral community. Plants are out, animals are in, and all interests—human and nonhuman—are equal.)

2. In principle, there's a straightforward way to assess whether a particular course of action is justified. Should you adopt a dog from your local animal shelter? Well, consider how things are likely to go—for you, the dog, and anyone else who might be affected—depending on whether you adopt. It certainly takes some work to run this calculation, not least because it's difficult to be sure that you've considered all the potentially affected parties. But in principle, this is work we can do, and so the answers to our moral questions are within reach.

3. The theory provides a simple explanation of what's wrong with many practices that are increasingly seen as objectionable. For instance, what's wrong with doing painful research on (literal, actual) guinea pigs? In a great many cases, the odds of success are extremely low, the potential benefit to human beings would not be significant, and the suffering of the animals is extraordinary. In other words, it looks like the cost outweighs the benefits, and those are exactly the circumstances in which utilitarianism condemns an action.

Of course, the view also has its liabilities. For instance, many have objected that utilitarianism is an incredibly *demanding* moral theory. It's easiest to see this by noticing the category of action that doesn't figure at all in utilitarian thinking, namely, the category of *permissible but suboptimal* behavior. According to the classic version of utilitarianism, you either do the best or you act wrongly, and the best thing you can do in a situation may often be a lot.[1]

Suppose, for instance, that the best thing you can do is give almost all your money to effective charities that try to improve the welfare of animals. Admittedly, that probably wouldn't be best for you: you'd be out a lot of money; your life would be much harder as a result. However, given how much good your money could do for animals—say, by funding welfare improvements for animals on farms—any costs you incur will be outweighed even by small benefits to a sufficient number of animals. If utilitarianism is true and the calculation works out that way, then you ought to give, even at great personal expense.

Many people would regard this as a demanding result. And you might think that's a reason to reject utilitarianism. Before we accept that conclusion, however, we should note that our judgments about what's burdensome are going to be relative to what we regard as normal. Imagine a world where you were used to stealing to get whatever you want. In that world, following the "don't steal" rule would probably feel like it was asking a lot of you: all that stuff used to be free (to you, since you were just taking it), and now you have to pay! No fun. But obviously, it doesn't seem so demanding to us, who follow the "don't steal" rule, to follow it. We've built lives that simply take for granted that it's wrong to run off with other people's things. Likewise, we might think that when utilitarianism tells us that we have "extreme" obligations, the problem isn't with the obligations, but with us.

We're used to downplaying the interests of animals, so any pressure to play them up seems radical.

The point here isn't that we should be utilitarians or that we should endorse any particular conclusion about the ethics of giving to effective charities. Instead, the point is that we need to scrutinize the intuitions that we use both to support and criticize moral theories. None of them gets a free pass. Granted, if moral theories answer—at least in part—our intuitions about what is and isn't morally required, then utilitarians will need to do some work: they will need to explain why the tensions between utilitarianism and those intuitions are either (a) merely apparent or (b) such that the intuitions should give. But that may well be work that utilitarians can do.

The Rights View

A prominent alternative to utilitarianism—namely, the rights view—comes out of the Kantian tradition and was developed in greatest detail by Tom Regan.[2] It's a *deontological* position, which is a catch-all term for nonconsequentialist moral theories that try, first and foremost, to specify what makes actions right and wrong (as opposed to other theories, such as virtue ethics, which are primarily concerned with who you ought to be; more on virtue ethics later).

The basic idea behind Kantianism is that individuals are owed respect; we shouldn't use them as *mere means*. In other words, we shouldn't use them in a way that fails to give due regard to their autonomy, to their ability to choose how to act for one reason or another. So what's wrong with having someone do work on your house and not paying him at the end? According to utilitarianism, it's that you've done something that doesn't maximize utility. According to Kantianism, though, it doesn't matter if you *do* maximize utility by not paying. (Maybe it makes you wildly happy, and the person you've stiffed is too busy to realize that he hasn't been paid.) Instead, Kantianism implies that it's wrong not to pay because that amounts to using the person who did the work as a mere means: you aren't respecting his reasons for agreeing to do the work in the first place—namely, the expectation of payment.

The rights view builds on this basic idea that it's wrong to use others as mere means, though it places less emphasis on autonomy and more emphasis on the inherent worth of individuals. Here's the idea. Kantians sometimes argue that utilitarianism regards individuals as mere "receptacles of value." In other words, according to utilitarianism, what's valuable about you is your experiential states, your pleasures and pains. Those are the things that can be summed alongside the pleasure and pain of all other beings, thereby revealing what ought to be done. It's almost as though *you*—the individual, the container for your experiences—aren't valuable at all. According to Kantians, this violates our intuitions about the worth of individuals.

Regan runs with this contrast between valuing experiential states and valuing individuals. What matters, he thinks, is that individuals be recognized as having inherent worth, valuable in themselves, regardless of their usefulness to others. And because they have inherent value, they're entitled to a certain kind of treatment—namely, respectful treatment, which acknowledges their independent worth and which forbids their being used merely for others' purposes. As Regan summarizes it:

> Some nonhuman animals resemble normal humans in morally relevant ways. In particular, they bring the mystery of a unified psychological presence of the world. Like us, they possess a variety of sensory, cognitive, cognitive, and volitional capacities. They see and hear, believe and desire, remember and anticipate, plan and intend. Moreover, what happens to them matters to them. Physical pleasure and pain—these they share with us. But also fear and contentment, anger and loneliness, frustration and satisfaction, calming and imprudence. These and a host of other psychological states and dispositions collectively help define the mental life and relative well-being of those . . . subjects-of-a-life we know better as raccoons and rabbits, beaver and bison chipmunks and chimpanzees, you and I. The basic moral right to respectful treatment places strict limits on how subjects-of-a-life may be treated. Individuals who possess this right are never to be treated as if they exist as resources for others; in particular, harms intentionally done to anyone subject cannot be justified by aggregating benefits derived by others. . . . The rights view recognizes the equal inherent value of all subjects-of-a-life.
>
> (2004, xvi–xvii)

It's important to recognize that the rights view isn't committed to saying that nonhuman animals have every right that humans have. Suppose that human beings have a right to a basic education: it doesn't follow from this that monkeys have a right to a basic education, as they aren't harmed by not receiving the kind of education we offer. The idea is that each subject-of-a-life has a right to be respected as the kind of thing it is. Since all subjects-of-a-life can, by definition, experience pain and they are harmed by that experience, they have a right not to have pain inflicted on them to benefit others. But not all subjects-of-a-life have an interest in a basic education, and so not all subjects-of-a-life have a right to it.[3]

The rights view has a number of attractive features:

1. It captures the intuition that there are some bright moral lines that we just shouldn't cross. Suppose that we could make many people slightly better off by torturing one animal—for instance, we could bring some short-term pleasure to many people by letting them watch a cockfight, which usually ends with one rooster bleeding to death from an array of injuries. As long as there are enough people on one side of this moral equation, thereby tipping the scale in favor of their pleasure, the utilitarian has to say that such an action isn't just morally permissible, but is rather morally required: it's what we ought to do, morally speaking. This is a hard pill to swallow. The rights view explains why such actions aren't permissible: they fail to respect the individual who would be tortured, using that one as a mere means to benefit others. That seems like the correct result.

2. The rights view seems to allow us to draw a distinction between those actions that we absolutely *ought* to do, morally speaking, and those actions that it would be *good* to do but that aren't morally required. According to the rights view, as long as you aren't violating anyone's rights, you have some freedom: you don't have to spend all your time trying to make the world the best place it can possibly be; you can have your own projects and pursue your own good. (The rights view does insist that you ought to help those whose rights have been violated, but it doesn't necessarily require you to give up everything for them.)

3. The rights view is based on the powerful thought that there is something about the *individuality* of nonhuman animals that requires our moral response. It's the fact that they are, as Regan says, "subjects-of-a-life" that explains why we have reason to be concerned about how their lives go for them. We might think that one of the first steps in moral thinking is to recognize that you are neither unique nor alone in the world: it's full of other creatures with their own vantage points on reality, their own beliefs and desires, and so forth. Perhaps, then, we might want to say that what matters fundamentally isn't pain per se but individual subjects—and that's what the rights view calls us to recognize.

All that said, we shouldn't understate the ways in which this, too, is a radical moral theory, at least if judged in terms of its assessment of the status quo. As Regan makes amply clear, the rights view calls for the complete and immediate end of animal agriculture—industrial or small scale, humane or cruel. There are no permissible forms of animal farming according to the rights view: they all invariably involve using others as a mere means to our own ends, and that, Regan argues, is very seriously wrong. Likewise, the rights view calls for an end to animal experimentation, as well as keeping animals captive in circuses and most zoos. (Zoos that function as animal sanctuaries are the likely exception.) It also has significant implications for conservation policy. For instance, most conservationists see no problem with killing invasive species to save noninvasive ones or culling some members of a species to improve the welfare of others. But if the rights view is correct, then these actions involve using some individuals just to benefit others, and that's wrong.

Virtue Theory

We might worry that utilitarianism and the rights view don't capture everything that matters to us in the moral domain. Isn't there a lot more to being a good person than these theories discuss? What about the internal life of the person? What about your feelings and dispositions and character? What about cultivating the right kind of life, not just considering things on an action-by-action basis? If you find yourself asking these questions, then virtue theory may address your concerns. Virtue theory denies that we're going to be able to assess what we should do without thinking about the kinds of people we want to become, and it refocuses the discussion around that aim. It is, first and foremost, a theory about our characters, not about our actions—though, of course, it has something to say about that too.

What kind of people should we become? What sorts of characters should we form? Presumably, we should become people who exhibit some key virtues: honesty, compassion, courage, diligence, humility, and so on. We can then use that insight to assess actions. According to virtue theory, there may not always be one right thing to do. But when there is, it's because that's the action that the virtues favor. If a particular action is what kind, honest, temperate, judicious (etc.) people would do, then it's the right thing.

There are lots of ways of developing virtue theory, and this isn't the place to survey them all. For present purposes, what matters is the way that the virtue ethicist encourages us to think about moral problems. According to utilitarianism, even very bad people can know what they ought to do. To answer that question, they just need to know how to deploy the principle of utility. But according to virtue theory, bad people may *not* be able to know what they ought to do. It's good people—the morally wise—who are able to tell what's best. So instead of having a simple principle, such as "maximize utility," virtue theory tells us that it's only the virtuous who are going to know how, in a particular situation, to balance being just and merciful, kind and honest, etc. There isn't going to be a shortcut, where we can enter the information about a situation into an algorithm and have it spit out the correct answer. Instead, we have to do the hard work of becoming people with virtuous characters, and only then can we be trusted to know what to do in the hardest situations.

This is both quite compelling and remarkably disappointing. It's compelling insofar as it's a refusal to give pat answers in ethics. If nothing else, we can safely say that ethics is hard. In the kinds of cases that we bother to discuss, we discuss them precisely because there is so much disagreement about what ought to be done. It's only the morally wise who are going to be able to figure out how to balance the virtues, which often pull in different directions. (Sometimes, the kind thing isn't fair, or the honest thing isn't compassionate.) And since lots of us aren't morally wise, at least if we're honest with ourselves, confusion and disagreement are exactly what we should expect.

At the same time, there's a sense in which the virtue ethicist is punting. What should we do? Who knows! Ask the virtuous! But we often *identify* the virtuous by the courses of action they recommend. And if we don't know what's right, then we don't know who to count as virtuous. This sort of problem is especially serious when it comes to issues relating to animals, where seemingly good people differ so radically in their assessment of our obligations. On the face of it, then, the virtue theorist gives us little advice at all.

Virtue theorists say different things at this juncture, but one attractive maneuver is to dismiss this worry as too removed from the reality of virtue-based decision-making. Consider, for instance, the way that Rosalind Hursthouse—a prominent virtue ethicist—discusses the ethics of eating animals:

> Can I, in all honesty, deny the ongoing existence of [the suffering of farmed animals]? No, I can't. I know perfectly well that although there have been some improvements in the regulation of factory farming, what is going on is still terrible. Can I think it is anything but callous to shrug this off and

say it doesn't matter? No, I can't. Can I deny that the practices are cruel? No, I can't. Then what am I doing being party to them? It won't do for me to say that I am not actually engaging in the cruelty myself. There is a large gap between not being cruel and being truly compassionate, and the virtue of compassion is what I am supposed to be acquiring and exercising. I can no more think of myself as compassionate while I am party to such cruelty than I could think of myself as just if, scrupulously avoiding owning slaves, I still enjoyed the fruits of slave labor. . . . The practices that bring cheap meat to our tables are cruel, so we shouldn't be party to them.

(2006, 141–143)

The point here isn't that Hursthouse's conclusion is correct—though the argument is certainly worth considering, and we'll spend some time with it later (see Chapter 7). Rather, the point is that we can grant that there are large, unanswered questions about how human beings should relate to nonhuman animals. What's more, we can grant that there is massive disagreement about how to balance the various character traits that we judge to be morally valuable. Still, when you're doing your best to be morally serious, you probably have a good sense, at least in many cases, about what is and isn't virtuous. That's what Hursthouse is modeling here. So sure, you can be vulnerable to self-deception, you can do your best to excuse your own behavior, and you can try hard to suppress negative interpretations of your behavior. But you can also be intellectually honest, appropriately humble, and see your behavior as either admirable or objectionable, depending on the case.[4] Admittedly, this doesn't make collective moral deliberation particularly easy, as we may have a very hard time convincing one another to adopt our ideas about what cruelty is and isn't, or what honesty does and doesn't require. The virtue ethicist will just shrug. As we all know, ethics is challenging. We have to do our best, learning what we can from those who seem to be more virtuous than we are.

Care Ethics

Like virtue ethics, we can think of care ethics as a reaction against utilitarianism and the rights view. However, the reaction is importantly different. Virtue ethicists reject utilitarianism and the rights view because they want to put the focus on our characters. At least when it was first developed, care ethicists rejected these approaches because they saw them as overly patriarchal ways of understanding the ethical project. In part, they were skeptical of the traditional goal of moral theory: namely, providing a theory of value (what's good and bad) plus a theory of the right (why every right action is right and every wrong one is wrong). Care ethics is, in this sense, a "critical" theory of ethics, regarding other tasks as more important. But arguably, the original versions of care ethics didn't quite make it all the way to a fully critical stance—a point to which I'll return in a moment.

We can distinguish three important aspects of traditional care ethics. The first is that it's committed to *particularism*. Care ethics began as a feminist critique of traditional moral theories, such as utilitarianism. That theory is one of several that says if you have all the facts about a situation, you can simply apply their preferred principle to find out what people should and shouldn't do in that situation. Carol Gilligan and Nel Noddings were some of the first to argue that this amounts to privileging overly rational, individualistic, and "male" ways of thinking—to the exclusion of emotional, relational, and feminine ways of approaching ethics. On their view, there isn't any one principle that explains why all right actions are morally right and all wrong ones are morally wrong—that's what makes it a form of particularism. Actions are still right and wrong—they aren't denying that. They are saying, however, that you can't just feed the details of a situation into some "tell me the morally correct thing to do" machine, turn the crank, and get an answer.[5]

We might worry that this makes it difficult to know what we should do. But care ethicists think that these worries are overblown. This is because they offer us two different tools for assessing our obligations, which brings us to the second aspect of care ethics, namely, the importance of care itself.

Here's one way of thinking about it. Care has many dimensions. It can involve feeling certain emotions: being happy when a friend is happy and being sad when she's sad. It can involve empathizing with her: recognizing her as a distinct individual, being attentive to her situation, and attempting to understand her on her own terms. It involves wanting what's good for her. It involves being responsive to her needs—sometimes at considerable cost to yourself. Actions are good, on this view, if they flow from this kind of rich, multidimensional sort of care; they are bad if they flow from various attitudes that are incompatible with care, such as neglect or hostility.

Of course, there are plenty of cases where it's difficult to know exactly what caring requires of you. Am I enabling this person or simply being supportive? Am I caring for someone the appropriate amount, or am I caring too much and so letting others down? But regardless of our moral outlook, these kinds of cases are often tricky, so maybe it's no fault of care ethics that it doesn't give precise guidance on them.

This brings us to the third aspect of care ethics, which concerns the importance of relationships. Care isn't some abstract idea: it's a way of feeling and relating to another person. And the nature of that care, and the responsibilities it generates, are affected by the kind of relationship in which it occurs. My care for my parents is different from my care for my wife, which is different from my care for my children, which is different from my care for my students. We can't separate a discussion of care from a discussion of the special obligations that we have as parents, partners, and so on—not to mention the really complicated details of individual relationships. So the claim isn't just that we need to act out of care. Rather, it's that we need to care in ways that are sensitive to the special responsibilities we have, given the particular lives we lead.

There is something very attractive about this picture. It's hard to find a single principle that sums up our ethical obligations. Plainly, caring is very important to being a good person and to acting well in so many situations. And it obviously matters that we are sisters and children and parents and employees; any ethic that overlooks these relationships is missing something important. However, we might have two worries.

The first is that care ethics is a bit too anthropocentric: in its early days, it was focused on relations of care between humans *and other humans*. This was partly because those who developed it thought that caring relationships required a kind of reciprocity and they didn't think you could have that with the citizens of the nonhuman world.

The second worry is that care may not be enough to address all the moral questions we face. It seems right to pay closer attention to our emotions and relationships but a mistake to limit ourselves to caring. What about the various character traits that can help us rein in our tendency to care too much, such as honesty and civic responsibility and a sense of justice? Think about the mother who is convinced that she ought to lie to cover up her son's crime. She might be caring excellently and yet still acting wrongly. The care ethicist might agree, saying that the problem here is that she doesn't care enough about victims or that she cares for her son in the wrong way. But how are we going to explain why she isn't caring enough about the victims or the sense in which this is the wrong way to care? What explains why she's striking the wrong balance? It would be helpful to have other values to which to appeal— something else to tip the scales in favor of truth telling and explain why it's the right choice in this case. But care ethics just gives us one tool—care—and we might worry that this one tool isn't enough to do all the work that needs doing.

Care ethicists make various moves here. For instance, some simply say that care is only part of the moral story: we need an ethic of care *and* an ethic of justice. But others have thought that this isn't a game worth playing: there will always be another puzzle to address, and the back and forth only distracts us from more important issues, such as real-world oppression and marginalization. When you combine this concern with the worry about anthropocentrism, you get the basic motivations for ecofeminism.

Ecofeminism and Beyond

Like care ethics, ecofeminism is committed to particularism, the importance of caring, and the significance of relationships. However, it completes the critical turn: it goes much further than care ethics in rejecting the traditional conception of moral theory. It isn't that ecofeminists have nothing to say about right and wrong. Rather, it's that ecofeminists don't think that questions about right and wrong are the most important questions to ask, and may even distract us from more significant features of the ethical landscape. To explain the basic idea, Carol Adams and Lori Gruen— two ecofeminists—write this:

> Ecofeminism addresses the various ways that sexism, heteronormativity, racism, colonialism, and ableism are informed by and support speciesism and how analyzing the ways these forces intersect can produce less violent, more just practices. In the 1990s, ecofeminists worked to remedy a perceived problem in feminist theory, animal advocacy, and environmentalism, namely, a lack of attention to the intersecting structures of power that reinforce the "othering" of women and animals, and contribute to the increasing

destruction of the environment. Though sometimes called "utopian" or "concerned with too many issues," ecofeminist theory exposes and opposes intersecting forces of oppression, showing how problematic it is when these issues are considered separate from one another.

(2014, 1)

The crucial idea is that *power relations* deserve close attention, as the structural features of the social world are often as important—if not even more important—than whether any particular individual acts well or badly, rightly or wrongly. Ecofeminists are concerned, first and foremost, with structural critiques of the world in which we find ourselves, which they see as organized by various binaries that preserve positions of privilege and disadvantage: human/animal, male/female, black/white, high class/low class, cis/trans, and so forth. So ecofeminists don't want to worry about whether going vegan maximizes utility. (That is, they don't want to worry about the question: If the goal is to do the most good you can, is that best achieved, at least in the domain of diet, by becoming a vegan?) Instead, ecofeminists would prefer to think of veganism as part of a political movement, an attempt to resist the social realities that frame animals as food rather than as individuals, as consumable rather than as having their own lives and interests. Likewise, instead of asking whether you should avoid wearing fur, you might note—as Marti Kheel does—that women who wear fur are situated in a culture that "robs women of their own self-image and then sells it back to them in distorted form" (1993, 259). This doesn't necessarily excuse fur-wearing, behind which there's an enormous amount of suffering. But it keeps the context in view: wearing fur isn't *just* or *primarily* an unwillingness to attend to animals, even if it's that too.

None of this is to suggest that ecofeminists don't care about individual action: nothing could be further from the truth. It is, however, to say that ecofeminists frame the significance of individual action very differently, so they're less concerned with criticizing individuals than they are with criticizing the social conditions in which individuals make choices. In nonideal circumstances—namely, our actual circumstances—all the options that an individual has are bad. In such circumstances, there may be little point to criticizing, say, a researcher who has to use mouse models to get funding for cancer research. Still, there are good reasons to be worried about the institutions in which this choice makes sense.

It's hard to compare ecofeminism to traditional moral theories precisely because it's engaged in a different project. It doesn't answer many of the questions that we expected other theories to answer: there is no account of membership in the moral community; there is no theory of value or criterion of right action; there is no explanation for why individuals have the particular rights that they have or how, exactly, those rights should be traded off against others. This isn't to say that ecofeminists can't or don't answer these questions; they can and do. Rather, it's just to say that when they answer these questions, they aren't answering them in a distinctive way. Instead, they often borrow from more traditional moral theories to fill in details, or they develop novel answers that aren't shared by other ecofeminists. This isn't a criticism. Rather, it's a way of highlighting an important difference in what ecofeminists think ethics is about. For ecofeminists, ethics' main goal is to diagnose—and ultimately address—real-world oppression. It's all well and good to explore the precise boundaries of the moral community, and such projects have their place within the ecofeminist tradition. But they aren't primary, and it would be a mistake to expect the theory to deliver what it isn't designed to provide.

Ecofeminism isn't alone in taking the critical turn. It's also the hallmark of other liberation-focused ethics, such as antiracist and anti-ableist defenses of animals. Syl Ko, for instance, considers the way that antiracist scholars often criticize the animalization of black people. They contend that white people animalize black people because they assume that it's okay to inflict violence on nonhuman bodies. By animalizing black people, white people legitimate violence against them too. But Ko doesn't think this goes far enough. Not only does she argue that we need to reject the idea that it's okay to inflict violence on nonhuman bodies, but she also claims that the "human—animal divide is the ideological bedrock underlying the framework of white supremacy."

Why think that? It's worth quoting her answer at some length:

> The racial hierarchy and racism, not to mention the racial thinking it generates, was the novel way white, Western Europeans in the colonial period legally and morally placed groups outside the "human" zone. . . . Their notion of "the animal"—construed under their white supremacist framework as "subhuman," "nonhuman," or "inhuman"—is the conceptual vehicle for justified violence. . . . The human–animal divide (binary), where "the human" and "the animal" form oppositional poles and, thus, oppositional status-markers on a "chain of being," is not an objective model handed to us from the heavens. "The human" and "the animal" were placed through the positing of a racial system. In the same vein, racial categories tracking modes of "being" and degrees of superiority/inferiority are not part of an objective framework that must be in place for us to think about or conceptually arrange members of the world. Both of these frameworks, which are deeply intertwined, and cannot be made sense of independent of one another, were creations invented by a small percentage of people who took themselves to be the singular point of knowledge and, through centuries of violence, genocide, and control made their view of the world, themselves, and others universal.
>
> (Ko and Ko 2017)

In short: if we are committed to antiracism, then we need to be committed to challenging the human–animal divide, since it's part of the same comprehensive system that's used to oppress black people specifically and people of color generally. And with this thesis in hand, Ko goes on to make a range of arguments about the right approach to animal advocacy, strategies for achieving black liberation, the nature of veganism, and much else. Is she giving us a general moral theory, the kind of thing that's supposed to tell you whether it's okay to lie to a friend as long as you're doing it to protect his feelings? No. However, that isn't the goal, and from the perspective of those who have taken the critical turn, it's a mistake to focus on those kinds of issues as the core of ethics. What really matters is whether beings are free, whether they can escape the yoke of oppression, not whether we work out some details of interpersonal morality.

We see a similar approach from Sunaura Taylor, though from a disability studies perspective rather than an antiracist approach. One of the foundational assumptions of contemporary disability studies is that we need to challenge value systems that assign lower worth to individuals by virtue of not having the traits possessed by able-bodied people. Some people in the disability rights community reject the idea that disabled people are at all like nonhuman animals, but Taylor embraces it. She just points out that if we value the distinctive traits that disabled people possess, then we should value them in animals as well. Consider, for instance, the ways that she sees ableism supporting animal oppression:

> Ableism . . . fosters values and institutions that perpetuate animal suffering. The various animal industries that exist in this country (from factory farms to animal research) rely on the public belief that using animals is okay because they lack the capacities that would make their use wrong. These industries also rely on ideologies of nature to justify what they do (perpetuating the idea that it is simply natural to use animals for our benefit, for instance). But even ideas of nature and naturalness are bound up with ableism, because constructions of nature often conflate such things as health, normalcy, and independence with evolutionary fitness or ecological compatibility. Ableist values are central to animal industries, where the dependency, vulnerability, and presumed lack of emotional awareness or intellectual capacity of animals creates the groundwork for a system that makes billions of dollars in profit off of animal lives. The very norms institutions that perpetuate animal suffering and exploitation are supported by ableism.
>
> (Taylor 2017, 60)

The upshot is this. Ecofeminist, antiracist, and anti-ableist theorizing about animals essentially says, "don't focus so much on individual action, and attend instead to the structural features of society—its institutions, its laws, its value systems—that preserve exploitation." Once we do that, we can think about how individuals ought to respond to their own exploitation or the exploitation of others. However, that sort of reflection is secondary.

Contractualism

All the theories that we've considered thus far lead to some radical conclusions, at least relative to what many people believe, about our obligations to and regarding nonhuman animals. Is there a moral theory that *isn't* so revisionary? After all, we did say in the beginning that it matters whether a moral theory matches our considered judgments, and you might wonder whether we've just abandoned that thought, given how pro-animal all these theories seem to be.

Truth be told, though, there just aren't many candidates that uphold most of the status quo, at least with respect to animals. But of the options, contractualism is probably the most serious contender. There are different versions of contractualism, but the basic idea is that morality is a set of rules to which we would consent—*if* some other condition were satisfied. So, for instance, perhaps morality is the system of rules to which we'd consent *if we were perfectly self-interested and rational*, or *if we were free and equal*, or *if we were determined to live in accord with rules that others couldn't reasonably reject.*[6] Whatever the condition, the idea is that morality is a system of rules that's created by *agents*, by beings with the deliberative capacities of normal adults. Unsurprisingly, most versions of contractualism imply that other beings like that— other agents—have various important rights. If we were perfectly self-interested and rational, we would see that it's in our interest to live in accord with rules like "don't murder (other agents)." By agreeing to live by such rules, we give up the freedom to use lethal violence against others, but we effectively get the right not to have lethal violence used against us. It's rational to make this trade, and so all agents have that right. But you can't make such deals with tigers: they won't abide by them. So, it isn't in our self-interest, or rational, to give up the freedom to use violence against such animals.

What about young children and those with severe cognitive disabilities? You can't make deals with them, either. Do contractualists have to say that they don't have rights?

They usually don't think so. Some argue, for instance, that it wouldn't be rational for us to agree to arrangements that don't protect the vulnerable beings about whom we care deeply, such as young children and those with severe cognitive disabilities. But since humans generally don't have such strong attachments to animals, it can be rational for us to agree to arrangements that don't extend even further.[7] This move probably doesn't work, given how much some human beings care about some animals and how little some human beings care about other human beings. And it's unclear whether contractualists have any better options.

But even if we grant contractualists their views about the boundaries of the moral community, we should note that they generally don't think we can do anything we want to animals. Instead, they think that our duties to animals are indirect. This is a view they borrow from Kant—who wasn't a contractualist, but famously developed the indirect duty position, as discussed in Chapter 2. On Kant's view,

> if a man has his dog shot, because it can no longer earn a living for him, he is by no means in breach of any duty to the dog, since the latter is incapable of judgement, but he thereby damages the kindly and humane qualities in himself, which he ought to exercise in virtue of his duties to mankind.
>
> (2001, 212)

In other words, when it's wrong to harm animals, this isn't because they matter in and of themselves. Instead, it's because of their link to someone who actually does have moral standing—namely, some human being.[8]

As we saw in Chapter 2, though, indirect duty views provide overly complex explanations of seemingly straightforward cases. Moreover, they seem to have some strange implications. As Jennifer Swanson (2011) observes, the indirect duty view implies that the last person on earth has no reason not to torture animals for fun, as there's no chance that he will harm any human beings. Of course, the contractualist can say that the problem isn't in the risk of harm of a human being per se, but rather in the deformation of character; you aren't supposed to become a cruel person, and you would have to be a cruel person to torture animals for fun. However, this reply won't work. If you know, as the last person on earth does, that in performing a certain action you can't possibly harm anyone who matters morally, then it's very hard to see how your behavior would count as being cruel.

In any case, if we're looking for a moral theory that doesn't lead to such revisionary conclusions—that is, one that doesn't immediately condemn animal agriculture and much animal research—then contractualism is probably the best candidate. Of course, it isn't clear that that should be our goal! What's more, it's an open question as to whether contractualism's problems—such as not recognizing animals as beings to whom we have direct obligations—can be overcome.

Looking Ahead

I've tried to give you a sense of the frameworks that have been the most influential in recent animal ethics. There are certainly others, and others still that are likely to become prominent in the future. For instance, African, Indian, and Asian ethical traditions are only just now being put in dialogue with Western views, and it will be interesting to see how cross-cultural theorizing evolves. By and large, however, the frameworks you have are the ones that have shaped, and still continue to shape, the Western, English-speaking discussions about animal ethics.

To clarify: these are the frameworks that have shaped discussions about animal ethics *among philosophers*. They've had some influence beyond the philosophical world—perhaps most notably in activist circles—but essentially all the frameworks that we've outlined are rejected by most people who work with animals. You won't find many animal researchers who are committed to animal rights; it's the rare farmer who's a utilitarian; there probably aren't any conservation biologists who are committed to ecofeminism. I'm not saying that to criticize animal rights, utilitarianism, or ecofeminism; I'm just pointing out that if we want to understand the ethical principles that motivate people in animal industries, we'll have to look elsewhere. In invoking one of these theories, we are criticizing from the outside. Outside critiques are all well and good, but they are easy for people to ignore. If I'm a utilitarian and you aren't, you can always just respond to my utilitarian argument by saying, "Well, we disagree about utilitarianism, so that's that." If we want to criticize from the inside, invoking the kinds of reasons that our conversation partners accept, then we'll need to understand the way that those people think about their moral obligations. For one example of this project, see Chapter 9, which engages with contemporary research ethics.

Finally, let me just expand on what I said at the end of the last chapter. There are cases where it doesn't really matter which of these theories is true. This is because there are cases where most moral theories agree about what you should do, and that agreement is decent evidence that you really ought to do it. However, there are lots of cases where the moral theories *don't* agree about what you should do. Those cases are harder.

I don't know which moral theory is true. When I consider the arguments for and against each one, I don't see a clear winner. So when I do animal ethics, I use theories as though they were lenses; they bring particular features of the world into focus. And in the context of specific debates, some features seem more important than others. When our conversation partners are especially concerned about the consequences of various courses of action, it's helpful to think like a consequentialist; when we are trying to figure out how we, personally, are going to navigate a thorny moral choice, it's helpful to think like a virtue ethicist. "That's all well and good," someone might complain. "But who's right? Which view *should* we adopt?" And if I knew, I'd tell you. But I don't, so I can't.

Given that, I think what's important is that we be transparent about how we're reasoning. As I said in the introduction, moral reasoning isn't a private affair; it's something we do together. From my perspective, it doesn't always matter whether we appeal to the same moral theory in every case. Instead, what matters is that we always tell each other, as clearly and frankly as possible, about the moral assumptions we're making on any given day, in whatever conversation we happen to be having. Transparency means laying our cards on the table, not always playing the same hand. So when, in what follows, I do actually defend a position, I'll try to be as open as possible about how I'm reaching it.

Further Reading

Bykvist, Krister, Toby Ord, and William MacAskill. 2020. *Moral Uncertainty*. New York: Oxford University Press.

Crary, Alice. 2016. *Inside Ethics: On the Demands of Moral Thought*. Cambridge, MA: Harvard University Press.

DeMello, Margo. 2012. *Animals and Society: An Introduction to Human-Animal Studies*. New York: Columbia University Press.

Donovan, Josephine, and Carol J. Adams (eds.). 2007. *The Feminist Care Tradition in Animal Ethics: A Reader*. New York: Columbia University Press.

Garner, Robert, and Siobhan O'Sullivan (eds.). 2016. *The Political Turn in Animal Ethics*. Lanham: Rowman & Littlefield Publishers.

Gruen, Lori (ed.). 2018. *Critical Terms for Animal Studies*. Chicago: University of Chicago Press.

Palmer, Clare. 2010. *Animal Ethics in Context*. New York: Columbia University Press.

Shafer-Landau, Russ. 2018. *The Fundamentals of Ethics*. New York: Oxford University Press.

Notes

1. There are versions of utilitarianism that don't have this feature. For instance, there are versions of utilitarianism according to which you are only obligated to choose one of the options that's good enough, rather than the best (satisficing utilitarianism). And there are also versions of utilitarianism that give up on deontic categories entirely (that is, right and wrong) and simply rank actions in terms of how much utility they produce, with no further commentary (scalar utilitarianism). But these views haven't been particularly influential in animal ethics, so we won't say anything more about them here.
2. Apparently, his name is pronounced like Ronald Reagan, the fortieth U.S. president.

3. I've chosen this example carefully, as others are more complicated. Consider, for instance, the right to vote. Strictly speaking, nonhuman animals have no interest in being allowed to vote *themselves*—that is, horses have no interest in being allowed in the voting booth—but they may have an interest in being represented in political decisions.

4. It's standard to distinguish the so-called "moral" and "intellectual" virtues, and you might think I'm running them together here. Not so: I'm just assuming that when we're being morally serious, we'll also do our best to exhibit intellectual virtue.

5. They weren't simply rejecting the principle that you should maximize utility as a decision procedure; utilitarians often reject that too. Instead, they were rejecting the idea that there is any one principle that's the criterion for right action across the board.

6. Someone might object to the idea that morality is about enlightened self-interest, insisting that morality is essentially other-regarding, where the whole idea is that it serves as a corrective to self-interest. This is a challenge to one way of developing contractualism, but not all, given the "free and equal" and "reasonable rejection" approaches.

7. Depending on the version of contractualism, we may get different results. Suppose we think that we ought to act in accord with the rules to which we'd all agree if we were free and equal. If "we" here means everyone, animals included, then animals may end up with rights, as we have to assume *their* freedom and equality too. If the "we" here doesn't mean everyone, then we need some story as to why not. And crucially, it has to be a story that doesn't imply that, for instance, infants are excluded from the "we," since we certainly want our theory to imply that they have rights.

8. This is different from the view that we have *prudential* reasons to do what's good for animals. After all, it might matter how we treat animals because they're valuable to us, and treating them poorly sets back our own interests. This is, very roughly, the way that many producers talk about animal welfare in intensive agricultural systems: stressed pigs are unproductive pigs, so stress should be reduced. Stress isn't intrinsically bad from the perspective of such producers: it's bad because it makes pigs less productive. Likewise, not putting oil in your car isn't intrinsically bad: it's bad because it sets back our interest in having a functioning vehicle. In the pig example here, stress doesn't have moral value, but it does have prudential (self-interested) value.

References

Adams, Carol J., and Lori Gruen. 2014. *Ecofeminism: Feminist Intersections with Other Animals and the Earth*. New York: Bloomsbury Publishing.

Hursthouse, Rosalind. 2006. "Applying Virtue Ethics to Our Treatment of the Other Animals." In *The Practice of Virtue*, edited by Jennifer Welchman, 136–155. Indianapolis: Hackett Publishing.

Kant, Immanuel. 2001. *Lectures on Ethics*. Edited by Peter Heath and J.B. Schneewind. Translated by Peter Heath. Cambridge: Cambridge University Press.

Kheel, Marti. 1993. "From Heroic to Holistic Ethics: The Ecofeminist Challenge." In *Ecofeminism*, edited by Greta Gaard, 243–271. Philadelphia: Temple University Press.

Ko, Aph, and Syl Ko. 2017. *Aphro-ism: Essays on Pop Culture, Feminism, and Black Veganism from Two Sisters*. New York: Lantern Books.

Regan, Tom. 2004. *The Case for Animal Rights*. Berkeley: University of California Press.

Swanson, Jennifer. 2011. "Contractualism and the Moral Status of Animals." *Between the Species* 14(1): 1–17.

Taylor, Sunaura. 2017. *Beasts of Burden: Animal and Disability Liberation*. New York: The New Press.

6   Animal Agriculture and Aquaculture

OVERVIEW

This chapter is the first of three about animals as food. This one provides an overview of the history, economics, and welfare impacts of contemporary intensive animal agriculture and aquaculture—drawn exclusively from industry and industry-friendly sources. This chapter is very light on philosophy, but the empirical issues are so important—and so often misunderstood—that they need to be set out in some detail. So, after mapping out the rise of intensive animal agriculture, the chapter summarizes the lives of pigs, cattle, and chickens in contemporary production systems. Then, the chapter turns to aquaculture, which is far more complex because so many more species are involved. So, instead of trying to be exhaustive, the chapter simply offers a rough sense of contemporary fish farming by considering some representative examples.

In 1900, the U.S. population was around 80 million; in 2020, it was around 330 million—a fourfold increase. As you might expect, U.S. agricultural production has also trended upward. In 1900, some 10.8 million cows and 51.9 million pigs were slaughtered for food in the United States. In 2018, it was 33 million cows and 124.5 million pigs. But chickens didn't go up by the same factor. In 1909, there were 340 million chickens on farms in the United States. You can't even find data that disaggregates the broiler population (chickens raised for meat) from the layer population (chickens raised for egg production), as they weren't raised separately at that point. In 2018, by contrast, the laying hen population alone was 340 million, and 9.16 *billion* chickens were slaughtered for food—28 times as many. Producers aren't just keeping up with the country's population growth: Americans are eating—and exporting—more meat than ever before.

Yet fewer Americans are producing it. In 1900, some 38% of the U.S. labor force was involved in farming, and there were roughly 5.7 million farms. In 2018, roughly 1% of the U.S. labor force was involved in farming, and there were roughly 2.1

million farms. In other words, farm productivity skyrocketed: on average, each farm now produces roughly 230 times as many animals than it did at the turn of the 20th century. What's more, they're producing them much faster. In 1925, for instance, chickens went to market after 112 days, weighing 2.5 pounds, and having consumed 11.75 pounds of feed. In 2019, chickens went to market after 47 days, weighing 6.32 pounds, and having consumed 11.38 pounds of feed. In 1924, 435 million chickens were on farms in the United States, producing nearly 35 billion eggs each year, with each layer hen averaging 89 eggs in that period. In 2019, 240 million laying hens produced roughly 70.5 billion eggs, averaging 294 eggs per hen per year. In the span of 94 years, farmers got chickens to grow to twice the weight in less than half the time while feeding them less. And fewer laying hens managed to produce over three times the number of eggs than chickens 95 years prior.[1]

How and why did all these changes happen? To answer these questions, we need to tell the story of intensive animal agriculture. In essence, the intensive/extensive spectrum represents the inputs-to-land ratio. Are you raising animals in a way that involves using lots of land with a relatively small amount of money? That's an extensive system. The classic example is pasture-raised cattle, where the animals largely feed themselves and don't require much human management. But are you, on the other hand, raising animals in a way that involves using a relatively small amount of land and spending lots of money on housing, equipment, feed, medicine, and labor? That's an intensive system. The classic example here is probably contemporary broiler chicken production, where you might have a shed worth $2 million that houses 50,000 chickens requiring constant monitoring. By one estimate, 90% of global livestock are now raised in intensive systems, though the percentage is almost certainly higher in the United States, as most extensive farming occurs in the developing world. Many people now refer to intensive systems as "factory farms," but no one in the industry talks that way. By the end of the chapter, I hope you'll have a better sense of whether this language is appropriate.

In any case, the story we're telling concerns the rise of a relatively new model of raising and slaughtering animals, which is linked to a relatively new model of distributing and selling them. To understand how and why we ended up with intensive animal agriculture, it helps to have a sense of the history and economics that created it. (I'm going to tell the story of terrestrial animal agriculture—that is, farming land animals—though we'll discuss aquaculture—that is, farming aquatic animals—later in the chapter. We'll save fishing for Chapter 8.) Then, we'll turn to the basics of intensive farming in the United States. This chapter is heavy on empirical detail and very light on philosophy; it's the only chapter of its kind in the book. However, given the centrality of agriculture in so many discussions about animals, it's essential to understand what it's like and how we got the form of agriculture we have today. Moreover, we should recognize that this is an *animal-focused* survey of intensive animal agriculture. I'm not going to say anything about many important concerns that people have about animal ag, including its environmental footprint, its treatment of workers, its contributions to the development of antibiotic-resistant bacteria, and its role in recent pandemics. These are all significant in their own right; they deserve serious thought. However, they are important independently of our views about animals; we'd care about them even if animals were automatons. So, I ignore them here.

A Quick History

Let's begin when the United States began. In 1776, roughly 85% of U.S. citizens were farmers. For our purposes, the important points to note are, first, that their farms produced lots of different products and, second, that the animal products didn't travel very far. There were practical constraints on both fronts. If you plant wheat every year, the pests who enjoy wheat will flourish, and your yields will steadily fall. To avoid this, you're going to rotate your crops, planting wheat in one field one year, beans in it the next, barley the third year, and then back to wheat. You're also going to have to allow some of your land to rest, since you can't rely on artificial fertilizers to replace the nutrients that crops extract from the soil. And since allowing land to rest simply means letting a cover crop grow on it—which you'll later plow under to enrich the soil—you may as well allow cattle to graze there. Not only will they add additional fertilizer, but as they wander around, their hooves will aerate the soil.

Of course, you won't only keep cattle; you'll have some chickens and pigs too. Different species provide different goods—eggs and meat from chickens, pork and pork fat from pigs, beef and milk from cattle. This isn't just about satisfying certain gustatory (taste) preferences, but about insulating yourself from various risks. These animals are vulnerable to different diseases and predators, have different lifecycles, reach slaughter weight at different times of the year, and have market values that don't necessarily covary with one another. So, if you want a steady supply of food for yourself and a steady income stream from whatever else you can produce, it makes sense to raise more than one kind of animal.

Once you've turned your wheat into flour, it's got a decent shelf life. But in 1776, the same can't be said of most animal products. Once you slaughter and butcher an animal, you have hours before someone needs to use it; after that, it goes rancid. So, animals had to be killed quite close to the location where they were going to be eaten. Because there were very few ways to transport animals—it would, for instance, be nearly 100 years before cattle were being transported by rail—that usually meant herding them to the nearest town where they could be killed, butchered, and sold.

In the late 1700s, less than 10% of the U.S. population lived in cities, so most animals didn't have to be driven very far. However, the population density in cities meant far more demand than the immediate geographical area could supply, and the sheer number of animals who had to be killed created both nuisances and public health challenges. In New York City, for instance, animals were brought by ferry from Connecticut, Long Island, and the Hudson Valley to Corlears Hook and were then marched halfway across what's now Manhattan. Looking back on this era from 1865, one critic observed that New Yorkers in the late 1700s were regularly troubled by

the driving of cattle and other animals through the densely crowded streets at all hours, and frequently not only in the most repulsive and indecent condition, but also to the great jeopardy of human life; with the carting, and immense quantities, of every species of offal and [foul, putrid] matter produced by the slaughtering process; [and] with the brutal and barbarous transportation of lambs, calves, and small animals from ferry-boats and other landings through the city, to every direction, with the sufferings of these dumb beasts shamefully advertised.

("City Nuisances" 1865, 2)

City dwellers wanted meat, but they didn't want their streets running with blood, nor were they fond of the rats who were attracted to all the by-products of slaughter. Unsurprisingly, then, as soon as people could move slaughterhouses away from urban centers, they did. This created one of the important pressures on animal agriculture: namely, having to figure out how to meet consumer demand for meat, milk, and eggs from people who didn't want to see cattle, pigs, and chickens.

Toward the end of the 1850s, some 20% of the U.S. population lived in cities. When you combine the challenge of transporting animals with increased urbanization, you get a second important pressure on farmers: the need to produce more meat, more quickly, on the land surrounding cities. Around that time, farmers began "soiling" their animals: that is, confining them and controlling their food supply to get them to gain weight faster. Consider a report from 1852:

Two short-horned cattle, 2 1/2 years old, as nearly of the same quality and condition as possible, were weighed on June 14, and each found to be 78 stone. The one was turned out on good pasture; the other was put into a loose box . . . where it received cut grass, with the addition of 2 lb. of oilcake daily. The two cattle, with others likewise experimented on, were weighed every month; and, on October 22, the box-fed animal was found to have gained twenty-six stones, and the pastured one only thirteen. The saving in the consumption of food far more than compensated the cost of oilcake and attendance, so that the increased gain of weight, besides the accumulation of valuable manure, formed a clear advantage in favor of the box-feeding and soiling system.

(Caird 1968, 375)

This was part of a larger trend of farmers coming to think of their animals in more mechanistic, output-oriented terms. The idea is clear in the practical advice that farmers gave one another in periodicals. Here's an example from 1884:

It is not the hog that grows to the largest size to which we should always look for the greatest profit, for large hogs require time in order to attain size, but the object should be to secure stock from breeds that convert the largest proportion of feed into flesh in the shortest possible space of time.

(1884, 334)

By the early part of the 20th century, the linguistic transformation is even more dramatic, and you find essays with titles like "The Dairy Cow Is the Best Machine on the Farm." This shift makes sense when we recognize a third pressure on farmers: economics. The margins for farmers are slim, and if consumers won't pay more for your product, then one of the few ways to increase profits is to improve output relative to input. This simple reality encourages farmers to think about their animals as machines—as things the performance of which can be optimized.

Fast-forward to 1930, when roughly 40% of U.S. citizens are farming—down by more than half since the country's founding. In absolute terms, however, this was close to the peak of the total number of farms, which crested at nearly 7 million in 1935. (The country's incredible population growth explains this otherwise-puzzling fact.) Technology had changed the face of farming yet again. In the early 1900s, some chemists from Germany, Fritz Haber and Carl Bosch, figured out how to produce ammonia by fixing nitrogen from the air, a process that would ultimately result in massive amounts of relatively cheap nitrogen fertilizer, boosting crop yields dramatically. Moreover, the development of refrigerated railcars in the late 1800s made it possible to slaughter animals in one state and sell the meat in a different one. Both developments increased the incentive to specialize, with some farmers opting to grow grain and others choosing to raise large numbers of animals. The latter would sell them to centralized processors, who would then transport the meat across previously unimagined distances.

Specialization, however, brought its own challenges. Consider, for example, this 1930 circular about egg production, which may well be the first publication to discuss beak trimming—that is, the process of trimming off roughly a third of a layer hen's beak. The author begins by acknowledging the link between increasing number of chickens per square foot (in the jargon: increasing stocking density) and their displaying various "vices." He then goes on to say that farmers need new methods for managing chicken "vices," as the old ones won't do anymore:

> [Although] feather picking and cannibalism become a more serious problem as poultry keeping becomes more intensified, they are not new vices among chickens. The Complete Poultry Book published some fifty years ago [circa 1880] refers to feather picking as a "pernicious habit" and suggests that "the chopping block is the surest remedy, but for valuable fowls a wire bit passed thru the mouth like a horse's bit and held in place by being passed thru the comb, the wire being just large enough to prevent shutting the beak firmly together, will render the bird unable to grasp feathers, and it will soon abandon the habit." The chopping block or the bit is hardly practicable under present methods of poultry management [that is, large numbers of animals in relatively small spaces]; hence special precautions for prevention and control have become a necessity.
>
> (Kennard 1930, 20)

This brings him to the value of beak trimming:

> Removal of the tip of the upper beak often becomes necessary as a control and defensive measure *to save the flock*. The tip of the beak is removed to

the quick, leaving it tender and in such shape that it is impossible for a bird to grasp firmly either [the] feathers or flesh [of other birds, causing] the bird [to be] rendered harmless for about three weeks. During this time the birds usually forget their past vices and no further trouble results. . . . Tipping the beaks *need not hinder the birds from eating mash, nor affect egg production any more than handling for any other purpose.*

(Kennard 1930, 27 emphasis added)

The point is clear: beak trimming cuts down on the number of birds you lose (you "save the flock") without costing you in terms of egg production. This means that you can keep more chickens in a shed of the same size, which means getting more eggs without having to invest in a new building. So, profits increase.

Let's leap to the present day. Less than 1% of Americans are farmers, and while the number of farms has fallen from roughly 7 million to 2 million, their average size has tripled—from around 150 acres to 450 acres. However, these numbers are skewed by the many small family farms that still exist. According to the U.S. Department of Agriculture (USDA), small family farms—ones that have less than $250,000 of gross annual sales—are 231 acres on average and represent 88% of the farms in the United States. A good number of them are actually hobby farms, subsidized by other sources of income. The USDA considers "very large" farms to be those with more than $500,000 of gross annual sales, and those average 2,086 acres. However, many farms are truly vast. The largest one in the United States, owned by the Resnick family, is 190,000 acres. Lucrative farming has been consolidated into the hands of the few.

But though the number of farms has fallen, corn yields have gone up by a factor of nine since 1930. Soybean yields have nearly tripled. Today, some 36% of corn yields and 70% of soybean yields are used to feed animals. In large part, this increase in productivity is due to the development of modern fertilizers, pesticides, and the mechanization of agriculture. We can raise so many animals because we now have the means to feed them.

Strikingly, though, most of those animals aren't owned by the people who raise them. Instead, they're owned by enormous agribusinesses that contract out the work of bringing animals to slaughter weight, specifying exactly what animals are to be fed, the conditions in which they're to be kept, and the weight range at which they're to be delivered. This takes much of the risk off the agribusinesses. If there's a mass die-off in a chicken shed, they are out the cost of those birds, but they aren't responsible for the mortgage on the property. That's someone else's problem.

That being said, it's worth noting that relative to the number of birds being raised, a mass die-off is actually quite rare. Layer hens, for instance, would get sick more often if they couldn't be distanced from their own feces. Keeping them in cages means that their waste falls through the wires, keeping them cleaner and healthier (in one sense of that term), and therefore more productive. Moreover, producers now have access to inexpensive antibiotics that can stave off disease. Of course, "healthier" and "more productive" don't necessarily mean "better off, all things considered." While they are, for instance, less likely to succumb to infections, such infections are a concern because chickens are living in conditions that increase the odds of disease transmission. The welfare trade-off here favors profitability, not comfort. In any case, the point here is just that intensive systems are designed to keep animals growing or producing (eggs, milk), and they generally succeed.

And companies don't just optimize concentrated animal feeding operations (CAFOs) for productivity, where animals are housed while they are brought to slaughter weight; additionally, they carefully calibrate every aspect of the supply chain—"hatch to dispatch," as they say in the chicken industry—improving profitability at each step. Contracts to raise animals can be issued in a staggered way, ensuring that they reach slaughter weight at different times; this means that processing plants receive a predictable, steady supply throughout the year. Moreover, because the slaughter weights are specified in advance, slaughter itself can become a standardized, mechanized process, with modern plants killing 175 chickens per minute, roughly 1,100 pigs per hour, and one cow every 12 seconds. This consolidation is called vertical integration, where companies control every part of the process, either directly or indirectly, making it possible to produce the inexpensive and consistent products that consumers demand.

And to be clear, they really do demand it. In 1909, the average American was consuming about 120 pounds of meat per year. By 1960, that number had shot up to 177.5 pounds, with beef in the lead. By 2020, the total was around 242 pounds, with poultry the clear front-runner. In fact, in 2020, the average American was consuming 116.5 pounds of chicken alone—almost as much as all the meat that the average American was consuming in 1909. In part, this is simply because Americans can afford so much more than they once could. In 1901, the average hourly wage in manufacturing was 23 cents an hour. However, eggs were $0.22 a dozen, a round steak was $0.14 a pound, and pork chops were $0.13 a pound. Essentially, you had to work an hour to afford a dozen eggs. In 2003, by contrast, the average hourly wage in manufacturing was $15.30, eggs were $1.24 per dozen, a round steak was $3.94 per pound, and pork chops were $3.13 per pound. So now a person in the same kind of job works five minutes for eggs. At least when it comes to animal products, a dollar now goes much further than it ever has before.

However, it never seems to go far enough, and Americans appear to think that they are entitled to spend less while getting more. In 1970, the average hourly wage was $3.92, a round steak was $1.30 per pound, and pork chops were $1.16 per pound. But when, in early 1973, the cost of meat rose around 5% in a month, consumers called for a boycott, which led to meat sales dropping 80% in some places. Eventually, President Nixon placed caps on meat prices in response. Though less coordinated, there was similar outrage in the wake of COVID-19, which also drove up meat prices. Customers complained loudly on social media at changing prices, reserving particularly intense anger for restaurants that, in an attempt to cover costs, added surcharges to meaty menu items. Although people in the United States spend less on food as a percentage of their income than most people in the world, they have a strong sense that they shouldn't be spending any more.

Here, then, is the big picture. Animal agriculture was, at one time, something in which most people participated. It served relatively local communities. But over time, lots of things changed. People moved to cities. Farmers recognized that animals' productivity could be optimized. Crop yields increased. The railroads and refrigeration made it cheap to ship meat across long distances. Slaughterhouses became mechanized, and that meant it was important for the animals to be standard sizes. Antibiotics became commonplace. Corporations acted in their best economic interests, streamlining every aspect of the supply chain. Consumers came to expect more meat at lower and lower prices (when adjusted for inflation). And seen from one angle, the result is tremendously impressive. People have access to more animal products than ever before, at lower prices than ever before. Many major agribusinesses are proud of this and see continuing that trend as a moral imperative. Consider, for instance, a message from the chief executive officer (CEO) of JBS (one of the largest beef and pork processors in the world, named after its founder, José Batista Sobrinho):

> Our global population will reach a staggering 9+ billion by the year 2050, and as our world grows, so do the needs of her global citizens. Our collective challenge is to provide this growing world with the nutritious, safe, and affordable food it requires in a sustainable manner that respects our planet's resources and secures a strong, prosperous course for future generations. The JBS team stands ready to meet this, the great challenge of our time.
>
> (Nogueira)

But what does all this mean for the animals?

Animal Welfare in Intensive Systems

Despite its length, what follows is actually a fairly concise summary of some of the welfare issues in contemporary intensive systems. There are many other issues that I could describe. It's also important to recognize that I've drawn exclusively from industry and industry-friendly sources in describing the welfare problems in contemporary animal agriculture—agriculture textbooks, peer-reviewed articles from agriculture journals, documents from industry trade groups, and recommendations from the American Veterinary Medical Association (AVMA). This means that I've focused on welfare problems that can't be dismissed as being the fault of "a few bad apples." Rather, they are the routine consequences of the system functioning in the way it's supposed to function. I've gone this route because my goal is *not* to provide a survey of the welfare issues in intensive systems that's neutral or unbiased. Instead, I'm trying to provide a survey that's *biased toward the industry*. If we have concerns about intensive systems simply based on the way the industry describes them, then we won't have to worry about whether we're being misled by those who are opposed to raising animals for food.

Pigs

We begin with pigs. Most pigs in intensive systems spend their entire lives indoors. Female pigs—called "gilts" before they have any offspring and "sows" after—reach sexual maturity when five or six months old; they are artificially inseminated when they are six or seven months old. Since the 1970s, the standard has been to place these pigs into farrowing barns, which are filled with gestation stalls, for the nearly four months of their pregnancies. Standard gestation stalls are metal pens just wider and longer than the bodies of the animals they house; pigs are unable to turn around for that entire period. Being in individual pens ensures that the pigs don't hurt one another; being unable to turn around prevents them from defecating into their feeders. On one level, this is good for sow welfare. But stalls are also better for reproductive performance—more pregnancies per barn (because it's easier to ensure conception) and more piglets surviving per litter (because sows can't roll over on them). Stalls also make life much easier for producers, as the orderly rows make it convenient to feed, monitor, and provide care for the animals.[2] However, stalls certainly aren't cost-free, as their use means that the pigs spend the bulk of their lives in intense confinement. Pigs are highly social, like to root, and have a strong desire to build nests during their pregnancies. All those impulses are entirely thwarted in stalls.

Shortly before these pigs give birth, they're moved to farrowing (birthing) stalls. These are slightly wider metal pens, with space in a separate but adjacent pen for the dozen or so piglets to whom each pig will give birth. The piglets have access to the teats of their mothers through the bars of the farrowing stall, and they'll feed that way for two to five weeks. Then, the sows will be impregnated again and moved back to a gestation stall. The cycle repeats for three or four years, until either they fail to conceive or begin to suffer foot or leg problems (which can be caused by standing on slatted floors). At that juncture, they're sent off for slaughter.

What happens to the piglets? Before they're separated from their mothers, most piglets undergo three procedures, and most males undergo a fourth. First, their teeth are usually clipped, as they are extremely sharp and can injure both their mothers and other piglets. Clipping causes acute pain and can result in chronic pain, in the event that it leads to infection. Second, their tails are docked to reduce injury from other piglets, who may bite their tails if they are left long. Tail docking is stressful and painful, and docked tails can end up growing neuromas that are permanently sensitive. If given more space and sufficient enrichment—that is, things to do other than bite at the tails of other piglets—tail biting can be reduced without docking, though not eliminated.

Third, piglets are permanently identified in some way, either by notching their ears or tattooing, with ear notching being the most common method. Both options are painful; both expose the pigs to the risk of infection. (Ear notching, for instance, might include up to ten V-shaped cuts in one ear and five in the other.) Finally, the males will be castrated to minimize "boar taint" in the meat of sexually mature pigs—a gamey flavor that isn't popular with U.S. consumers. Like all the other procedures, castration is almost always done without drugs to alleviate pain, which is obviously acute in the moment. And then there's the healing process, with pigs' behavior indicating that they are uncomfortable for days.

When it's time to inseminate their mothers again, the piglets are moved to a weaner unit. The separation alone is stressful, and the move disrupts natural social groupings, which can lead to heightened aggression. This problem is made worse by the fact that stocking densities in weaner housing tends to be high, and there's rarely much enrichment.[3] Even in the EU, where there's tighter welfare regulation, more than 80% of pigs don't end up in housing with species-appropriate enrichment.

After three to six weeks, the pigs are moved to finishing barns. They weigh about 50 lbs. then; they will weigh about 280 lbs. four months later. That's when, at six months old, they'll be shipped off for slaughter. Most finishing barns are made of a series of group pens with slatted floors, allowing waste to fall through, but also creating risks of injuries to pigs' feet and legs. These pens allow for social interaction, but, of course, that can also lead to aggression and its subsequent harms. (That said, though, the aggression usually doesn't last more than two days after pigs have been introduced to one another.) Although there are many relatively small issues with group housing—for instance, dominant pigs eating most of the food, which can be managed by attentive farmers—boredom remains the main one. The slatted flooring, which is used to allow waste to drop through, makes it difficult to add enrichment: it simply isn't feasible to add extensive bedding materials so that pigs can build nests or forage material so that they can root, as these would clog the drains; likewise, the slatted flooring means it isn't possible to create spaces for wallowing. In the EU, some producers have tried hanging chains from the side of the pigs' crates, just to provide pigs with something to chew on and play with. The chains are appealing to producers, since they don't need to be replaced. But for that very reason, they're less good for pigs, who prefer softer things with which to engage, such as rope, wood, or balls.

Being transported for slaughter is one of the most stressful events in pigs' lives. They are often deprived of food and water in advance of the trip, ostensibly to prevent digestive issues during the ride. The vibration from the road can exacerbate existing leg injuries, and they can be exposed to extremes of heat and cold. Pigs are delivered to a holding pen, from which they are prodded down a chute. Then, they are stunned unconscious, sometimes in a gas chamber with CO_2, but typically with an electric shock or a captive bolt gun. Then, they are hoisted upside down on a conveyer belt and carried to workers who will slit their throats. If stunning isn't done properly—which certainly occurs, given the incredible pace of the line—then pigs can be partially or fully conscious for these final moments. In rare circumstances, they can even fall from the conveyer belt, very much alive, into the "blood pit" below.

Cattle

Essentially, we only want one thing from pigs: pork. But in the case of cattle, we want two things: dairy products and beef.[4] And although there are important connections between the dairy and beef industries, they're importantly independent too. This is because animals who are excellent milk producers aren't necessarily the best beef producers, and vice versa. Farmers optimize for the products they want, and that has meant generations of selective breeding to create dairy cows who are optimized for milk production and beef cattle who are optimized for beef production. Let's begin with dairy.

As with pigs, most dairy cows spend most of their lives indoors. Remember the gilt/sow distinction? There's the same thing with cattle: heifers are female cattle who haven't had a calf; after giving birth, they're called cows. Not all heifers are used for dairy; some are used to breed beef cattle or are raised for beef themselves. But if they are going to be used for dairy, then heifers are artificially inseminated at 12 or 13 months old, having their first calf some 9 months later.

During their pregnancies, heifers and cows are generally kept in group maternity pens with straw bedding. On some farms, the animals stay in these pens for calving as well, though it's also common to move them into individual stalls. Either way, dairy calves are usually separated from their mothers very quickly—sometimes just an hour after birth, and almost always within a day. If left longer, as would be natural for them, both the cow and calf become more distressed upon separation. (However, separation's being *less* distressing doesn't mean that it *isn't* distressing. On one visit to a dairy farm, I heard a cow bellowing at the other end of the barn and asked whether she was okay. The farmer told me that she'd had her calf just a few hours before I'd arrived; now, she was trying to find him. She never would.)

The fates of calves vary. The female calves are the most valuable to the dairy farmer, as they'll form the next generation of milk producers. The males are more complicated. Some of them are sold for veal, and many more for beef. In some circumstances, it doesn't make financial sense for farmers to raise them to the point where they could be sold, given feed and veterinary costs. So, they are shot shortly after birth. Most calves, though, are moved to individual hutches after being born, isolated from other cattle, where they'll spend the next two months. They're often fed just four or five liters of milk, which is less than half of what they'd drink if with their mothers. (Normally, calves would feed on and off throughout the day, but they're usually just fed twice daily until they're eight or nine weeks old. Less than 7% of calves in the United States are fed three times a day.) Then, they'll move into some kind of group housing until they are sold or ready for insemination.

After cows have calves, they lactate. Nearly 80% of lactating cows end up in one sort of indoor stall system or another. Roughly half of those are tie-stalls—that is, stalls they can't leave—which obviously limits behaviors that enhance well-being, such as social interaction, walking, grooming, and grazing. But whether or not they can come and go, dairy cows are steadily being bred to be larger, so if they're housed in a system that was designed 30 or more years ago, as so many were, they often don't fit well in the spaces available to them. What's more, low quality or poorly maintained flooring can result in stumbles and falls that can leave them permanently lame. It's hard to know exactly how common clinical lameness is across the dairy industry, as estimates vary so dramatically. However, it looks to be a problem for at least 15% to 25% of cows while they are still on farms. (That said, a study on dairy cows arriving at slaughter facilities found nearly 40% to be lame. So, either the estimate on farms is low or transportation causes many new injuries. And, of course, both could be true.)

Over 80% of U.S. dairies dock the tails of their cows. Over 90% dock using an elastrator band—essentially, a thick rubber band that causes the tail to fall off after three to seven weeks—and most farmers say they dock for cow hygiene reasons. But studies don't indicate that there is much benefit for the animals—or for worker health, for that matter. Arguably, the main motivation is that tail docking makes it much more convenient to milk cows, which has to be done twice per day. This is itself a welfare issue, as dairy cows produce so much milk that their udders are regularly engorged to the point of soreness. In any case, tail docking is painful and stressful, and as with pigs, can lead to chronic pain if neuromas develop. It also leaves them more vulnerable to flies, since they can't use their tails to shoo them away.

Roughly 80% of U.S. dairy cows are dehorned on an annual basis. Dehorned cattle are less likely to injure handlers and one another's udders, flanks, and eyes. However, only 30% of dairy farmers use pain relievers when dehorning, despite it being painful and stressful. Studies suggest that it takes a full week for inflammation, cortisol levels, indications of restlessness, and normal behaviors (such as play) to return to baseline levels. Pain mitigation is recommended by the AVMA, but most don't use it because of the cost.

The average dairy cow lives about five years, which means that she delivers two to four calves before being sent to slaughter. There are, of course, some producers who have slaughter facilities on-site, but most don't for a combination of financial and regulatory reasons. On average, animals travel between six and seven hours to slaughter facilities, though audits have revealed cases where animals have traveled for nearly two days. By law, though, you "may not confine animals in a vehicle or vessel for more than 28 consecutive hours without unloading the animals for feeding, water, and rest," which provides strong incentive to keep travel times down ("Title 49" 2011, §80502).

As with pigs, cattle are delivered to a holding pen. They are eventually prodded down a chute. At the end of the chute each cow is restrained so that she can be rendered unconscious with a captive bolt stunner—essentially, a pneumatic gun that fires a steel rod into the skull—as the law requires that cattle be unconscious before actually being killed. However, if the stunning devices are defective or poorly maintained, or if they aren't placed properly on the animal's skull, she'll still be conscious when she's hoisted up and her throat is cut.

The path to slaughter for beef cattle is a bit different. Typically, beef calves remain with their mothers on pasture until they're weaned at six or seven months old. About a third of the heifers stay on that pasture to produce the next generation of cattle, but the rest will go to a different pasture where their feed is supplemented so that they put on weight faster. At that point, they are typically sold and sent to a feedlot for finishing, where they will be brought up to 1,200 to 1,400 pounds. At around 18 to 22 months old, they'll be sent to be processed.

Each stage of raising beef cattle presents its own welfare challenges. One of the early ones is castration. (Before male cattle are castrated, they are called bulls; afterward, steers.) This is done for the sake of meat quality, uniformity, and ease of management—including reproductive management, since the animals aren't separated by sex. Physical castration is the most common method, as opposed to the chemical option, where a toxic agent is injected directly into the testes. There is, of course, the acute pain associated with physical castration, which is generally done without anesthetic. (Only 30% of calves castrated at less than six months get an analgesic, and only 20% of veterinarians report using any kind of pain reducer at the time of castration.)

There are two main methods of physical castration: the Burdizzo clamp and the band method. With the Burdizzo, you crush the spermatic cords one at a time, which cuts off the blood supply. This method causes less pain in the long run, but also requires more training to employ correctly. Cortisol is generally raised for up to two weeks, immune response is affected for over a month, and inflammation persists for more than two months.[5] The band method slows the blood supply rather than cutting it off entirely, but eventually causes the testes to die as well. However, it causes more lasting pain, as evinced by changes in behavior for a full month and wound sensitivity, inflammation, and abnormal posture for nearly three months. Being castrated is likely among the most stressful events in a steer's life.

There are also welfare issues associated with more routine aspects of the lives of beef cattle. For instance, when on pasture, they can be without shelter or without adequate access to it. Indoor feedlots can lead to all the issues that come along with space constraints. Mud in both indoor and outdoor systems can lead to foot disease and may prevent cattle from lying down, making it difficult for them to rest, and half the cattle on feedlots have knee and hock injuries. And if mud doesn't cause problems, dust can: a third of culled cattle have lung lesions at slaughter. What's more, feeding itself can be a welfare issue. If cattle are fed a disproportionate amount of grain relative to roughage, they can have digestive issues and liver abscesses. But feeding roughage is expensive, so not everyone provides cattle with a proper diet. There are a surprising number of ways in which the well-being of cattle can be compromised.

Chickens

Finally, we turn to chickens. As with cattle, there are really two industries here: the egg industry and the broiler industry. Let's begin with egg production.

Chicks are born in a hatchery. Not long after, they are put on conveyor belts to be examined by chicken sexers, who determine whether they are male or female. Because the breeds that are good egg producers aren't excellent meat producers, there is no use for the males, so they are killed immediately, usually by being dropped into high-speed grinders.

After the females have been identified, they are trucked to a grow-out facility—essentially, a large barn with plenty of feed where the chickens are free to roam the floor. These immature chickens—pullets—will stay there for roughly 18 weeks before being moved to a laying facility. During their first week or so in the grow-out facility, their beaks will be trimmed. This involves removing roughly a third of the upper beak, or sometimes both the upper and lower beak. There are several ways to do it, but in the United States, hot-blade trimming is the most common. The contraption looks a bit like a guillotine, and the blade is heated close to 1300°F so that it both cuts and cauterizes at the same time. (If the beak grows back, as it sometimes does when the procedure isn't performed properly, the beak will just be trimmed again when the bird is five to eight weeks old.)

Unsurprisingly, this is a painful practice that disrupts normal behavior: it makes it more difficult for chickens to clean their feathers; it also makes it harder for them to eat and drink immediately after. The argument for it is that farmers are trying to avoid feather pecking, other pecking injuries, and cannibalism. This process isn't necessary in extensive systems, where chickens aren't stocked so densely. However, the very features that make systems intensive also make the trimming essential, and it reduces overall chicken mortality. (Reducing overall chicken mortality is obviously good from the perspective of producers. It is good for the chickens, however, only insofar as they have lives worth living; it is bad otherwise.)

At the end of the 18 weeks, about three-quarters of hens will be moved to a laying facility, which means moving into cages: typically, six hens per cage and 80 square inches per hen. This isn't enough space to flap or stretch their wings. The cage floor doesn't allow them to scratch, and they don't have enough room to preen themselves as much as they'd like. However, cages make hens far more productive, as it's easier to ensure that all hens are getting enough food, and any aggressive hens are only able to hurt five other hens.

Hen productivity starts to fall off after several months. At that juncture, their productivity can be extended just a bit by induced or forced molting—that is, by withholding food or water, or more commonly now, by only offering low-nutrient foods. Chickens molt each year naturally, which involves eating much less, losing their feathers, and not producing eggs. After a few weeks, their appetite returns, as does their plumage and productivity. Induced molting essentially brings this process on artificially, thereby causing a spike in egg production afterward. It also causes distress, aggression, and frustration; it makes birds more vulnerable to disease; and when molting is induced rapidly, it can lead to bone mineralization, which makes bones more prone to breaking. Of course, it also means more eggs from fewer chickens, since farmers don't need to raise as many birds as they otherwise would to meet demand. This sort of trade-off is everywhere in the industry: the more productive animals are, the fewer of them you need; but of course, the more productive they are, the worse their lives tend to be.

In any case, while an induced molt might extend the lives of chickens by several weeks, eventually egg production drops below the cost of feeding and housing the hens. At that juncture, they're trucked away for slaughter. Chickens are grabbed by their legs, five per catcher's hand. Then, they're placed in crates and loaded into the truck. This process is stressful, as hens are skittish in normal circumstances and strongly dislike being handled. Their wings and legs can be broken as a result. What's more, the truck ride itself is hard on the birds: some 30% of caged hens' bones break during the trip.

When the hens arrive, they are usually dumped onto a conveyor belt, hung upside down, and brought to electric water baths—the cheapest method of stunning. Then their necks are cut. This process doesn't always go as it should, given the speed at which chickens are killed. So, they can be partially consciousness when they're scalded, which is supposed to remove their feathers. Sometimes, in fact, they are barely stunned and their necks aren't cut at all, so they are fully conscious when they go into the boiling water.

When it comes to broiler chickens, the numbers are staggering. In 2019, over 9.2 billion chickens were raised in the United States, and the average broiler complex processed 1,000,000 to 1,250,000 birds per week. In the same year, broilers reached an average market weight of 6.32 lbs. in 47 days—not even seven weeks. During 2018 and 2019, however, 5% of those birds never made it to market; they died beforehand at some point in the supply chain. Producers pull dead chickens from their sheds every day.

Most broiler chickens are housed in a 16,000-square-foot building with 20,000 to 25,000 other chickens. This leaves between 0.64 and 0.8 square feet per chicken once they're grown—which certainly isn't enough space for preening, turning, wing flapping, ground scratching, feather ruffling, or wing stretching. In houses with 25,000 birds, there's barely enough room for each bird to stand—and they will never go outside to get more room. The house has a bedding of organic matter that's disinfected between flocks, but nevertheless, footpad dermatitis is common, and is considered within industry standards as long as it covers less than half the footpad area. Industry standards demand that the ammonia in the air from chickens' urine and feces not exceed 25 ppm at bird height, though there's evidence that even 10 ppm raises some issues, and chickens seem to be averse to ammonia-heavy conditions after just 15 minutes of exposure. At 25 ppm, ammonia levels lead to respiratory disease, affect olfaction, and may harm chickens' organs.

Chickens eat more, and so grow faster, when it's light. So, producers are incentivized to keep the lights on all the time, even though this is stressful for the birds. Chicken houses are supposed to provide darkness for four hours a day, but this darkness may be provided in one-hour increments. Chickens' eyes probably don't develop normally in such environments, and compromised vision may explain some premature mortality if those birds are unable to find food.

Most, however, find it in spades, because producers want them to gain weight rapidly. Indeed, broilers have been bred to grow at a dramatic rate, which makes them subject to a host of welfare problems. For instance, their large muscle mass and short legs complicates their gait and therefore compromises their stability. The National Chicken Council (NCC), an industry trade group, has welfare guidelines that it uses for audits. Even the best auditing score for evaluating chickens' gait only requires that the chickens be able to walk five feet, with no requirement that the gait be normal.

In any case, at the end of their lives, broilers suffer the same fate: they are caught and placed in crates (usually by hand, but sometimes with enormous vacuums that deposit the animals directly into trucks), they are trucked without food or water to a slaughter facility, and then killed. As with layer hens, the slaughter process doesn't always go as it should due to the speed at which chickens are killed. This isn't news to the industry. It's considered acceptable for 500 birds per flock of 25,000—that is, 2%—not to be effectively stunned or bled out. That is, it's acceptable for those birds to be scalded alive. There were some 9.2 billion chickens killed for meat in 2019. 2% of 9.2 billion is 184 million chickens.

Aquaculture

So far, we've just considered terrestrial animal agriculture—that is, animals raised for food on land. However, enormous numbers of aquatic animals are raised for food as well: carp and salmon, shrimp and oysters, and an untold number of other species. For the sake of space, we won't explore the history of the industry, though as you might imagine, much of the consolidation and intensification of aquaculture has to do with the powerful economic incentives that favor the present system. Instead, we'll just try to get a sense of the shape of the industry, highly diverse though it is. We'll also have a more international perspective than we did when discussing terrestrial agriculture, as it's almost impossible to talk about aquaculture without talking about China.

In 2016, inland aquaculture—that is, aquatic animals not raised in sea pens, but instead in manmade ponds and tanks on land—generated 51.4 million tons of aquatic animals. (Unlike terrestrial animal agriculture, no one reports headcounts; they only report tonnage. However, you can calculate the headcounts by dividing the tonnage by the average slaughter weight of the animal. All the headcount estimates in this section were generated using that method.) Most of this is finfish aquaculture, which makes up 92.5% of all inland aquaculture.[6] When you add in the mariculture output—a form of aquaculture produced in confinement in the oceans—the globe produced 80,031,000 tonnes of seafood in 2016. This represents an extraordinary number of animals. For instance, grass carp are particularly popular in China, and 6 million tonnes of them were produced: that's more than 3 billion carp. Of crustaceans, white-legged shrimp are the most-farmed animal, with 4.2 million tonnes produced: that's roughly 210 *billion* shrimp. (Humans kill more shrimp each year than all terrestrial farmed animals combined.)

The world's main exporter is China, which, in 2016, exported 14% of the global share of fish products (followed by Norway with 7.6%). The world's main importer, however, is the United States, which in the same year imported 15.1% of the global share of fish products (followed by Japan with 10.2%). While the United States itself is still more heavily invested in the capture of wild fish relative to fish farming, production is ramping up here too. In 2017, for instance, the United States produced 626 million pounds of aquacultured products, with over 10% growth in the sector every year for the preceding decade. By contrast, though, the United States imported 3.4 billion pounds of edible fish imports from East and South Asia in 2017 (including 1.1 billion pounds of shrimp). Ninety-one percent of American seafood consumption is derived from imports, and well over half of that is farmed. How are all these animals created, raised, and killed?

To create the next generation of fish, producers have to strip the eggs out of the last one. This involves pulling a fish out of the water and squeezing her eggs out of her. Then, you strip the milt (fish semen) out of a male and mix the two together so that the eggs are fertilized. In a guide to trout production, the authors note that "[in] the case of rough handling and unprofessional stripping fish may be hurt or even injured. . . . If fish is stripped [in the wrong way] its internal organs such as spleen or liver may be damaged which can result in mortality" (Hoitsy et al. 2012, 11). By that standard, much stripping is rough or unprofessional, as 25% of stripped fish die as a result of this process. And whether or not the process results in death, manual handling is stressful, as is being removed from the water. Small-scale producers don't process as many fish, and so probably do less harm to the ones they strip. In large-scale aquaculture, however, the rate of injury is no doubt higher.

The eggs then go to a hatchery, where the fish are born. In the case of grass carp, for instance, this means they spend their first 20 to 25 days in a shallow pool. Then, they are caught with nets to ensure that carp of the same size are moved to grow-out facilities. They're placed in plastic bags filled with oxygenated water with up to 500 other fingerlings (baby fish). Many don't survive the journey, though, and it's considered normal to lose up to 10% in the 24 hours post-bagging. At that point, they're moved either to inland or mariculture environments.

The most common type of inland aquaculture facilities globally are earthen ponds. These can take many forms, but one common method is to co-opt parts of wetland ecosystems to develop shallow, aerated, and drainable wide trenches for the fish. However, there are also fully indoor production systems, outdoor open tanks, and any number of other alternatives, each with their own advantages and disadvantages both from a production perspective and from a welfare perspective. Mariculture, by contrast, takes place in the sea, and the fish are restrained in enormous pens made of netting. Worldwide, though, nearly 60% of marine and coastal aquaculture is devoted to shelled mollusks, not fish, partly because fish are more vulnerable to disease in open environments of that kind.

Humans don't raise many carnivorous *terrestrial* species for food, but they do raise carnivorous aquatic species. In the United States, even carnivorous fish are fed diets composed of less than 50% fishmeal or fish oil, and globally, aquaculture uses about half a pound of wild fish to produce one pound of aquacultured seafood. However, because fishmeal and fish oil are generally produced from very small fish, this statistic doesn't really give us a sense of the number of wild fish used to produce a single farmed fish, and estimates there vary considerably.[7] It seems likely, though, that bringing any one member of a farmed carnivorous species up to slaughter weight involves killing several other aquatic animals.

Fish spend the grow-out period—that is, the time between leaving the hatchery and reaching slaughter weight—in fairly barren environments, usually without any enrichment at all. They are typically fed by automatic feeders, and as with terrestrial animal agriculture, eating provides one of the few sources of stimulation. (Even this, however, isn't uniformly positive, as the feed itself can create welfare issues. Salmonid fishes grow faster on high-fat diets, and producers have a financial incentive to use soybean meal rather than fishmeal, as the former is cheaper. However, this combination can cause intestinal inflammation and diarrhea.)

Unsurprisingly, many factors can affect the welfare of aquatic animals. Most obviously, the water's characteristics are especially important: temperature, gas concentrations, pH levels, salinity, the presence of pollutants, and so on. There are also concerns about things like lighting, noise, and vibrations, which can significantly increase stress. However, perhaps the most pressing issues are the ongoing threats of both parasites and diseases—to the point that they are generally considered to be the main hurdle to further aquaculture development, though not because producers regard these problems as unacceptable from a welfare perspective. Instead, they threaten the profitability of the industry, given how many fish they kill. While not all parasites clearly compromise welfare, some do. Salmon lice, for instance, can cause bleeding, open sores, and even expose the skull. This is enormously stressful and also puts fish at greater risk of additional infections.

In the United States, farmed fish aren't protected by the Humane Methods of Slaughter Act (HMSA), which requires, among other things, that land animals not be sensible to pain when they're slaughtered. (Things are no better in the EU: Directive 2010/63, which is the EU's equivalent of the HMSA, also excludes farmed fish.) The HMSA also tries to ensure that cattle aren't transported to slaughter with broken legs and that workers minimize their use of electric paddles to move livestock toward stunning. Without such protections, producers are largely making decisions based on economic considerations, which means that they transport a great many animals at high stocking densities to slaughter facilities. We don't know much about the way that different methods of transport affect fish welfare or precisely how stressful transport is. But when you put fish in a small tank, water quality can deteriorate pretty quickly, which can lead to problems like hypoxia (low oxygen levels in the water, which is far worse for some species than others; tilapia are not hypoxia resistant while carp are). And many studies have demonstrated that even short transport durations can significantly increase fish's cortisol levels. The stress likely comes from being handled, captured, and suspended in an environment with worsening water conditions.

For some time, fish were killed by adding carbon dioxide to the water, which is a relatively simple and inexpensive process. It was obvious to producers, however, that this was highly aversive for the fish, as members of some species would literally try to leap out of the water to escape. So now, stunning has become the standard method, either by electrical shock or physical impact. In larger slaughter plants, these methods are largely automated, with fish being pumped into the machines that stun them. Large salmon plants, for instance, can process 6,500 fish an hour. Regardless of species, and whether terrestrial or aquatic, there is little doubt that many animals suffer when slaughter happens at such extraordinary rates.

Taking Stock

Despite all this detail, we've only just scratched the surface. There is far more to say about the way we raise and slaughter the animals we've discussed. Moreover, there are many animals we've simply ignored: I've said nothing at all about sheep, goats, turkeys, guinea pigs, horses, rabbits, kangaroos, frogs, turtles, octopuses, and many others. The material in this chapter is meant as a basic orientation, not an exhaustive resource.

Still, I think it's enough to respond to skepticism about welfare problems in intensive systems. Consider this passage from Loren Lomasky, a noted political philosopher:

> [Why] do so many people categorically reject . . . factory-farming? I can think of two explanations. First, one may imaginatively put oneself in the position of the cooped-up bird or the steer waiting to be stunned and slaughtered and respond with a shudder. Such emotional responses are understandable, but I do not believe that they carry much epistemic weight. Second, disturbing videos of meat-packing operations are typically secreted out and made public by groups that are stridently anti-meat. It can, I believe, be safely assumed that the items they release for general viewing are those that most strongly support their own agenda and are not representative of the full range of industry practices.
>
> (2013, 192)

Lomasky is wrong. You don't need to imagine yourself as a farmed animal to be troubled by their plight: there is excellent evidence that they are living in circumstances that impose serious welfare costs. Moreover, we don't need to listen to activists to be worried about contemporary intensive systems. As I said earlier, I've drawn exclusively from industry sources in describing the welfare problems in contemporary animal agriculture. Still, you can see why people refer to intensive animal agriculture as "factory farming." And in these factories, do most animals have lives that were worth starting? I say they don't. But even if you think otherwise, perhaps, we can agree that their lives aren't good enough.

Further Reading

Anderson, Virginia DeJohn. 2006. *Creatures of Empire: How Domestic Animals Transformed Early America*. New York: Oxford University Press.

Carr, John, Shih-Ping Chen, Joseph F. Conner, R.N. Kirkwood, and Joaquim Segalés. 2018. *Pig Health*. Boca Raton: CRC Press.

Duncan, Ian J.H., and Penny Hawkins. 2010. *The Welfare of Domestic Fowl and Other Captive Birds*. Heidelberg: Springer Netherlands. https://doi.org/10.1007/978-90-481-3650-6.

Engle, Terry, Klingborg, Donald J., and Bernard E. Rollin. 2019. *The Welfare of Cattle*. Boca Raton: CRC Press.

Genoways, Ted. 2015. *The Chain: Farm, Factory, and the Fate of Our Food*. New York: Harper.

Gillespie, Kathryn. 2018. *The Cow with Ear Tag #1389*. Chicago: University of Chicago Press.

Leonard, Christopher. 2014. *The Meat Racket*. New York: Simon & Schuster.

McMullen, Steven. 2016. *Animals and the Economy*. New York: Palgrave.

Norwood, Bailey F., and Jayson L. Lusk. 2011. *Compassion, by the Pound: The Economics of Farm Animal Welfare*. New York: Oxford University Press.

Ogle, Maureen. 2013. *In Meat We Trust: An Unexpected History of Carnivore America*. New York: Houghton Mifflin Harcourt.

Pachirat, Timothy. 2013. *Every Twelve Seconds*. New Haven: Yale University Press.

Robichaud, Andrew A. 2019. *Animal City: The Domestication of America*. Cambridge, MA: Harvard University Press.
Specht, Joshua. 2020. *Red Meat Republic: A Hoof-to-Table History of How Beef Changed America*. Princeton: Princeton University Press

Notes

1. There are similar changes with other species. In 1935, pigs weighed an average of 232 pounds at the time of slaughter. By 2018, that number was at 286 pounds. In 1929, cattle averaged 955 pounds at the time of slaughter. By 2018, they averaged 1,352 pounds. In 1924, the average milk production per cow was 4,167 pounds. In 2017, the cows produced 22,914 pounds of milk on average *per year*. (This numbers exclude the milk suckled by calves. Also, you might think milk production will be reported in gallons, but that's not the way the USDA does it. If you're curious, though, each gallon weighs about 8.5 pounds.) https://downloads.usda.library.cornell.edu/usda-esmis/files/cz30ps66x/jd473517g/bk128k88x/mcprsb19.pdf
2. There's actually evidence that group housing, where pigs can move freely and interact with one another, actually reduces the number of stillbirths, and is better for reproductive performance generally: www.ncbi.nlm.nih.gov/pmc/articles/PMC4698681/.
3. This is where tail biting can become a particularly serious problem, and in extreme cases, can lead to death. Studies report that between 2% and 12% of pigs experience *severe* tail biting damage when they aren't docked.
4. We also want a range of other products from pigs, dairy cows, and beef cattle, with leather being the most obvious example. However, those are generally by-products. If we want to understand why intensive systems have the features they do and why animals' welfare is compromised in the ways it's compromised, we'll do better to focus on the products that intensive systems are supposed to generate as efficiently as possible.
5. Around 85% of beef cattle don't need dehorning, as they are bred not to have horns. However, for those who do, castration tends to be done at the same time as dehorning, so the pain is compounded. Around the same time, a bit under half of beef operations brand their cattle.
6. However, this percentage is dropping as we farm more crustaceans.
7. For one attempt to do the calculations, see www.countinganimals.com/the-fish-we-kill-to-feed-the-fish-we-eat/.

References

1865. "City Nuisances: The Slaughterhouses of New York." *New York Times*, December 18.
1884. Farm, Field, and Fireside, 7(76). https://idnc.library.illinois.edu/?a=d&d=FFF18840401
2011. "Title 49—Transportation." *GovInfo*. www.govinfo.gov/content/pkg/USCODE-2011-title49/pdf/USCODE-2011-title49-subtitleX-chap805-sec80502.pdf.
Caird, James. 1968. *English Agriculture 1850–1851*. Second edition. London: Frank Cass & Co. Ltd.
Hoitsy, György, András Woynarovich, and Thomas Moth-Poulsen. 2012. "Guide to the Small Scale Artificial Propogation of Trout." *FAO*. www.fao.org/3/a-ap341e.pdf.
Kennard, D.C. 1930. "'Chicken Vices' and 'Tipping the Beaks'." In *Poultry*. Ohio Agricultural Experiment Station, Special Circular 28. http://hdl.handle.net/1811/71946.
Lomasky, Loren. 2013. "Is it Wrong to Eat Animals?" *Social Philosophy and Policy Foundation* 30(1–2): 177–200. doi: https://doi.org/10.1017/S0265052513000083.
Nogueira, Andre. "CEO Welcome." *JBS*. https://jbssa.com/about/ceo-welcome/.

7   Production and Consumption Ethics

OVERVIEW

This is the second of three chapters about animals as food. Now that we have an understanding of what animal agriculture and aquaculture are like, we can turn to the moral issues they raise. In particular, this chapter separates three ethical issues that are typically run together: first, the ethics of *producing* animal-based foods; second, the ethics of *purchasing* animal-based foods; third, the ethics of *consuming* animal-based foods. As we'll see, while most moral theories condemn the production of animal-based foods, the ethics of purchasing and consuming them are more complex. As we'll also see, though, there is at least one way of navigating that complexity that's worth considering.

The last chapter gave you an overview of intensive animal agriculture: what it's like and how it came to be. This chapter brings us back to ethics, and it's devoted to two questions. First, how should we assess intensive animal agriculture and aquaculture? Second, depending on our assessment, what should we say about purchasing and consuming products from those systems?

To be clear, that second question is *not* a different way of asking whether we're morally obligated to be vegans. That's an important question, but I don't tackle it here, and I don't really explore it elsewhere in the book. This is because I think it's unhelpful to frame the central ethical issue here in terms of whether we should adopt a particular diet. Let me explain why.

When people talk about veganism, they're usually talking about a diet that involves strictly avoiding animal products: no meat, no eggs, no dairy, no exceptions. If that's what you mean by "veganism," then a good *argument* for veganism has to establish that you ought to abstain from eating *all* animal products *all the time*. And if we go looking for such an argument, then we'll have to spend a lot of time thinking about weird questions, or questions that are so specific that they can distract us from the choices that most people actually face:

- "Well, would you eat a pig if the two of you were stranded on a desert island, and it was your life or Porky's?"
- "What about eating crickets? Is that okay?"
- "Is it fine to eat roadkill?"
- "My mom raises chickens in her backyard and treats them absolutely fabulously. Is it really wrong to eat their eggs?"
- "My Uncle Bill has a ranch where he raises, slaughters, and processes cattle. They have lives that are the envy of most animals. Sure, they die before they would naturally, but they are killed quickly and humanely, and anyway, death is just one day. Is it okay to have one of Uncle Bill's steaks if he offers it to me?

These are perfectly good questions. It's worth thinking about moral views that might forbid killing animals even to save human lives. It's worth thinking about whether insect farming is actually bad for them and whether there are good arguments against even the best extensive systems—like Uncle Bill's ranch—as well as whether it's okay to eat what's served to you by a family member. But if we focus on those kinds of questions, then we're probably going to lose sight of the big picture. As we've seen, most of the animal products in the United States come from intensive systems. Unsurprisingly, then, when most people in the United States are making decisions about what to eat, they are almost always choosing between eating meals that include animal products from intensive systems, on the one hand, and eating plant-based meals, on the other. That's where the action is, morally speaking. In this chapter, then, we're setting aside extensive systems, not because they aren't important, but because they supply so few of the animal products that are available in grocery stores and restaurants. We're also ignoring the fishing industry—though not aquaculture—because the ethics of catching wild animals is different from the ethics of raising captive ones, as we'll see in the next chapter. Our goal is to think through the ethical issues associated with the most common animal-based foods: the cheese on your pizza, your burger from McDonald's, the bacon next to your eggs.

There's a second reason why it's good to begin with the ethics of intensive animal agriculture (and aquaculture, though I won't keep mentioning it explicitly) and then turn to the ethics of purchasing and consuming the products from intensive systems. The reason is simple: it's one thing to produce meat, dairy, and eggs; it's a different thing to buy them; it's yet another thing to eat them. These are different activities. What's more, they often aren't done by the same person. The odds are good that you aren't a farmer, a slaughterhouse worker, or an agribusiness executive. The odds are also good that there have been lots of cases where you've consumed animal-based foods without buying them. That said, you often buy what you eat, so we can afford to be a bit sloppy about the distinction between purchasing and consuming. However, we can't be sloppy about the distinction between purchasing and consuming, on the one hand, and producing, on the other. Those are very different kinds of actions that are typically done by entirely different people. So, it would be surprising if the ethical issues associated with them were the same.

The Ethics of Production

All that said, let's start with the ethics of production—that is, with our assessment of intensive animal agriculture. What should we say about it? Let's see what happens if we apply some of the moral theories that we discussed back in Chapter 5.

Suppose, for instance, that we are considering intensive animal agriculture ("animal ag" for short) from a utilitarian perspective. Of course, intensive animal ag isn't one action; it's a complex industry with many, many agents involved. So, it wouldn't make much sense to apply the version of utilitarianism that we discussed earlier, which is designed to assess individual actions. However, we can consider animal ag using a variant of utilitarianism: namely, rule utilitarianism. According to rule utilitarianism, we should follow rules such that, if most people followed them, utility would be maximized. Our question, then, is whether things are as good as possible in virtue of having a norm that permits intensive animal ag. In other words: Is utility maximized by allowing factory farming? Is utility maximized by *not* having a rule that *forbids* factory farming?

It's hard to see how. When we consider the sheer number of animals and the scope of their suffering (nearly 10 billion land animals raised and slaughtered in the United States each year, not to mention all the aquatic ones) relative to the U.S. population (around 330 million as of this writing), it becomes clear that animal products would have to generate an *enormous* amount of utility for it to be worth permitting the industry. After all, it's important to remember that a world without intensive animal agriculture isn't a world without animal products, much less a world without food. People would just have access to fewer animal products, plus a wide range of plant-based options. And even if people don't care for plant-based foods as much as they like animal products, it's unlikely that those plant-based products would actually result in *negative* utility. (A veggie burger probably won't hurt you.) Instead, they would just result in *less* utility. (You might enjoy the veggie burger slightly less than you would enjoy a beef burger.) So, the *relevant* benefits to human beings are only the benefits represented by that difference—which seems small indeed.

We can make the point a bit more vividly by considering some back-of-the-envelope calculations. The average broiler chicken weighs a bit over 6 pounds when slaughtered, providing something like 3.5 pounds of meat. If we assume that a serving of chicken is four ounces, then that represents 14 servings. If broiler chickens live, on average, 47 days, then we are looking at roughly one serving for every three days of a chicken's life. So now we face the question: Is the benefit of eating a single serving of chicken worth the experiences that a broiler chicken has over the course of three days? If we think not, then rule utilitarianism will condemn broiler production: people are not, on average, getting enough of a benefit from eating chickens to offset the cost, on average, to those chickens.[1] And assuming that we make the same judgment when it comes to the trade-offs for other species, rule utilitarianism will condemn intensive animal agriculture generally.[2]

Does intensive animal agriculture look better if we're Kantians? To the contrary, it looks much worse. Here's the way Christine Korsgaard summarizes the Kantian idea that we're committed to respecting animals, which means not using them in ways that cause them to suffer:

> Each of us regards himself or herself as an end in itself, a being with inherent value, and on that ground demands recognition and respect from others who are also capable of valuing. What . . . we demand, when we demand that recognition, is that our natural concerns—the objects of our natural desires and interests and affections—be accorded the status of values, values that must be respected as far as possible by others. And many of those natural concerns—the desire to avoid pain is an obvious example—spring from our animal nature, not from our rational nature. That it is wrong to make an animal suffer is something you already believe, since there is an animal— yourself—whose suffering you declare to be morally objectionable.
>
> (2009, 5–6)

The idea here, in short, is that since we value aspects of *our* animal nature (our bodies and what's good for them), we're committed to valuing animal nature wherever we find it. That is, if we think that our *own* ability to suffer provides others with a reason to treat us with respect, then it also provides us with a reason to treat *others* with respect—including animals. And as Korsgaard would argue, intensive animal agriculture doesn't meet that standard.[3]

Can we defend intensive animal agriculture as virtue ethicists? We might argue that it's compassionate to try to provide a desirable product at an affordable price to anyone who wants it. And intensive animal agriculture does that. However, there is nothing about virtue ethics that allows us to limit our moral concern to human beings, and so we'll have to ask whether intensive animal ag is compassionate to the animals. We will need to assess whether it's just to treat animals as though their interests were trivial. We'll have to determine whether we are being truthful with ourselves and others about the nature and costs of intensive animal agriculture. Again, then, intensive animal ag looks worrisome.

I could make similar points about the other moral theories that we canvased in the last chapter. For the sake of space, however, let's consider those points made and turn our attention to the only moral theory that has a shot at defending factory farming: namely, contractualism. Recall that according to one version of contractualism, morality is a system of rules to which self-interested, rational agents would agree under certain idealized circumstances (including, for instance, having full information about empirical matters). No agent is going to agree to a set of rules on which *she* has no right to moral consideration, so every agent will have standing. And many contractualists have thought that self-interested, rational agents would exclude animals from the contract—that is, they wouldn't endorse rules that give standing to animals.[4] But if animals don't deserve direct moral consideration, then there probably isn't anything wrong with intensive animal agriculture.

Or so it might seem. But there are ways of criticizing animal agriculture that don't depend on animals deserving any direct consideration at all, much less equal consideration. For instance, there seems to be a link between cruelty to animals and cruelty to humans, with one of the more disturbing pieces of evidence being that rates of domestic violence are higher in communities with slaughterhouses, even after controlling for other variables. Moreover, intensive animal agriculture has significant environmental costs: it's responsible for some 14% of all carbon emissions, significant land use (which means evermore deforestation as animal agriculture grows), and water pollution (which has been linked to significant die-offs of aquatic life). There are also public health concerns, including air quality issues that disproportionately affect members of historically marginalized communities. (Do a quick Google search for info about North Carolina hog farms.) Additionally, there are worries about the increasing threat of antibiotic-resistant bacteria due to low-level ("subtherapeutic") antibiotic use in animal feed. Lastly, there are links between intensive animal agriculture and the threat of pandemics. Some zoonotic diseases, such as H1N1, were incubated in intensive chicken farms, and as I write this, in the summer of 2020, there are rumblings about human deaths due to a new swine flu that is circulating in China. Granted, most zoonotic diseases are ultimately traced to wildlife, but there is still a sense in which intensive animal agriculture is responsible for their making the jump to human beings: it displaces poor farmers who can't compete, which incentivizes their participation in the wildlife trade, increasing the likelihood of human/wild animal interaction. It's unclear that fully informed, fully rational, and purely self-interested agents would agree to rules that sanction a system with these consequences. So, even contractualism may condemn intensive animal ag after all.

To be clear, these objections to intensive animal ag are relevant regardless of the moral theory we invoke. Going back to virtue ethics for a moment, just to illustrate the point, we could ask whether it's wise to produce food with so many known negative externalities for the environment and whether we are exercising self-control and temperance in opting for a production system that delivers far more meat than is good for us from a nutritional perspective. However, according to most other moral theories, we don't need to discuss anything other than animal-focused criticisms of intensive animal ag to reach a conclusion about it. These objections are especially relevant here precisely because we are considering a version of contractualism that denies that animals are members of the moral community—a commitment that isn't shared by utilitarianism, Korsgaard's Kantianism, or virtue ethics.

Obviously, there are other moral theories to consider, but I doubt that any of the standard options will be much more friendly to intensive animal agriculture. So what should we conclude? Intensive animal ag is, of course, an enormous success by its own standard, producing an incredible amount of inexpensive meat, eggs, and dairy products. However, it's hard to deny that the lives of animals in these systems alternate between being desperately boring, highly stressful, and acutely painful. These aren't lives we would tolerate for the animals we care about. If, for instance, we were to find out that cats and dogs were being treated in these ways, there would be an uproar.

What's more, it's difficult to argue that we *need* intensive animal agriculture. After all, even if some people need to consume animal products for health reasons, there is no good evidence that Americans need to consume as many animal products as they currently do. Most health researchers agree that Americans eat too much meat and would be better off eating more vegetables. And while extensive systems couldn't satisfy the current demand for animal products without creating lots of other problems (such as deforestation), they may well be able to satisfy a lower and healthier level. Granted, products from extensive systems are more expensive. But even if some people need animal products to be inexpensive for, say, food security reasons, it doesn't follow that we need a market-based solution to that problem. Governments already subsidize animal products. In principle, they could enhance existing food security programs to ensure that animal products remain affordable for low-income consumers. Finally, it's hard to see why we would need intensive animal agriculture to preserve the traditions and food cultures that people value. Again, having access to less meat (per dollar spent) doesn't mean having access to none.

I am cautious by temperament. I'm wary of criticizing the status quo. I tend to think that it's altogether too easy to assume that some alternative would be better, as we're often unaware of all the considerations that support existing practices and institutions. When it comes to intensive animal agriculture, though, I just don't know how to defend it without assuming that the interests of animals are completely trivial *and* that we should ignore all of intensive animal ag's negative side effects. I can understand arguments for extensive systems: I can see why we might think that death isn't particularly bad for nonhuman animals, and how many animals can be given decent—if not ideal—lives on farms that are well-designed and well-run. I feel the weight of nutritional arguments for the continuation of animal product consumption. I understand sociocultural arguments for the continuation of practices that are bound up with eating animals. But I struggle to see how we can take animals seriously, as individuals deserving moral concern, and not criticize intensive systems. If animals matter, then factory farms should go.

The Ethics of Purchasing and Consuming

You might disagree. But let's just assume, for the sake of argument, that we've settled the basic moral question about the ethics of production. Given as much, it might seem like a simple affair to tackle the ethics of purchasing and consuming animal products. We can just jump from the one to the other, right? If it's wrong to farm animals in intensive systems, then doesn't it follow that we shouldn't purchase or consume products from those systems? Well, maybe. However, it's more difficult to show this than you might think. To see why, we'll revisit a few moral theories. And I should warn you: things are going to get technical fairly quickly. However, I'll remind you of the main thread as we go and remember that the complexity is the point; I'm trying to explain why it's hard to jump from the ethics of creating animal products, on the one hand, to the ethics of purchasing and consuming them, on the other.

Utilitarianism

Again, let's begin with utilitarianism. Here's the simple utilitarian argument for abstaining from products from factory farms:

1. You ought to do whatever maximizes expected utility.
2. By abstaining from purchasing and consuming animal products from intensive systems, you maximize expected utility.
3. So, you ought to abstain from purchasing and consuming animal products from intensive systems.[5]

The crucial premise is the second one. If it's true, it's because what you buy and eat somehow affects what happens on farms; your actions send some signal to which producers are responding. However, it's pretty clear that that isn't true across the board: there are plenty of cases where consuming animal products sends *absolutely no signal* to producers to the effect that they ought to reduce production levels, and yet you would clearly benefit from consuming animal products. For instance, your roommate goes out of town, leaving his leftover Kung Pao chicken in the fridge. It will go bad before he returns, and he just expects you to throw it out long before then. No one will know if you eat it, and you really like Kung Pao chicken. So if the goal is to maximize expected utility, you should eat it. This act will have no negative effects (for animals, for the environment, for you, etc.) and some decidedly positive ones (e.g., gustatory pleasure, satiation of hunger, nutrition, free lunch, etc.). And if you don't like this example, it's easy to generate other ones: think about the buffet lunch at the office for the boss's birthday, where whatever people don't eat is thrown away. The upshot: the simple-act utilitarian argument for abstaining from products from factory farms doesn't work.

This No Signal Objection is based on the gap between purchasing and consuming: sometimes, you can eat without purchasing, and in those cases, your actions may not send any signal to producers at all. It's important to recognize, though, that the utilitarian can still *discourage* consuming products from factory farms. The utilitarian can say that even if it isn't clearly wrong to eat the leftovers in the Kung Pao chicken case, there are strong reasons to abstain. For instance, in realistic cases, it's often difficult to determine whether your eating the leftovers won't make a difference—it's always possible that it might weaken your resolve to abstain where your choosing animal products *wouldn't* maximize expected utility, or that others might learn about your behavior and have *their* resolve weakened. So, the utilitarian can affirm that it's morally *prudent* to adopt a rule of abstaining in all circumstances, even if there are cases where indulging isn't obviously morally impermissible.

It may indeed be morally prudent to adopt that rule, but let's just note that we are now out of the domain of moral requirements. After all, the point of the Kung Pao chicken case is *not* that you are in a morally ambiguous situation. Rather, the point is that in that case, you're *morally obliged* to eat the leftovers. So, the utilitarian has to say that it's morally prudent to adopt a rule that will, in some cases, tell you to do what's morally wrong. Fair enough: no rule of thumb is going to be perfect. But if the goal was to establish that it's always wrong to consume products from factory farms, then that ship has sailed. In the wake of the Kung Pao chicken example and ones like it, the conversation will now be about how frequently you can discern whether your actions make a difference, as well as your commitment to acting the right way when your actions *do* make a difference. Some people won't be able to stick to their guns when it counts. Others will. So, there's no longer any general utilitarian conclusion about the wrongness of consuming animal products from intensive systems, and there will even be some variety in terms of what it's morally prudent for particular people to do.

So much for the simple utilitarian argument against purchasing and consuming products from factory farms. Maybe the mistake was the one we mentioned earlier: namely, running together purchasing and consuming. Utilitarians can retrench, insisting that even if consuming animal products is sometimes okay, it's never okay to purchase them. In defense of that conclusion, they can offer a very similar argument:

1. You ought to do what maximizes expected utility.
2. By abstaining from purchasing animal products from intensive systems, you maximize expected utility.
3. So, you ought to abstain from purchasing animal products from intensive systems.

Unfortunately, this argument faces a problem too even if we approach things as utilitarians and so concede that first premise. Here it is. When you buy some chicken at the grocery store, no one goes out back to slaughter a new chicken to replace whatever you bought. In fact, the odds are very good that when you buy some chicken at the grocery store, nothing at all happens on the farmer's end; there is absolutely no change in production levels. But if that's the case, then there are *net benefits from purchasing*: namely, whatever increase in utility you get from having chicken over your other options.

To see why production doesn't invariably respond to purchasing, we need to recognize, first, that grocery stores want to maximize profit, not minimize food waste. Sometimes, of course, minimizing food waste is the way to maximize profit. But quite often, they need to allow some waste to make more money. That's the basic story when it comes to almost all fresh products: you need to have plenty of it available to capture every possible sale, and to do that you have to accept that you'll throw a lot of it away. Second, grocery stores don't order individual chicken breasts from their suppliers; they order truckloads of chicken products. As a result, they have to think in terms of whether it's worth buying one more or one fewer truckload. Third, there are innumerable small fluctuations in demand, and grocery stores can't simply alter their ordering every time there's a tiny increase or dip, as that level of precision would itself be costly. So, in addition to the waste that stores tolerate to maximize sales, there is waste that stores tolerate to have manageable and consistent relationships with their suppliers.

To be clear, the idea is *not* that because there's waste in the system, your purchases don't make a difference. Rather, the idea is that because of the scale of the system, stores are incentivized *not to pay attention to the actions of any one consumer*. (We're assuming that you're buying normal amounts of food. If you clear out the entire meat case, the ordering manager will notice!) What happens, then, when *you* buy some chicken? This line of reasoning says: probably nothing to chickens, and yet you benefit, which means that utility is maximized by purchasing. This is the Causal Inefficacy Problem: your purchases don't make a difference to production levels.

What can utilitarians say about this problem for their argument? Here's the standard move. Granted, you don't *know* when your purchases make a difference, but maybe you don't need to know. Alastair Norcross, for instance, argues that there are *thresholds* where changes in demand result in changes in ordering, and because hitting one of those thresholds would make a huge difference, the expected utility of purchasing animal products is still negative. In other words, maybe it's the case that nothing changes depending on how you shop, but something would change if 10,000 people shopped differently; it might be the case that many fewer chickens would be raised as a result.[6] And by not purchasing animal products, you make it slightly more likely that we'll hit that 10,000-people-shopping-differently threshold.

In other words, while the probability of making a difference may be very low, the *size* of the difference you'd make *if* you made a difference is huge. And since you don't know whether you're the threshold shopper—the person whose purchase makes a difference as to whether the threshold is hit—then we should do what utilitarians normally do under uncertainty. We should take the probability of making a difference and multiply it by the size of the difference you would make if you *were* to make a difference. That gives us the expected utility of purchasing. Here's the way Norcross explains it:

> Suppose that the industry is sensitive to a reduction in demand for chicken equivalent to 10,000 people becoming vegetarians. For each group of 10,000 who give up chicken, a quarter of a million fewer chickens are bred per year. It appears, then, that if you give up eating chicken, you have only a one in 10,000 chance of making any difference to the lives of chickens, unless it is certain that fewer than 10,000 people will ever give up eating chicken, in which case you have no chance. Isn't a one in 10,000 chance small enough to render your continued consumption of chicken blameless? Not at all. While the chance that your behavior is harmful may be small, the harm that is risked is enormous. The larger the numbers needed to make a difference to chicken production, the larger the difference such numbers would make. A one in ten thousand chance of saving 250,000 chickens per year from excruciating lives is morally and mathematically equivalent to the certainty of saving 25 chickens per year.

> (2004, 232–233)

In other words:

1. If 10,000 people stop buying chicken, 250,000 chickens will be saved.
2. So, you have a 1 in 10,000 chance of saving 250,000 chickens.

3. A 1 in 10,000 chance of saving 250,000 chickens is equivalent to (the expected effect is) saving 25 chickens.
4. If you can save 25 chickens, you ought to stop buying chicken.
5. So, you ought to stop buying chicken.

Call this the Order Threshold Solution to the Causal Inefficacy Problem. If the Order Threshold Solution works, then we can set aside one of the most significant hurdles for the utilitarian argument against purchasing animal products.

But does it work? I'm not so sure. My main worry is the move from Premise 1 to the intermediary conclusion on Line 2, which is supposed to follow from it. Sure, it might be true that if 10,000 people stop buying chicken, 250,000 chickens will be saved. However, it doesn't follow that *you* have a 1 in 10,000 chance of saving 250,000 chickens. The probability of your making a difference might be much, much lower, since it might be all but certain that grocery stores don't adjust their ordering in response to the actions of individual consumers. So, the *average* effect is one thing; you get it by dividing the impact of hitting a threshold by the number of individuals required to hit a threshold. However, what matters here is the *expected* effect; you get that by looking at the probability of making a difference and multiplying it by the effect of hitting a threshold. And we have good reason to believe, based on the considerations discussed earlier about the incentives for grocery stores, that the probability of your making a difference is extremely low. Granted, if we didn't know anything about how grocery stores work, then it would be sensible to use the average effect as a proxy for the expected effect. But we do know something about how grocery stores work, and so we can tell that the average effect isn't a great proxy.

Here's what all this means: If the probability of your making a difference is very low—say, 1 in 10 million, rather than 1 in 10,000—then the calculation won't work out the way Norcross suggests. Instead, it will work out that not buying chicken is basically equivalent to sparing a chicken from one day of its life. (The math: 1/10,000,000 chance of making a difference × 250,000 chickens = 0.025 chickens; 0.025 × 47 days, which is the average time to slaughter weight = 1.175 days.) Now, we have to compare the net utility gained by a human being when she consumes chicken and the net utility in one day of a chicken's life. Does that human being gain more than the chicken loses? I'm inclined to think not, but the truth is that it's a complicated empirical issue, and I'm not totally sure what to say about it. However, what's pretty clear is this: if we assume that the probability of your making a difference is even lower—say, 1 in 100 million, or one in a billion—the math will work out in favor of buying chicken (assuming that the person likes chicken).

It might seem terribly cold and heartless to think this way, but that's not my fault: that's just the way utilitarianism works. In any case, the big takeaway here is just that things are tricky. Utilitarians *might* have a good argument against purchasing animal products from intensive systems, but it depends on complex empirical and theoretical questions about the probability of your making a difference. Until we know what those probabilities are, we just can't say much more.

The Rights View

Proponents of broadly Kantian views, such as the rights view, will be thrilled with this result. This isn't because they want to defend animal product consumption, but because they're critical of utilitarianism. Indeed, the most famous proponent of the rights view, Tom Regan, mentions all this empirical complexity as a reason to prefer the rights view over utilitarianism. By his lights, it's a mistake to get lost in such calculations just to decide whether it's okay to purchase products from intensive systems. Instead, he argues:

> To treat farm animals as renewable resources is to fail to treat them with the respect they are due as possessors of inherent value. . . . Since . . . the current practice of raising farm animals for human consumption fails to treat these animals with respect, those who support this practice by buying meat exceed their rights. Their purchase makes them a party to the perpetuation of an unjust practice. [Abstaining from purchasing animal products] is not supererogatory; it is obligatory.
>
> (Regan 2004, 345–346)

On the face of it, then, Regan's argument goes something like this:

1. Animals possess inherent value.
2. If a being possesses inherent value, then it's unjust to treat her as a renewable resource.
3. Raising animals for human consumption treats them as renewable resources.
4. So, it's unjust to raise animals for human consumption.
5. If a practice is unjust, then it's wrong to be "a party to the perpetuation" of it.
6. By purchasing animal products, you become party to the perpetuation of an unjust practice.
7. So, it's wrong to purchase animal products.

Obviously, this argument is going to rule out much more than purchasing products from intensive systems. That's the point of Premise 3: *all* animal agriculture treats animals as renewable resources, and so we get the conclusion in Line 4: it's unjust to raise them for human consumption. And on the assumption that purchasing isn't the only way to be "a party to the perpetuation of an unjust practice"—for instance, you can also be a party by eating meat you didn't pay for—you can rule out (most) animal product consumption too.

What should we say about Premises 5 and 6, though? On one interpretation—which certainly isn't the only one—you become a party to the perpetuation of an unjust practice if you *cause* that practice to continue. So, for instance, we might say that I'm party to the perpetuation of an unjust practice if some injustice wouldn't occur if I were to shop differently. But if that's the right reading, then the Causal Inefficacy Problem crops up again. The odds are good that you don't make a difference, so it isn't the case that, by purchasing animal products, you become party to the perpetuation of an unjust practice.

Regan could get around this problem with a much stronger claim: he could say that if a practice is unjust, then it's wrong to take *even the tiniest chance* of contributing causally to its happening. The Even the Tiniest Chance Premise will get the conclusion that the rights view is supposed to deliver—namely, a moral obligation to be vegan—but it faces some pretty serious problems. First, it seems entirely insensitive to the much more likely *good* consequences that said actions may have. If you are buying a meal for a homeless person and the person wants a hamburger, you can be quite confident that you'll better respect and satisfy that person's desire—and provide more calories—if you buy that person a hamburger rather than a black bean burger. If the odds are extraordinarily low that you're causing any harm by buying the beef patty, why shouldn't the good consequences be relevant?

Second, let's grant that you can act wrongly by taking a tiny chance of being party to the perpetuation of an unjust practice. If so, then it follows that the vast majority of our actions are morally wrong. Since causal chains are so complex, most of our actions involve a very small chance of being party to the perpetuation of an unjust practice, even if those actions have no obvious relationship to the objectionable behavior. For instance, when I order black coffee at the coffee shop, I support a business that sells animal products: many of the products there aren't vegan. Of course, I'm not *buying* a nonvegan product, so you might not think that *I'm* supporting the perpetuation of an unjust practice. Still, my money might be *subsidizing* the sale of those products, allowing the shop to sell them at a lower price than they could if they weren't making money from the sale of black coffee. So, I'm taking a minuscule chance of being party to the perpetuation of various unjust practices (such as dairy production; egg production, via their baked goods; and so forth). This would mean that it's morally wrong for me to buy that cup of black coffee, and that just seems implausible.

Third, the Even the Tiniest Chance Premise seems like an arbitrary way to develop Regan's argument. At some point, "the tiniest chance" is hard to distinguish from no chance at all. So, Regan now owes us an account of why even the tiniest chance is important enough to make it wrong to purchase and consume animal products. If he appeals to the expected impact of purchasing, then he can no longer say that the rights view is superior to utilitarianism in the way it grounds the duty to abstain from purchasing products from factory farms. (Recall that it's supposed to be an advantage of the rights view that it doesn't require us to answer difficult empirical questions about the likelihood of your actions having an impact.) But what other option is available? Unfortunately, the answer to that question isn't clear.

Let's take stock. We got ourselves into this mess because we accepted a causal interpretation of "being party to an unjust practice," a phrase that appears in the crucial premises of Regan's argument. But surely other interpretations are available, and perhaps the rights theorist can use one of those to argue that we ought to abstain from animal products from factory farms. I'll just consider one popular alternative: the idea that you are party to an unjust practice if you *benefit* from it.

The first thing to note is that this alternative also implies that the vast majority of our actions are morally wrong: since causal chains are so complex, I benefit from lots and lots of unjust practices. Consider this: most of my students eat meat, and as a result of their having had meaty meals, they come to my class energized and ready to talk; so, I benefit from their animal product consumption, and so from their support for an unjust practice. If I'm party to an unjust practice as a result, then I'm in trouble just by teaching them. But that's implausible.

The second thing to notice is that I don't always benefit from purchasing animal products, so this view implies that purchasing isn't always wrong. Imagine a case where I buy milk that's gone bad and I get sick from drinking it. I'm worse off for having purchased the milk, and so it seems bizarre to say that I've benefited. However, it shouldn't work out that my actions are morally okay simply because I got sick!

Would it be better if we said "don't *try* to benefit from unjust practices"? This would help with the teaching objection, as I'm not trying to benefit from an unjust practice when I teach my classes. However, I'm not sure whether it helps with the milk objection. Am I trying to benefit from an unjust practice when I buy milk? Maybe so, but now it isn't so clear that it's wrong to do that. I suspect a lot of well-meaning shoppers reason like this: "If I thought that not buying some milk would make a difference, I wouldn't buy it; but since it doesn't make a difference, I'm going to enjoy it." To my ears, while the shoppers are trying to *benefit* from an unjust practice, they aren't trying to *support* it. And we might think that it's supporting, rather than benefiting, that's the moral problem. If you would support harms to animals that you could prevent, not only does that mean you would cause harm, but it also means that you aren't that concerned about animals. But if you are just willing to benefit when it doesn't make a difference, then I can hear that as a kind of savviness. The thought is something like "let's focus our moral energies on cases where our actions matter, not where they just have some symbolic value." And that thought doesn't seem so crazy to me.

We could, of course, try to help Regan out by considering several other possible interpretations of the idea of being party to an unjust practice. Perhaps some of them would fare better. My own view, for what it's worth, is that many of them are going to have similar problems. Either they will assume you make a difference when you don't, or they will imply that the vast majority of our actions are morally wrong. Of course, there are probably some rights theorists who are happy to embrace that second option. "That's the price of living in an unjust world," they might say. "We do the wrong thing all the time!" And fair enough; they can take that view.

But if they do, I start to lose my grip on the conversation. I thought the goal here was to get some guidance on what we should do, to distinguish the right actions from the wrong ones. However, if it turns out that almost everything I do is wrong, I don't really get the point of talking about "right" and "wrong" anymore. If it's really true that I shouldn't do something, then it's got to be the case that I can avoid doing it. But if someone argues that the only way to act morally is, say, to opt out of living in a capitalist system, then while there is some sense in which I can do that—I could go live in the woods, at least for a while—that clearly isn't feasible. The sense in which I "can" do it is irrelevant for practical decision-making. I want to hold myself and others to standards that are reasonable given our actual situations, not radically idealistic ones. So, I think our ethic should be sensitive to what's *feasible* for ordinary people, not to what it's in-principle-possible for people to do.

Granted, some people will think exactly the opposite; they will say that feasibility is too concessive to the status quo, that it's good to have an ethic that pushes us. So I don't raise this point as a decisive challenge, but just as a way of flagging that there are larger issues behind this debate, questions about what, exactly, morality is *for*. Still, I think these sorts of worries are enough to justify setting the rights view aside, at least for now.

At this juncture, we have a few options. We could, of course, keep investigating different objections and replies to the utilitarian or rights-view-based argument for abstaining from products from intensive systems. Alternatively, we could turn to other moral theories, or perhaps just plausible moral principles, trying to assess whether they will allow us to reach the same conclusion. I'm not sure, though, how much we would learn from all that, as I suspect the same issues would recur. We would continue to debate the efficacy of individual purchases, the symbolic significance of purchasing and consuming animal products, and the demandingness of our ethic. These are worthwhile issues. However, I think we've done what we came to do: namely, show that it's complicated to move from the ethics of creating animal products, on the one hand, to the ethics of purchasing and consuming them, on the other.

Notice, though, that some of the complexity is due to the goal: establishing a moral *obligation* to abstain from purchasing and consuming animal products. In what remains, let's see how things go if we set this objective aside, exploring other ways of approaching the ethical issues here.

Virtue and Self-Examination

I think it's useful to start with the way that virtue ethicists approach this topic, not because we want to commit ourselves to the virtue ethical framework, but because they have some insights into the way we might frame the moral issue. As I mentioned in Chapter 5, Rosalind Hursthouse offers what's probably the best-known virtue-based argument against buying products from factory farms. It begins by calling the reader's attention to the suffering involved in intensive animal agriculture, and she then writes this:

> Can I, in all honesty, deny the ongoing existence of this suffering? No, I can't. I know perfectly well that although there have been some improvements in the regulation of factory farming, what is going on is still terrible. Can I think it is anything but callous to shrug this off and say it doesn't matter? No, I can't. Can I deny that the practices are cruel? No, I can't. Then what am I doing being party to them? It won't do for me to say that I am not actually engaging in the cruelty myself. There is a large gap between not being cruel and being truly compassionate, and the virtue of compassion is what I am supposed to be acquiring and exercising. I can no more think of myself as compassionate while I am party to such cruelty than I could think of myself as just if, scrupulously avoiding owning slaves, I still enjoyed

the fruits of slave labor. . . . The practices that bring cheap meat to our tables are cruel, so we shouldn't be party to them.

(Hursthouse 2006, 141–143)

If we interpret this as an argument for our having a moral obligation to abstain from purchasing or consuming animal products from intensive systems, then we will immediately get bogged down in many of the same issues that the utilitarians and rights theorists face. After all, the notion of "being party" to objectionable practices is hard to spell out. Should it be given a causal interpretation? Then either most consumers aren't party to factory farming or they are party to too much, as complicity abounds. And if it isn't given a causal interpretation, then we face the same sorts of problems that made trouble for the rights view: for instance, we end up with a principle that successfully links production and consumption by saying that it's wrong to benefit from unjust production, but then we have to say that just about everything we do is wrong.

But what's important here, I think, is not so much the particular way that Hursthouse is linking her actions as a consumer to intensive animal agriculture. Instead, what's important is the way that she deliberates. She's examining herself, turning over her own beliefs, values, and motivations. Whatever else we might say about virtue ethics, it seems to go right in asking us to scrutinize ourselves. There is something important about the idea that, at least in one mode, ethical deliberation is kind of self-reflection, a highly personal activity that involves investigating who we are and who we aspire to be.

However, there is something a bit foreign about the precise *way* that Hursthouse reasons in this passage, as so few of us, I think, ever invoke the virtues directly when we are thinking about how to live. Instead, we attend to our emotions, to the way that information and experiences have shifted our perspective, and to reflections on our identities, both actual and aspirational. I see a more familiar form of moral reasoning in a piece by Grace Boey, who was an undergraduate when she wrote an essay trying to explain why, despite doubting that her actions make a difference, she decided to abstain from consuming animal products:

What gave me the final push was really this: I just felt *sad* every time I looked down at my plate. The reason why I started feeling so sad was because . . . so much of [information about intensive animal agriculture] had seeped into my brain that I could no longer live with eating the stuff I knew to be produced in this way. That's why giving up meat was so easy for me: where I used to see a pork chop on a plate, I now see a tail-less, crusty-eyed, psychotic sow. And it's important to me that I keep this aversion going: I have no wish to remain in the system I don't believe in, even if it should make [no impact].

For me, this is what animal abstinence in a broken system boils down to: integrity. Emotion and some cognition may have been the spark, but the desire for integrity is what really keeps this flame going. And that's why I keep pictures of battery cages in my phone, [since] I don't spontaneously visualize miserable hens when peeking into patisseries. When I opt out, I act in accordance with my own values about how the world should be—which is, free of the system. Whether or not the "virtue" of such integrity makes for a strict moral requirement, it certainly important to my own project of self-integration and identity that I pursue it.

(Barnhill et al. 2017, 27)

Let's pause and appreciate Boey's process here. First, she's taken the time to understand what intensive animal agriculture is like; she isn't simply responding to a few stray facts. Second, Boey hasn't *siloed* that understanding, keeping it completely separate from her emotional life. Instead, she's allowed the information to alter her feelings—which, of course, many people don't. It's easy to take in information and, essentially, put in a box, so that it doesn't complicate the way you experience the rest of the world. Boey isn't doing that because, as she says at the end, she is interested in the "project of self-integration"—she's trying to avoid becoming the kind of person who organizes her mental life in ways that spare her psychological discomfort.

Third, Boey's emotional shift is accompanied by a perspectival shift: whereas, previously, a pork chop was a pork chop, she now sees it as having a story, as part of an animal with a very particular—and dark—history. This doesn't seem to be totally voluntary, because it seems to be a product of her understanding and her emotions; however, it isn't entirely *in*voluntary either. Boey recognizes that it would be easy to allow herself to return to the ordinary, socially dominant way of seeing pork chops. So, fourth, she takes steps to preserve her perspectival shift: she keeps those photos on her phone, so that she doesn't forget—or what might be worse, remember without feeling anything.

Finally, she has a story about how all this fits together. She wants to live in a way that's more reflective of how she thinks the world should be, which means allowing actions that might not make a difference—like eating a pork chop—to have symbolic significance in her life. For her, eating a pork chop is not performing an action that has some very low probability of triggering an order that might adjust pig production levels. Instead, eating a pork chop is a way of *saying* something to herself and others. It says: "I'm okay with the way sows are treated on factory farms." And obviously, that isn't the message that Boey wants to send, whether to herself or anyone else.

I don't exactly know how to categorize Boey's approach to ethics. There are links between what she's doing and both care ethics and ecofeminism, but she's obviously not framing things in terms of care, nor focusing on the kind of structural critique that we'd expect from an ecofeminist analysis. But however we categorize Boey's approach, let's recognize that she's making the conversation personal. She's encouraging us to have a dialogue with ourselves about who we are and want to be. It involves asking whether we know what Boey knows, whether we share her feelings when we look at our plates, and whether we share her values. What's more, we have to ask whether we hope to become the kind of person whose beliefs, feelings, and values are woven together in the way that hers are.

Frankly, I feel most comfortable doing ethics in the way that this chapter began, setting out principles and considering their implications. There is something attractive to me about the structure and the order. By contrast, Boey is inviting us to do ethics in a way that focuses squarely on our identities, that occupies itself with emotions, perceptions, and the narratives we tell about our lives. As a result, her approach is messy. It doesn't allow us to specify either what people's duties are or why they have them. It doesn't let us talk at some level of generality about "people's" duties—about the responsibilities of unnamed persons who happen to face choices like ours. It doesn't let us abstract away from the details of particular individuals' lives. And to be clear, this is *not* because Boey is telling us that we have to pay more attention to how much money people have, or their specific nutritional needs, or something like that; the problem isn't one that you can solve by adding more information. Instead, she's just giving up on the project of doing ethics for other people. Boey's approach is decidedly from the first-person perspective. She's showing us how she's reasoning, for herself and about herself, and she's inviting us to do likewise. If we're willing, we can follow her lead, reasoning the same way for and about ourselves. But we can't do it for anyone else.

I think there's something valuable about the way I do ethics. I see ethics as a project that we do together, looking for reasons we can share. The goal is to come up with moral guidelines that seem sensible to everyone who actually cares about living with others based on mutually agreeable standards. But that isn't the only conception of ethics, and even if it's valuable, it doesn't have to be the only approach that's worth pursuing. Boey is offering a different and more personal option. In a sense, she's encouraging you to ask whether, knowing what you now know, you can look at a pork chop in the same way. She's welcoming you to ask whether you *want* to see it the same way. This is ethics as self-examination, as aspiration toward our ideals. I hope you accept her invitation.

Further Reading

Abbate, Cheryl. 2019. "Veganism, (Almost) Harm-Free Animal Flesh, and Nonmaleficence: Navigating Dietary Ethics in an Unjust World." In *The Routledge Handbook of Animal Ethics*, edited by Bob Fischer. New York: Routledge.

Bramble, Ben, and Bob Fischer. 2015. *The Moral Complexities of Eating Meat*. New York: Oxford University Press.

Chignell, Andrew, Terence Cuneo, and Matthew C. Halteman (eds.). 2014. *Philosophy Comes to Dinner: Arguments on the Ethics of Eating*. New York: Routledge.

Harper, Breeze A. 2010. *Sistah Vegan: Black Female Vegans Speak on Food, Identity, Health, and Society*. New York: Lantern Publishing & Media.

Holdier, A.G. 2016. "The Pig's Squeak: Towards a Renewed Aesthetic Argument for Veganism." *Journal of Agricultural and Environmental Ethics* 29(4): 631–642.

Lamey, Andy. 2019. *Duty and the Beast: Should We Eat Meat in the Name of Animal Rights?* New York: Cambridge University Press.

Lowe, Dan. 2016. "Common Arguments for the Moral Acceptability of Eating Meat: A Discussion for Students." *Between the Species* 19(1): 172–192.

Podgorski, Abelard. 2020. "The Diner's Defence: Producers, Consumers, and the Benefits of Existence." *Australasian Journal of Philosophy* 98(1): 64–77.

Saja, Krzysztof. 2013. "The Moral Footprint of Animal Products." *Agriculture and Human Values* 30(2): 193–202.

Notes

1. If we think that the benefit of a serving of chicken to a human being is not worth the experiences that a broiler chicken has over the course of those three days, then we are committed to saying that there is more suffering than pleasure over the course of those three days. After all, if we thought that there were more pleasure than suffering, then we would have to say that intensive broiler production is justifiable, at least in principle. (Utilitarians are all about maximizing, so it wouldn't be justified if there were any way of producing even more net utility. So then it becomes an empirical question about whether there is another animal production system that provides more net utility overall.) It seems clear to me that there is more suffering than pleasure over the course of those three days, but truth be told, I'm not sure how to offer a rigorous argument for that conclusion; the best I can do is refer you to the description I gave in the last chapter of broiler chicken production. Of course, you might think that this is an objection to the conventional utilitarian approach: we shouldn't be worried about how much pleasure chickens are eking out from, say, feeding; we should just be interested in minimizing the amount of suffering, regardless of how much pleasure may be associated with it. That view has a name: *negative* utilitarianism. If we are negative utilitarians, then the case against intensive animal agriculture is a slam dunk.

2. The move from broiler production to intensive animal agriculture generally is actually somewhat complicated. For instance, while it's very plausible that broiler chickens have net negative lives, it's less clear what to say about beef cattle. I am not saying that beef cattle have net positive lives; I'm just saying that I don't quite know how to demonstrate that they have net negative lives. Essentially, let's suppose we assess whether a life is net negative or net positive by dividing a life into moments, giving each one a positive or negative score, and then summing all those scores. For beef cattle, it seems plausible that many of those moments are going to be just barely positive. And because they live a fairly long time, it's an open empirical question whether the positive outweighs the negative, or vice versa.

3. In my view, Korsgaard makes her argument against intensive animal agriculture more controversial than it needs to be. Her case against it relies on the principle that "you should not bring a creature into existence if you know in advance that the creature's life will not be worth living" (2018, 221). But questions about whether lives are worth living are notoriously difficult to answer, and while I agree that the lives of many farm animals are not worth living, this adds unnecessary complexity. It should be enough to say "you should not bring a creature into existence if you know in advance that you plan to use that being in a way that's deeply disrespectful." This version is also preferable because it allows her to criticize extensive animal agriculture too, on the assumption that it is deeply disrespectful to an animal to kill her in her prime for your economic benefit.

4. There are a few reasons why contractualists have thought that self-interested and rational agents would probably insist on rules that provide standing to humans but not to nonhumans. First, agents probably won't be willing to endorse rules that don't grant moral status to infants or those with severe cognitive disabilities—they wouldn't be rules we would care about, given our affections for our own children and family members. Second, agents have self-interested reasons to agree to rules that protect the senile, comatose, and brain damaged, as they themselves may end up in such a situation. Third, contractors have reason to endorse rules that promote virtue in themselves and others, at least insofar as virtue serves the end of the contract process: namely, establishing rules that lead to a stable society. But animals aren't rational agents, most people don't care about nonhuman animals nearly as much they care about human beings, agents don't have to worry about becoming animals themselves, and society seems fairly stable in spite of the ways we use animals.

5. For arguments along these lines, see Matheny (2002), Norcross (2004), and Singer (2009).
6. There are problems with this assumption. For the details, see Fischer (2020).

References

Barnhill, Anne, Mark Budolfson, and Tyler Doggett. 2017. *Food, Ethics, and Society: An Introductory Text with Readings*. New York: Oxford University Press.

Fischer, Bob. 2020. *The Ethics of Eating Animals*. New York: Routledge.

Hursthouse, Rosalind. 2006. "Applying Virtue Ethics to Our Treatment of the Other Animals." In *The Practice of Virtue*, edited by Jennifer Welchman, 136–155. Indianapolis: Hackett Publishing.

Korsgaard, Christine M. 2009. "Facing the Animal You See in the Mirror." *The Harvard Review of Philosophy* 16(1): 4–9.

Korsgaard, Christine. 2018. *Fellow Creatures: Our Obligations to the Other Animals*. New York: Oxford University Press.

Matheny, Gaverick. 2002. "Expected Utility, Contributory Causation, and Vegetarianism." *Journal of Applied Philosophy* 19: 293–297.

Norcross, Alastair. 2004. "Puppies, Pigs, and People: Eating Meat and Marginal Cases." *Philosophical Perspectives* 18: 229–245.

Regan, Tom. 2004. *The Case for Animal Rights*. Berkeley: University of California Press.

Singer, Peter. 2009. *Animal Liberation: The Definitive Classic of the Animal Movement*. New York: Harper Perennial.

8 Fishing

OVERVIEW

This is the third of three chapters on animals as food. This one tackles the fishing industry, which is importantly different from animal agriculture and aquaculture because it targets wild animals. If we assess industrial fishing based on the number of animals killed, it looks like it's among the worst ways that humans harm nonhuman animals. But if we focus on the amount of suffering caused, then depending on what we say about the amount of suffering in nature, the fishing industry may be doing more good than harm on balance. The chapter wraps up with another look at how best to navigate the complexities of eating as an individual, arguing that even if we don't condemn the fishing industry, we could still have reasons to avoid its products.

Through many months of reporting on fishing, I was struck by the age-old consistency of the vocation: the typical workday for a fisherman hadn't changed since the days of Galilee. It was backbreaking labor punctuated by crushing boredom. You shot your net, cast your line, waited, waited more, then hopefully hoisted or reeled in a catch. Over the past century, however, technology has transformed fishing from a type of hunting into something more akin to farming. With highly mechanized ships that operate more like floating factories, the industry became brutally efficient at stripping the seas of virtually everything in them.

By 2015, about ninety-four million tons of fish were caught each year, more than the weight of the entire human population. Much of the credit and blame goes to the building boom in the 1930s of purse seiners. These ships surround an entire school of fish with a deep curtain of netting, sometimes nearly a mile around, with a thick wire that runs through rings along the bottom of the mesh. After setting the net, the ship hauls in the bottom wire, and the net is pursed, or cinched, like a laundry bag. A crane lifts the net out of the water, the fish are dumped into a gaping funnel, sorted (often by conveyor belt), and swallowed into the ship hold.

World War II spurred engineers to develop lighter, faster, more durable ships that could travel farther on less fuel. Submarine combat propelled innovation in sonar, helping illuminate the dark fathoms. Finding fish became more a science of spreadsheets than an art of dead reckoning. Subzero onboard freezers freed fishermen from their race against melting refrigerator ice. Innovations in plastics and monofilaments lengthened fishing lines from feet to miles. Lightweight polymer-based nets enabled super-trawlers to rake the ocean with the ruthlessness of two tanks rolling through a rain forest, a mesh of steel cables strung between them . . . These technological advances, as well as the industrialization of fishing, are a big reason why catches from the high seas rose 700 percent in the last half a century. They also partly explain why many of the world's fish stocks are at the brink of collapse.

(Urbina 2019)

We've now said a bit about the ethics of raising animals for food in intensive systems. So far, though, we haven't said anything about industrial fishing, which is the other main way that we put meat on the table. It isn't the only other way, of course, even if we restrict our attention to fish: there's recreational angling and various kinds of small-scale operations. But we're letting the numbers tell us what to prioritize, and by that standard, our focus should be squarely on industrial operations.

Fishing by the Numbers

That being said, it's actually quite difficult to know exactly how many fish are killed annually by the fishing industry. One of the difficulties is methodological: as mentioned in Chapter 6, it's standard to report fishery production in tons, not individual heads. The Food and Agriculture Organization of the United Nations (FAO)'s most recent report estimates that fisheries caught some 97 million tons of fish in 2018.[1] So, if you want to estimate the number of lives at stake here, you start by dividing the tonnage of each species by their average weights. But that only gives us part of the picture. To get a fuller one, we need to factor in both discards and "IUU" fishing—that is, illegal, unreported, and unregulated fishing.

Very roughly, "discards" are all the fish you caught but didn't want and so threw away.[2] Most of these animals die in the process, and their bodies are usually tossed back in the water. We don't have particularly good data on discard rates, as they aren't well documented. The best available research is a 2019 report from the FAO; it estimates that just shy of 11% of the total global catch is discarded. Many, many animals are just collateral damage in our quest for seafood.

But discards are only part of the undercounting problem: there is also illegal, unreported, and unregulated (IUU) fishing. Given the vastness of the ocean and the nature of the activity, the scope of such fishing is extremely difficult to estimate. The FAO often cites a number from a 2009 study that put the upper bound at 26 million tons of fish. If that estimate were correct, that would mean that these fish represent nearly a quarter of all the wild fish killed for food each year.

Based on FAO statistics from 2007 to 2016, one advocacy group crunched the numbers and estimated that given an average catch of 77 million tonnes during that period, fisheries were killing between 790 billion and 2.3 trillion fish per year.[3] For the sake of simplicity, that estimate excludes discards and IUU fishing. Moreover, it's based on an average catch that's 20 million tonnes lower than the most recent year for which we have data. So, it's reasonable to assume that the fishing industry kills at least a trillion animals per year, and perhaps dramatically more. It's very difficult to get a good estimate of the number of animals killed by terrestrial animal agriculture, but you often hear numbers around 90 billion per year.[4] It's clear, then, that the fishing industry kills a great many more animals.

It also might seem clear, therefore, not only that industrial fishing is morally wrong, but that it's the most significant way that people harm animals.[5] But are these claims true? This chapter is devoted to exploring the issues that come up when we try to answer this question.

Calculating Harm

Let's begin with the harm question, returning to the overall moral assessment later. Is fishing the most significant way that people harm animals?

Tallying Lives Lost

The simplest way to answer this question is to compare (a) the number of lives lost as result of fishing with (b) the number of lives lost due as a result of animal agriculture (which is probably the other contender for the tragic title for "Most Harmful"). If we do that, then fishing probably "wins" an unfortunate competition. However, while there's obviously something plausible about the idea that we should compare the number of lives lost, there are also objections to this method of counting. The first is that while the loss of life certainly seems significant, there are, as we saw in Chapter 4, plenty of puzzles that make it difficult to defend that judgment across the board. It may turn out that death itself isn't bad for anyone; that death isn't bad for nonhuman animals specifically; or that while death is bad for nonhuman animals, it isn't *that* bad for many of them. Second, though, and more importantly, we might think that even if death is bad, it isn't the only thing we care about: suffering matters too, and perhaps even more. So, if we are looking for a proxy for the total harm that an industry causes, perhaps we should be focusing on the suffering of nonhuman animals rather than the number of lives lost.

Suppose, then, that we try to figure out how much suffering wild-caught fish endure compared to other animals. Just providing a list of the ways that various industries harm animals isn't very helpful. What we need is a single scale that we can use to represent all the impacts on animals. This would allow us to compare the negative impacts of fishing on fish with the negative impacts of intensive animal agriculture on chickens, pigs, and cows. One option—which has its limits, but so do all the alternatives—is to try to quantify the total amount of suffering caused by the fishing industry, measured in some unit of time, which we can then contrast with the total amount of suffering caused by some other form of food production. Obviously, this is enormously difficult to do in any precise way. So, we will simply have to stipulate some numbers that are not completely unreasonable and see what results from the process. If it turns out that one industry is dramatically worse than another—say, by a factor of ten—then we can be fairly confident that despite uncertainty about the specific numbers we chose, it's still reasonable to say that "Industry A is worse than Industry B." If it turns out to be a close call, then we should probably withhold judgment. In any case, we won't know what we should say until we try to do the calculations.

Consider, then, that while some wild-caught fish suffer for hours or days on long lines or gill nets, most don't: their swim bladders explode as a result of coming to the surface too quickly, or they suffocate within minutes on the deck, or they are crushed under the weight of other fish. However, we don't want to underestimate the total amount of suffering, so let's use a fairly high estimate: we'll suppose that, on average, a wild-caught fish suffers for an hour before dying. Then, we can aggregate all those hours to come up with the total amount of suffering that fishing produces, expressed in "life years." (That is, take all the hours, divide by 24 to get the number of days, and then divide by 365 to get the number of years.) Using this method and the fishing estimates with which we began, the fishing industry causes, on an annual basis, roughly 114 million life years of suffering, using the conservative estimate of the total kill count.

Globally, though, over *6 billion* layer hens are killed each year, each of whom lives between 12 and 24 months in very unpleasant conditions.[6] (See Chapter 6 for details.) So, we don't even need to factor in broiler chickens—who easily outnumber layers by a factor of six or seven—to see that the life years of suffering due to the chicken industry are much, much higher than those produced by the fishing industry. Now, it looks like the chicken industry wins the "Most Harmful" title.

Factoring in the Badness of Death

We reached this conclusion by focusing on the harms that are directly caused by each industry. However, we might think that we've forgotten an important detail. It certainly matters that chickens have lives that involve significant pain. At the same time, though, when chickens are killed, we might argue that they aren't losing anything: their lives are so bad that they are better off dead. In the case of fishing, by contrast, fish are robbed of lives that might be quite good, where they are free to pursue their own interests. And it's worth remembering that many fish would have had very long lives indeed. Salmon, for instance, can live 3 to 8 years; tilapia, 9 to 11 years; Atlantic cod, as many as 25 years; and bluefin tuna, up to 30 years. If we were to factor in positive experiences as well as negative ones, then the calculation would change radically.

Let's just suppose, for instance, that the average wild-caught fish lives just two years and that each fish is caught at the midpoint of her life. Then, we wouldn't just be aggregating one hour of suffering per fish killed. We would also need to factor in a full year of lost life, with all the pleasures it would have contained. Based on the sheer number of fish killed, the scales would tip back squarely "in favor" of fish. Strikingly, this follows even if we think that it's much less likely that fish are conscious than that chickens are conscious. Suppose that whatever probability you assign to chickens being conscious, you only assign one-tenth that probability to fish being conscious. Still, even given the lower-bound estimate of the number of fish killed each year by the fishing industry—1 trillion—that would still mean 100 billion life years lost. So, if we think that chickens are better off dead and fish are robbed of lives worth living, then industrial fishing is indeed the most harmful activity.

Recall that we started off comparing the sheer number of lives lost. We then thought that this might not capture what's most relevant, so we turned instead to the amount of suffering. At that juncture, we recognized that we should also factor in what animals are losing as a result of their deaths. Having done all that, can we say that, of the two industries, fishing is worse than farming?

No. There remains one important complication. In thinking about what fish lose as a result of their deaths, we made it sound like they were each losing a full year of good life. But in Chapter 4, we raised the possibility that most wild animals don't have lives that are worth living. And if their lives *aren't* worth living, then rather than losing a year of pleasures, we might think that they, like chickens, are being benefited by their deaths.

Wild Animal Suffering

This may sound crazy, but there are some good reasons to take it seriously. Let's consider them in some detail.

We'll begin with the idea that we mentioned in Chapter 4: namely, that insofar as nature optimizes, she optimizes for fitness, not welfare. Again, as Richard Dawkins puts it, "Nature is not interested in suffering one way or the other unless it affects the survival of DNA" (1996, 132). So, unless animals' fitness would be improved by some mechanism that would make them experience less suffering, we should expect that their lives are as hard as they appear to be. And they appear to be hard indeed.

Animals suffer due to parasites, disease, exposure to environmental conditions (for instance, excessive heat or cold), injury, hunger, the threat of predation, and as a result of actually being eaten. To give just one fish-specific example, consider algae blooms. Some types of algae produce neurotoxins that disorient fish, leaving them vulnerable to predators, while others produce toxins that damage fish's organs. Even if those injuries aren't fatal, they significantly increase the likelihood that fish will contract infectious diseases. In the years leading up to 2017, a particularly bad algae bloom wiped out 100 million Pacific cod off the coast of southern Alaska—70% of the population.

However, these reminders of wild animal suffering don't show that suffering predominates in nature—that is, that most wild animals have lives with more pain than pleasure, or *net negative* lives. That conclusion is made more plausible, though, when we consider what it means for nature to optimize for fitness rather than welfare. There are, for instance, different reproductive strategies in the animal kingdom. Though it's a spectrum and we are simplifying quite a bit, it's safe to say that humans are "K-strategists": we have few offspring and we invest a great deal in the ones we have. Most animals, however, are "*r*-strategists": they have hundreds, thousands, or even millions of offspring; invest very little in them; and only a few of them survive.[7] Essentially, *r*-strategists ensure the survival of their species by winning a war of attrition. A mouse might have 1,000 pups over the course of her lifetime, but there aren't 1,000 times as many mice each generation; likewise, a tuna might lay a million eggs over the course of her lifetime, and yet the seas aren't completely full of tuna. The vast majority of offspring die relatively young.

How do they die? There are, of course, many ways to go. Some of the unlucky offspring die of starvation or thirst; others are eaten by predators relatively soon after birth; others still will contract diseases and wither away. And prior to their deaths, all these individuals will experience the ordinary stresses of trying to find food and shelter from the elements, trying to evade predators, and so on.

In other words, the lives of *r*-strategists' offspring are nasty, brutish, and short. Someone might doubt, however, that this shows that suffering *predominates*. Granted, the critic might say, there is *extensive* suffering in the wild. However, it isn't yet clear that most animals live *net negative* lives. It could still be the case that animals enjoy more pleasure than pain, even if not much more.

While this is possible, it seems unlikely. First, we should be suspicious of our own intuitions here, since we know that we romanticize and idealize nature. When we picture animals in the wild, we tend to imagine them as we see them in nature documentaries: bears lumbering through the woods, monkeys chattering among themselves in the canopy of the rainforest, hawks soaring above the pines. That is, we tend to focus on mature animals who have survived all the threats that killed off all their siblings. Moreover, we tend to picture them healthy and well, rather than disease-ridden, hungry, or severely injured. And, of course, there is a powerful cultural narrative according to which what's natural is good. Animals are *supposed* to be out there in the wild, experiencing whatever it offers (or doesn't, as the case may be). Obviously, we don't want that for ourselves: we spend an enormous amount of time fighting against nature: humans quickly kill animals who pose a threat to them, and we are in the midst of an enormous war against the microorganisms determined to occupy our bodies; we are hardly consistent with respect to the idea that "natural is good." The point here is just that we probably shouldn't trust our intuitive sense of the lives of wild animals—we know that it's skewed by factors like the one just canvassed.

Second, we tend to overestimate the quality of our *own* lives—which suggests that we may not be attentive to all the factors that compromise the lives of wild animals, whose lives are not that much harder. Consider this depressing survey from David Benatar (2006, 70–71):

We tend to ignore just how much of our lives is characterized by negative mental states, even if often only relatively mildly negative ones. Consider, for example, conditions causing negative mental states daily or more often. These include hunger, thirst, bowel and bladder distension (as these organs become filled), tiredness, stress, thermal discomfort (that is, feeling either too hot or too cold), and itch. For billions of people, at least some of these discomforts are chronic. These people cannot relieve their hunger, escape the cold, or avoid the stress. However, even those who can find some relief do not do so immediately or perfectly, and thus experience them to some extent every day. In fact, if we think about it, significant periods of each day are marked by some or other of these states. For example, unless one is eating and drinking so regularly as to prevent hunger and thirst or countering them as they arise, one is likely hungry and thirsty for a few hours a day. . . . The negative mental states mentioned so far, however, are simply the baseline ones characteristic of *healthy* daily life. Chronic ailments and advancing age make matters worse. Aches, pains, lethargy, and sometimes frustration from disability become an experiential backdrop for everything else. Now add those discomforts, pains, and sufferings that are experienced either less frequently or only by some (though nonetheless very many) people. These include allergies, headaches, frustration, irritation, colds, menstrual pains, hot flushes, nausea, hypoglycaemia, seizures, guilt, shame, boredom, sadness, depression, loneliness, body-image dissatisfaction, the ravages of AIDS, of cancer, and of other such life-threatening diseases, and grief and bereavement. The reach of negative mental states in ordinary lives is extensive.

Given all these factors that decrease our own well-being, despite our relatively comfortable circumstances, it would be stunning if things weren't substantially worse for wild animals.

Third, and as suggested by the previous point, animals don't need to be experiencing *acute* suffering to have negative lives overall; less intense negative affective states will do the trick. Moreover, there's good reason to think that the frustration of various desires and drives is unpleasant. That is, after all, one of the best explanations for why it's evolutionarily valuable for organisms to have unpleasant experiences: they motivate them to do things that are difficult and taxing. The unpleasantness of hunger drives us to find food even when we have low energy levels due to its absence; fear of threats drives us to take all sorts of precautions that are themselves labor-intensive. If it were tolerable to be hungry or fun to realize that someone wants to eat you, you wouldn't try so hard to find food or avoid being eaten. So, while most animals probably aren't experiencing excruciating pain throughout most of their lives, most animals are probably experiencing a great many negative affective states.

Fourth, it's easy to fall into a simplistic way of assessing whether a life is net negative. We start by taking the moments of a life and rate them as being, on balance, positive or negative. Then, look at all the moments and see whether the positive ones outnumber the negative ones, or vice versa. If we do that, then maybe it will work out that there will be enough positive (or at least neutral) moments to outnumber the negative ones. But this neglects the *intensity* of suffering relative to the intensity of pleasures. It's nice for a fish to munch on some seaweed, but it isn't *that* nice. By contrast, it's really awful to be fleeing from a predator and then to be terrified for some time thereafter that you haven't really gotten away. The thought here is that the amount that seaweed contributes to well-being is far less, in absolute terms, than having to flee detracts from well-being. This is confirmed by experimental evidence on the aversiveness of pain: animals work much harder to avoid pain than they work to have positive experiences. This suggests that pain sets back their lives in a way that's much worse than any benefits provided by simple pleasures. Once we factor in the intensities of the moments, whether positive or negative, it becomes harder to maintain that the lives of wild animals are net positive.

So here, in sum, is the case for the view that suffering predominates in nature. There is plenty of evidence that animals experience suffering in nature: we know quite a lot about the parasite loads that many animals carry; the pandemics that sweep through their populations; the stresses imposed by hunger, cold, and predation; and much else. That alone doesn't show that most wild animals have net negative lives. Instead, that conclusion is supported by what we know about natural selection more generally: namely, that it promotes fitness, not welfare—as made vivid in the contrast between r- and K-strategists. Because most species are r-strategists and yet populations aren't skyrocketing, we know that the vast majority of animals die relatively young. Additionally, we know that we idealize and romanticize nature; we know that we're inclined to underestimate how many negative experiences *we* have; we know that that net negative lives are not necessarily lives consumed by excruciating suffering, but by more modest negative affective states; and we know pain makes a disproportionately large (negative) contribution to well-being. All this makes it quite plausible that, at least in hedonic terms, most wild animals have net negative lives.

We might conclude, then, that most wild fish have lives that aren't worth living. Given this, our harm calculations change. As opposed to saying that fishing causes the most harm, fishing may instead be benefiting the animals it kills. On this view, while the fishing industry is motivated by profit, it may in fact be engaging in mercy killing, sparing wild fish from even worse fates. Granted, it's bad for fish to twist on a hook for some period of time before being hauled out of the water, it's bad for them to asphyxiate on the deck of a boat, and it's bad to be crushed under the weight of the other fish that are poured on top of them. Moreover, those in the fishing industry aren't saints: they aren't fishing out of compassion for the fish! However, regardless of the ways in which the industry harms fish, it's also bad for fish to be chased by predators, to die slowly as a result of the work of parasites, or to contract diseases that slowly kill them. And when we consider the scope of the harms to which wild animals are vulnerable, it becomes more plausible that it's better for fish to be killed by humans than to live a longer life in the wild.

If this is right, then it isn't just relevant to the question of whether the fishing industry is the most significant way that people harm animals. It's also relevant to the question of whether the fishing industry is doing something morally wrong at all. If it's indeed the case that wild fish are better off dead than alive, then while we might still criticize the fishing industry for acting for the wrong reasons—the industry certainly isn't motivated by concerns about wild animal suffering—we may not be able to fault the industry for what it does.

Resisting the Radical Conclusion

This is a radical conclusion, and as with all radical conclusions, we should be very careful before accepting it. How might someone object to the line of thinking that seemed to support it?

One possible objection is that fishing has various other negative consequences for aquatic ecosystems. For instance, people often argue that the problem with the industry is that it's slowly emptying the oceans. The FAO estimates that over 90% of wild fish stocks are either fully exploited or overexploited, and some estimate that, absent intervention, we may face a fishless ocean by 2048.

But this objection isn't very compelling. If most wild fish have lives that aren't worth living, then perhaps it's better for the oceans to be empty. That's the point of the main argument: although it *seems* as though it's good for fish to be left alone, appearances are deceptive; in fact, their lives are very bad, to the point that they are better off dead.

The critic might argue that emptying the oceans would result in the widespread destruction of marine ecosystems, and it seems likely that such extensive oceanic changes would have ramifications for life elsewhere on the planet. What are the odds that the consequences will be good? Presumably, not very high. What seems more likely is that collapsing fish populations would cause immense suffering among the incredible number of other animals who depend on fish for their survival. So, we might think that even if our focus is solely on preventing suffering, there is a reasonable case for devoting attention to fish: efforts to scale back fishing are, among other things, efforts to save the marine ecosystems on which so much life depends.

But it's easy to see the problem with this new attempt to condemn fishing. This argument relies on the assumption that the creatures who eat fish have lives worth living, but, of course, the same concerns about suffering in the wild apply to them. Second, while collapsing ecosystems may be bad for fish (and others) in the short run, the arguments we've been considering suggest that they would prevent far more suffering in the long run, as they would prevent so many net negative lives from coming into existence. So again, we're left with a striking and disturbing conclusion: rather than being the worst thing we do to nonhuman animals, emptying the wild—whether aquatic or terrestrial—may actually be a good thing.

So, let's consider a more fundamental objection to the radical pro-fishing conclusion. This objection is based on something we said in Chapter 4. Though we haven't said it explicitly, the conversation so far has assumed that hedonism is the correct theory of well-being: we've been sliding from (a) the claim that fish have more, and more intense, negative experiences than positive ones to (b) the idea that their lives are bad on balance. That makes sense if hedonism is true. But the desire satisfaction theory allows that if someone would rather stay alive despite the suffering he's experiencing, then he's better off alive. As long as that desire is strong enough, it can trump various desires not to be in pain. So, if fish care enough about surviving, then their lives could be good on balance, even if they experience more suffering than pleasure. Likewise, perfectionists could say that the ability to live a life in the wild is so valuable that it is, in general, worth any costs associated with it.

The problems for this move also go back to Chapter 4: namely, the objections we already raised against these theories of well-being. In the case of the desire satisfaction theory, the worry is that it's hard to know what desires to attribute to fish, and in any case, it's unclear whether those desires would be sufficiently informed to be relevant to their well-being. In the case of perfectionism, there's a puzzle about why life in the wild would be so remarkably valuable. I'm not saying that these are insuperable challenges; still, it would take some work to respond to either of them.

Here's one more way to resist the conclusion that emptying the wild would improve the world: maybe we shouldn't be willing to accept such a radical conclusion without far more evidence. It isn't enough that there's a decent argument for a pessimistic hypothesis about the plight of animals in the wild. Perhaps we shouldn't accept so bold a conclusion based on some considerations about the prevalence of disease and injury, the suffering associated with predation, and general points about reproductive strategies—however plausible those points may be. Instead, someone might contend, we need more detailed ethological studies before endorsing the view that so many animals live lives that are bad on balance. Since this conclusion can be used to justify something like emptying the wild, it needs a lengthy empirical defense. It can't just be a reasonable thing to believe.

This is a kind of precautionary argument, and unfortunately, it looks like it can be turned right around on the critic. The upshot of the objection is this: fishing certainly *seems* to harm lots of fish, and we shouldn't suddenly think it's okay because it's reasonable to believe that suffering predominates in nature. But we might just as well say "consider what happens if suffering *does* predominate, and we *don't* fish." Then, there would be an untold number of additional life years of suffering. It seems bad to take that kind of a chance. Moreover, let's notice that we probably wouldn't be resisting so much if we were talking about *helping* wild animals rather than killing them. Imagine if we had considered all the same arguments for believing that many wild animals live lives that are bad on balance and then said: "So, where we can help them without much cost to ourselves, we should." We might all nod our heads. But if the evidence for wild animal suffering is good enough to justify our having some responsibility to help, why isn't it good enough to justify not condemning the fishing industry?[8] Even the best objection we've got, then, doesn't give us a knock-down, drag-out argument against emptying the wild.

We've gone down a dark path, and let's pause to assess how we got here. Essentially, we started with the idea that we should do morality by the numbers, comparing the number of lives lost—or the number of life years of suffering—to decide what should count as the worst thing we do to nonhuman animals. And to settle that issue, we have to consider what the lives of wild fish are like. If they are good on balance, then fish aren't just being harmed by the way they're killed; they're also harmed by being robbed of valuable futures. But if the lives of wild fish *aren't* good on balance, then they aren't being harmed by death. (If your life is not good on the balance, then it seems to follow that you would be better off dead; and if you would be better off dead, then death isn't a harm to you.) So, if the lives of wild fish aren't good on balance, then industrial fishing is not the worst thing that we do to nonhuman animals, and may in fact be morally permissible.[9]

A Relational Angle?

We might wonder whether we got off on the wrong foot. Will things look different if, say, we took a more relational view of the situation rather than a strictly numerical one? Maybe it's the case that simply because wild animals are wild, we have some duty to leave them to their own devices, not to interfere with their lives. We don't have the kind of relationship with them that would make intervention appropriate. So, whether or not we would be benefiting them by killing them, we might just say that it isn't our place to get involved. We can still condemn industrial fishing, therefore, even if we can't say that it's the worst of the things that humans do to nonhuman animals.

This relational idea has something going for it. Many people have the idea that we shouldn't tinker with ecosystems, that we should allow wild animals to live their lives in peace. Sue Donaldson and Will Kymlicka (2011), for instance, have argued that we can think of wild animals as occupying sovereign nations, with a right to self-determination that we ought to respect. From such a perspective, fishing is a bit like invading a country and killing its citizens—not because they were about to attack us, but because we like the way they taste.

However, I'm not sure that this relational view will actually provide the resources to condemn fishing. Instead, I think it just helps us think about why terrestrial animal agriculture is particularly bad.

To see why, let's recall this chapter's epigraph. In it, Urbina says that "technology has transformed fishing from a type of hunting into something more akin to farming." And in context, you can see why he says it: his point is that fishing has slowly become more like harvesting grain than, say, deer hunting. But in some crucial respects, fishing remains dramatically *unlike* terrestrial animal agriculture. The nature of the relationship that we have with wild-caught fish is different from the relationship that we have with, say, hogs on a hog farm. For instance, if we didn't breed hogs, they wouldn't exist. But wild fish exist regardless of whether we try to catch them. Moreover, we didn't construct—and have no realistic ways to change—the environments that wild fish inhabit. We did construct—and can change—the environments in which hogs live their lives. In the case of hogs, we can put an end to an enormous amount of suffering either by radically changing our farming practices or by ending farming altogether. In the case of wild fish, we can only put an end to the suffering that we cause. We can't prevent fish from coming into existence (unless we kill even more fish), and we can't prevent the suffering that results from their natural environment. Of course, maybe we should just leave wild fish well enough alone, and "doing the best we can for them" just means not interfering with their lives. Or maybe we should kill as many fish as we can to minimize the total amount of suffering in the world. We'll have to think about both possibilities. For now, the point is just that the situations are different.

A relational perspective suggests that we have certain responsibilities to hogs that we don't have to fish. Hogs are entirely dependent on us: they wouldn't exist without us, and we determine how their lives go.[10] As a result, we might think that it's particularly horrific that we keep creating them and treating them so badly. There are obviously important differences, but consider the contrast between people who neglect their own children and people who don't bother to do anything for the needy children of faraway strangers. Most of us are, of course, in that latter camp: we don't donate to famine relief efforts, we don't produce medical supplies for those in the developing world, etc. However, almost none of us are in the former camp: if we have kids, we take good care of them. In some small way, this might reveal something about the contrast between farming and fishing. Intensive farming—whether terrestrial or aquatic—involves imposing significant suffering on beings who are entirely dependent on you, with essentially no compensation. That makes it particularly awful.

This analogy is suggestive, and it leads me to think that the relational view may not condemn fishing after all. If wild fish do, in general, have net negative lives—lives that are bad on balance—then perhaps the ethics of fishing looks a bit (a *bit*) like the ethics of dealing with strangers whose lives are very bad, but who can only be helped in violent ways. Consider, for instance, a fictional World War II narrative. A Nazi is on a train that's bringing prisoners to a concentration camp. He knows that when they arrive, those poor souls will be tortured at length before being killed. He has an opportunity to sneak back to the car where the prisoners are being held, close the air vents, and use a canister of nitrogen to displace all the oxygen. This would cause the prisoners to die quickly and relatively painlessly. There are no alternatives: if he were to open the doors and let people jump out, the guards would mow everyone down, and they would bleed out slowly by the train tracks; if he does nothing, he knows what will happen at the camp. Even in such circumstances, I don't think we can blame someone for being horrified at the thought of killing all those prisoners. Moreover, we can be skeptical that violence is the best way to deal with a situation, no matter how bad that situation seems. At the same time, though, we can always worry that being unwilling to use violence is a kind of moral squeamishness. As awful as it would be to kill those prisoners, the alternative seems worse. So, while I don't know whether the Nazi is morally *obligated* to kill the prisoners, I suspect that it's permissible. Likewise, while I don't want to say that we *ought* to fish, I doubt that it's wrong, assuming that wild fish have lives that are bad on balance.

Here's the upshot. The relational way of framing things doesn't clearly imply that fishing is wrong. Instead, it compares farming and not fishing and supports the view that farming is much worse. It also suggests that while we can't really blame people for being critical of the fishing industry, it may still be a good thing to fish, at least given the assumption that wild fish have net negative lives. So, it seems that the conclusion we reach about wild animal suffering has enormous implications for the way we assess the ethics of fishing. If it turns out that wild animals don't live net negative lives, then fishing is morally heinous: it is the worst thing we do to nonhuman animals. But if wild animals do have net negative lives—as the evidence suggests—then things are murkier. While the realities of the fishing industry are ugly indeed, the industry may—entirely unintentionally—be doing an enormous amount of good.

Fishing and You

Let's conclude by reflecting, very briefly, on what you personally should do when it comes to purchasing and consuming wild-caught fish (and products made from them).

Obviously, if we think that fishing is wrong, then many of the issues here are going to be the same as the ones that we considered in the last chapter. There are reasons to think that your actions as a consumer make no difference at all. If those reasons apply equally well to the fishing industry—and I don't see why they wouldn't—then that makes trouble for some types of arguments against purchasing and consuming wild-caught fish. There may be ways around this problem by appealing to various other moral principles—including, for instance, the idea that we shouldn't be complicit in wrongdoing, or that we shouldn't benefit from it—but it's difficult to spell out these principles in ways that don't result in a general condemnation of our actions as consumers. Insofar as we think that we often act permissibly when we shop, that's a strike against those principles.

But if we *don't* think that fishing is morally wrong, then on the face of it, the ethical issue for you, as a consumer, seems simple: if it's fine to fish, then it's fine to eat the fish who are caught. And if we think that emptying the wild is actually good for the animals who were in it, then we may feel even more comfortable with buying and eating the fish whose bad lives were cut short. On one level, I think that's right. I also think, however, that it's worth thinking more broadly about the ethics of eating, rather than always beginning with questions about whether a particular way of getting animal-based foods is morally wrong. We can think about eating as a political act, not just a moral one, and that changes the way we understand it.

Here's the idea. Eating has become politicized in much of the developed world. When actions are politicized, we don't get to decide what they mean to others. We can say whatever we want about our reasons, but they don't determine how our actions are interpreted. Post-politicization, our actions have a symbolic significance of their own, quite apart from the intentions behind them. (Think, for instance, of the way people interpret someone's decision not to use the pronouns that a trans person prefers. This someone might say that he's just trying to use language based on his own views about sex and gender, and that he values transgendered people as much as he values anyone else. But it doesn't matter what he says: he will only be heard as transphobic. The meaning of his decision isn't his to determine.) As a result, our actions align us with causes, whether we mean to be so aligned or not. We don't get to decide what certain actions say about what we stand for.

How are we aligning ourselves if we choose to eat animals—whatever the animal and whatever the history of that animal? What does the action of eating animals say about what we stand for? I suspect that to eat animals is to stand squarely within the mainstream of the culture, to do what most people do, to be normal. It's to align ourselves with the status quo. And to abstain, therefore, is to reject the mainstream to some extent or other. It's to opt out.

So let's suppose that there are devastating problems with all the arguments against eating animals. Let's imagine, in other words, that purchasing and eating animals is permissible always and everywhere. *Even still*, it would be very hard to make the case that, in general, it's a good thing to eat animals due to the symbolic significance of that act. We certainly have reasons to want the food system to change in a dramatic way: recall all the arguments against intensive animal ag in Chapter 7. So, even if it's fine to eat wild fish specifically, based on considerations about wild animal suffering, we find ourselves in a situation where most instances of eating animals have the same kind of symbolic significance—they align us with or against the mainstream—and very few instances of eating animals are likely to align us with an industry that's doing any good. Moreover, most people don't think very much of the differences between animals and methods of production, as most people aren't paying attention to them. So, if you eat one kind of animal, with one history, then people will interpret it as a blanket permission to eat any animal, with any history. Your actions say: "If it's okay sometimes, it's okay all the time—or at least it isn't terrible." In such circumstances, we have a political reason to opt out across the board. We have reason to say: "I'm not going to agonize about whether this particular action is morally permissible. I'm just going to form habits that make it easy for me to abstain all the time, and in so doing, push back against the status quo."

This reason isn't decisive. If it turns out that you need to eat some tuna for health reasons, or maybe just to placate Grandma, the political consideration may be outweighed. But it's there just the same. And crucially, this way of thinking about the ethical issues discourages us from getting lost in the weeds here. Consumer ethics is hard; animal ethics is harder still. I don't have great faith in my ability to sort these things out, despite devoting my career to them. I am, however, reasonably confident that I don't get to decide what I stand for when I act in one way or another, and I'm pretty sure I know what I stand for if I eat animals. It doesn't follow from this that it's always wrong to eat them. It does mean, however, that if we are looking for a simple way through the moral complexities here, we have one available. We can recognize eating as a political act, think about the social significance of eating animals, and then ask ourselves what we stand for.

Further Reading

Greenberg, Paul. 2011. *Four Fish: The Future of the Last Wild Food*. London: Penguin Books.
Kaldewaij, Frederike. 2013. "Does Fish Welfare Matter? On the Moral Relevance of Agency." *Journal of Agricultural and Environmental Ethics* 26(1): 63–74.
Leeuw, D., and A. Dionys. 1996. "Contemplating the Interests of Fish: The Angler's Challenge." *Environmental Ethics* 18(4): 373–390.
Michaelson Eliot, and Andrew Reisner. 2018. "Ethics for Fish." In *The Oxford Handbook of Food Ethics*, edited by Anne Barnhill, Mark Budolfson, and Tyler Doggett, 189–208. New York: Oxford University Press.
Pauly, Daniel. 2019. *Vanishing Fish: Shifting Baselines and the Future of Global Fisheries*. Vancouver: Greystone Books.
Zanette, Liana Y., and Michael Clinchy. 2019. "Ecology of Fear." *Current Biology* 29(9): R309–R313.

Notes

1. www.fao.org/3/ca9229en/CA9229EN.pdf
2. People often think that bycatch estimates are what matter—that is, the estimates of non-target species. Not so: some bycatch is kept and sold, which means that it goes into the number mentioned earlier. What matters is what people throw away.
3. http://fishcount.org.uk/studydatascreens/2016/numbers-of-wild-fish-A0-2016.php
4. See, for instance: https://faunalytics.org/fundamentals-farmed-animals/.
5. Even if we use a simple numerical standard, there are other candidates. There are, for instance, lots of animals harmed by habitat destruction and lots more killed as pests. However, it's enormously difficult to estimate those numbers, and nothing I'll say turns on whether fishing is, in fact, the cause of the most harm. So, I'll set this issue aside.
6. See: www.poultrytrends.com/.
7. These terms come from a certain model of population dynamics, where r is the maximum rate of growth and K is the carrying capacity of the habitat.
8. My hunch is that it's because the fishing industry is actually doing something, while most people have no intention of lifting a finger to help wild animals. We prefer inaction to action, though it's difficult to explain why one should be preferable to the other.
9. I say "may" rather than "is" because questions about whether death harms someone are distinct from questions about the ethics of killing. There can be decisive moral reasons not to kill someone even if death wouldn't harm her. Still, if death wouldn't harm someone, then one major argument against killing that individual no longer applies.
10. There are wrinkles here, in that it isn't entirely true that we have no responsibility for fish coming into existence. It is true that we don't have any control over *whether* any fish come into existence, but we do have some influence over *which* fish come into existence. Our fishing changes when fish die, which changes when fish breed, and so changes which fish hatch (or otherwise come into the world). So fishing does create some responsibility for the existence of particular individuals, and perhaps even populations (depending on how we individuate populations). However, it's not clear how this way of affecting fish populations could be considered wrong, as lots of our actions affect which future people come into existence. After all, lots of our actions have predictable (though usually unintentional) impacts on when people have sex. But we generally don't think that's wrong in and of itself. If it's wrong, it's wrong for other reasons.

References

Benatar, David. 2006. *Better Never to Have Been: The Harm of Coming into Existence*. Oxford: Oxford University Press.

Dawkins, Richard. 1996. *River Out of Eden: A Darwinian View of Life*. New York: Harper Collins.

Donaldson, Sue, and Will Kymlicka. 2011. *Zoopolis: A Political Theory of Animal Rights*. New York: Oxford University Press.

Urbina, Ian. 2019. *Outlaw Ocean*. New York: Alfred A Knopf.

9   Institutional Animal Care and Use Committees

OVERVIEW

You are a professor at a university. How do you get permission to use animals in your teaching and research? What standards are employed to assess whether that use is acceptable? This chapter answers those questions, and in so doing, serves as an introduction to some ethical issues associated with institutional animal care and use committees. In particular, the chapter considers whether common uses of animals would pass the test if the committees' own standards were applied more rigorously. The answer, it seems, is: probably not. And once we understand why, we can see the value of having a wider range of perspectives involved in the vetting of animal use.

Here's a perfectly ordinary event at my university. A professor and some students hop into a van, drive to some nearby pond, and set up sunning traps. Essentially, a sunning trap is an inner tube with a ramp on either side, both of which lead up to a plank that goes across the top. Turtles get the impression that they're climbing onto a stable log where they can rest in the sun. However, the plank that crosses the inner tube isn't stable: it's a "trigger board" with a rod through the center, allowing it to spin. When the turtles put their weight on one side, the board flips, dropping them into a net below. There they wait for collection.

Eventually, the students bring the turtles back to a lab. The professor anesthetizes the turtles with tricaine—otherwise known as MS-222, which is made less acidic by adding baking soda, sparing the turtles the skin irritation that they'd otherwise experience. The professor pinches the turtles' legs to see whether they're still responsive, and if they aren't, she injects a much higher—and fatal—dose of tricaine. (In the language of *The Guide for the Care and Use of Animals*—the document that, essentially, governs animal use on university campuses—these turtles are only exposed to "Category C" pain and distress, that is, the transitory variety. This is true, or is supposed to be true, of whatever they experience during trapping, as a result of handling, and due to the injection.) The students place the turtles in plastic bags and store them on ice until it's time to dissect them. When that time comes, the turtles are removed from the bags and decapitated. Then, the students start learning about the signs and symptoms of parasites.

Granted, this isn't the only thing they're learning. They're also being trained on how to capture, transport, anesthetize, and euthanize these animals. They're learning how to distinguish between normal tissue and diseased tissue, between normal gut contents and cysts. They're getting experience with the tools and techniques of necropsy. They're supposed to be gaining confidence in their ability to work with real animals. They are in a parasitology lab, and that means capturing, transporting, killing, and dissecting wild animals to study the particular parasites they carry.

In the grand scheme of things, the professor and students aren't killing that many turtles. However, the story matters because it brings out some important features of contemporary animal research ethics. In particular, it helps us think through how decisions regarding animals are *supposed* to be made in these contexts, as well as how they're *actually* being made.

Let's be perfectly clear here. The goal of this conversation isn't to argue that animals should never be used in educational settings. (It's certainly possible, though, to make the case for that conclusion. If, for instance, animals have the right not to be used as mere resources for the benefit of others, or if we should assess actions based on whether they maximize utility, then it will be very hard to argue that most pedagogical uses of animals are justified.) In this chapter, we aren't concerned with assessing the ethics of animal use in research and teaching from the perspective of any of the moral theories that we discussed in Chapter 5. That's a worthwhile project, and we'll take it up in the next chapter. Here, the goal is to understand how those people think about the ethics of animal care and use, assessing some common practices by their own standards. In short, while we may ultimately conclude that there are serious moral problems with almost all pedagogical uses of animals, we're going to assume for the time being that lots of uses are morally permissible. At this juncture, the goal is just to understand *what's* being valued in the current system, as well as *how much* it's being valued relative to everything else.

Animal Research Regulation in the United States

To get some perspective on the subject, it's worth having a bit of background regarding contemporary animal research and its regulation.

In the United States, animal research is regulated by multiple agencies. The first and most important is the U.S. Department of Agriculture (USDA), which is empowered by Congress through the Animal Welfare Act. The Animal Welfare Act is a federal statute from 1966 that was crafted to protect just a few kinds of animals in research contexts: dogs, cats, monkeys, guinea pigs, hamsters, and rabbits. It's been amended several times since then and now regulates the use of many kinds of animals in lots of contexts: teaching and experimentation, purchase or transportation that crosses state lines, and all animal use that's supported by federal funds.

However, the Animal Welfare Act still isn't a general piece of animal protection legislation; it isn't designed to protect *all* animals. The USDA's interpretation of the

Animal Welfare Act is given by the Animal Welfare Regulations, and as the Animal Welfare Regulations make clear, even the now-broader version of the Animal Welfare Act is quite narrow. This is because the Animal Welfare Regulations use a very specific definition of "animal":

> Any live or dead dog, cat, nonhuman primate, guinea pig, hamster, rabbit, or any other warm blooded animal, which is being used, or is intended for use for research, teaching, testing, experimentation, or exhibition purposes, or as a pet. This term ["animal"] *excludes*: Birds, rats of the genus *Rattus* and mice of the genus *Mus* bred for use in research, and horses not used for research purposes and other farm animals, such as, but not limited to livestock or poultry used or intended for use for improving animal nutrition, breeding, management, or production efficiency, or for improving the quality of food or fiber.
>
> ("Final Rules" 1989, emphasis added)

In essence, this means that the Animal Welfare Regulations only cover mammals, and not even all of those. Most notably, it excludes mice and rats bred for research—which make up the vast majority of the animals used in research in the United States—and agricultural animals.

This matters for plenty of reasons, but one of them is that this exclusion makes it surprisingly difficult to know how many animals are used for research purposes in the United States. According to a report from the USDA's Animal and Plant Health Information Service (APHIS), 780,070 animals belonging to covered species were used in 2018 ("Annual Report" 2020). But since that estimate ignores the most common species—perhaps the most significant ones being mice, rats, and zebrafish—we need to do some work to get a more accurate number.

We can get a ballpark figure by extrapolating from UK statistics, where researchers are required to report on rodents and fish. There, 3,443,768 animals were used for the first time in procedures in 2018: 79.6% of these animals were rodents and 14.7% were fish. The animals covered in the United States under the Animal Welfare Act were just 0.6% of the total number of animals used in the UK ("Annual Statistics" 2019). So, if we assume that the percentages in the United States mirror those in the UK—that is, if we assume that the APHIS report is only counting 0.6% of all animals used for research purposes—then we should estimate that 130,011,666 animals were used for research in the United States in 2018. Hardly a trivial number.

In any case, the second major regulatory player in the United States is the Office of Laboratory Animal Welfare (OLAW), which enforces U.S. Public Health Service (PHS) policy as part of the U.S. Department of Health and Human Services. For the most part, OLAW's job is to ensure that organizations comply with PHS policy, which is basically summed up by two documents: the *U.S. Public Health Service Policy on Humane Care and Use of Laboratory Animals* and the *Guide for the Care and Use of Laboratory Animals*. Essentially, these documents cover all activities involving vertebrate animals—mice and rats are *not* excluded—that are operated by organizations that receive federal funds. So even if a particular researcher isn't on a federal grant—something from the National Institutes of Health or the National Science Foundation—she still needs to follow the guidelines in these documents.

There are a few other players in the mix, including a nonprofit called AAALAC International that accredits organizations as having met certain higher welfare standards, as well as several national professional societies that provide guidance about specific species. But if you only know about the Animal Welfare Regulations and PHS policy, you know enough to have a pretty good sense of the restrictions on contemporary animal use in research and teaching.

It's important to realize, though, that researchers don't get approval from the USDA or OLAW directly. Instead, there are institutional animal care and use committees—IACUCs (pronounced *eye-uh-kucks*)—at each institution that does research and teaching with animals, and it's the job of those committees to evaluate proposed uses. IACUCs are usually made up mostly of scientists who themselves use animals in research and teaching, but there is always at least one nonscientist member.[1] So, while researchers are ultimately bound by policy set by the USDA and OLAW, in practice, they answer to the members of their local IACUCs.

Among other things, IACUCs are supposed to apply the standards given in *The Guide for the Care and Use of Animals*, more commonly known as the *Guide*. In its first chapter, that document says:

> Using animals in research is a privilege granted by society to the research community with the expectation that such use will provide either significant new knowledge or lead to improvement in human and/or animal well-being. It is a trust that mandates responsible and humane care and use of these animals.
>
> (National Research Council 2011, 4)

The *Guide* doesn't say exactly what counts as "significant" or "new" knowledge, what would count as improvement in human and/or animal well-being, or what it means to be "responsible" or "humane." It accepts that there will have to be many hard conversations among researchers about how to interpret those standards. (Presumably, members of the public should be in on these conversations too, since "society" grants the privilege to do this research in the first place. More on this later.) However, the *Guide* does provide one tool that, in the estimation of its authors, "represent[s] a practical method for implement[ing these] principles" (2011, 4): namely, the 3Rs.

According to the 3Rs, first proposed by Russell and Burch (1959), those involved in research with animals should strive to (a) *replace* animals with nonliving models, (b) *reduce* the number of animals used in research, and (c) *refine* animal care and use practices so that animals are better off. Obviously, there are lots of contexts in which animals can't be replaced by cell cultures or digital models. And if, for instance, you're studying the effects of pain itself, you can't refine your methods to the point where they're painless. The goal is to minimize the negative impacts on animals given legitimate research objectives. And which are those? Presumably, the ones that would lead to "significant new knowledge or lead to improvement in human and/or animal well-being."

So the big picture here is this. If you're at a university and you want to use animals, whether for research or teaching, then you have to justify that use to a committee that's mostly composed of your peers. And in essence, you do that by showing that your plan is in line with the Animal Welfare Regulations and PHS policy. If the IACUC approves your plan—called a protocol—you're good to go.

Turtles Revisited

Back to turtles. Let's begin by making two very basic observations. The first is about the justification for using live animals. The second is about how the professor determines the number of live animals who are going to be used.

The first observation is that, in principle, it's possible to teach about capturing, transporting, killing, and dissecting wild animals without actually doing any of those things. It's also possible to teach people about the differences between the parasites that plague wild animals without actually killing any wild animals. Students can read books, they can look at images, they can watch videos, and they can practice various skills using lifelike models. It's even possible to increase people's confidence with real animals this way. If it weren't possible, it would be strange that professors spend time preparing students for fieldwork—that is, going out and doing the trapping and transporting—by talking to them about what they should expect, and how to operate, in the different situations they might encounter.

To be clear: I'm not saying that you can, by reading books and using models, get *exactly the same* educational benefits that you get from working with living (and once living) animals. Instead, I'm saying that, at least in this context, you can't justify using live animals *simply* based on a concern to teach information or skills because that information and those skills can be taught without harming any additional animals. Instead, you have to value teaching that information and those skills *in a particular way*, perhaps based on the thought that the experience of working with real animals provides a certain kind of know-how that's otherwise unavailable, but perhaps for some other reason entirely.

Granted, it isn't unreasonable to value teaching certain information and skills in a particular way. If we didn't know this already, we all learned it during the COVID-19 pandemic, when schools around the world were forced to move their classes online. This was an enormous educational loss. While it's true that plenty of content *can* be taught remotely, there are reasons why so many people prefer face-to-face instruction: it makes it easier to build relationships between teachers and students; it eliminates certain distractions; it provides opportunities for quick and costless feedback; it makes it easy to do certain kinds of activities that are awkward or impossible online. It's perfectly sensible to recognize and value these advantages. But, of course, we can't simply point to the value of face-to-face instruction to justify preserving it during a pandemic. Identifying what matters is the first move in the conversation. Then, we need to weigh those values. During the pandemic, we made the collective judgment that it was worth sacrificing certain educational goods for the sake of public health. When assessing parasitology labs, then, we need to weigh what matters too. We know that student learning is important, but student learning isn't the only thing at stake—a point to which we'll return.

Let's make a second observation about capturing and euthanizing turtles. Suppose we grant that professors can't replace these animals with alternatives, such as books, digital models, physical models, or what have you. The next question, then, is whether they can reduce the numbers, which is the second of the 3Rs. How would they do that? This also turns out to be a question about values related to education. To see why, we need to recognize that the number of animals killed doesn't depend directly on the number of students. It isn't as though each student goes out and collects her turtle, brings him back to the lab, and goes through the process described earlier. Instead, there are practical constraints that require students to form groups—such as the limited number of sunning traps—and each group goes out and collects a certain number of animals. But while that creates a lower bound for group size, determined based on the number of students relative to the equipment available, it doesn't give us the upper bound. That's a pedagogical decision. Teachers decide that the group shouldn't be "too big" relative to the educational aims mentioned earlier.

For what it's worth, though, I've never actually seen professors think much about the upper bound of group size when asking for permission to capture and euthanize wild animals. When they submit a protocol to the IACUC, they probably expect their colleagues to agree that smaller groups are better than big ones for educational reasons, as well as that it's generally fine to do whatever's best for students. So, nothing needs to be said about group size.

In any case, the upshot here is that there are two questions we can ask about the justification for capturing and euthanizing wild animals for pedagogical purposes. The first is whether wild animals need to be captured and euthanized at all. To answer this question, we have to assess whether the pedagogical objectives can justify confining and killing animals. The second question relates to the number of animals being captured and euthanized. Can professors achieve the relevant pedagogical objectives with fewer animals? If so, then according to the 3Rs, they should. If not, then they may proceed.

These two observations help us appreciate several important points:

- People explicitly appeal to certain values to justify animal use. However, there are also implicit values at work, and it takes a bit of digging to reveal them. In this case, the values are pedagogical: professors want certain kinds of educational experiences for their students.
- It's easy for these implicit values to remain implicit because, in general, those who use animals are justifying themselves to people who use them for similar purposes. It's easy for values to go unnoticed—or to be confused for practical constraints—when everyone takes them for granted. That's why it matters that there's a nonscientist member on the IACUC, as that person hasn't been socialized into the scientific community. Being socialized into a community involves learning that community's values, and participating in a community often involves taking those values for granted as you act. Simply by virtue of being an outsider, the nonscientist member is in a better position to recognize values for what they are.

- When values are implicit, people aren't careful to explain why they should be respected in a particular case. When it comes to using turtles, for instance, no one feels any obligation to find and cite peer-reviewed educational research saying that to achieve certain educational outcomes, students need to be able to physically interact with live animals as opposed to reading books, working with models, watching videos, and so forth—much less that they need to physically interact with live animals a certain amount. In fact, no one feels any pressure to cite any educational research at all.
- IACUCs aren't composed of individuals who are there, first and foremost, to represent the interests of animals. Instead, they are largely composed of individuals *invested in using animals* who have a job: namely, ensuring that animal use meets certain professional standards. Obviously, many of those professional standards are in place to protect the welfare of animals, but there is a sharp difference between the two approaches. If IACUCs were composed of people whose task it was to represent the interests of animals—animal advocates— then you would expect them to ask whether certain educational benefits are worth the impacts on the well-being and lives of those animals. Instead, however, IACUCs simply *grant* that those educational benefits are worth trying to secure and then check whether professors are meeting certain professional standards as they pursue them. An animal advocate would ask: Is this worth the price? IACUC members, by contrast, generally ask: *Given* that it's okay to use animals for this or that purpose, is the researcher going about her work in a way that meets professional expectations?

Ethics Training

Let's pause here for a moment. Essentially, I've just said that there are cases where the people charged with assessing whether animal use is ethical aren't asking basic ethical questions. Instead, they're simply assuming answers to those questions. Why?

There are many answers to this: sociological, psychological, historical, and so on. But part of the answer is that we don't train the members of IACUCs to ask those questions. While most of them do receive ethics training, not all do, and what they do receive is pretty thin.

Suppose that you're appointed to your institution's IACUC. What training will you be required to complete? The answer, at present, is one of the basic orientation courses provided by an organization like the Collaborative Institutional Training Initiative (CITI). The course is focused almost entirely on legal and procedural matters. Here is a sampling of the learning objectives for the most recent version:

- Identify the agencies that regulate the use of animals in research, testing, and teaching, and state what species each agency regulates.
- Identify the documents that guide organizational policies related to animal husbandry, housing and caging environments, veterinary care, occupational health and safety, and physical plant.

- Discuss the process and possible outcomes of full committee review of animal use protocols.
- State reasons why IACUCs cannot administratively extend protocol approval past the expiration date.

The closest that the course comes to addressing truly ethical issues is when it says that individuals ought to be able to "[c]ompare the relationship between animal welfare regulations and the ethical treatment of animals, in contrast to the ethical treatment of human subjects involved in research." It turns out, however, that the relevant information here is also procedural. It concerns matters such as: Does a nonscientist member of the committee have to be present for a quorum? (Yes for institutional review boards, or IRBs, which focus on research on human subjects; no for IACUCs.)

This kind of ethics training is like the annual ethics training that many businesses require their employees to complete. These online courses are really just a way of delivering memos about relevant laws and organizational policies. It's "ethics training" in the sense that you're being told what you must and shouldn't do, but it's obviously very different from the kind of ethics that we've been doing here. When a business requires you to take an online ethics course, the laws and policies aren't up for debate, nor is their interpretation. For instance, in the annual ethics training at my university, faculty and staff are informed that you can't hire someone to cater your luncheon just because he happens to be your husband. This is a perfectly reasonable policy; I have absolutely no objection to it. The point is just that you aren't supposed to ask questions about the wisdom of the policy; this sort of ethics training isn't designed to promote ethical *deliberation*, the skill of critically assessing rationales for, and interpretations of, the principles we live by. Instead, it's designed to reduce policy violations, and it tries to do that by providing information about the relevant policies.

However, some ethics training *does* try to promote ethical deliberation. It aims to increase sensitivity to moral considerations, to encourage critical reflection on proposed ways of balancing those considerations, and to foster transparency in ethical decision-making. It does the first by identifying and clearly distinguishing between our various values and ways of valuing. It does the second by exploring moral theories, which try to explain why we ought to act in some ways, avoid acting in others, and exercise good judgment in the rest. It does the third by insisting that ethical decisions be justified by arguments, which make explicit the reasoning that supports a course of action, and thereby make that reasoning subject to evaluation by the rest of the community. This is how philosophers do "ethics training" with their students—or, more colloquially, how they teach ethics. It's what I'm doing with you. Where institutional ethics training teaches you policies with which you need to comply, philosophical ethics training is designed to help you *do ethics*.

Why focus on the difference between these two methods? Isn't it enough to give good guidelines when it comes to research? Not obviously. When it comes to hiring caterers, knowing that you can't hire family members is all the information you need. By contrast, assessing proposed animal research isn't so mechanical. The skill of ethical deliberation is relevant to reflecting on, debating, and ultimately making collective decisions regarding the responsible and humane care and use of animals. After all, the members of IACUCs face difficult decisions about how to interpret the moral terms that are essential to their decision-making, such as "responsible" and "humane." Moreover, we can't simply expect the 3Rs to answer the hard questions for us, as they only push the questions back a step. The ethics of replacement might be straightforward: it's better, morally speaking, not to use animals rather than to use them. As the *Guide* acknowledges, though, things are more complex when it comes to refinement and reduction. ("Refinement and reduction goals should be balanced on a case-by-case basis" [National Research Council 2011, 5].) These are often in tension, and while the *Guide* provides some indication of preferred trade-offs—for instance, it strongly discourages reusing animals in multiple experiments to avoid using more animals overall—it leaves many questions open.

Imagine a case where employing a more painful procedure would mean not needing to use as many animals. (For instance, if a researcher is trying to develop a new method for assessing stress, there's a question about when she ought to euthanize the animals she's using to develop the technique. The longer she's allowed to go, the more she can learn from each individual. But in turn, the more each individual suffers.) When is it acceptable to intensify the harms to those few animals for the sake of not harming others? Likewise, imagine cases where using many animals would allow researchers to minimize the cost to any individual, though the cost would remain nontrivial. When is it acceptable to harm a new individual just for a small reduction in suffering for others? The *Guide* doesn't answer these questions and instead leaves them for IACUCs to work out. Without training in moral deliberation, there is a real risk that the members of IACUCs will simply defer to the judgment of researchers rather than independently assessing the merits of the protocol.

There are similar points to make about the many value-laden terms that are important in the animal research literature, including "species appropriate," "welfare," and "due consideration." Or take the distinction between saying that researchers "should" do something and that they "must" do it, an issue that gets a few paragraphs in the beginning of the *Guide*. When the *Guide* says you "must" do something, you don't get to say that your circumstances are exceptional; that's no excuse for not following the policy. When it says you "should" do something, though, the *Guide* says: "Should indicates a strong recommendation for achieving a goal; however, the Committee recognizes that individual circumstances might justify an alternative strategy" (National Research Council 2011, 8). While this explanation of "should" leaves open the possibility that other strategies may be appropriate, it says nothing about the kinds of considerations that might justify a course of action other than the one that the committee recommends. Consider, for instance, the claim that animals should be given "adequate resources for thermoregulation" (National Research Council 2011, 43)—that is, animals should be given the means to be able to regulate their own temperatures. It's easy to imagine protocols that would make it difficult to provide these resources for an extended period. Suppose that the animals in question regulate their temperature by burrowing into wood shavings, which are normally provided as bedding. But maybe the researchers are studying the impact of some bacteria on these animals and they don't want any complications caused by having other biotic materials in the cage. So, they make the environment barren. Should a protocol like this be approved? Why or why not? The answer to this question requires moral deliberation; you can't just consult the *Guide* for the answer.

So we have, I think, very good reasons to want the members of IACUCs to receive training in moral deliberation, not just information about the policies that they are supposed to enforce. But this may not be a conclusion that everyone welcomes. Some researchers (and administrators) would insist that promoting (philosophical) ethics training may lead IACUC members to forget their role. The task of the IACUC is to oversee animal research on the presumption that animal research is justified. If there are perspectives from which animal research *isn't* justified, then why encourage a way of thinking that makes them salient? If a committee were in charge of overseeing travel-abroad programs, it wouldn't be a good idea to train its members in a way that led them to think that perhaps we shouldn't have travel-abroad programs in the first place.

I say that because I can imagine the objection, but not because I find it compelling. To the contrary, I think we *absolutely* want people overseeing travel-abroad programs who are open to abandoning the whole enterprise. Wouldn't it be a bad thing to have people in charge of travel-abroad programs who didn't care about student safety, the quality of the educational experience, and fair pay for tour providers? If, for instance, a travel-abroad program happens to be such that one of every three students comes home injured, you would hope that the leaders would be willing to shut it down. Likewise, you would hope that the members of IACUCs would be sensitive to the moral costs and benefits of the research they assess.

What's more, let's remember what the *Guide* says about animal research:

> The decision to use animals in research requires critical thought, judgment, and analysis. Using animals in research is a privilege granted by society to the research community with the expectation that such use will provide either significant new knowledge or lead to improvement in human and/or animal well-being. It is a trust that mandates responsible and humane care and use of these animals.
>
> (National Research Council 2011, 4)

These statements indicate that the *Guide* itself recognizes circumstances in which animal research *in general* wouldn't be justified: if such research rarely provided either significant new knowledge or led to improvement in human and/or animal well-being, then it would violate the public trust. The privilege to do research in the first place wouldn't have been earned. Is the *Guide* at fault for raising this possibility—indeed, for framing the ethics of animal research in these terms? Presumably not. If the *Guide* is saying, essentially, that the scientific community should recognize that there are conditions under which animal research would be wrong, it can't be a mistake to introduce ways of thinking that could challenge animal research generally.

It seems to me, therefore, that the members of IACUCs need more ethics training. This doesn't mean educating them more about policies and procedures. Instead, it means giving them the tools to engage in ethical deliberation, and then encouraging them to do it.

Turtles Re-revisited

In any case, let's imagine ourselves as members of a particularly thoughtful IACUC, and suppose we want to think harder about whether we should let professors capture and kill turtles for parasitology labs. How should we proceed? How should we decide when lethal use is justified?

The answer isn't completely clear. The *Guide for the Care and Use of Animals*, for instance, doesn't say anything at all about when *educational* uses are justified. All it says is that animal *research* is justified when it produces significant new knowledge or improves well-being. How do these goals relate to educational uses?

Education is supposed to produce knowledge—which means the information is new to the individual who gets it—and, of course, some of what people learn is significant. However, it would be a mistake to say that education is justified because it produces significant new knowledge *in one individual*, where that knowledge is already had by many others. If that were the view, then we could justify repeating any experiment, no matter how much pain it causes, as long as someone new was there to learn from it. But no IACUC would allow, for instance, students to repeat painful experiments on chimpanzees simply for the educational benefits of having done the experiments themselves. So IACUCs are sensitive, at least to some degree, to concerns about balancing educational benefits and costs to animals.[2] We can't simply say that because students would learn something, it's okay to capture and kill animals.

Of course, producing significant new knowledge isn't the only thing that can justify animal use. Maybe training with animals improves well-being. If so, whose? If, for instance, the training involves lab mice, then it isn't the mice's well-being, who appear to be worse off as a result. If we assume that animals in the wild have lives worth living and the training involves wild animals, then it isn't their well-being either. If we assume that animals in the wild *don't* have lives worth living and the training involves wild animals, then the animals may actually be better off and the training may be justified on that basis—though, of course, this is as uncomfortable a conclusion to draw here as it was when we were discussing wild fish (see Chapter 8).

For the sake of argument, though, let's assume that the animals used for training purposes have lives worth living. Then, we won't be able to appeal to their well-being to justify the training. Perhaps we could appeal to the well-being of other members of the species who will be handled less roughly, and killed less painfully, by individuals with more experience doing this kind of work. If that's the idea, though, then it's a pretty weak justification. For instance, there are probably lots of students taking these classes who have no intention of going into fieldwork, so that's an argument for making this on-the-job training as supposed to classroom training. What's more, it seems really unlikely that animal use *always* improves animal well-being even for those individuals who do want to make fieldwork part of their career (even if it often does), as lots of the methods are largely failproof. Again, then, that training could be done on-the-job rather than in the classroom as new hires shadow experienced ones.

Perhaps it's more plausible to say that educational uses of animals promote *human* well-being, on the assumption that learning and skill acquisition are good for people. (Not everyone would agree. Consider, for instance, the author of Ecclesiastes 1:18: "For in much wisdom is much vexation, and those who increase knowledge increase sorrow.") However, this brings us back to the first problem. Presumably, if it's good for human beings to learn how to capture and euthanize turtles *simply because they are learning something*, then it's also good for human beings to learn how to do all sorts of horrifying studies—since in those cases as well, they'll be learning something. Consider Harry Harlow's famous maternal deprivation studies, done at the University of Wisconsin Madison from the 1930s to the 1950s. He took infant monkeys away from their mothers and placed them alone in cages, albeit with surrogate "mothers" made of metal wire. He gave a talk about his research in 1965, during which he described the impact on the monkeys this way:

> No monkey has died during isolation. When initially removed from total social isolation, however, they usually go into a state of emotional shock, characterized by . . . autistic self-clutching and rocking. . . . One of six monkeys isolated for three months refused to eat after release and died five days later. The autopsy report attributed death to emotional anorexia. A second animal in the same group also refused to eat and would probably have died had we not been prepared to resort to force-feeding. . . . Our data indicate that the debilitating effects of three months of social isolation are dramatic.
>
> (Harlow et al. 1965, 92)

No IACUC would approve this research now, and no IACUC would let professors repeat Harlow's studies for pedagogical purposes. But if not, then the view can't be that anything goes as long as students learn something. There are constraints.

Where are we? The goal was to determine how we are supposed to assess whether it's okay to capture and kill turtles for a parasitology lab. However, unless we just assume that any pedagogical objective is a good reason to capture and kill wild animals—which seems patently false—we will have to say that it's okay to capture and kill turtles for a parasitology lab only because wild animals generally have lives that aren't worth living, so euthanizing them can plausibly be construed as mercy killing. That is not an argument that's going to carry the day during the average IACUC meeting.

All that said, and as I mentioned earlier, no one blinks an eye when professors ask for permission to do things like this. So, despite these philosophical concerns, most IACUCs clearly aren't reasoning about the situation in the way we're laying things out here. Instead, as I suggested, they are granting that it's fine to trade the lives of some animals for certain educational benefits, assuming that you take reasonable steps to minimize the pain that those animals experience. For them, the only question to consider is whether professors are going to take those reasonable steps.

Notice, though, that even if we grant this approach, we're still left with the question of the number of animals. In other words, the goal so far has just been to capturing and killing—not capturing and killing some specific number of animals. And here again, the 3Rs—that call for replacing animal models, reducing animal numbers, and refining methods—seem relevant. The simplest way to reduce animal numbers is to increase the number of students per group. Unfortunately, IACUCs don't insist on this. But they should.

In any case, the general point here is *not* that if we let the *Guide* be our guide, it's impossible to justify killing turtles to teach students about parasites. There may well be some good argument for that practice that we haven't considered here. Instead, the point is *when we invoke the standards that animal researchers use to assess animal research*, we realize that there are values at stake that are rarely made explicit during the deliberations in which IACUCs engage. We've focused on educational values here, but there are other examples for other uses of animals. And notably, because these values aren't made explicit, no one is even *trying* to explain why it's okay to kill animals for certain pedagogical benefits, even though that justification is one that someone ought to provide. Why isn't anyone trying to provide it? One possibility is that the members of IACUCs aren't trained to engage in ethical deliberation, but just to apply policy. But if it's true that, as the *Guide* says, animal use is a privilege rather than a right—a privilege that's granted by the public—then we, as members of the public, are entitled to a satisfying story about the rationale for animal use.

Further Reading

Botero, Maria, and Donna Desforges. Forthcoming. "The Role of Moral Values in Evaluation of the Use of Non-Human Animals in Research." *Society and Animals*: 1–18.

Carbone, Larry. 2019. "Ethical and IACUC Considerations Regarding Analgesia and Pain Management in Laboratory Rodents." *Comparative Medicine* 69(6): 443–450.

Curzer, Howard J., Gad Perry, Mark C. Wallace, and Dan Perry. 2016. "The Three Rs of Animal Research: What They Mean for the Institutional Animal Care and Use Committee and Why." *Science and Engineering Ethics* 22(2): 549–565.

Gluck, John P., and Barbara Orlans. 1997. "Institutional Animal Care and Use Committees: A Flawed Paradigm or Work in Progress?" *Ethics and Behavior* 7(4): 329–336.

Hansen, Lawrence Arthur. 2013. "Institution Animal Care and Use Committees Need Greater Ethical Diversity." *Journal of Medical Ethics* 39(3): 188–190.

Houde, Lisa, Claude Dumas, and Thérèse Leroux. 2009. "Ethics: Views from IACUC Members." *Alternatives to Laboratory Animals* 37(3): 291–296.

Landi, Margaret S., Adam J. Shriver, and Anne Mueller. 2015. "Consideration and Checkboxes: Incorporating Ethics and Science into the 3Rs." *Journal of the American Association for Laboratory Animal Science* 54(2): 224–230.

Nobis, Nathan. Forthcoming. "Why IACUCs Need Ethicists." *ILAR*.

Stichter, Matt. 2012. "Justifying Animal Use in Education." *Environmental Ethics* 34(2): 199–209.

Notes

1. This is simplifying the situation a bit, but not in a way that matters here. PHS policy requires a nonscientist member; the Animal Welfare Regulations don't. But since most institutions that do research covered by the regulations are also doing research covered by PHS policy, they go by the stricter code, which here means having the nonscientist member.
2. One possibility, which I won't explore in any detail here, is that IACUCs might be doing the same kind of cost/benefit analysis when it comes to the turtles, but since they don't think of death as a harm for nonhuman animals, they are only counting the transitory pain and distress caused by trapping, transporting, and anesthetizing. However, that idea doesn't sit very comfortably with the thought that researchers ought to reduce the number of animals used in lethal studies. If death isn't a harm (and animals can be killed painlessly), why ever worry about how many animals a researcher kills?

References

1989. "Final Rules: Animal Welfare; 9 CFR Parts, 1, 2, and 3." *USDA National Agricultural Library*. www.nal.usda.gov/awic/final-rules-animal-welfare-9-cfr-parts-1-2-and-3.

2019. "Annual Statistics of Scientific Procedures on Living Animals, Great Britain 2018." *Gov.UK*. www.gov.uk/government/statistics/statistics-of-scientific-procedures-on-living-animals-great-britain-2018.

2020. "Annual Report Animal Usage by Fiscal Year 2018." *USDA*. www.aphis.usda.gov/animal_welfare/annual-reports/Annual-Report-Summaries-State-Pain-FY18.pdf.

Harlow, Harry F., Robert O. Dodsworth, and Margaret K. Harlow. 1965. "Total Social Isolation in Monkeys." *Psychology* 54: 90–97. www.ncbi.nlm.nih.gov/pmc/articles/PMC285801/pdf/pnas00159-0105.pdf.

National Research Council. 2011. *Guide for the Care and Use of Laboratory Animals: Eighth Edition*. Washington, DC: The National Academies Press. https://doi.org/10.17226/12910.

Russell, W.M.S., and R.L. Burch. 1959. *The Principles of Humane Experimental Technique*. London: Methuen.

10 Animal Research

OVERVIEW

When, if ever, is it morally acceptable to use animals to develop therapies for human benefit? This chapter explores this question by focusing on the case of cystic fibrosis research. While this research has often been horrible for animals, it's probably acceptable from a utilitarian point of view, as so many humans have benefited. If animals have rights, though, then this research probably isn't justified. So, we take a closer look at arguments against the thesis that animals have rights, trying to figure out what it would take to make those arguments work. The chapter wraps up with some reflections on whether a commitment to animal rights is compatible with excusing people who support animal research, even if the research itself is wrong.

Dr. Dorothy Andersen earned her medical degree in 1926, graduating from Johns Hopkins in a class with just five other women. She took a surgical internship at Strong Memorial Hospital, which later became a one-year teaching position at the University of Rochester, with which Strong is affiliated. She applied for a surgical residency at Strong, but that position had never been given to a woman before, and she was rejected on that basis. So, she moved to Columbia University, where she took up research on the endocrine system and female reproduction, eventually earning her doctorate for that work. In 1935, she moved to the Babies Hospital at Colombia–Presbyterian Medical Center—now the Morgan Stanley Children's Hospital of New York–Presbyterian—where she was responsible for performing autopsies. On one occasion, she was presented with a child who had died of malnutrition, presumably because of celiac disease, where the intestines are hypersensitive to gluten and, as a result, patients have a hard time digesting food. To her surprise, though, she found damage in the child's pancreas, on which celiac disease has no impact. After reviewing hundreds of pathology slides from other ostensible celiac patients, she realized that there were really two diseases here, not one. In 1938, Anderson published a report where she gave a name to the novel condition: "cystic fibrosis of the pancreas."

Cystic Fibrosis and Humans

That disease—which we now simply call cystic fibrosis, or CF—is a genetic disorder that afflicts some 30,000 people in the United States and between 70,000 and 100,000 worldwide. The problem, in essence, is that a protein doesn't function properly in the cells that make certain secretions, such as digestive enzymes, mucus, and sweat. That protein—the cystic fibrosis transmembrane conductance regulator (CFTR)—serves as a channel across the membrane of cells, preserving the right balance of chloride ions in and on the cell's surface. When the protein isn't functioning properly, you get too much chloride in the cell, making the cell's secretions thick and sticky. The effects aren't trivial. The mucus clogs the lungs, making it very difficult to breathe, and forcing patients to cough constantly. CF patients are also highly vulnerable to bacterial infections, which exacerbate both problems. Eventually, the infections lead to scarring in the lungs, which means a permanent loss of lung function. If you imagine spending your whole life breathing through an airsickness bag, you'll get a glimpse into what it's like to have CF.

Or, at least, you'll get a glimpse into one dimension of it. The lung issues don't explain why CF was considered a childhood disease, why it was once common for infants not to reach their first birthdays. This thick, sticky mucus also damages the pancreas, which affects both insulin and digestive enzyme production. One of the signs of CF in infants is terrible and persistent diarrhea after weaning. These digestive problems result in malnutrition, with all the developmental problems associated with it.

In the early 1950s, Anderson started working with Paul di Sant'Agnese, and together they realized that they could identify CF patients by checking the salt content in their sweat.[1] This allowed them both to identify more CF patients and to develop protocols for improving their well-being. By the mid-1950s, doctors recognized that they needed to treat lung infections, encourage kids to cough up mucus, and make sure that children's diets were appropriate for their condition. With the help of antibiotics, CF patients began to live longer and longer. By 1962, doctors were predicting that many kids would live to be ten. In the 1970s, with the development of lung transplants, the median age of death got into the teens.

My brother was born in 1985, and after he'd presented all the standard symptoms, he was diagnosed with CF in Houston, Texas. When we got back to Bay City, the small town where we were living at the time, a well-meaning doctor introduced my mother to a woman who'd lost her young twins to cystic fibrosis. That woman had buried both her children before they'd finished elementary school. (Thanks to new steroids and other therapies, many CF patients were living into their twenties by that time, but news travels slowly in that part of the country.) In 1989, we moved to Rochester, New York, and I have many memories of wandering the halls of Strong Memorial Hospital—where Dorothy Andersen was an intern, and where she was unjustly denied a residency. My brother was in and out of that place more times than I can count.

When my brother was four, researchers discovered the gene responsible for CF, which launched a new age of CF research. In 1993, the U.S. Food and Drug

Administration (FDA) approved dornase alfa, which thinned that sticky mucus in the lungs. In 1997, the FDA approved tobramycin, which was an antibiotic in aerosol form, shortening the persistent lung infections that CF patients battle. In 2004, researchers demonstrated the benefits of inhaling hypertonic saline. In 2006, ivacaftor entered clinical trials, a drug that improves the functioning of the CFTR protein, allowing it to operate more effectively as a chloride channel. Then came elexacaftor, which increases the number of CFTR proteins on the surface of cells, essentially creating more chloride channels, which means that no one of them needs to work as efficiently. We next got tezacaftor, which realigns the CFTR protein on the cell surface, helping those channels to form properly. Finally, in 2019, the FDA approved a therapy that's a combination of these three drugs, Trikafta, for people with CF who meet a few common conditions—satisfied by roughly 90% of CF patients. Time will tell, of course, but Trikafta promises to be a dramatic development in CF care. There is reason to hope that, in virtue of such therapies, we will come to think of CF as akin to diabetes—a serious condition, to be sure, but one that can be managed. Perhaps the life expectancy of CF patients will be reduced by 10% or 20% rather than 50% or 60%.

When you spend a lot of time with someone with CF, you get used to having your conversations interrupted by fits of coughing, the body doubled over, and ended by a rush to the sink to spit up green and brown mucus. (In a cruel twist, laughter tends to set off the hacking.) You do everything a bit more slowly or for shorter periods of time. You might take several breaks while raking the lawn or while taking a walk. I remember visiting my brother one Christmas when he was trying to exercise more regularly, which is especially important for people with reduced lung function. He got on his bike, pedaled hard for about 30 seconds, and then collapsed on the ground, wheezing uncontrollably for five minutes.

My brother went on Trikafta as soon as it became available. It has been nothing short of life-changing. His back used to ache all the time, the muscles spasming from all the coughing. But his back doesn't hurt anymore. He used to need a nap after a bit of yard work or a busy day at the office. Playing with his young son used to leave him exhausted. Now he can make it through the day. He's taken up cycling again and can now go out for 30 miles. He called me one afternoon and said, "I guess this is what it's like to be able to breathe."

Cystic Fibrosis and Animal Research

From the perspective of CF patients and their families, these developments are extraordinary. But they've come at a steep price for nonhuman animals. We have many of these transformative therapies because of animal research.[2] In that research, animals are used as models for human biological phenomena: for instance, the progression of a disease in an animal is used as a proxy for the progression of a disease in a human being in hopes that what's true of the former can be generalized to the latter. Consider early research on lung transplants, most of which was done on dogs. The Russian surgeon Vladimir P. Demikhov worked on the procedure throughout the late 1940s, experimenting on 67 canines. Only six dogs survived for more than two days, and none for much longer. There were similar efforts, and only marginally better results, throughout the 1950s. The animal who survived the longest made it 30 days postoperation. At first, anyway, things didn't go any better when researchers at the University of Mississippi eventually got permission to try the procedure on a human being. After practicing on hundreds of animals, they were allowed to try lung transplants on a 58-year-old man. He died 18 days later of kidney failure and infection. Obviously, things have improved dramatically since then, but not without the use of many other animals as experimental subjects, and dogs remained the main model well into the 1990s.

However, the main CF-specific animal research has been done on members of six species: zebrafish, mice, rats, rabbits, ferrets, and pigs. Most animal research begins with mice, as they are such inexpensive and convenient research subjects. But mice are sufficiently different from human beings that they are often poor models for human beings. So, as Figure 10.1 suggests, researchers slowly move toward species whose members are more similar to human beings in the relevant respects, taking on the additional practical complexities—such as housing pigs versus housing mice— only when they've exhausted the simpler options.

In all these cases, using these animals as models means genetically modifying them to have CF. Many genetic disorders are studied using "knockout mice"—that is, mice created without a particular gene. The first knockout mice for CF research were generated in 1992, but mortality rate was high: only 5% made it to maturity. This is especially striking because mice don't have most of the symptoms associated with CF; for them, the primary manifestation is in the intestines. So, rather than

Disease	Human	Pig	Ferret	Rabbit	Rat	Mouse
Spontaneous Lung Infections	✔	✔	✔	?	X	X
Impaired Growth	✔	✔	✔	✔	✔	✔
Intestinal	✔	✔	✔	✔	✔	✔
Exocrine Pancreatic	✔	✔	✔	?	X	X
Endocrine Pancreas	✔	✔	✔	?	?	X
Hepatic	✔	✔	✔	?	?	X
Gallbladder	✔	✔	✔	?	NA	X

Figure 10.1 A checkmark indicates that members of that species with CF are known to present with the relevant symptom. "X" indicates that members of that species with CF are known not to present with the relevant symptom. The figure is drawn from Rosen et al. (2018).

dying of lung infections, we can assume that most of these mice simply couldn't digest enough food to survive. (While some were surely euthanized before starving to death, many probably weren't, as it's unlikely that they were under 24-hour surveillance.) Over the years, researchers learned how to produce mice with better survival rates, as well as with more of the symptoms traditionally associated with CF, such as high levels of mucus production in the lungs. While this was better for the researchers, it probably wasn't better for the mice. Surviving to maturity just means living with cystic fibrosis, though without many of the therapies that make CF tolerable for human beings, followed by euthanization when the experiment is over.

As useful as mice have been, though, pigs and ferrets have proven to be the best model of the disease. In addition to the intestinal problems, members of both species develop lung infections within a few weeks of birth, and their lungs scar in much the way that human lungs do. They also have pancreatic problems and they contract liver and gallbladder disease. This means that very few of the piglets and pups survive long enough for the research to reveal anything about the impacts of CF on mature animals: almost all of them have intestinal blockages at birth and are never able to pass feces; so, their stomachs become distended, and the vast majority die within a few days. There is no doubt that these animals suffer as a result, experiencing significant pain and discomfort over the course of their abbreviated lives. Surgeries and antibiotics can extend the lives of some of these animals, though surgery itself is something that compromises welfare, at least in the short run. Moreover, survival simply means facing other challenges, such as gastric ulcers, digestive problems, and, most notably, severe lung infections.

Researchers aren't sadists. In their view, this work must be done for the sake of current and future CF patients, and articles that discuss animal models usually include sentences like these:

Animal models that reproduce the human cystic fibrosis disease phenotypes are *required* to effectively develop methods to treat the disease.
(Fisher et al. 2011, 311, emphasis added)

Animal models are *essential tools* for understanding and comprehensively investigating CF pathophysiology.
(Semaniakou et al. 2018, emphasis added)

If they're right, then there is at least one moral theory that wouldn't condemn such research: namely, utilitarianism. As one defender of animal experimentation puts it:

Last year, there were 3.79 million procedures carried out on animals in the name of science in Great Britain. It sounds like a huge number . . . [but it needs to be contextualized.] There are around 360,000 new cases of cancer in the UK each year. Around 850,000 people currently live with dementia. Over 4 million people have diabetes in the UK. Around 7 million people are living with cardiovascular disease. And an estimated 17.8 million people— about one in four people—live with a musculoskeletal condition such as osteoporosis or osteoarthritis. Patients benefit from research, past and present, aimed at understanding and treating diseases. Such research has made it possible for many people to live with, rather than die from, their illness.

(Holder 2018)

And while this passage doesn't mention CF specifically, it's easy to show that the same point applies. Although no one knows the exact number, and no one has even tried to get a ballpark figure, it's probably safe to say that tens of thousands of animals have been used for CF research since the disease was discovered. As we mentioned earlier, however, there are 70,000 to 100,000 people with CF worldwide, and each year, there are 2,000 to 3,000 babies born with the disease. So, it doesn't take long for the number of human lives to outstrip the number of nonhuman animal lives.[3]

Potential Problems With Animal Research

There is, however, a standard objection to the idea that this research is necessary. In short, it says that however bad the other options are—that is, those that don't involve using animals—they are probably still better than using animals, given the many problems with making inferences from research on animals to conclusions about human beings. Let's consider a few of these issues.

Some of them are general problems with the published results that we see in many domains of science; these aren't animal research–specific issues. They include:

- Providing insufficient detail about study design. This involves not including basic information about the number of animals used, the number of animals removed from the study (for whatever reason), the number of animals euthanized for welfare reasons, etc.
- Underreporting results. Many papers don't mention how many studies were done in total in the results for each one, but only mention the results for the study that shows the desired effect. This is, in part, a rational, albeit objectionable, response to the realities of the practice of science, where getting funding depends on publishing in journals, and journals are more inclined to publish positive results (A is correlated with B) as opposed to negative ones (there is no relationship between A and B).
- Not reporting potential conflicts of interest. Even though many studies are funded by groups with a vested interest in certain outcomes, the vast majority of these studies don't report any conflicts. Of course, we shouldn't make too much of the fact that research was funded by a drug company; however, we shouldn't ignore it either, given the very real incentives, both personal and professional, for researchers to secure external funding.

Additionally, though, there are lots of problems that *are* specific to animal research. The basic idea behind using animals as models is simple: if things work in a certain way in these animals, then they probably work that way in human beings. So, if chloride transport works in a certain way in the cells of ferrets, then it probably works that way in the cells of human beings. Hence, if a drug fixes problems with chloride transport in ferrets, then it will probably fix that problem in human beings. However, it turns out that this isn't true. Instead, it looks like no more than 10% of therapies that work on animals are ultimately approved for human use. Translation has been most successful for cardiovascular disease, where some 18% of therapies get approved for human use. But when it comes to many other diseases, the numbers are remarkably low. With Alzheimer's disease, only 0.4% are ultimately successful in human beings; with stroke, only 0.1%.

Sometimes, this is because of differences in the way that the condition is created in the model—that is, the animal—versus the way that the condition tends to develop in human beings. When it comes to stroke research, for instance, no one simply waits for older mice to have strokes spontaneously. Instead, they are induced by head trauma or by increasing blood pressure artificially, which leads to quite different results in young, healthy animals than it does in older human adults. Moreover, to make the procedure more humane, anesthesia is sometimes used, but that, of course, is an additional confounding variable. In other contexts, the problem is that it's easy to make too much of apparent genetic similarity. In complex adaptive systems, even small genetic variations can lead to very significant differences in overall function. (Not incidentally, this may explain why it wasn't until 2016 that anyone understood why mice don't develop the respiratory problems typically associated with CF— over 25 years after mouse models became standard in CF research. It was only a puzzle because it seemed to researchers that mice *ought* to develop these problems, based on their physiology.)

What do critics propose instead? In short, statistical and computer modeling, paid clinical trials (with humans who consent to be research subjects), stem cell research, "organs on chips," and any other option that technological innovation and ethics boards make available. And in many cases, researchers do use such options for precisely the reasons we've just considered: they are concerned about translation too, and they are glad to take advantage of other options that may improve their outcomes.

However, we shouldn't be too quick to dismiss animal experimentation as some outmoded and backward research program. As Larry Carbone points out:

> Animal studies do not exist in a vacuum. They are conducted and interpreted with studies in cell and tissue culture, in human populations, in human volunteers, and in computer models. When that complex edifice leads to important discoveries and drugs, it is difficult to tease out the relative contribution of each research methodology. It is impossible to determine how much slower these discoveries would have been without animals, if they could have happened at all. It is even harder to look forward to as-yet-unknown knowledge and what studies will be most productive in its discovery. An enormous concern is about what we miss by overreliance on animal models. But that concern surely applies to overreliance on any of the research methodologies mentioned here, and even to the interwoven edifice of multidisciplinary research.
>
> (2013)

Moreover, it's easy to forget the slow and cumulative nature of scientific research. Nature doesn't share her secrets freely. And while there is a narrative that emphasizes the role of the genius in scientific discovery, making dramatic progress after a burst of insight, most scientific progress is produced by trial and error, slowly building on the work of past scientists. Rather than standing on the shoulders of giants, the scientific enterprise involves adding one pebble after another to the heap, and it takes decades (or longer) to make the mountains that the rest of us enjoy. So, while the failures of different animal research programs may look like evidence that something is amiss, those failures may just be normal science at work—slow and steady, often revealing what not to do, but thereby suggesting what to try.

So where does that leave us? For starters, this defense doesn't imply that all animal research gets a pass, as many active scientists would grant. No one is defending third-rate experimental designs, failure to be transparent about methods, or trying a new procedure simply because no one's ever tried it before. Pro–animal research scientists regularly criticize one another for the shortcomings of their work, and the cumulative nature of science provides no shield against those challenges. However, this defense does complicate any quick inference from past failures to the falsity of the specific claims that we considered earlier:

> Animal models that reproduce the human cystic fibrosis disease phenotypes are *required* to effectively develop methods to treat the disease.
>
> Animal models are *essential tools* for understanding and comprehensively investigating CF pathophysiology.

So, it may be time to stand back from questions about the *utility* of animal research and think in other terms about the moral issue here. Suppose that animal research does in fact offer us important medical advances that couldn't be had any other way. Would that be enough to show that it's morally justified?

Research and the Rights View

According to animal rights theory, the answer is clear: No. Tom Regan summarizes the position this way:

> Lab animals are not our tasters; we are not their kings. Because these animals are treated routinely, systematically as if their value were reducible to their usefulness to others, they are routinely, systematically treated with a lack of respect, and thus are their rights routinely, systematically violated. This is just as true when they are used in studies that hold out real promise of human benefits. . . . It is not just refinement or reduction that is called for, not just larger, cleaner cages, not just more generous use of anaesthetic or the elimination of multiple surgery, not just tidying up the system. It is complete replacement. The best we can do when it comes to using animals in science is—not to use them. That is where our duty lies, according to the rights view.
>
> (1986, 188)

Though the rights view might seem rabidly antihuman, its proponents regard this accusation as unfair. As Regan puts it elsewhere:

> The rights view plays no favorites. No scientific practice that violates human rights, whether the humans in moral agents or moral patients, is acceptable. . . . Those who accept the rights view are committed to denying any and all access to these "resources" on the part of those who do science. And we do this not because we oppose cruelty (though we do), nor because we favor kindness (though we do), but because justice requires nothing less.
>
> (Regan 2004, 393–394)

From the perspective of the rights view, justice simply places constraints on the way we can learn about all animals—human and nonhuman. It's often the case that the best way to learn about something is profoundly unethical, as demonstrated by dark episodes in the history of medicine, such as the Nazis' research on hypothermia and the Tuskegee syphilis study. But those cases demonstrate that the value of the knowledge doesn't justify the violation of rights. The heart of the rights view is that we should extend this same observation to nonhuman animals, based on the thought that there is no principled basis for affirming human rights while denying rights to individuals who are similar in morally relevant respects—namely, being experiencing subjects-of-a-life.

Obviously, not everyone's convinced. Consider Carl Cohen's response to the rights view:

> [Do you support the work that saved] tens of thousands of human children from diphtheria, hepatitis, measles, rabies, rubella, and tetanus (all of which relied essentially on animal subjects)—as well as, now, AIDS, Lyme disease, and malaria? I surely do. If you would join me in this support we must conclude the defense of animal rights is a gigantic mistake.
>
> (1997, 94)

There is an expression in philosophy that sounds pretty strange when you first hear it: "One person's *modus ponens* is another person's *modus tollens*." In this context, however, the meaning is pretty straightforward. Here's how Regan is reasoning:

1. If animals have rights, then animal research is unjust.
2. Animals have rights.
3. So, animal research is unjust.

This is an instance of modus ponens, an inference form that says if A is true, then B is true; A is true; therefore, B is true. By contrast, Carl Cohen—a staunch defender of animal experimentation—reasons as follows:

1. If animals have rights, then animal research is unjust.
2. Animal research isn't unjust.
3. So, animals don't have rights.

This is an instance of modus tollens, an inference form that says if A is true, then B is true; but B isn't true; so, A isn't true. On Cohen's view, it's so obvious that we should do research on animals to benefit human beings that there *must* be something wrong with any argument for animal rights. The task is just to figure out where that argument goes wrong.

If we want to generate objections to the rights-based argument against animal research, then we might start by drawing a distinction between moral *agents* and moral *patients*. Moral agents are autonomous beings who can act for moral reasons, and so have moral obligations. Moral patients are the members of the moral community, and so matter morally, but they aren't moral agents. So, both moral agents and patients should figure in our moral deliberations, but we can only hold moral agents accountable for their actions. With that in mind, we might make the following assumption: *rights entail obligations*. In other words, having rights means having certain moral responsibilities, which implies that you can't be a rights holder unless you're a moral agent. (Moral patients don't and can't have moral responsibilities, so they don't have rights.) But many people deny that nonhuman animals are moral agents, and if that's right, then animals don't have rights.

You can probably generate the main objection to this argument yourself. Human infants and those with severe cognitive disabilities seem to have rights, yet they aren't moral agents. Indeed, we often refer to human infants and those with severe cognitive disabilities when explaining the difference between being a moral agent at a moral patient. A normal adult human is the classic example of a moral agent; her infant child is the classic example of a moral patient—the child matters morally, but can't be held responsible for anything. If we want to maintain that the child has rights, as we should, then this is the wrong way to criticize the rights view.

To be fair to Cohen, he recognizes and dismisses this option himself. Instead of appealing to the moral agent/moral patient distinction, he says this:

> Animals . . . lack [the] capacity for free moral judgment. [That is, they aren't moral agents.] They are not beings *of a kind* capable of exercising or responding to moral claims. Animals therefore have no rights, and they can have none.
>
> (Cohen 1986, 866 emphasis in original)

This might seem like a different way for Cohen to make the same point we discussed earlier. However, there is a crucial difference. True, human infants can't respond to moral claims, but we might think that they're beings *of a kind* that's capable of responding to moral claims: they are, after all, human (as opposed to being plants or rocks), and human beings are the sorts of things that can respond to moral claims. So, we might conclude that infants are moral beings, even if they aren't yet capable of doing the things that are characteristic of moral beings. Animals, by contrast, aren't moral beings; they just aren't that kind of thing.[4] We can call this "the kinds argument," and it promises to draw the distinction that Cohen wants: no animal has rights because no animal is the appropriate sort of being that can have them, whereas all humans are. The upshot? We can't violate the rights of animals, as they don't have any. Of course, this is compatible with saying, as Cohen does, that there are important constraints on the way that we treat nonhuman animals; we must be humane. Still, he thinks that most animal research can proceed.

However, this step from "animals don't have rights" to "most animal research is permissible" is actually more complicated then Cohen suggests. After all, even if animals don't have rights, it could still be the case that most animal research can be criticized on the basis of being unproductive and inhumane. In other words, as long as there are *some* constraints on what we can do to nonhuman animals, we still have to show that we are meeting those constraints before we can claim to be acting in a permissible way. But given the worries about animal experimentation that we discussed earlier, we might conclude that it rarely provides much in the way of human benefit. And given the suffering it often involves, we might conclude that it's rarely humane. (Moreover, we can link these two points: the less information we can expect to get from research, the less suffering we can justify and the easier it is to condemn research protocols as inhumane.) The upshot: as long as animals matter to some degree or other, we may not need to show that they have rights to criticize a lot of animal research.

But let's set this point aside and focus instead on the "kind" argument itself. Does this do the work that Cohen needs it to do? Short answer: not obviously.

The central problem, it seems, is this. The easy thing is to say that moral agents have rights and no one else does. Then, if you want to know why moral agents have rights, you just point to the fact that they are moral agents. Obviously, though, Cohen can't say that. If he did, his view would imply that human infants don't have rights, and that's no way to make friends and influence people. So, he makes the move to kinds, to the importance of being human. As a result, the *motivation* for the view is clear. However, what isn't clear is *why* being human is morally important; that is, it isn't clear what would *explain* its importance. After all, there are human beings who will never develop the capacities that ground moral agency, whether because they have medical conditions in virtue of which they won't survive infancy or because they have such severe cognitive disabilities that they will never become moral agents. Hence, it will never be appropriate to hold them morally responsible for their actions. So, Cohen can't say being human is special because every human is going to have the relevant capacities.

And anyway, even if Cohen *could* say that being human is special because every human is going to have the relevant capacities, he shouldn't. Imagine someone saying, "We shouldn't experiment on fish embryos because eventually, they will become creatures who can experience pain." This is a bad justification for not experimenting on fish embryos, since *while they are still embryos*, they lack the capacity to suffer. What seems to matter is the capacities they have *now*, while we are considering doing something to them, not the capacities they will probably have in the future. Likewise, we should look for properties that infants have *now* that explain why they have rights—not properties that they will have in the future.

Here's a fanciful thought experiment that really drives the point home:

Two perfectly normal people, Jack and Jill, decide to have a baby. Jill gets pregnant and eventually gives birth to a daughter, who they name Anomaly.

Unbeknownst to them, however, there was a large random genetic mutation at a very early stage in Anomaly's development—so large, in fact, that Anomaly isn't human, at least on a standard conception of what it is to be a human. For instance, though Anomaly is still fertile—that is, were another of her kind to exist, she would be able to produce viable offspring—it's impossible for her to reproduce with a human. But despite Anomaly's unusual genetic mutation, she looks like a normal infant. Her DNA has, in the jargon, the same phenotypic effects.[5]

Imagine being Anomaly's parents: I'll bet you'd be quite convinced that she has rights. But it turns out that she isn't human. So if being human is what matters, that she doesn't have rights. This seems like an unacceptable conclusion.

How can Cohen respond while staying committed to the kinds argument? The obvious thing is to say that being human *isn't* what matters. Instead, what matters is being a *moral* being—*that* kind of thing, whether human or not. But now he's back to the old problem of those with severe cognitive disabilities. This view seems to imply that those with severe cognitive disabilities are of the wrong kind, since if their condition is genetic (and if your nature is determined by your genome), they aren't moral beings.[6]

Cohen might reply: "Look, those with severe cognitive disabilities are *not* of the wrong kind; they are still human, and human animals are moral animals. That's what matters." Unfortunately, though, we can modify Anomaly's case to show that this move won't help either:

Two perfectly normal people, Jack and Jill, decide to have a baby—Anomaly. Same story: genetic mutation, not human, etc. The wrinkle is that although Anomaly looks and behaves like a normal infant and will develop physically in a normal way, her mutation will limit her cognitive capacities; mentally, she will never develop beyond the abilities of an average two-year-old.

In this new version of the case, Anomaly isn't human, nor is she of the kind (assuming that your genome determines your kind) that's inherently a *moral* being. So, it looks like Cohen would have to say that Anomaly doesn't have rights. And again, if you were Anomaly's parents, I suspect you'd disagree.

Giving Up on Explanations

Does Cohen have any better options? Perhaps, though he never really develops the alternative that he suggests. Here's what he writes:

Rights are universally human; they arise in a human moral world, in the moral sphere. In the human world moral judgments are pervasive; it is the fact that all humans including infants and the senile are members of that moral community—not the fact that as individuals they have or do not have certain special capacities, or merit—that makes humans bearers of rights.

Therefore, it is beside the point to insist that animals have remarkable capacities, that they really have a consciousness of self, or of the future, or make plans, and so on. And the tired response that because infants plainly cannot make moral claims they must have no rights at all, or rats must have them too, we ought forever put aside. Responses like these arise out of a misconception of [rights themselves]. They mistakenly suppose that rights are tied to some identifiable individual abilities or sensibilities, and they failed to see that rights arise only in the community of moral beings, and that therefore there are spheres in which rights apply and spheres in which they do not.

(Cohen 1997, 97)

In this brief passage, Cohen is trying to step back from the particular debate—the controversy about whether animal experimentation can be justified—and instead broach a more general question about how rights talk works in the first place. In essence, he's challenging the idea that rights talk is the sort of thing we should try to explain, or at least that it's the kind of thing we should try to explain fully. Let's pause and mull this over for a minute.

The main argument for the rights view, and for many other standard theories in animal ethics, often begins with the observation that infants, those with severe cognitive disabilities, and the comatose deserve moral consideration. However, those individuals lack the more sophisticated capabilities that normal adults enjoy. This is supposed to motivate the idea that the correct explanation for membership in the moral community—not just in the case of these individuals, but generally—must be some simpler trait, such as being sentient, or being an experiencing subject-of-a-life. The next step is to observe that animals also have that trait, and so it can only be mere prejudice, the sin of speciesism, that leads us to deny them moral consideration.

Cora Diamond argues, rather famously, that this line of argument rests on a mistake. She rejects the idea that *any* nonmoral trait can, in and of itself, explain why an entity matters morally. Instead, she thinks that recognizing something as morally important depends on our being willing to see it as falling into a category that's *already* moral, that already says something about our relationship to that thing. So, for example, to see an entity as human is to see her as important from the get-go, as an entity about which it would be bizarre to ask, "Why are you relieving its pain?" If we see an entity as human, we don't see "it" as an *it*; instead, we see "it" as *him* or *her*, as *someone*, and as someone whose suffering provides a reason to offer aid. As she puts it:

We cannot point and say, "This *thing* (whatever concepts it may fall under) is at any rate capable of suffering, so we ought not to make it suffer". . . . That "this" is a being which I ought not to make suffer, or whose suffering I should try to prevent, constitutes a *special* relationship to it.

(Diamond 1978, 470, emphasis in original)

It's really important to understand what's going on here. According to just about everybody in conversations about animal ethics, we need to explain *why* things matter morally, and we do that by appealing to nonmoral, empirically detectable traits, such as having the capacity to suffer. Despite their disagreements, utilitarianism and the rights view are unified in this point. Diamond is saying: give up on explanation. Things matter morally because we relate to them in a certain way, a way that's reflected in the categories we use, that *presupposes* their moral importance.

If Diamond is right, then a remarkable conclusion follows. This standard move in animal ethics, to appeal to infants and those with severe cognitive disabilities, might actually be self-undermining. This is because it can lead us to abandon the thick, morally laden categories—*human* and *animal* and *thing*—that underwrite our willingness to respond to suffering or injustice or anything else. Instead, we can find ourselves looking around and noticing some beings with the capacity to suffer, some beings without it, and no story at all about why we should care one way or the other. Diamond's thought, essentially, is that when we forget the ordinary categories that we've long used to carve up the moral world and just think about the presence or absence of certain capacities, we will be left with nothing but the search for consistency, which we can just as well achieve by denying moral consideration to newborns and the senile. Sure, *you* may not want to do that. I know I don't. But as Diamond recognized—and as many disability rights advocates have argued—once we stop thinking about human lives as special, there is a real risk that we will start to assess them in terms of their sophistication, or their balance of pleasures and pains, or their contributions to society, or any number of other sorts of factors. We may lose our grip on the sacredness of being human.

Diamond's view is radical. She thinks that something's having a particular physiological trait—like the capacity to feel pain—doesn't itself give you any reason to care about what happens to that thing. It's only once you categorize it *in a certain way*—as a fellow creature, or perhaps as a person—that it develops this significance. Cohen isn't saying anything as radical. But he is, I think, pushing in this direction, even if he doesn't quite know it. He's saying that there's some kind of mistake in wanting explanations for every single human's moral importance, for looking at each individual human being and saying: "You must have some specific property, or we won't count you as mattering." Instead, Cohen seems to think that it's enough for some of us to have this very important property—this property of being the kinds of beings who create a moral world—and the rest of us can matter without having any special property at all. For Cohen, community membership does the work, just as categorization does the work for Diamond.

The obvious question for Diamond is: What determines how things get categorized? Just our whims? Diamond wouldn't exactly say that, but she does think that there isn't a decisive rational basis for these categorizations: they are, instead, determined in large part by our willingness to see others in particular ways, to be moved by them, to be open to them having an effect on our sentiments. As a result, she thinks that expanding the moral circle—coming to see more individuals as morally important—isn't going to be accomplished by rational argumentation as much as by emotional engagement. It will be poetry, rather than proofs, that do the work.

We might ask something similar of Cohen: What determines who gets into the moral community? And maybe he could take a page from Diamond here, saying that there is no rational basis for the boundary; there are only the facts about the scope of our affections. It turns out that we are deeply invested in children and those with severe cognitive disabilities quite independently of whether they have the properties that allow us to create a moral community; we aren't, however, as invested in the well-being of nonhuman animals. So, the moral community is roughly the human community, even if "being human" isn't a morally relevant property in any traditional sense of that phrase.

Of course, it's worth wondering whether our affections really are limited in the way that this reply suggests. If they aren't, then the moral community might be much larger than Cohen imagines. It's worth remembering that there were times when it would have seemed very plausible to people that we couldn't really care about anyone who wasn't a member of our sex or tribe or race or religion. Might it be possible to add species to that list, as one more category that seemed enormously important, but turns out not to be?

I'm not sure. People sometimes surprise us with their flexibility. (Likewise, they sometimes surprise us with their *in*flexibility.) But suppose the answer is yes, species is just one more category that we can learn to ignore as morally irrelevant, and we can indeed come to care about the fates of nonhuman animals in a way that we care about human beings who are unlike us in various respects. Then, this spells trouble for Cohen's "we need to understand the nature of rights" objection to animal rights.

Whatever we say about this particular issue, though, it's worth recognizing that there remains something disappointing about the Diamond/Cohen approach. We started doing animal ethics because we wanted to *reduce* arbitrariness: we wanted to think more systematically about animals and get a better handle on our obligations to and regarding them. But if the Diamond/Cohen line is correct, then there are cracks in the foundation of this project: sure, we can reduce arbitrariness in our thinking *given the categories that we are already using*, but the choice between different ways of viewing animals doesn't seem to have any rational basis.

Maybe that's true. As Hume says in a very different context: "It is not contrary to reason to prefer the destruction of the whole world to the scratching of my finger" (1739, 637). Hume's point here is that our preferences and desires can take whatever shape they take without violating the dictates of reason. It might be *tragic* that you prefer the destruction of the whole world to a scratch on your finger, but it isn't irrational. And if the categories that are used to shape the moral world—*human* and *animal* and *thing*—are structured by our preferences, by our willingness to engage (or not), then perhaps it isn't surprising that they don't lend themselves to rational assessment. But again, it seems disappointing, as it seems to undermine our motivation for doing ethics in the first place. If there's arbitrariness in the foundations, then who cares if there's arbitrariness elsewhere?

Conclusion

Let's take stock. If it turns out that animal research is essential for certain medical developments, then given the number of animals used versus the number of people who stand to gain, some animal research is almost certainly justified from a utilitarian perspective. So, if we're going to criticize animal research generally, we'll probably need to appeal to animal rights. (Of course, we might not think that we should criticize animal research generally, but we're trying to figure out how the challenge would go if we wanted to make it.) The question then becomes: What's the best criticism of the view that animals have rights? We considered three answers. The first, which is the least promising, simply says that you have rights if you're a moral agent, no nonhuman animal is a moral agent, and so no nonhuman animal has rights. The second, which is more sophisticated, but still seems to be vulnerable to serious objections, says that you have rights if you're the right kind of being—the moral kind—which is a distinctively human property. The third move is to give up on the idea of explaining why all humans have rights and no animals have them, simply saying that what matters is community membership, being one of us. That option is certainly the most radical and gives up much of what drove us to do ethics in the first place. We might conclude, then, that if we're sympathetic to the basic argument for animal rights, then these criticisms don't give us good reasons to change our minds. The rights-based challenge to animal research stands.

Out of curiosity, though, we might wonder whether there's a way to stick with the rights view and still give the go-ahead to animal research. Here's one possible story. Even if we go in for the rights view, it doesn't follow that we have to *blame* everyone who supports animal research.[7] After all, it's possible to say that those who are in favor of animal research are supporting rights violations and so are acting wrongly. Still, they might be acting excusably, such that no one could fault them for their choice. Imagine, for instance, that you borrowed $100 from a wealthy friend of yours, someone who definitely doesn't need the money, and you promise to pay it back by Friday. But when Friday rolls around, it occurs to you that if you pay the money back today, you won't be able to afford a present for your daughter on her birthday. So, you don't return the money, you purchase the present, and you thereby break your promise. You've acted wrongly: you violated your friend's right to have his money back on the agreed-upon day. You probably agree, though, that you acted excusably. Sure, you should have paid the money back, but no one can blame you for prioritizing your daughter's happiness in these circumstances.

Maybe something similar is true when it comes to animal experimentation. Sure, animal experimentation violates the rights of nonhuman animals, and it's wrong for that reason. But when you look at your children, your parents, or your own survival, perhaps you can be excused for supporting rights violations. Maybe no one can blame you for prioritizing the people you love.

This view tries to split the difference between saying that animal research isn't blameworthy because it's permissible, on the one hand, and saying that animal research *is* blameworthy because it's wrong, on the other. It says that animal research is wrong but not blameworthy because we have an excuse. And on one level, I find this attractive. I think it's important to preserve the idea that there is something awful about the research we do on animals. I don't have CF myself, but I think I have a pretty good sense of what it's like to live with it. And on that basis, I wouldn't wish the experience on anyone, human or nonhuman. When I imagine the experience of a piglet who's too weak to feed, suffering from intense abdominal cramping as her belly becomes more and more distended, I think: she shouldn't have been created; no one should have brought her into existence.

However, I'm not fully satisfied by the "wrong but excusable" line. In short, I just doubt that we can spell out the details in a satisfying way. When I gave the example involving your wealthy friend, the cost to him is trivial: it just doesn't matter whether he gets his $100 back today or next week. But when it comes to the animals we use as research subjects, the costs to them are extreme: they stand to lose everything, and invariably do. Moreover, this is exactly the kind of case that the rights view is designed to address: one where we're inclined to benefit the many at the expense of the few, and the few will suffer more for it. So, I tend to think that it's going to be quite difficult to explain why, given the rights view, it would even be excusable to support wrongful practices like animal research.

What should we then say? I'm not sure. I am sure, however, that I'm thankful for the drugs that have transformed my brother's life. If they weren't available and it was my call whether to proceed with animal research to develop them, I would give the green light. Perhaps we should say, on that basis, that I'm altogether too partial, altogether too speciesist. Or perhaps we should reassess the arguments that led us to the rights view.

Further Reading

2019. *Animal Experimentation: Working Towards a Paradigm Change*. Edited by Kathrin Herrmann and Kimberley Jayne. Leiden: Brill.

Beauchamp, Tom L., and David B. Morton. 2015. "The Upper Limits of Pain and Suffering in Animal Research." *Cambridge Quarterly of Healthcare Ethics* 24(4): 431–447.

Carbone, Larry. 2004. *What Animals Want: Expertise and Advocacy in Laboratory Animal Welfare*. New York: Oxford University Press.

DeGrazia, David, and Jeff Sebo. 2015. "Necessary Conditions for Morally Responsible Animal Research." *Cambridge Quarterly of Healthcare Ethics* 24(4): 420–430.

Ferdowsian, Hope, L. Syd M. Johnson, Jane Johnson, Andrew Fenton, Adam Shriver, and John Gluck. 2020. "A Belmont Report for Animals?" *Cambridge Quarterly of Healthcare Ethics* 29(1): 19–39. Cambridge: Cambridge University Press.

Fouts, Roger. 1998. *Next of Kin: My Conversations with Chimpanzees*. New York: William Morrow.

Garrett, Jeremy. 2012. *The Ethics of Animal Research: Exploring the Controversy*. Edited by Jeremy Garrett. Cambrigde, MA: MIT Press.

Nobis, Nathan. 2016. "Tom Regan on Kind Arguments against Animal Rights and for Human Rights." In *The Moral Rights of Animals*, edited by Mylan Engel Jr. and Gary Comstock, 65–80. Lanham: Lexington Books.

Pound, Pandora. 2020. "Animal Models: Problems and Prospects." In the *Routledge Handbook of Animal Ethics*, edited by Bob Fischer, 239–252. New York: Routledge.

Slicer, Deborah. 1991. "Your Daughter or Your Dog? A Feminist Assessment of the Animal Research Issue." *Hypatia* 6(1): 108–124.

Streiffer, Robert. 2014. "The Confinement of Animals Used in Laboratory Research." In *The Ethics of Captivity*, edited by Lori Gruen, 174–192. Oxford: Oxford University Press.

Notes

1. When Houston became a major hub for CF research, doctors needed sweat samples from children who were potential CF patients but who might not be well enough to run around. So, they would take them for a drive with the A/C off and the windows rolled up, letting the brutal summer heat produce enough sweat for the test.
2. Throughout this chapter, when I talk about "animal research" and "animal experimentation," I just mean nontherapeutic animal research and experimentation. Research is nontherapeutic when it isn't trying to benefit the individual on whom the research is being done. So if I try out a new drug on a very sick person who stands to benefit from that drug—and she consents—then I am doing therapeutic research, which doesn't seem morally objectionable at all. Nontherapeutic research, by contrast, aims to benefit someone other than the research subject. In the case of human beings, we can sometimes justify nontherapeutic research if people are willing to be experimental subjects, perhaps because they care enough about victims of the relevant disease. But in the case of nonhuman animals, we can't get their consent—or, at least, can't get their informed consent. This alone doesn't necessarily imply that nontherapeutic research on animals is morally wrong, but it does make clear that a standard way of justifying nontherapeutic research—namely, the informed consent of the subjects of research—isn't available.
3. The argument is even better we don't look at lives, but instead look at life years of suffering. Granted, the nonhuman animals used in research may suffer more intensely, but most of them also live very short lives—typically measured in hours or days, not months or years. So, the total numbers of life years of suffering is going to be dramatically lower than the total number of animal lives lost, further skewing things in favor of animal research. Of course, I've been assuming that the relevant form of utilitarianism is act utilitarianism, as opposed to rule or virtue utilitarianism. Does the calculus change then? To show that it does, we would need to establish that the side effects of allowing animal research are bad enough that they outweigh any benefits to human beings that come directly from the research. So, for instance, maybe the following is true: maybe the only people who would allow animal experimentation are also the kind of people who would support animal agriculture, which (let's suppose) has huge costs in terms of utility. Given as much, we ought to say that it's vicious to support animal experimentation because of the link between supporting animal experimentation and supporting animal agriculture. However, it isn't clear that this is true, as there seem to be many people who are opposed to animal agriculture while remaining somewhat sympathetic to at least some animal experimentation.
4. Not everyone agrees with this—see Mark Rowlands (2012)—but we'll assume that it's true for the sake of argument.
5. Thanks to Travis Timmerman for this idea.
6. Someone could insist at this juncture that your nature is determined by your soul, not your genome. For criticisms of this, see Chapter 2.
7. Thanks to C.E. Abbate for suggesting this way of defending the rights view.

References

Carbone, Larry. 2013. "The Utility of Basic Animal Research." *Ethics of Medical Research with Animals*, January 14. http://animalresearch.thehastingscenter.org/report/the-utility-of-basic-animal-research/.

Cohen, Carl. 1986. "The Case for the Use of Animals in Biomedical Research." *The New England Journal of Medicine* 315(14): 865–870.

Cohen, Carl. 1997. "Do Animals Have Rights?" *Ethics and Behavior* 7(2): 91–102.

Diamond, Cora. 1978. "Eating Meat and Eating People." *Philosophy* 53(206): 465–479. www.jstor.org/stable/3749876.

Fisher, John T., Yulong Zhang, and John F. Engelhardt. 2011. "Comparative Biology of Cystic Fibrosis Animal Models." In *Cystic Fibrosis: Methods in Molecular Biology*, edited by M Amaral and K. Kunzelmann, 311–334. Totowa, NJ: Humana Press.

Holder, Tom. 2018. "In Defence of Animal Testing." *Understanding Animal Research*, September 11. www.understandinganimalresearch.org.uk/news/communications-media/in-defence-of-animal-testing/.

Hume, David. 1739. *A Treatise on Human Nature: Being an Attempt to Introduce the Experimental Method of Reasoning Into Moral Subjects*. Auckland: The Floating Press, 2009.

Regan, Tom. 2004. *The Case for Animal Rights*. Berkeley: University of California Press.

Regan, Tom. 1986. "The Case for Animal Rights." In *Advances in Animal Welfare Science*, edited by M.W. Fox and L.D. Mickley, 179–189. Washington, DC: The Humane Society of the United States.

Rosen, Bradley H., Marc Chanson, Lara R. Gawenis, Jinghua Liu, Aderonke Sofoluwe, Alice Zoso, John F. Engelhardt. 2018. "Animal and Model Systems for Studying Cystic Fibrosis." *Journal of Cystic Fibrosis* 17(2): 28–34.

Rowlands, Mark. 2012. *Can Animals Be Moral?* New York: Oxford University Press.

Semaniakou, Anna, Roger P. Croll, and Valerie Chappe. 2018. "Animal Models in the Pathophysiology of Cystic Fibrosis." *Frontiers in Pharmacology* 9.

11 Zoos

OVERVIEW

How good are the arguments that are typically offered in defense of zoos? This chapter tries to answer that question. Along the way, it draws a sharp contrast between valuing animals as individuals and valuing animals as instances of species. This difference explains many disagreements between animal advocates and conservationists about certain standard practices in zoos. The chapter makes a number of practical recommendations concerning ways that zoos could be improved. It concludes with some personal reflections on the ethics of visiting zoos—or, rather, on visiting zoos more ethically.

Magdeburg, Germany. May 2008. A Siberian tigress named Kolina gives birth to three healthy cubs. That same day, the zoo director, Kai Perret, had all three cubs euthanized, their bodies frozen, and later had them delivered to University of Göttingen for dissection. Then, he had the cubs' father, Toskan, castrated. Why?

In short: genetics. The zoo had acquired Kolina and Toskan a year and a half earlier to breed them, and everyone was thrilled when she got pregnant. However, testing later revealed that Toskan wasn't a pure Siberian tiger; he had Sumatran ancestry as well. This made the cubs worthless. First, they couldn't be used to breed the next generation of Siberian tigers. Second, no other zoo would be willing to display them as Siberian tigers, so they couldn't be traded to enhance some other aspect of the Magdeburg collection. And third, if kept at the Magdeburg Zoo, they would have taken up valuable space and resources. The staff considered aborting Kolina's pregnancy, but decided that it would be too risky. So after she delivered, they gave each cub a lethal injection.

Zoos and Their Animals

This story isn't unique. "Management euthanasia," as it's called, occurs at zoos around the world. This particular case made the news, though, because two animal rights organizations filed charges. In response, the major zoological associations came out in support of the Magdeburg Zoo. The World Association of Zoos and Aquariums (WAZA), for instance, provided a statement that said:

> [Conservation] management takes on many forms and can, on occasion, include the euthanasia of individuals. Humane euthanasia, as a component of population management, and based on scientific analysis of the ex situ (i.e. captive population) to ensure its long-term sustainability, is supported by WAZA as acceptable.
>
> (Hance 2010)

Nevertheless, the individuals involved were found guilty, and the zoo was fined €8,100. The district court judge said that there were "no sufficient reasons to kill less valuable, but totally healthy animals" (Hance 2010). This prompted a strong response from the zoological community, the members of which perceived it as an attack on their conservation work. In another statement, WAZA responded to the verdict:

> WAZA sees the conviction of the three Zoo Magdeburg staff on the premise that humane management euthanasia for conservation purposes is not a "reasonable" course of action to be a repudiation of international consensus on what constitutes best conservation practice. In light of the fact that the consumptive and terminal use of both wild and domesticated animals for the purposes of food production and recreation is viewed as being acceptable and reasonable in modern society, this judgement can only be regarded as an act of legal and moral hypocrisy.
>
> (Groch 2015)

This case is fascinating for several reasons. First, it's interesting because there's actually some controversy about how to distinguish subspecies. There are plenty of cases where you can find, within a single subspecies, the same degree of genetic difference that people use to justify the existence of a new subspecies in some other context. So, while the cubs were killed because they were mongrels, that judgment isn't entirely uncomplicated. Second, WAZA's point about moral hypocrisy seems quite compelling: if it's morally acceptable to kill animals for all sorts of other reasons—including our just wanting to eat them or have them as trophies on our walls—what's so bad about euthanizing some tiger cubs for conservation purposes?

Third, and perhaps most significantly here, there's the tension between two radically different perspectives on the value of nonhuman animals. From the zoo's perspective, those cubs were valuable *as instances of a subspecies*, as tokens of a type, as examples of a kind. From the perspective of the animal rights organizations, those cubs were valuable *as individuals*. In saying this, I'm obviously not saying that the zoo *only* cared about the cubs as instances of a subspecies. They cared about them as individuals too, as demonstrated by the fact that they were concerned about their welfare: the zoo staff euthanized the cubs via lethal injection, rather than via some torturous method, such as starving them to death. For the zoo, though, their *primary* value was as instances of a subspecies, and when the staff learned that the cubs weren't pure Siberian tigers, they no longer saw them as having lives worth preserving. From the perspective of the zoo, the value they attached to the cubs as individuals wasn't enough to justify the resources and opportunity costs that would have been required to give them decent lives. It was more important, from the zoo's perspective, to breed other tigers who could help preserve the Siberian tiger species. The reverse is true for the animal rights organizations: for them, the primary value of the cubs was as individuals; any additional value derived from their subspecies was secondary, and clearly of much less importance.

Once we appreciate this contrast, it's much easier to understand why zoos do the things they do:

- It explains why, in 2015, the Copenhagen Zoo made a similar decision and killed a healthy, 18-month-old giraffe named Marius: his subspecies isn't endangered in the wild, the zoo already had a number of giraffes of his kind, and no other zoo was interested in taking him. So, a zookeeper got him to lower his head by offering him a piece of rye bread, and then a veterinarian fired a bolt gun into his skull. After publicly dissecting him, the staff fed him to the lions.
- It explains why it's common for zoos to trade animals, which means dividing animal family groups and then introducing new individuals who may or may not get along with the animals who remain. The Association of Zoos and Aquariums (AZA), a North American industry group, for instance, has nearly 500 "species survival plans," the advisors for which are responsible "for developing a comprehensive population Studbook and a Breeding and Transfer Plan which identifies population management goals and recommendations to ensure the sustainability of a healthy, genetically diverse, and demographically varied [zoo] population" ("Species Survival"). The primary objective here is the preservation of species, not preserving ties between individual animals.[1]
- It explains why zoos keep animals in captivity who would likely live much longer in the wild. In protected areas of Africa and Asia, for instance, wild elephants live more than twice as long as elephants in European zoos. The median lifespan for female African elephants is 17 years if born in a zoo, versus 56 years in the Amboseli National Park. Granted, this isn't a general rule: Tidière et al. (2016) found that 84% of the mammalian species they studied lived longer in captivity. The point here is just that being a member of that smaller, unlucky group isn't enough for zoos to decide that those animals shouldn't be kept in captivity. In general, zoos are willing to compromise the lifespans of individual animals for the sake of species health.
- It explains why zoos keep animals who may prefer very different environments than the ones that zoos can provide for them. Snow leopards, for example, are highly solitary animals who seem to value patrolling their territory. Their home ranges vary dramatically depending on the availability of prey, but even when prey is abundant, they regularly survey an area between 30 and 65 km^2. The two snow leopards in New York's Central Park Zoo occupy no more than half an acre, or roughly 0.002 sq km., most of which puts them in sight of human

beings. And the Central Park Zoo is doing relatively well by industry standards. Many zoos give their big cats much less space.

- Finally, it explains why organizations that spend an enormous amount of time, energy, and money to save some animals have no problem killing other animals to feed them. Lions eat nearly 500 pounds of beef per week, and bears are often given a chow that's a mix of horsemeat, fish meal, and various plant-based ingredients. However, cattle, horses, and forage fish (such as sardines and mackerel, which are converted into fish meal) aren't threatened or endangered species, and so aren't deemed nearly as important as the animals who represent relatively rare species in zoos.

Given the costs that zoos impose on particular animals, we'd hope that zoos are right to value animals first and foremost as instances of species, rather than as individuals. What's more, we'd hope that they're achieving their stated conservation aims. The San Diego Zoo, for example, which is often ranked as the top zoo in the United States, says that its vision is to "lead the fight against extinction" and understands its mission as being "committed to saving species worldwide by uniting our expertise in animal care and conservation science with our dedication to inspiring passion for nature" ("San Diego Zoo"). How well are zoos living up to such aspirations?

Should Species Matter?

Let's begin with the idea of valuing animals as instances of species. The obvious worry here is that species don't feel anything; they aren't the kinds of things that can suffer. There may be a sense in which you can hurt a species, but it's an analogical one. Whatever species are, they can't bleed, they don't experience pain, and they don't care what happens to them. On the face of it, then, it seems strange that species would matter more than the individuals who represent them.

Of course, it wouldn't be so strange if animals weren't sentient. There are lots of cases where the type is more important than any instance of it. Just the other day, I dropped a glass jar on the floor, sending splinters of glass flying in a million directions. I was unhappy. Truth be told, though, that glass jar didn't really matter; what mattered was my being able to have jars like it, jars of the same type, as they are particularly good for bringing my lunch to and from work. So I got another, and life is just as good as before. When it comes to glass jars, it's just obvious that the type matters more than the token, the kind more than the instance of the kind. However, sentient individuals aren't like individual glass jars. Sentient individuals care about what happens to them; glass jars—and species—don't.

Granted, species can be valuable *to human beings* in ways that make us think about particular animals as being like individual glass jars. We can value species because they carry information about evolutionary history. We can value them as features of ecosystems that we want to preserve or to restore to some previous state. We can value species as aesthetic objects—we want there to be tigers, because we think they are beautiful, but we don't care which tigers they are. And, of course, we can value them in lots of other ways as well. And when we do, individual animals don't necessarily seem to be that important. What matters is the evolutionary information, or the ecosystem, or the aesthetic object. As we've discussed many times throughout the book, though, there are good reasons to challenge the idea that our interests determine whether and how animals are morally important. So, even if we don't particularly care about animals as individuals, and their value to us is akin to the value that attaches to a given glass jar, they can still be morally important—indeed, more important than the thing we actually care about (namely, their respective species).

This mismatch between the value we assign and the value things have shouldn't be particularly strange; it's actually a common phenomenon and the setup for countless jokes on sitcoms. A character learns that the head baker at his bakery has just died. But rather than being sad for the baker and his family, the character is awkwardly disappointed because he will no longer be able to get his favorite cakes. He knows he's expected to care about the baker—you know, as a person with infinite worth, etc.—but in fact, he cares more about her as a means to an end, as he can only think about whether she wrote down her recipes. Perhaps we are like that character. If so, we shouldn't be.

Still, it could work out that while it's a mistake to value species more than individuals in general, it isn't a mistake when it comes to *endangered* species. In those cases, the thought goes, the sheer rarity of the species increases its value such that it's worth sacrificing the interests of individuals to preserve it.

This thought isn't absurd. Consider a parallel. During the last 30 years of his life, Claude Monet produced some 250 oil paintings depicting the water lilies near his home in Giverny, France. Given Monet's stature as a painter, they are all valuable. However, they aren't nearly as valuable as the 25 paintings that make up "Haystacks," a series that Monet did from 1890 to 1891 and which are generally regarded as his finest work. (In 2019, one painting from the series sold for $110.7 million at Sotheby's, a famous art auction house, which was the highest price ever for an Impressionist painting.) But now imagine that 249 of Monet's paintings of water lilies are destroyed in a fire; only one remains. It's quite plausible that in virtue of it being so rare, and perhaps in virtue of the others being lost in such a tragic way, the last waterlily painting might actually be more important than any of the "Haystacks" paintings. In fact, it would seem totally reasonable to go to much greater lengths to preserve the last waterlily painting than any member of the "Haystacks" series, as it's now one of a kind, even if that required destroying one member of the "Haystacks" series. Similarly, then, we might think that it's worth killing hogs to feed the last polar bear, since in virtue of being the very last one, that bear is extraordinarily valuable.

In the case of art, then, it seems plausible that there are cases where rarity increases value, and as a result, it's permissible to make sacrifices that we would otherwise regard as unacceptable. However, it's a bit hard to imagine the same reasoning being applied to people. Imagine that there is a nurse whose job it is to process the applications to get on a heart transplant list. One afternoon, two applications come in at the exact same time, and the nurse has to decide which should go first. The only difference she notices between the patients is that one is Apache, a rare Native American tribe, while the other is Latino. Should she put the Apache person higher on the list than the Latino person? Does the fact that the Apache ethnic group is more rare give the nurse adequate reason to treat that individual as more valuable? I'm inclined to think not and to say that she should just flip a coin.

Even if you disagree and think that she ought to prioritize the member of the rarer ethnic group, now imagine there being some other differences. Suppose, for instance, that the Latino individual has never had a heart transplant, while the Apache has (this would be that person's second). Or suppose that the Latino individual has two dependents, while the Apache has none. Does the rarity outweigh these considerations too? Presumably not. So, while the value of nonsentient objects might vary dramatically based on rarity, I suspect that it doesn't work that way when it comes to people, and ordinary moral considerations basically carry the day. On the assumption that animals are more like people than they are like nonsentient objects, we should probably say the same thing about animals. As a result, we should be suspicious of the idea that species preservation is more important than the basic interests of animals—in zoos or anywhere else. And if that's right, then we have good reason to doubt that many standard practices in zoos are morally justified—including the ones mentioned at the beginning of this chapter—as they would be very difficult to defend without the assumption that species preservation is morally primary.

Zoos' Conservation Mission

But suppose I'm totally wrong about this. Let's suppose, in other words, that it's completely appropriate to value individual animals as instances of species first and foremost (which is compatible with valuing the individual animals as individuals—just not with valuing them *chiefly* as individuals). Still, we're left with the question of whether zoos are living up to their aspirations when it comes to conservation. Are zoos "lead[ing] the fight against extinction," either individually or collectively?

They certainly claim to be. However, a lot depends on what we mean by "conserving species." WAZA defines conservation as "securing populations of species in natural habitats for the long term" (Barongi et al. 2015, 12). And if that's the way we think about conservation, then it doesn't really matter whether zoos are able to preserve examples of species within their confines; what matters is that their efforts result in stable populations in the home range of the relevant species. (After all, the goal is not to run Noah's Ark, where species only exist as living museum specimens, preserved indefinitely in captivity.) And there is some evidence of success along this dimension. For instance, the International Union for Conservation of Nature (IUCN), a coalition of over 14,000 environmental organizations, gives zoos and aquariums some credit for the recovery of 16 of the 64 vertebrate species on its IUCN Red List of Threatened Species. By and large, this is based on breeding programs that aim to reintroduce animals to the wild. And there are, of course, some famous success stories where a species was on the brink of extinction and breeding programs seem to have prevented that particular loss: think, for instance, of the California condor, the red wolf, the Arabian oryx, and the black-footed ferret. However, we need to keep these successes in perspective. Even if zoos have been responsible for making certain species *less* threatened, that doesn't mean those species aren't still in danger. And unless the trendlines turn dramatically, there will continue to be more habitat loss, which means fewer places for wild animals. There will continue to be more animal migration as a result of that loss, which means new competitors for the habitat that remains. Climate change isn't going to be reversed anytime soon, which means ongoing changes to the ecosystems on which animals depend. And in many parts of the world, the wildlife trade shows no sign of abating, which often targets the very species that conservationists are trying to protect.

Moreover, while we know about the success stories, we don't have a good sense of just how often zoos try and fail to preserve species. How often do breeding programs fail to preserve the necessary degree of genetic diversity? What percentage of reintroductions are successful? And how should we assess what counts as a successful reintroduction anyway? Is it enough to have the species existing somewhere, or must it exist in its native range? If the former, then the Arabian oryx is a success story, as it now lives wild in the United States. If the latter, though, then it's a failure, as there are no more wild Arabian oryx on the Arabian Peninsula.

Let's also recognize that much of zoos' conservation work involves financial contributions. WAZA, for instance, boasted in 2015 that zoos and aquariums raise roughly $350 million for wildlife conservation every year. However, let's also recognize that this is a remarkably small portion of what conservation work requires. Consider this 2011 estimate—though it's a bit old now, the numbers haven't changed dramatically since then—which discusses the cost of conservation:

> World governments have committed to halting human-induced extinctions and safeguarding important sites for biodiversity by 2020, but the financial costs of meeting these targets are largely unknown. We estimate the cost of reducing the extinction risk of all globally threatened bird species . . . to be U.S. $0.875 to $1.23 billion annually over the next decade. . . . Incorporating threatened nonavian species increases this total to U.S. $3.41 to $4.76 billion annually. We estimate that protecting and effectively managing all terrestrial sites of global avian conservation significance [and global conservation significance for other taxa] increases this to U.S. $76.1 billion annually.
>
> (McCarthy et al. 2012, 946)

It may be the case that every bit helps, but $350 million is less than half of 1% of the $76 billion that this estimate suggests is required. There is a real worry, then, that zoos and aquariums are fighting a losing battle, one that requires vastly more resources than they can possibly secure.

In sum, then, even if we grant that zoos are correct to see species preservation as being of chief importance, we might still criticize zoos for not doing all that much to advance species preservation. The accusation here isn't that zoos aren't even trying, although that's true of some. For the most part, though, many zoos are genuinely doing their best. But their best may not be good enough.

Zoos' Educational Mission

All that said, it may not be fair to assess the conservation efforts of zoos solely—or even primarily—based on their *direct* contributions to preserving species. After all, zoos have an indirect strategy as well: education. If people can come to think and feel differently about wildlife and conservation work as a result of visiting zoos, then perhaps they will vote differently, or donate money they wouldn't otherwise, or engage in other activities that, we hope, improve the lives of nonhuman animals. However, some recent reviews of the literature aren't terribly encouraging on this front. Nygren and Ojalammi, for instance, take stock of a decade of empirical research into the educational impacts of zoos and conclude that "the overall evidence that the visitors learn about conservation and biodiversity, and even more importantly, that this learning results in behavioral changes, remains quite weak" (2018). In part, this is because there are methodological disagreements. For instance, researchers don't see eye to eye about which changes in visitors ought to be measured, making it difficult to aggregate results across studies. As they point out, for instance, different researchers have focused on different changes that zoos might try to effect in their visitors. Unfortunately, though, it isn't clear what the relationships are between the outcomes that people have studied, such as "pro-environment sentiment," "conservation ethos," "conservation intentions," "conservation mindedness," "conservation caring," "conservation attitudes and behavior," "environmental intentions," and "biodiversity literacy." Moreover, most studies just look at zoo visitors by themselves, as opposed to comparing zoo visitors with people who don't attend them. Without a control group, it's hard to know whether any apparent effects are genuine.

However, the deeper issue is that the vast majority of people simply visit zoos rather than take tours or participate in classroom-style learning, and they visit primarily for entertainment rather than education. Godinez and Fernandez (2019) essentially show that these unstructured visits to zoos have very little impact compared to repeated visits that involve structured educational activities. While zoo educational programs can make a difference, especially for those who are already conservation-minded, zoos as a whole don't seem to have much impact, and it's hard to get excited about the impact they do have. Smith et al. (2008), for instance, assessed the impact of visiting a zoo by determining how frequently people report recycling paper for the sake of hawk conservation. There are, of course, connections between resource use and hawk habitats, but it's hard to believe that this is the kind of behavior that zoos were hoping to promote.

What's more, there is entirely unsurprising evidence that people are much more likely to be interested in conservation activities that are directed toward species with which they've connected at the zoo, which results in a strong bias toward "charismatic" species—that is, the kind of animals we find cute, or awe inspiring, or what have you. However, these are also the species for which it's the least difficult to generate support via other means. Moss et al. ran a series of conservation workshops in schools for 7- to 11-year-olds, finding that participation "correlated with a positive, measurable and statistically significant impact in the student learners, particularly in terms of conservation-related knowledge but also student attitude to conservation and zoo-related issues" (2017, 33). So, it doesn't look like actually visiting zoos is necessary to yield these kinds of effects.

In fact, it doesn't look like we need anything so expensive or time-consuming. For instance, the literature on nature documentaries seems to show many of the same effects to be produced by showing people well-made films, and a recent review found that many different kinds of images of animals "can have positive effects on people's attitudes to animals, altering their emotional responses and willingness to protect them" (Thomas-Walters et al. 2020, 1138). Indeed, some related research seems to show impacts that are much larger than anything that zoos report. Jacobsen (2011), for instance, assessed whether Al Gore's *Inconvenient Truth* documentary led to an increase in people buying carbon offsets, finding that in the first two months after it was released, there was a 50% increase in offset purchases within a ten-mile radius of movie theaters that were playing it. Admittedly, the increase didn't last—it was back to baseline after a year—but that's still a significant effect. If a good conservation documentary could do anything similar, it would be remarkable.

Let's take stock. While the staff at zoos are genuinely concerned about the welfare of the animals under their care, it remains the case that zoos aren't in the business of maximizing welfare per se; they are willing to make trade-offs for the sake of conservation goals. The most charitable explanation for this is that they are primarily concerned with preserving species.[2] If so, then zoos had better be correct to value animals first and foremost as instances of species rather than as individuals. What's more, they had better be achieving their stated conservation aims. So far, we've challenged both ideas: there are problems, morally speaking, with the idea that species matter more than individuals, and it's unclear that zoos are doing as much as they claim to advance the cause of species. What's more, the accomplishments for which they do deserve credit—some successful species reintroductions, for instance, and some educational work—don't obviously justify the sheer number of animals kept in captivity. In principle, anyway, much of the conservation work could be done through universities rather than zoos, and it's possible that many of the educational outcomes could be achieved via other strategies, including options as simple as having people view documentaries. So, if we assume that we shouldn't permanently confine animals without good reason, then we have cause to doubt that zoos have met their burden.

Of course, we might not be convinced that confinement per se is bad for animals, or at least not for all animals. (It's one thing to confine toads; it's another to confine orcas.) And even if we *do* think that confinement itself is bad for many animals, we might not think that it's nearly as bad for animals as life in the wild, as discussed in Chapter 8. So, we may conclude that it's permissible for zoos to confine animals *not for any of the reasons they cite*, but because life in the wild is difficult enough that confinement in zoos is preferable.[3] However, *if* life in the wild is so bad that animals are better off in confinement, then this also suggests that zoos are acting objectionably insofar as they try to preserve species in the wild—since that amounts to trying to make more animals suffer all the wild's challenges. The upshot is that zoos appear to be in an uncomfortable moral predicament. On the one hand, *their* reasons for confining animals aren't very compelling. On the other, *better* reasons for confining animals are in tension with one of their central aims—namely, preserving species in the wild.

Objections to Zoos

It's also important to recognize that zoos are vulnerable to challenges from some of the moral theories that we discussed earlier (see Chapter 5). There is, for instance, a decent utilitarian argument against zoos. Consider the animals harmed to feed zoo animals. Once we tally up all their suffering, it's likely that the scales tip in favor of abolishing keeping predators on display. Moreover, utilitarians might argue that zoos are incompatible with the long-term goal of reducing speciesism. Remember: utilitarianism isn't just concerned with the consequences over the next few days, weeks, or years; instead, utilitarianism is concerned with the consequences as far out as there are consequences. If it turns out that having zoos supports the idea that animals are, simply by virtue of being animals, less valuable than human beings, then zoos support speciesism. Perhaps they do support that it, since they appear to be based on the assumption that it's acceptable to privilege species preservation over the good for individual animals. Given that we reject similar views about human beings, this sounds like a speciesist arrangement. And if persistence of speciesism results in lower net utility because it allows us to continue treating animals poorly, then zoos can be criticized on this basis.

Things are no better, and arguably worse, if we approach things from a Kantian perspective. From that angle, the fundamental wrong is treating individuals as means to our ends, ignoring their interests along the way. As we saw at the outset, though, by privileging species over individuals, zoos do exactly that. Karen Emmerman nicely points out that there are also powerful ecofeminist objections. She argues that it's important to highlight:

> the immorality of separating bonded pairs, social groups, and families through inter-zoo transfers and captive breeding programs. As theorists who consider relationships of love and care central to moral life, ecofeminists strongly object to the ways zooed animals' relationships with their conspecifics are regularly broken up to serve zoos' interests.
>
> (Emmerman 2020, 384)

We could go on, but this is enough to make the basic point. The positive case for zoos is difficult to make, and there are some powerful arguments against their continuation. We might conclude, on that basis, that abolition is the way forward: we should have a world without zoos.

A World Without Zoos?

I'm not sure that a world without zoos would be better than the status quo. For the sake of argument, though, let's just consider what abolishing zoos might mean for the animals currently in captivity.

For many of the animals currently in captivity, simply releasing them into the wild, even in their native range, might just be a death sentence. The carnivores have never had to hunt; the plant eaters have never had to avoid predators. None of them have had to learn how to avoid disease vectors and parasites. So, without extensive training for reentry into the wild, which simply may not be possible for many animals, we shouldn't be confident that they would flourish. Moreover, it's worth remembering that releasing these animals simply means putting them in competition with the animals already in those ecosystems, which means increasing the pressures on animals who already face an enormous number of threats to their welfare. (For more on this, see Chapter 4.)

A better plan may be to move animals to sanctuaries, where the animals are free to roam while still being protected from human interference. It's worth recognizing, however, that there are two very different kinds of sanctuaries. One sort of sanctuary is essentially a fenced wild space. However, this leaves you with the problem of feeding the carnivores. If all the animals from one zoo go to a single space, the lions will flourish (for a time) while the other species are decimated. And if you don't have predators, then you face different challenges. Consider Oostvaardersplassen, a Dutch animal preserve that occupies 15,000 acres about half an hour from Amsterdam. Dutch biologists tried to re-create the ecosystem that would have been there thousands of years ago, stocking it with cattle, red deer, horses, foxes, geese, and other wildlife. After a few mild winters, however, the populations of these animals exploded, vastly outstripping the available food supplies. As a result, thousands of animals starved, and sharpshooters had to go in and cull more than half the population. Of course, this problem could be avoided in a sanctuary for former zoo animals by universal reproductive control—that is, if every animal were spayed or neutered. However, if we think that animals have a right to sexual autonomy, a kind of right to sexual self-determination, then spaying and neutering would violate that right.[4] In any case, this creates new welfare problems, as you now have an increasingly lonely environment for elderly animals, as animals steadily die off due to disease, parasites, predators who find their way past the fences, and so on. (On that note, it's worth remembering that one of the few advantages of zoo life is veterinary care; animals in an unmanaged sanctuary will suffer without it.)

There are problems, then, for unmanaged sanctuaries. So, we might opt instead for managed sanctuaries, as are now common for animals who were previously on farms. There, the animals will be provided with food, shelter, and medical care, but they will have dramatically more room and much less human contact overall. This would be enormously expensive, and it's unclear how it could possibly be funded. But even if that problem were solved, these facilities would still face the problem of feeding the carnivores. How, exactly, is it just to liberate some animals on the backs—or, rather, with the backs—of others?

Regulating and Improving Zoos

I'm not claiming that there is no best-of-a-bad-lot option here. However, rather than try to figure out which of these suboptimal plans is the least objectionable, let's just acknowledge that zoos aren't going away anytime soon. So while it's valuable to consider the shape of a world without zoos, we also need to consider how to improve the institutions we have, whatever their problems. So, let's set aside the issue of abolition and consider the status quo. What would make it better?

Let's start with the basics. Right now, zoos in the United States are regulated under the Animal Welfare Act (AWA). Congress gave the U.S. Department of Agriculture (USDA) the job of enforcing the AWA, a task carried out by one of the agencies within it: namely, the Animal and Plant Health Inspection Service (APHIS). One of APHIS's jobs is to determine who needs "exhibitor certification," that is, permission from APHIS to display animals for the public. Here's the answer:

> Individuals or businesses with warm-blooded animals that are on display, perform for the public, or are used in educational presentations must be licensed as exhibitors with APHIS. Licensed exhibitors include circuses, zoos, educational displays, petting farms/zoos, animal acts, wildlife parks, marine mammal parks, and some sanctuaries. The animals involved in the exhibition may include domestic and exotic animal species.
>
> ("Regulated Businesses")

Why only warm-blooded animals? As discussed in Chapter 9, the AWA isn't a general piece of animal welfare legislation; it only applies to warm-blooded animals, and not even all of those—it exempts, for instance, animals who are raised for food. So, the AWA doesn't protect many animals who are kept in captivity and displayed to the public—including snakes, lizards, crocodiles, and turtles—which means that APHIS doesn't police their activities. As a result, there is no government entity that keeps track of how many reptile houses, serpentariums, and alligator farms there are or how they treat their animals.

A first step would be to close this loophole in the AWA. Granted, APHIS's oversight doesn't make everything marvelous for animals, but it does provide a legal recourse against the worst offenders. Moreover, we might think that the lack of legal recognition is itself a moral problem, even if there weren't welfare issues to worry about. There are two reasons to object to a legal regime that doesn't recognize all nonhuman animals as deserving some basic consideration. First, the law shouldn't be arbitrary, and there is no reason to draw a line between warm-blooded and cold-blooded animals: if the former deserve legal protection, then so do the latter. Second, there's an expressive concern. Although there are good reasons not to equate the law with morality, it remains the case that people use the law as moral cover: if something is legal, then it can't be *that* bad. By not regulating the captivity and care of cold-blooded animals, U.S. law communicates that we don't need to worry about those animals nearly as much, if at all. Now, it would be too much to ask of the law that it only ever communicate the truth; the law can't be blamed for the way it's misused by the public. However, if the law is arbitrary—covering some species but not others, and not for any good reason—then this expressive failure is an additional moral problem. Lawmakers can't say that people are misusing the law, because the law is written to be misused. The arbitrariness is there because of the biases of (former, though also probably current) lawmakers against certain kinds of animals.

Let's suppose that, by some miracle, we were able to close this loophole in the AWA and get protection for cold-blood animals. The next step would be to recognize that the AWA is not a guide to best practices; rather, it sets certain bare minimum standards that need to be met. Here are some examples of the kinds of standards to which APHIS holds exhibitors:

- Primary Enclosures—Animals must be housed in structurally sound enclosures that are in good repair and meet APHIS's minimum space requirements. The floors must protect the animals from injury. The cages must be dry and clean and allow animals easy access to food and water.
- Feeding and Watering—Animals must be provided with nutritious, palatable food that is free from contamination, properly stored, and served in a clean receptacle. Potable water must be made available twice daily for 1 hour if it is not available all the time.
- Outdoor Shelter—Animals must be protected from sunlight, precipitation, and extreme temperatures.
- Adequate Veterinary Care—Programs of disease control and prevention, euthanasia, and veterinary care must be established and maintained under the supervision and assistance of a veterinarian. A caretaker also must observe the animals daily.

("Pre-License")

These are a fine start, but they still leave much to be desired. APHIS sets very modest minimum enclosure sizes.[5] Although APHIS recommends enrichment, it doesn't require it, meaning that animals can, in principle, occupy otherwise-empty enclosures assuming that other standards are met. APHIS requires that food be "palatable," not desirable. APHIS provides minimal guidance about species-specific needs. And so on.

By contrast, the AZA publishes detailed Animal Care Manuals for many species. The one for jaguars, for instance, says that "to the fullest extent possible, management under human care should emulate circumstances an animal might encounter in nature" and then goes on to provide pages of information about jaguars' natural environment (*Jaguar Care*). This is characteristic of AZA recommendations, which are always indexed to the relevant species. As opposed to providing an acceptable temperature range for enclosures across all species, the AZA provides species-specific recommendations. It insists that enclosures meet the psychological needs of animals. It demands that animals be kept in groups that meet their social needs.

That said, the vast majority of organizations with animal exhibitor licenses in the United States—which, to the average person, are just zoos—lack AZA accreditation. In 2018, there were 2,640 exhibitors in the United States. This number includes AZA-accredited zoos, but there are no more than 136 of those ("Aquarium Statistics"). In the United States, anyway, most animal exhibitors are only bound by the standards that APHIS specifies. If we really wanted to improve things for animals, we would look for ways to make AZA accreditation the standard, rather than the exception, in the current industry. Ideally, this would involve amending the AWA so that the AZA standards have the force of law. Short of that, it would be helpful to have financial incentives. At present, it costs $10 to apply for a license to exhibit animals, and the most expensive license fee (determined, essentially, by how much business the organization does) is only $750. (The cheapest is just $30.) So we might imagine an arrangement where exhibitor licenses cost dramatically more, and audits are much more involved, unless organizations demonstrate that they can and will treat their animals as the AZA recommends. And minimally, it would be good to have better enforcement of the standards currently on the books (or, rather, better enforcement of less arbitrary versions of those standards, which should be extended to cover cold-blooded species). As it is, APHIS is only required to inspect animal exhibition facilities once every three years or if there's a complaint. And given the public's lack of knowledge about the factors affecting animal welfare, we should expect far fewer complaints than could be submitted.

While we're dreaming, let's go one step further. Some zoological organizations are quite explicit about the way they think about the trade-offs involved between animal welfare and conservation. WAZA, for instance, actually provides a decision schema for making these judgments, as seen in Figure 11.1.

Two observations about this image. First, it captures the idea that there are thresholds: zoos shouldn't allow welfare to drop below some minimum standards, and they should only pursue conservation goals above some level of importance. Second, it captures the idea that as a zoo is less and less able to provide good welfare for the members of a particular species, the importance of the conservation goal ought to increase. That is, it takes a weighty conservation goal to justify relatively low animal welfare; as animal welfare increases, though, less significant conservation goals can justify keeping animals in captivity.

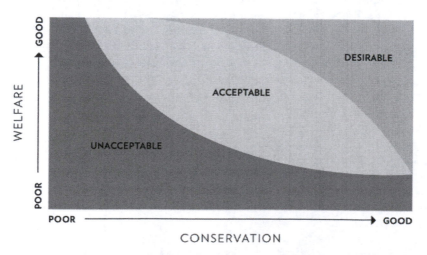

Figure 11.1 A decision schema for considering the intersection between the separate dimensions of animal welfare and conservation.

Source: (Mellor et al. 2015, 54).

However, this decision matrix is ambiguous, allowing for two distinct interpretations. On one interpretation, we count the benefits of captivity against the costs. This means comparing, on the one hand, the benefits of medical care, easily accessible food, and freedom from predation against the costs of having a small enclosure (when compared to the terrain that the animal would otherwise like to explore) without much novel stimulation (boredom is bad for animals too). This makes it much easier to justify keeping animals in captivity, because conservation goals don't need to be as pressing if we can offset the welfare costs with corresponding welfare benefits. On another interpretation, though, we *only* count the costs of captivity. The question becomes: Is the conservation goal important enough to justify imposing the cost of captivity on this animal, regardless of any benefits the animal may receive? This obviously makes it harder to justify keeping animals in captivity. The first interpretation allows zoos to say, "We aren't *only* harming animals; indeed, we're probably benefitting them on net, and the good we do for them is relevant to justifying their captivity." The second interpretation forces zoos to say, "We *are* harming animals, and we had better be doing enough conservation-wise to make that harm acceptable." I want to suggest that the second interpretation is the one that zoos should adopt, largely as a check against their impulse to place too much weight on species over individuals.

For the sake of having a concrete example of these two decision procedures in action, let's now return once more to the Central Park Zoo, which, as of this writing, displays three California sea lions. In 1975, there were only 90,000 of them on the California coast; by 2008, however, their population has more than tripled, fully rebounding thanks to the protections provided by the Marine Mammal Protection Act (MMPA). And as a result, they are no longer considered endangered. In and of itself, that doesn't necessarily mean that, by WAZA's standards, California sea lions shouldn't be displayed. There could be other reasons why those standards would permit their captivity. However, the fact that the population has fully rebounded does suggest that the welfare of those sea lions should be quite high if they are to be held captive.

Is their welfare quite high? I'm not sure. Those sea lions are in the center of the zoo, visible from all sides, in a space that's dramatically smaller and more uniform than the one they would range over in the wild. These seem like costs of confinement. If we interpret the decision matrix in the first of the two ways we outlined, the way that says, "But remember the benefits!," then we should next observe that the sea lions are fed and receive veterinary care. They are free from the threat of predation. They have formed relationships with members of the zoo staff. What's more, the zoo's website indicates that at least one of them was "rescued," and so on the assumption that the alternative was death, a life in captivity may have been best for her specifically.

I worry, though, that this interpretation of the matrix makes it too easy to allow our own values to take precedence, to suppose we know—when it's controversial—that animal autonomy isn't that important. Yes, one of the sea lions was "rescued." But was rehabilitation an option? Could she have been released? Was the decision not to release her made for her sake? Another sea lion in the enclosure was "born in the

Bronx" (*Central Park* "California"), no doubt at the Bronx Zoo. If she was going to be separated from her family anyway, why wasn't she released? If zoos were to employ the second interpretation of the decision matrix—the one that only weighs the importance of the conservation goal against the costs to animals—it seems less likely that the Central Park Zoo could justify permanently confining these sea lions. And no doubt something similar is true for many other animals in many other zoos.

I readily admit: it's unclear to me whether, on balance, these particular sea lions are best off in captivity. This is because I have lingering worries about the suffering of wild animals in their natural environments; again, see Chapter 8. Still, I tend to think that we should set up our decision-making so that it favors liberty over confinement. Things would be better for animals in zoos if the AWA had fewer loopholes, and better still if AZA-style standards were the norm. Finally, I think things would be better if the burden of justification were higher for keeping sentient beings in captivity. We shouldn't be too quick to trust ourselves to make decisions that are in the best interests of animals.

Zoos and You

Having said all that, let's close with a more personal question. Should you go to zoos? Is it okay to make a day of it with your family?

We could tackle this question the same way that we tackled questions about the ethics of purchasing and consuming animal products in Chapter 7. Then, we might talk for a while about whether your actions make a difference, and if so, the difference they make. Or we might discuss whether going to zoos constitutes supporting unjust practices. And there are interesting issues to explore here. For example, while your dollars might be helping to prop up zoos, they are also helping to ensure that animals have all the resources they need. What's greater when you buy a ticket to the zoo: your impact on the continuation of that zoo or your impact on the welfare of individual animals? That, no doubt, is a complex empirical question, and it would take some work to sort it out. Likewise, even if we think that zoos are unjust institutions and actively engage in various unjust practices, it's also true that they materially aid animals both within their walls and in the wild. When, if ever, is it permissible to support unjust institutions that also do good things, especially good things that no one else is well-positioned to do?

I confess, however, that I don't find these questions terribly interesting. And that's probably because my relationship to zoos is just so different from my relationship to animal products. Hence, while we can think about them in the same way—as consumer ethics issues—they certainly don't feel the same. I face questions about what to eat regardless of who I am, regardless of where I am. But not so with zoos. Those questions come up because I'm a dad. So in what remains, I'm going to set aside the consumer ethics angle, focusing on a more relational one.

As I write this, my children are five and ten years old. As you might imagine, there are lots of conversations about animals in my house. My kids know my concerns about the way animals are treated; they understand that I have objections to many aspects of the status quo. And to different degrees, they sympathize with those concerns and objections. However, they still get excited by the idea of going to the zoo or an aquarium, and when the permission slip comes home to go on a field trip, they really want me to sign it. Zoos, for them, still represent the opportunity *to be in the presence of wild animals*—the ones they can usually only see in books and on nature documentaries. That is overwhelmingly appealing to them, even if cages aren't.

I think there is something wonderful about their desire to be in the presence of animals, wild or otherwise. I want my children to be the kind of people who take delight in recognizing that animals are looking back at them, that these are individuals who aren't just watched, but watch. These are beings who feel and want things, just like my kids. So, I want to cultivate their impulse to be near animals, not quash it. Moreover, I don't really blame them for wanting to be near wild animals. Children are surrounded by depictions of wild animals: the artwork on their walls, the characters in their stories, the subjects of the shows they watch. And as a result, my children have forgotten more about Komodo dragons and leopards than I will ever know about them. *Of course* they want to see these animals.

So it seems to me that the real question is: When I allow my children to go to zoos, or take them myself, how should I do it? Because rightly or wrongly, those trips will take place from time to time. What, then, would make them better? What would make them worse?

I don't have crisp answers here. What I can say, however, is this. When I have taken my children to zoos, I've mourned for a lemur hiding in the upper reaches of his enclosure. I've looked at a turtle in a tiny terrarium, and I've felt the weight of our collective callousness, our inhumanity. And I've tried to communicate some of that to my kids without crushing them:

> *He's amazing, isn't he? Do you see his eyes? Do you see how he's following us? He knows we're here. What do you think it's like, looking out from that cage? What do you think he thinks?*
>
> *Where do you think he came from? How do you think he got here? The sign here says that they're all boys. Where's their mother? I wonder if they miss each other.*
>
> *You're right: he's so strong. And beautiful. And probably fast. Not much room to run, though. Wish he had more.*
>
> *Who do you want to see next? Isn't it crazy that we can walk a few steps and see so many different animals? Sometimes I can't really believe it. What do you think it's like, being a lion who can see a wolf on the other side of the path?*

I'm not saying that having these conversations makes it morally permissible to visit zoos. I am saying, however, that if we're going to visit zoos with our children, it seems important to help them take up the perspective of the individuals they see. In so doing, we give them the opportunity to question the institution that makes that seeing possible, that exposes animals to their stares. Moral education is difficult, and I'll be the last to say that I make good choices about how best to raise my kids. Still, if we allow our children to enjoy things to which we object, we should also give them the tools to criticize those things—and us—down the line. Our hands won't be clean, but it's better than nothing.

Further Reading

1996. *Ethics on the Ark*. Edited by Bryan G. Norton, Michael Hutchins, Elizabeth F. Stevens, and Terry L. Maple. Washington, DC: Smithsonian Institution Press.

Braverman, Irus. 2013. *Zooland: The Institution of Captivity*. Stanford: Stanford University Press.

Gray, Jenny. 2017. *Zoo Ethics: The Challenges of Compassionate Conservation*. Ithaca: Cornell University Press.

Jamieson, Dale. 2003. "Against Zoos." In *Morality's Progress: Essays on Humans, Other Animals, and the Rest of Nature*, 166–175. Oxford: Oxford University Press.

Jamieson, Dale. 2003. "Zoos Revisited." In *Morality's Progress: Essays on Humans, Other Animals, and the Rest of Nature*, 176–189. Oxford: Oxford University Press.

Notes

1. Inbreeding often results in unhealthy animals that can't be bred to continue the species. So, while it might look as though being concerned with health is essentially equivalent to being concerned with individual well-being, this isn't necessarily the case. Obviously, zoo staff do care about individual well-being to some degree or other. The point is just that we should understand the significance of "health" in this context, where it isn't just about preventing some particular individual from experiencing discomfort, but about ensuring that a sufficient number of individuals can propagate the species.

2. The uncharitable explanation: zoos are, first and foremost, part of the entertainment industry, and unusual animals are good for business.

3. Of course, the "nature is awful" defense of zoos only works for animals who are captured and brought to zoos, not animals bred in captivity. The ethics of breeding animals is a separate moral issue.

4. See David Boonin (2011).

5. The AWA doesn't provide many species-specific definitions apart from cats and dogs. All it says is that "enclosures shall be constructed and maintained so as to provide sufficient space to allow each animal to make normal postural and social adjustments with adequate freedom of movement." In the case of cats, however, this is actually defined to mean 6 ft.^{3} (and 3 ft.^{2} of floor space). So, we shouldn't make too much of "sufficient space" here.

References

2015. *Committing to Conservation: The World Zoo and Aquarium Conservation Strategy*. Edited by Rick Barongi, Fiona A. Fisken, Martha Parker, and Markus Gusset. Gland: WAZA Executive Office.

2016. *Jaguar Care Manual*. Silver Spring, MD: Association of Zoos and Aquariums. https://assets.speakcdn.com/assets/2332/jaguar_care_manual_2016.pdf.

"About San Diego Zoo Global." *San Diego Zoo*. https://zoo.sandiegozoo.org/about/about-san-diego-zoo.

"California Sea Lion." *Central Park*. www.centralpark.com/things-to-do/central-park-zoo/california-sea-lion/.

Boonin, David. 2011. "Robbing PETA to Spay Paul—Do Animal Rights Include Reproductive Rights." *Between the Species* 13(3). https://doi.org/10.15368/bts.2003v13n3.1.

Emmerman, Karen. 2020. "Moral Arguments Against Zoos." In *The Routlege Handbook of Animal Ethics*, edited by Bob Fischer, 381–393. New York: Routledge.

Godinez, Andrea M., and Eduardo J. Fernandez. 2019. "What is the Zoo Experience? How Zoos Impact a Visitor's Behaviors, Perceptions, and Conservation Efforts." *Frontiers in Psychology* 10: 1746. https://doi.org/10.3389/fpsyg.2019.01746.

Groch, Sherryn. 2015. "WAZA backs German Zoo Convicted of Animal Rights Violation." *Action for Dolphins*, April 2. https://blog.afd.org.au/uncategorized/waza-backs-german-zoo-convicted-of-animal-rights-violation/.

Hance, Analysis Jeremy. 2010. "Guilty Verdict Over Euthanizing Tigers in Germany Touches Off Debate about Role of Zoos." *Mongabay*, August 11. https://news.mongabay.com/2010/08/guilty-verdict-over-euthanizing-tigers-in-germany-touches-off-debate-about-role-of-zoos/.

Jacobsen, G. 2011. "The Al Gore Effect: An Inconvenient Truth and Voluntary Carbon Offsets." *Journal of Environmental Economics and Management* 61: 67–78.

McCarthy, Donald P., Paul F. Donald, Jörn P.W. Scharlemann, Graeme M. Buchanan, Andrew Balmford, Jonathan M.H. Green, Leon A. Bennun, Neil D. Burgess, Lincoln D.C. Fishpool, Stephen T. Garnett, David L. Leonard, Richard F. Maloney, Paul Morling, H. Martin Schaefer, Andy Symes, David A. Wiedenfeld, Stuart H.M. Butchart. 2012. "Financial Costs of Meeting Global Biodiversity Conservation Targets: Current Spending and Unmet Needs." *Science* 338(6109): 946–949. https://doi.org/10.1126/science.1229803.

Mellor, D.J., S. Hunt, and M. Gusset (eds.). 2015. *Caring for Wildlife: The World Zoo and Aquarium Animal Welfare Strategy*. Gland: WAZA Executive Office.

Moss, Andrew, Carrie Littlehales, Anya Moon, Charlotte Smith, and Chris Sainsbury. 2017. "Measuring the Impact of an In-School Zoo Education Programme." *Journal of Zoo and Aquarium Research* 5(1): 33–37.

Nygren, Nina V., and Sanna Ojalammi. 2018. "Conservation Education in Zoos: A Literature Review." *Trace: Finnish Journal for Human-Animal Studies* 4. https://doi.org/10.23984/fjhas.66540.

"Pre-License Application Package: Class C- Exhibitors." *USDA*. www.aphis.usda.gov/animal_welfare/downloads/forms/APHIS_Form_7003-7003A_Class-C_AppKit.pdf.

"Regulated Businesses (Licensing and Registration)." *USDA*. www.aphis.usda.gov/aphis/ourfocus/animalwelfare/SA_Regulated_Businesses.

Smith, L., S. Broad, and B. Weiler. 2008. "A Closer Examination of the Impact of Zoo Visits on Visitor Behaviour." *Journal of Sustainable Tourism* 16(5): 544–562.

"Species Survival Plan Programs." *Association of Zoos & Aquariums*. www.aza.org/species-survival-plan-programs.

Thomas-Walters, L., C. McNulty, and D. Veríssimo. 2020. "A Scoping Review into the Impact of Animal Imagery on Pro-environmental Outcomes." *Ambio* 49: 1135–1145. https://doi.org/10.1007/s13280-019-01271-1.

Tidière, Morgane, Jean-Michel Gaillard, Vérane Berger, Dennis W.H. Müller, Laurie Bingaman Lackey, Olivier Gimenez, Marcus Class, and Jean-François Lemaître. 2016. "Comparative Analyses of Longevity and Senescence Reveal Variable Survival Benefits of Living in Zoos across Mammals." *Scientific Reports* 6. https://doi.org/10.1038/srep36361.

12 Pests

OVERVIEW

Humans kill an untold number of animals each year because they view those animals as "pests." This chapter takes a deep dive into the ethics of killing rodents as pests by assessing the common reasons given for their extermination. This involves estimating rodent populations, calculating the relative value of human and nonhuman lives, and mapping out some different ways of thinking about rights. In addition, the chapter looks at nonlethal ways of trying to manage rodent populations, none of which seem particularly promising. We wrap up with some thoughts about the prospects for resolving the difficult issues that the chapter raises.

When rats come across a new food source, they don't consume as much they can. Instead, they nibble a bit, waiting to see whether it makes them sick. Or they watch others nibble, checking for ill effects. This behavior is obviously adaptive; it protects rats from poisons and pathogens. Or, at least, it protected rats from the poisons and pathogens that were common in their evolutionary history, where a short wait tended to reveal whether a food source was contaminated.

However, the "nibble and wait" strategy isn't as reliable as it once was. This is because those who want to manage rat populations—a euphemism for "kill as many rats as possible"—use slow-acting poisons. Anticoagulants are particularly popular, thinning the blood and eventually causing fatal hemorrhages. A nibble isn't enough to have this effect; it takes some time for rats to build up the necessary concentration of the poison in their systems. Once they do, though, death is slow and painful, taking anywhere from 5 to 15 days. Rats' lungs fill up with blood, making it difficult to breathe. Their kidneys shut down, which causes fatigue, confusion, and nausea. They bleed throughout their intestinal tract, leading to persistent bloody diarrhea. They bleed into their body cavity, making all motion painful. It isn't a nice way to go.

It is, however, a cost-effective way to kill. Anticoagulants are cheap, and in the 1990s, they were used for roughly 95% of rat control efforts in the United States.

Other methods have shifted that percentage down a bit—dry ice in burrows, which asphyxiates rats, and traps that ultimately drown them in alcohol, among many other less common strategies—but anticoagulants remain enormously popular, killing millions upon millions of rats each year.

Why are people so determined to kill rats? There are essentially three reasons. First, people don't *like* being around rats. They are widely seen as filthy and disgusting, and a 2016 study found that people are more depressed as a result of being around rats than they are due to being around crime.

Second, rats are expensive. They chew through wires, causing power, phone, and Internet outages—and, on occasion, fires.[1] Rodents also contaminate food, and one estimate from the 1980s suggested that rodents cost human beings some $300 billion in food losses annually. Rodents also burrow under sidewalks and roads, which can cause them to collapse.

Third, rats are disease vectors, carrying dozens of diseases that they can transmit to both humans and domesticated animals. They are a reservoir for *Leptospira*, a genus of bacteria that causes leptospirosis. Leptospirosis typically isn't fatal, but in developing countries, it kills roughly 10% of those who contract it, causing kidney and liver failure, pulmonary distress, cardiovascular irregularities, and other serious symptoms. It's a particular threat in slums, where people are at greater risk of coming into direct or indirect contact with rat feces (where the indirect contact is often via water contamination).

There are some obvious questions to ask. Are these good reasons to kill rats? If so, are they good reasons to kill so *many* rats? If so, are they good reasons to kill rats *using standard methods*?

As we explore these questions, we'll be thinking through a way we categorize nonhuman animals that rarely gets much attention: namely, as pests. Pests are just those animals who have undesirable effects on humans (or, more commonly, things of concern to humans), and animals categorized this way are typically seen as "to be eliminated." And as Peter Singer pointed out in *Animal Liberation*,

> the very word "pest" seems to exclude any concern for the animals themselves. But the classification "pest" is our own, and a rabbit that is a pest is as capable of suffering, and as deserving of consideration, as a white rabbit who is a beloved companion animal.
>
> (1999, 233)

So, this classification needs to be examined. While this chapter takes a deep dive into one particular "pest," rats are hardly alone in being seen as problems; the members of any species can, in the right context, be categorized as pests. In Florida, people are determined to kill iguanas; in Maryland and Delaware, there are systematic efforts to eradicate nutria; throughout the southeastern United States, feral hogs are the targets. And while we have to consider each case on its own merits—the impacts of Asian carp in the Mississippi River are different from those associated with the brown tree snake in Guam—we can still learn something about the kinds of arguments that are offered, and their strength, by zeroing in on rats. Indeed, we need to zero in, because otherwise it's difficult to appreciate the complexities behind the charges that people level at pest species. So, that's exactly what we'll do.

Three Good Reasons to Kill Rats?

Let's begin by thinking more carefully about the three main concerns about rats: disgust, expense, and disease. More generally, these are concerns about psychological well-being, property, and physical health. Let's take them in turn.

Psychological Well-being

Psychological well-being has many dimensions, some more significant than others. It includes, for instance, freedom from very deep fears. My grandmother had a paralyzing phobia of mice: she would faint in terror when she saw one in the house. Given that impact on her psyche, she had a fairly strong reason not to want mice around. And, of course, we usually aren't obliged to share our living spaces with anyone, and certainly not with individuals we find terrifying; so, it seems fine for her to exclude rodents from her living space. Fear matters, and it certainly justifies distancing yourself from the individual of whom you are afraid.

However, it's also true that it usually isn't okay to kill someone because you find him terrifying. Fear isn't a blank check. We need to consider whether your fear is reasonable, whether it's grounded in a genuine threat. This, of course, is familiar from so many recent discussions of police violence. Yes, sometimes the police are genuinely afraid of the individuals they encounter. However, if the police are afraid as a result of prejudice, ignorance, or something equally objectionable, then their fear doesn't justify their use of force. The claim here, of course, is *not* that killing a rat is equivalent to a police officer using unwarranted lethal force. Instead, the point is just that in our interactions with other humans, it matters whether threats are real, not simply whether they are perceived. So, unless things are very different when it comes to nonhuman animals, whether it's okay to kill rats depends on how likely it is that they can make you worse off. Fear itself—absent a corresponding threat—isn't much of a reason to end their lives.

Is there any reason to think that things are very different when it comes to nonhuman animals? Things would probably be very different if animal lives had almost no value; then, it wouldn't be very important to protect them with norms like, "Don't kill out of fear alone." Things would also be very different if death isn't bad for animals. Then, while it would be important not to cause them to suffer, it would be fine to end their lives. But even if the lives of nonhuman animals are less important than those of human beings, there's no reason to think that they are completely insignificant (see Chapter 2). And while death may not be as bad for animals as it is for human beings, it's far from obvious that it isn't bad for them at all.[2] (See Chapter 4.) So, fear alone doesn't seem to justify killing. And if fear doesn't, it would be surprising if other emotions and attitudes could do the trick. Fear is a particularly powerful response, and so if we can't justify killing on that basis, then we shouldn't expect distaste, discomfort, and similar feelings to make killing okay. So, we can set aside the first of the three complaints about rats, at least if offered as a justification for killing them. If "you're scary" is the only criticism we can level at rats, then we should get over it, rather than kill them as a way of maintaining our own psychological comfort.

Property Damage

In *Home Alone*, with thieves on the way, the young Kevin McCallister famously says: "This is my house; I have to defend it!" And while he might not *need* to defend his house, morally speaking, property rights do seem to *justify* some violence. Sometimes, you can use force to prevent others from damaging or stealing your belongings. Maybe that's the story with rats: we're entitled to use force against them because they're damaging our property.

"Entitled to use force" is one thing; "lethal management" is another. Was Kevin McCallister entitled to put a nail through Harry's foot to stop him from taking a TV? Was Kevin entitled to use a blowtorch on Marv's head to stop him from stealing some jewelry? Probably not; Kev should have just called the cops. (Worse movie, better ethics.) Likewise, while our property rights might justify the use of force, they probably don't justify *as much* force as we use against rats. If killing is *ever* justified to protect property, it's definitely the option of last resort, and we almost never exhaust all available options before using lethal force against rats.

So let's aside a simple property rights–based defense of killing rats. Instead, let's think more generally about how serious property damage is. Initially, anyway, we might actually think that property damage is much less significant than psychological well-being, as property loss doesn't necessarily bother anyone. If rats eat a bunch of grain that was going to be thrown out independently or chew through wires that haven't actually been used in ages, then although property is being destroyed, there is some sense in which no one is being harmed. However, there are certainly other cases where property damage puts people at real risk. If rats chew through an electrical cord and cause a fire as a result, people could be very seriously injured—or perhaps even die.

Something similar is true in more modest cases where rats cause power outages. For some people, of course, a power outage is merely an inconvenience. But there are, of course, people who depend on electricity for important things. If I rely on a medicine that has to be kept cold and my refrigerator goes out, I may well be in trouble. And, of course, there are much more indirect ways in which a power outage can be a problem. If rats make a nest in my car, chewing through wires and defecating in the air filter, then I'm on the hook for the cost of the repairs.[3] I may not have that money, and if not, these small issues have a way of snowballing. Many people have found themselves homeless thanks to such small twists of fate. A rat chews through some electrical wiring, the cost of the mechanic eats up the money that was set aside for rent, it's hard to catch up, and a crisis begins.

The problem, of course, is that it's tremendously hard to take the step from these plausible observations to some general conclusions about the appropriate way of handling rats in any given human space. Most obviously, this is because it's really hard to quantify the risks involved. If we had reliable statistics on the problems that can be directly attributed to rats and a decent method of measuring the severity of those problems, then we could make some progress. That would be enough to get a sense of the human toll. However, it wouldn't be enough to settle what we should do, not least because it wouldn't tell us how to think about the relationship between the costs that rats impose on human beings and vice versa.

It would simplify things considerably if we had a single scale that we could use to represent the costs to all parties involved. Then, given that we could get the relevant empirical information, we could make a straightforward assessment of whether humans are harmed more severely by rats than rats are harmed by humans. What's more, if we accept some form of consequentialism, then that alone may be enough to tell us what we should do.[4]

One way to do this would be to put a dollar value on the life of each rat. Then, we could look at the total amount of property damage, measured in dollars, and compare it to the total value of the rats we kill (where by "the total value of the rats we kill," we mean, "the number of rats we kill multiplied by the dollar value that we've assigned to each life"). However, there are two methodological worries here. The first worry is that this approach inclines us to count morally irrelevant costs and ignore morally important ones. For instance, they incline us to count morally irrelevant costs by counting damage to things that aren't morally important but have economic value, such as grain that would have gone to waste anyway (for whatever reason). They also lead us to ignore morally important costs, such as the risk of disease that's caused when rats chew on economically insignificant things, such as garbage. The second methodological concern is that the method is speciesist, since while there won't be much resistance to putting a dollar value on a rat's life, there often *is* resistance to putting a dollar value on a human life. There are ways of addressing both methodological issues, but it may be better to opt for a scale that more directly compares the value of human and rat lives.

Let's play things out given this second methodology. Suppose we knew, for instance, that one human life is worth 1,000 rats' lives. And suppose we knew that each rat in your home raises the absolute risk of your dying by 1%. Then, we could do some math and conclude that if the goal is to do whatever maximizes expected value, you ought to kill any rat you see. After all, any rat would be worth exactly one rat life, but we can also think about it as jeopardizing 1/100th of a human life, which is worth (according to our assumption) ten rat lives. So again, if the goal is to do whatever maximizes expected value, eliminating each rat is the right move.

Of course, we don't know that any of the assumptions in this argument are correct. We don't know the relative value of human and rat lives, we don't know the risk to which each rat exposes you, and I don't think we know that we ought to do whatever maximizes expected value. So the point isn't that you ought to go kill rats; instead, it's that if we knew all that stuff, then, given consequentialism, the ethical issues here wouldn't be so complicated. But we don't know all that stuff, so the issues are complicated indeed.

However, I do think we know lots of other things that are relevant to the conversation, at least if we set aside a narrowly consequentialist perspective. One of them is that property damage is enormously irritating, and we all certainly want to avoid it.

But another is that human beings have steadily increased their numbers, taken control of more land, and in so doing, created habitats that are fantastic for rodents. Much of the human world is full of warm, cozy nooks where rats are quite safe from (nonhuman) predators. These spots give rats access to reliable food sources, nesting materials, and all the other things that rodents enjoy. So, it's no surprise that rats occupy them, and since they aren't doing it maliciously, but are only fighting for survival, we can't exactly blame them for their choices.[5] I think that this historical perspective suggests that we should be wary of any quick defense of killing rats, but it doesn't tell us anything about the limits of what we should tolerate. We might think, for instance, of rats as innocent threats. They do indeed expose us to risks of varying severity, but since we can't hold them accountable for it, we have to think carefully about how to navigate both their innocence and the danger they pose to us. But while that's all well and good, it doesn't tell us much until we get a better sense of the threat they pose.

Human Health

With that in mind, let's turn away from property damage to the final and, presumably most important, reason that people kill rats: namely, the health risks they pose to people directly, not via property damage. What sort of risks do rats pose to human health? How serious are the threats?

Again, it's hard to find reliable data on how often people contract diseases that can be directly attributed to rodents. However, we do know that there are at least 60 diseases that rodents transmit to both human beings and domesticated animals, including leptospirosis, hemorrhagic fever, Lassa fever, and salmonella infections.[6] We've already said a bit about leptospirosis, so let's just get a quick sense of the others.

The symptoms of hemorrhagic fever include intense headaches, back and abdominal pain, fever, chills, nausea, and blurred vision. If the disease goes untreated, patients' blood pressure can drop precipitously, they can go into shock, their heart can leak blood, and they can suffer acute kidney failure. The risk of death depends on the virus that causes the fever, and one of the main strains has a mortality rate below 1%. For the other, however, 5% to 15% of patients die. There are some 200,000 cases globally each year, and roughly 24,000 people succumb to it.

Between 100,000 and 300,000 people contract Lassa fever each year. Roughly 20% have very serious symptoms, including hemorrhaging from their mouths, eyes, and nose; severe difficulty breathing; and frequent vomiting. Pregnant women who contract the disease are at risk of having their babies suffer from encephalitis, a condition where much of the brain doesn't develop. Though it's hard to know how many people die as a result of the disease, the cause of death tends to be multiorgan failure.

Salmonella infections can cause vomiting, cramps, diarrhea, fever, and headaches, among other symptoms. There are approximately 1.35 million infections in the United States each year, but only 420 deaths. In other countries, however, things are worse, and roughly 160,000 deaths are attributed to it annually. The disease is generally transmitted through food contaminated by feces, and while it's impossible to know exactly how many of these deaths are directly attributable to rats, they are surely responsible for some portion of them.

In all these cases, though the diseases can be contracted in other ways, rodent control is still considered a central part of risk management—that is, we lower the incidence of the disease by killing as many rodents as possible. There are several reasons why the United States has so few deaths that can be attributed to rodents, including a good sanitation system and fairly reliable access to healthcare. One of the reasons, though, is that Americans are very good at eradicating mice and rats. It's in poorer countries—and especially the urban centers in those countries, where rodents and people are living in close quarters, often with poor sanitation—where a relatively large number of people succumb to these illnesses. While these threats have basically been eliminated in much of the developed world, they're still quite deadly elsewhere.

If we invoke the consequentialist approach that we discussed earlier, then we can start to make progress on our ethical assessment by comparing these numbers to the number of rat deaths. Just how many rats are we killing to save human lives? Unfortunately, it's extremely difficult to answer this question, as no one keeps track of the number of rats we kill. Moreover, no one even attempts to determine how many human *deaths* should be directly attributed to rodents (among all the possible ways that people could have contracted particular diseases), much less how many human lives are saved by killing rodents. So, we just have to do our best with some rough estimates.

We can get a ballpark figure on rodent *populations*—not deaths—by looking at those cities where some estimates have been offered. In Paris, for instance, one study found that there are three rats for every two people; in New York, it's roughly one rat for every four people. In Mexico City, however, it's more like six rats per person, and in parts of central China, as many as nine per person. If we add in the few remaining data points and take the average across urban environments, we get an estimate of three rats per person in cities across the globe. Since roughly 55% of the global population lives in cities, that gives us nearly 13 billion urban rodents. Let's suppose that pest management efforts only manage to kill 1% of urban rodent populations—which is certainly far less than the real percentage, though, of course, no one knows what the real percentage is. Then, we get an estimate of 130 million annual rodent deaths in cities.

Now, how many human lives are saved as a result of these rodent deaths? Again, we don't know. However, if we look at the various diseases that the Centers for Disease Control (CDC) lists as transmitted by rats, then we discover, for instance, that hemorrhagic fever with renal syndrome kills 24,000 people a year; Lassa fever, some 5,000 a year; leptospirosis, a bit over 500,000 per year; and so on. The grand total across all such diseases is about 600,000. Now recall our assumption that pest management efforts only manage to kill 1% of urban rodent populations. Let's suppose that we're *saving* a corresponding percentage of human lives: that is, 1% of the 600,000, or roughly 6,000 human lives per year. In other words, let's suppose that we are barely killing any rats relative to the total rat population but that we are saving a huge number of human lives for each percentage of the rat population we kill. This is about the most generous set of assumptions we can make *in favor* of pest management. Given all this, and rounding things off, this means that the price of saving one human life is around 22,000 rodents. The question then becomes whether it's really the case that a human life is worth 22,000 rats' lives.

Of course, no one should take this particular number too seriously. We've made lots of assumptions that we know to be wrong. The rodent population estimate is extremely rough, as it's based on so little data. Moreover, we are seriously underestimating the number of rodent deaths and massively overstating the relationship between rodent deaths and lives saved. The odds are very good that we have to kill a huge percentage of the rodent population to make even a tiny reduction in the percentage of human deaths, as most of those deaths occur as a result of poor sanitation (where rats have contaminated the water supply) and limited access to medicine, not the number of rats per se. After all, it doesn't take many rats to contaminate drinking water, so you have to kill a lot of rats to reduce the risk of infection. And once people are infected, the risk of death is mostly determined by access to medicine. Consider that the plague—which is a rodent-borne disease—once killed somewhere between 50% and 60% of people infected, whereas it now kills no more than 10%. The plague has become a treatable condition, not because the disease is any less serious if untreated, but because we have effective treatments. Something similar is true for all other rodent-borne diseases. In any case, and finally, it's also possible that we're seriously overestimating the number of actual human deaths. The vast majority of deaths attributed to rodents are due to leptospirosis, but the death estimates vary dramatically, and most are lower than the one I've used. So if I had to bet, I'd say that the price of saving the human life is at least ten times greater than that 22,000 estimate.

Do We Have Good Reason to Kill So Many Rats?

Just for the sake of argument, let's suppose I'm right, and the price of saving a human life is around 220,000 rats—not 22,000. That's a lot of rodents' lives. Still, even when the numbers get very high, there's something uncomfortable about the thought that we would let people die to save rats. On this basis, perhaps, some philosophers, such as Martha Nussbaum, simply accept that we need to make trade-offs here, and rats should be on the losing end. On her view, it's sensible for a nation to strive to better its citizens, setting policy in ways that help human beings achieve flourishing lives. However, she argues:

> That cannot be a realistic policy goal for all animals. . . . Even if we narrow the group of creatures [to those who can suffer], there will very likely be pervasive conflicts, since creatures threaten one another's safety and since fostering the good of one creature may actually create a greater threat to another. . . . It would be nice to think that rats could all be shipped off to a rat community where they could live untroubled lives without infecting or endangering other animals; something like this probably can be done with field mice—they can be trapped harmlessly and released back into the wild. But killing rats does not seem to be a heinous moral evil, and it may in many cases be the least of the evils. A complete ban on killing therefore seems implausible.
>
> (Nussbaum 2001, 1541)

In other words, we might hope to move toward a world where we make everyone—human and nonhuman—able to hit some basic benchmarks for flourishing. That is, we might strive for a world where every creature, regardless of species, is able to have a life that's good enough (even if not great). However, while she thinks that's a reasonable goal for human beings, it isn't a reasonable goal for nonhuman animals, since the good for them is in tension with the good for us. So, as she says elsewhere, "the primary goal should be painless humane killing, if there has to be killing—and there might have to be, to prevent the spread of disease or damage to human children and other animals" (Nussbaum 2006, 371).

Nussbaum's idea here is that our obligations are somehow ranked. Yes, we should do the best we can for rats, but not at the expense of significant risks to human beings. This leads to an obvious question. What might explain the general priority of humans over nonhumans here?

From a moral perspective, Nussbaum doesn't have much to say about the general priority of humans over nonhumans. In short, she accepts something like the Principle of Equal Consideration of Interests, but then insists that "more complex forms of life have more and more complex (good) capabilities to be blighted, so they can suffer more and different types of harm" (361). As a result, we get the view that while human beings don't matter more than nonhuman animals per se, human beings have a wider range of interests that have to be factored into our moral deliberations. So, while humans aren't more morally important in principle, they will often be privileged in practice.

However, that's not the full version of her answer, because she thinks that there's a political dimension to this issue as well. It's an intriguing proposal, so let's sketch it as a contrast to the broadly consequentialist perspective that we've been considering so far. Essentially, Nussbaum thinks that from a political perspective, it would be unjust to opt for a full species egalitarianism, where all animals are truly equal. How does she get there?

The basic idea behind her capabilities approach is that each individual should have the opportunity to flourish, where flourishing involves the development of a range of capabilities. These capabilities are species-specific, so there are capabilities unique to human beings and different ones unique to rats, lemurs, and parrots. Justice requires that individuals have the opportunity to live lives that are good enough—that is, where they are able to develop each of their capabilities to some threshold, even if not to the maximum degree.

However, there are two wrinkles when it comes to human beings. First, Nusbaum thinks that some capabilities have to be had equally to be had to a sufficient degree. Certain political capabilities, for instance, might be the kind that you don't have enough of if you don't have as much as other people. So, it's a more complicated thing to achieve justice for human beings than it is for nonhuman animals. To achieve justice for a particular animal, you only need to consider the situation for that particular animal and any others on whom she depends (members of her pack or school or herd). However, to achieve justice for a human being, it isn't enough to look at those local facts. You also need to consider the broader sociopolitical context in which that human being is situated.

Second, Nussbaum thinks that we have to talk about implementing principles of justice in real-world political institutions in ways that recognize the diversity of humanity. If it isn't reasonable to expect people to take an idea seriously, based on their religious convictions or philosophical scruples, then we don't get to appeal to it in our political deliberations, and those political deliberations are essential to realizing the just world for which she thinks we should be striving. As she puts it, following the political philosopher John Rawls, there is an important difference between people's "metaphysical" ideas—their overall worldview that might tell them, among other things, whether God exists and what the relationship between human beings and animals is—and their political views. In theory, we can agree about lots of things in politics without agreeing about metaphysical matters, as our very different worldviews can still support a single set of judgments about how, practically speaking, we ought to live together.

With all that in mind, she says this about the idea of equal dignity across species:

> An idea of cross-species dignity is not a political idea that can readily be accepted by citizens who otherwise differ in metaphysical conception. It is a divisive metaphysical idea, in contradiction with many religious ideas of the soul, and so forth. So let us simply say that the idea of equal cross-species dignity is an attractive idea, indeed from many points of view a compelling idea, but that we do not need to rely on it in our political overlapping consensus. We may rely, instead, on the looser idea that all creatures are entitled to adequate opportunities for a flourishing life.
>
> (Nussbaum 2006, 384)

Putting the pieces together, we get the following view. Because we wouldn't have justice for human beings if we were to make laws based on moral assumptions that people can reasonably reject, we shouldn't regulate our lives together based on the idea that all animals are truly equal. Instead, we should adopt a more modest ideal: namely, that all nonhuman animals are entitled to adequate opportunities for a flourishing life. But since Nussbaum thinks that it isn't unjust to kill rats when they threaten human health, killing them must be compatible with giving rats adequate opportunities for flourishing. At the very least, then, she's committed to saying something like "the importance of securing justice for human beings is going to dictate what counts as giving rats adequate opportunities for flourishing." In other words, it can be just to shorten the lifespans of rats—we can pass the test of having given them adequate opportunity for flourishing—if we are killing them for the sake of advancing justice for human beings. Unlike the broadly consequentialist approach we were considering earlier, where we just look at the numbers of lives at stake, Nussbaum thinks we need to look at what justice requires for human beings, which then dictates whether certain moral ideals determine what justice demands. All animals are equal? Too controversial. All animals deserve a shot at a flourishing life? Yes. But let's be clear: a shot at a flourishing life is not the same thing as having inviolable rights (and is, in fact, compatible with lots of killing).

We might think that this inegalitarian approach is going to be a feature of any political conception of justice. Essentially, the idea behind this conception of justice is that what's just has to be the kind of thing that reasonable citizens could come to see as just, at least if they were willing to reason cooperatively about how their society ought to be organized. However, some philosophers propose that we abandon this idea, accepting that what's just doesn't depend on what reasonable people would accept, but on whether things are actually the way they ought to be—whether the laws and institutions that structure public life are responsive to the moral rights of the individuals governed and affected by them. That's the basic idea behind the "political turn" in animal ethics, the idea that we need to think far more seriously about how our political institutions ought to be revised if they are to recognize the rights of animals. How does this alternative work?

Perhaps the most famous proposal is due to Sue Donaldson and Will Kymlicka (2011). They argue that a just society would recognize that animals fall into three broad categories, which are fuzzy at the edges, but clear enough to be useful. First, there are animal citizens: that is, all the domesticated animals who are, in one way or another, part of human society. This includes companion animals, of course, but also the animals we raise for food and other animal products (leather, etc.). Those animals should be given versions of all those rights that are appropriate for human citizens. This doesn't mean that dogs get to go to the voting booth, but it does mean that canines should have people who represent their interests in the political process. Next, there are wild animals, who Donaldson and Kymlicka see as forming sovereign nations, deserving the right to self-determination. Essentially, then, we should leave wild animals to themselves, allowing them to live their lives as they see fit. In the middle, though, are liminal creatures—the animals who live in and around human societies but aren't exactly part of them. This broad category includes all those animals we tend to classify as pests.

Do we have to let liminal animals live among us? Donaldson and Kymlicka say that we're free to exclude some of them. However, others need to be allowed to stay—rats among them. Donaldson and Kymlicka write:

> [Some liminal animals] are almost exclusively identified with human settlement. Examples include European starlings, house sparrows, house mice, and Norway rats, amongst others. Unlike other [species], *it's not obvious that [these animals] can thrive outside the context of human settlement.* . . . [These liminal animals] live amongst us regardless of whether we invite them, actively support them, or want them as part of the community. Many humans see very few benefits to the presence of these animals and have subjected them to rigorous campaigns of suppression and control. Yet, even more than for other [species], we must accept that *they belong here amongst us*: they have no wilderness option. And deportation almost certainly results in death.
>
> (2011, 221 emphasis added)

And human-caused death, on their view, isn't an option. That would be unjust. So what can be done? Donaldson and Kymlicka uniformly support nonlethal methods of control, recommending live trapping and relocation. Moreover, to alleviate some of the stress of being moved, they favor providing food and water until the animals are "able to fend for themselves" (2011, 246).[7]

How did we get here? We started off with the idea that even if the price in terms of rats' lives of saving a human life is fairly high, we might be opposed to letting people die to save rats. One way to argue for that idea is to invoke Nussbaum's framework, which allows us to say that, at least when killing rats advances the cause of justice for human beings, it ought to be done.[8] However, Nussbaum's approach isn't without its detractors, and there are other political approaches to justice—such as the one that Donaldson and Kymlicka develop—that will make it much harder to defend killing.

Options Other Than Death

At this juncture, it's worth pausing to consider the prospects for nonlethal rat management. Donaldson and Kymlicka think we should relocate at least some rats, though they don't consider a wide range of cases. How promising is that strategy?

There are several things to say here. The first is that, at present, there is no feasible way to relocate all the rodents who currently carry various diseases. There simply isn't the political will for it. After all, it's one thing for you to live-trap a mouse who's taken up residence in your basement; it's something else to call on your city to live-trap the millions of rodents who make their homes across the urban landscape. Second, even if this could be done, it's hardly obvious where these rodents could go. After all, any site that would be viable for rodents would almost certainly have an existing rodent population, one that would be harmed significantly by the influx of new animals competing for resources. (The harm wouldn't be trivial, given the way that their social and familial groups affect their ability to thrive in a given space.) Presumably, there is something objectionable about deporting people who threaten us to a country that's foreign both to us and to them, and on top of that, one where they will cause others to starve. If so, relocation—that is, deportation—seems like a bad option.

One alternative is to use the standard strategies for reducing rat populations in an area: namely, exclusion and sanitation. In other words, you block entry points and you remove food sources. But it isn't clear that the strategies would be acceptable in a rights-respecting regime. Let's recall that according to Donaldson and Kymlicka, "it's not obvious that [certain liminal animals] can thrive outside the context of human settlement," and so "we must accept that they belong here amongst us." This makes it seem like rodents have some claim to live their lives in human spaces, and this creates trouble for the idea that it's okay to try to prevent them from cohabiting with us.

After all, if rodents have a right to live among us because it's where they can thrive, and if they can thrive among us because we often *don't* exclude them and we leave food sources available to them, then perhaps they have a right to human homes and trashcans—or, at least, to human-provided shelter and sustenance. Of course, providing continued access to human homes and trashcans, or to other shelters and sustenance, would just exacerbate all the concerns that we discussed at the beginning of the chapter—psychological well-being, property damage, and public health. The odds are good that we would end up in a situation with even stronger reasons to kill rodents. So, providing continued access to human homes and trashcans doesn't seem like a good way to go.

We might pin our hopes on sterilization, which, at least initially, seems both realistic and rights-respecting. All female mammals are born with oocytes, which are the precursors to the eggs that females ovulate. If you can kill an animal's oocytes, you make her sterile. ContraPest does just this, and it's been put to use in a number of U.S. cities to reduce rat populations. A 2017 study done by Senestech, the company that produces ContraPest, claims that when tested in "a complex urban environment," their product "reduced the seasonal population peak by 67% after 133 days of baiting" without any additional pest management strategies (Pyzyna et al. 2017). Of course, reducing the population *peak* by 67% is not the same as reducing the *population* by 67%; apparently, the overall population was down by about 42% (Molteni 2017). Still, that's a significant reduction. Even if other techniques are more effective—such as anticoagulants—the welfare improvements might make the trade-off worthwhile.

It's important to recognize, though, that even if this is the best solution available, it's still less than ideal. Sterilization deprives female rats of the opportunity to raise young, which is an activity that seems to be deeply significant to many animals, and insofar as we think that being able to engage in species-specific behavior is an important dimension of animal welfare, we should recognize this as a cost. Indeed, it may well be a rights violation: it's unclear why reproductive freedom shouldn't be one of animals' basic rights, as we generally take it to be a basic right for human beings. Moreover, we don't know much at all about the impact that sterilization drugs have on mating behavior. In the case of white-tailed deer, a popular sterilization drug doesn't prevent female deer from cycling and male dear from mating with them, leading to an extended rutting season. Anyone who's seen does frantically running from bucks should be concerned about parallel issues for rats.

There's an obvious retort. After all, we are choosing between evils here. Maybe we're going to violate the rights of rats regardless of what we do. But given the choice between killing them and setting back their sexual and parental autonomy, it's obvious that killing is the more serious rights violation. Moreover, because sterilization reduces populations by preventing rodents from coming into existence, it ultimately results in many fewer rights being violated, since the alternative is allowing many more rats to exist and, ultimately, to be killed. The upshot, then, is that there is no cost-free way of managing rodent populations, and even if sterilization is the most promising from a welfare perspective, it remains that it probably isn't either politically or financially feasible in many locations in the short term. So, since we will be making choices in nonideal circumstances for the foreseeable future, the best we can probably do is lobby for methods that involve quick and relatively painless deaths.

Conclusion

Here at the end, let's stand back and think more broadly about the difficulty of improving the plight of rats. When we're confronted with difficult trade-offs that affect human beings, we can ask the human beings what they want. The fact that we can't do this with animals is particularly troubling, especially if we think that animals have rights. People, after all, can *waive* their rights, telling us that they will *allow* what would, without consent, be a rights violation. This happens all the time. For instance, we need blood from some people to save the lives of others. It would be unjust to tie people down and take their blood without their consent. But when we face a public health crisis, we can ask people to donate blood, and quite often, they will. Consent has this ability to eliminate trade-offs, to turn a dilemma into an opportunity where people's goodwill can be on display.

Unfortunately, though, we can't do anything so straightforward with rats. The question we want to answer is this: Of all the far-from-ideal options available for protecting human health (at least from the perspective of rats), which would they prefer? Obviously, rats can't tell us. We have to decide for them.

What's more, it isn't very clear how we ought to make that decision. Perhaps certain people could be designated as representatives for these animals, and their job would be to speak on animals' behalf. However, it's very hard to know why we should trust these people's judgment.

First, there are basic empirical questions to which we don't have answers, including ones about the extent of rats' suffering in the wild. After all, this entire conversation has been based on the assumption that it's bad for rats to be killed, but perhaps that's a mistake. Second, there are philosophical puzzles: we have very little insight into the minds of rodents, we are a long way from having a widely accepted theory of animal well-being, and it's far from obvious how to balance various goods for animals when they conflict. The representatives' judgments might tell us a lot about their own philosophical commitments, but not necessarily about what, ultimately, ought to be done. Someone might say: "Just let the representatives vote!" But while that might be the democratic thing to do, it doesn't eliminate the basic worry, which is that we would learn more about ourselves than about what would be good for rats.

There is, at this juncture, something tempting about a kind of laissez-faire approach, where we simply let rodent populations be at their natural levels and encourage people to take the precautions necessary for their health. Perhaps the best we can do is leave rats alone. But if we go that route, it would only exacerbate the problems that lead people to want to kill rats in the first place unless there were massive changes in the way people think about rodents. Those kind of shifts are possible, at least in certain circumstances. In Cambodia, for instance, some people regard rats as beloved companions, and they've trained rats to detect the land mines that were scattered by Americans during the Vietnam War, as well as by Cambodians during the civil wars that followed. One former soldier told an anthropologist, "I thought of rats as pests, but now I think of them as my very best friends" (DeAngelo 2020). Plainly, though, the circumstances that changed his mind aren't going to be replicated everywhere, nor would we want them to be. So it's safe to say that in the world we now occupy, leaving rats alone would be a recipe for a renewed commitment to rodent control.

It seems to me, then, that we're in the difficult situation of having to make decisions about what would be best under massive uncertainty, since the alternative—the laissez-faire option—is pretty clearly worse. In a dark sense, I think the best-case scenario here would be that the lives of liminal animals are bad enough that they are better off dead, and so falling prey to one of our rodent control methods, awful though they often are, is still better than continued existence. Then, we could simply—if regretfully—maintain the status quo. However, despite all the arguments that I gave in Chapter 8, I'm still not sure that most rats are better off dead. My gut still says we need to look for ways to minimize the number of their deaths. But my gut has been wrong before.

Further Reading

2013. *Trash Animals: How We Live with Nature's Filthy, Feral, Invasive, and Unwanted Species*. Edited by Kelsi Nagy, and Phillip David Johnson II. Minneapolis: University of Minnesota Press.

Anderson, Elizabeth. 2005. "Animal Rights and the Values of Nonhuman Life." In *Animal Rights: Current Debates and New Directions*, edited by Martha Nussbaum and Cass Sunstein. New York: Oxford University Press.

Cochrane, Alasdair. 2016. "Life, Liberty, and the Pursuit of Happiness? Specifying the Rights of Animals." In *The Ethics of Killing Animals*, 201–214. New York: Oxford University Press.

Donovan, Josephine. 2015. "Pest Control." *Between the Species* 18(1). https://digitalcommons.calpoly.edu/bts/vol18/iss1/10.

Meerburg, Bastiaan G., Frans W.A. Brom, and Aize Kijlstra. 2008. "The Ethics of Rodent Control." *Pest Management Science*, 64: 1205–1211.

Nieuwland, J., M.A.A.M. van Gerwen, and F.L.B. Meijboom. 2019. "Rumble in the Urban Jungle: Moral Dilemmas in the Management of Liminal Rodents Perceived as Pests." In *Sustainable Governance and Management of Food Systems: Ethical Perspectives*, edited by Eija Vinnari and Markus Vinnari, 247–252. Wageningen: Wageningen Academic Publishers.

Palmer, Clare. 2003. "Colonization, Urbanization, and Animals." *Philosophy & Geography* 6(1): 47–58.

Simmons, Aaron. 2007. "A Critique of Mary Anne Warren's Weak Animal Rights View." *Environmental Ethics*, 29.

Smit, F. J. L. 2015. "Ethics in Rodent Control." In *Rodent Pests and Their Control*, edited by Alan P. Buckle and Robert Henry Smith, 316–329. Boston: CABI.

Van Gerwen, Maite A.A.M., J. Nieuwland, H.V. van Lith, and F. Meijboom. 2020. "Dilemmas in the Management of Liminal Rodents—Attitudes of Dutch Pest Controllers." *Animals* 10(9): 1614. https://doi.org/10.3390/ani10091614.

Warren, Mary Anne. 1997. *Moral Status*. Oxford: Clarendon Press.

Yeates, James. 2010. "What Can Pest Management Learn from Laboratory Animal Ethics?" *Pest Management Science* 66: 231–237.

Young, Stephen M. 2011. "On the Status of Vermin." *Between the Species* 13(6). https://digitalcommons.calpoly.edu/bts/vol13/iss6/8.

Notes

1. These are problems associated with many rodents. In fact, squirrels are the #1 cause of power outages in some areas: www.publicpower.org/periodical/article/infographic-top-causes-power-outages.
2. There are actually some views in which death is worse for animals than it is for human beings. Christine Korsgaard (2018) considers the possibility that because human lives have a narrative structure, it's important for those narratives to end—that is, for people to die. This makes there be something fitting and appropriate about human death that is absent for nonhuman animals. That being said, I once had a conversation with Benjamin Mitchell-Yellin where he suggested that human lives can have a narrative structure without it being good for them to die, as not all narratives need to end. He compared the narrative structure of human lives to those of soap operas, which can be continually renewed with new plot twists and new characters, all without losing what makes them distinctively themselves.
3. This happens more often than you might think and was a particularly large problem during COVID-19, when people were driving their vehicles much less frequently.
4. I would say that it "would" be enough to tell us what to do, except that we haven't said anything about costs to individuals who aren't either humans or rats.
5. Can we ever blame rats for their choices, or nonhuman animals more generally? It seems very plausible that we can blame some animals for some choices, though the most compelling cases are ones where we have established relationships with companion animals—for instance, your dog chewing up the furniture even though he knows full well that he shouldn't. I'm not sure what to say about rats specifically, and even less sure what to say about rats in the contexts that are of interest here.
6. It would be interesting to consider in detail the risks that rats pose to domesticated animals, but as important as that is, it's beyond the scope of this chapter. In principle, it could turn out that we ought to kill rats to stave off threats to the well-being of other animals under our care, but it would take some work to show this, and I'm not sure how the argument would go. So, I'll just focus on the direct tensions between humans and rats.
7. To be fair to Nussbaum, after she says that killing rats is justified, she immediately notes that "sterilization and other nonviolent methods are morally preferable" (371; also 385–388).
8. We said nothing about whether killing rats is a particularly effective way to do that relative to, say, improving sanitation and access to healthcare. But even if it isn't particularly effective all on its own, let's just grant here that it could still make sense as a best-of-a-bad-lot option or as part of a comprehensive effort (that is, including other strategies).

References

2017. "Hemorrhagic Fever with Renal Syndrome (HFRS)." *CDC*. www.cdc.gov/hantavirus/hfrs/index.html.

2019. "Lassa Fever." *CDC*. www.cdc.gov/vhf/lassa/.

2020. "Salmonella." *CDC*. www.cdc.gov/salmonella/.

DeAngelo, Darcie. 2020. "How Rats Are Overturning Decades of Military Norms." *Sapiens*, July 7. www.sapiens.org/culture/land-mine-detection-rats/.

Donaldson, Sue, and Will Kymlicka. 2011. *Zoopolis: A Political Theory of Animal Rights*. New York: Oxford University Press.

Korsgaard, Christine. 2018. *Fellow Creatures: Our Obligations to the Other Animals*. New York: Oxford University Press.

Molteni, Megan. 2017. "NYC's Newest Weapon Against the Rats? Sterilization." *Wired*, March 14. www.wired.com/2017/04/nycs-newest-weapon-rats-sterilization/.

Nussbaum, Martha C. 2006. *Frontiers of Justice: Disability, Nationality, Species Membership*. Cambridge: The Belknap Press.

Nussbaum, Martha. 2001. "Animal Rights: The Need for a Theoretical Basis." *Harvard Law Review* 114(5): 1506–1549. https://doi.org/10.2307/1342686.

Pyzyna, Brandy, Gary Witmer, Shane Siers, Ashley DeDecker, Nicholas Trulove, Cheryl A. Dyer, and Loretta P. Mayer. 2017. "The Efficacy of ContraPest®, a Contraceptive Bait, for the Management of Wild Rats (Rattus norvegicus and Rattus rattus)." *Wildlife Fertility Control*. www.wildlifefertilitycontrol.org/wp-content/uploads/2017/10/The-efficacy-of-ContraPest-a-contraceptive-bait-for-the-management-of-wild-rats-Rattus-norvegicus-and-Rattus-rattus-Brandy-Pyzyna.pdf.

Singer, Peter. 1999. *Animal Liberation*. Second edition. London: Pan.

13 Companion Animals

OVERVIEW

Living with animals raises all sorts of difficult moral questions. After a quick survey of some of those problems, this chapter dives into an issue facing many companion animal guardians: namely, whether to allow their cats to roam outside, where they are bound to hunt and kill some wild animals. This allows us to consider a range of puzzles in companion animal ethics, including the nature of our relationships with companion animals, the risks to which we can permissibly expose others, and foundational questions about the choice to live with animals in the first place.

According to the American Pet Products Association, U.S. consumers spent over $72.5 billion on their animals in 2018. But the money doesn't tell the whole story about our devotion. In one survey of 2,000 people, over 60% said they'd leave their partner for their animal, 54% said they'd give a finger to save their dog or cat's leg, and 25% said that they'd lose a limb to save their animal's ability to walk. Twenty-three percent were actually willing to lay down their own life to save their furry friend. Even more—32%—said they'd kill someone if it came to it (Radbil 2016).

Who knows whether people *really* feel as strongly for their animals as this survey suggests. Either way, some conservatives are concerned about human/animal attachments. A recent *National Review* piece, for instance, worried that people are turning to their animals to fulfill their basic emotional needs (Routledge 2018). Do young people view animals as "safe" relational investments? Since your animal probably won't reject you, a nonhuman companion is, relative to a human one, a less risky way to address your loneliness? Or is there a kind of emotional laziness at work, where people like not having to negotiate or compromise with our companion animals? We're glad not to have to work on the parts of ourselves that cause trouble in human relationships?

I have no idea whether we love our companion animals too much or whether we use them as Band-Aids in the midst of the "loneliness epidemic" that's been discussed by so many social scientists. I bring all this up, however, just to highlight the sheer range of questions that companion animals raise. On the one hand, when, if ever, should someone be willing to kill for their dog? On the other, is there something unfortunate about having an animal as your primary companion? Whatever we say about these questions, what will our answers reveal about our understandings of humans, animals, and the values realized in companion animal relationships? Claude Lévi-Strauss, a French anthropologist, once said that animals are "good to think"— an expression that means, very roughly, that we can learn a lot about ourselves by investigating our relationship with them. Though this is probably true generally, it's an especially plausible claim about companion animals.

But while we might "think" companion animals to understand ourselves, we should also think about them for their own sakes, as our preferences and practices have significant consequences for their lives. Here's a sampling of the many difficult moral questions that companion animals raise:

- Is it okay to selectively breed animals to have traits that human beings find appealing? If people like dogs with long, slender legs or pug noses, is it permissible to "create" beings like that? After all, lots of people object to the idea of "designer children," where technology promises to allow us to choose the color of our children's eyes, or their IQs, or any number of other features. The thought is that we should somehow accept children as they are, that part of parenting is recognizing the distinctive nature and value of the people we create naturally. Should we have the same approach to the nonhuman animals with whom we live?

- Speaking of creating nonhuman animals, it is okay to breed cats and dogs (or any other animal) at all? There are, after all, far too many cats and dogs who don't have homes, and most shelters have to euthanize animals on a regular basis because it's so difficult to place them. In this context, is it ever permissible to create new animals?

- Whatever we say about the ethics of creating animals, how should we think about the ethics of living with them? For instance, is it okay to declaw a cat if her claws are a nuisance to you? What if you wouldn't be willing to keep her otherwise? That is, is it okay to declaw a cat if the alternative is sending her to a shelter—where she may well be euthanized—or abandoning her outside? Is it okay to confine your dog to a crate to prevent him from making a mess while you're away at work? When, if ever, is it acceptable to use a choke collar? Is there something morally problematic about having a large dog in a condo? Is there something morally off about having a cat in a small apartment?

- Set aside cats and dogs for a moment. How should we think about all the moral issues associated with living with relatively unusual animals: ferrets, iguanas, parrots, turtles, and tarantulas? How well do human homes accommodate their needs? To what degree should they be considered domesticated? Should training be required before people are allowed to purchase or adopt certain animals? Who should administer that training? What should it include?

- Many of the animals we keep eat other animals. Cats, of course, are obligate carnivores—they need to eat meat to survive—as are many reptiles. Is it morally okay to kill some animals to feed our companion animals? Should we force animals to be vegan, or only keep animals who are naturally vegan?

- Should you spay or neuter your cats and dogs? If so, why? Is there a moral difference between neutering a cat so that he doesn't spray and neutering a cat so that he doesn't sire a litter of kittens? If animals have rights, wouldn't they have a right to sexual autonomy? If so, then wouldn't spaying and neutering violate that right? When, if ever, would it be appropriate to infringe upon that right?
- Many countries have universal healthcare, distributing the cost of healthcare across the population and thereby ensuring that everyone can access it. While there is private health insurance for companion animals, there is no country that provides universal healthcare for them. Is this an injustice? Is there something wrong about making these costs fall entirely on individual citizens? Relatedly, there is a child tax credit; should there be a companion animal tax credit?
- How should we make decisions regarding the end of life for our companion animals? When, if ever, should we euthanize them? What factors are relevant to deciding whether their lives are still worth living? And whose choice should that be? Should veterinarians be able to decide that a companion animal is in too much pain to continue living, even if the family isn't ready to let the animal go?

And, of course, there are dozens of other topics we might explore. Unfortunately, we can't examine them all in the detail they deserve. Instead, we'll just zero in on one issue that's received considerable attention in the news over the last several years, one that also allows us to touch on many of these questions along the way—namely, the "cat wars." In short, many environmentalists think that cats should be permanently confined indoors, while many cat owners happily allow their cats to roam freely outside, insisting that their kitties ought to be allowed to roam. Who's right?

The Cat Wars

Here's the basic issue. Many cats like to go outside. But when let outside, they kill wild animals—small birds, mammals, reptiles, and amphibians. And they don't just kill a few; they seem to kill *a lot*. A now-famous 2013 study estimated "that free-ranging domestic cats kill 1.3–4.0 billion birds and 6.3–22.3 billion mammals annually" *in the United States alone* (Loss et al. 2013). Cats are thought to have contributed to at least 63 vertebrate extinctions, and they are thought to pose a hazard to many threatened vertebrates. And "free-roaming" cats—namely, cats who are allowed to roam unattended—can contribute to the deaths of wild animals even if they don't kill those animals directly. For instance, when cats don't manage to kill their prey, they may still injure those animals, making them more vulnerable to lethal threats down the line. Cats are also causes of stress for wild animals. Even if they don't kill or injure prey, they still surprise and chase them. A study in the UK looked at the way blackbirds respond to cats in the area, even if they weren't actively being chased. The researchers found that blackbirds made significantly fewer visits to their nests when cats were present, which means that they brought less food to their nest-bound young. So fear isn't just bad for the adult birds, as a form of stress—it's also bad for their offspring, who are hungrier and more vulnerable as a result of standard feline activity. Finally, cats create dangers for wildlife that have nothing to do with their hunting behavior, as cats can spread infectious diseases, such as *Toxoplasma gondii*, *Sarcocystis neurona*, and *Bartonella* bacteria. The upshot: while it's good for cats to go outside, should we keep them indoors anyway, confining them for the sake of wild animals?

The mainstream view in the United States is that cats should be kept indoors:

> The Humane Society of the United States: "Our ultimate goal is to dramatically and humanely reduce the number of cats outdoors, leading to much less risk and harm to the cats, no predation of birds and wildlife and the elimination of potential public health concerns and nuisance-related issues" ("Common Ground").
>
> People for the Ethical Treatment of Animals (PETA): "In order to be responsible, conscientious neighbors to wildlife (who were here long before most of us and our cats), we need to get serious about . . . keeping cats safe indoors" ("14 Billion").
>
> Texas Parks & Wildlife: "We like cats, but the best place for pet cats is inside where they will be safe and healthy and live long happy lives. Also, that will allow the neighborhood wildlife to lead safer, healthier lives too" ("Cats Inside!").
>
> American Bird Conservancy: "Domestic cats can make wonderful pets. But when allowed to roam outdoors, these introduced predators have serious consequences. Cats . . . kill approximately 2.4 billion birds every year in the U.S. alone, making cat predation by far the largest human-caused mortality threat to birds. Our Cats Indoors Program educates the public and policy makers about the many benefits to birds, cats, and people when cats are maintained indoors or under an owner's direct control" ("Cats Indoors").

This consensus is striking because the groups have such different ideological commitments. It isn't as though U.S. avian advocacy groups are the only ones insisting on keeping cats indoors.[1] But widespread agreement about something doesn't make it true. So let's ask: Is it true that people ought to keep their cats indoors? Or, more accurately, is it true that people ought to permanently confine their cats indoors for the sake of wildlife?

This question is interesting in its own right; it's a practical problem that many cat owners face. But it's also interesting because it draws our attention to some general puzzles in companion animal ethics. How should we understand our relationships with the animals with whom we live? What burdens can we impose on them—either for their own sakes or for the benefit of others? And should we be keeping these animals in the first place?

Should We Permanently Confine Cats?

Let's begin by trying to push back against the consensus that we ought to permanently confine cats. There are five considerations that seem relevant:

1.   The scope of the harm that should be attributed to the cats people own
2.   Different understandings of "confinement"
3.   The impacts of confinement on cats
4.   The plight of wild animals
5.   The nature of our relationship with our feline companions

On the first point, it's important to distinguish between the impacts caused by owned and unowned cats—that is, cats under someone's control as opposed to stray and feral cats. A meta-analysis focused on the United States suggested that the vast majority of wildlife mortalities (89% of mammals and 69% of birds) should be attributed to unowned cats, not owned ones. Moreover, not all owned cats hunt: one U.S. study tracked cats' activities with kitty cams (tiny cameras mounted on their bodies) and found that only 44% of them pursued prey. Granted, there are cases where owned cats have done most of the damage. For instance, a study on gray catbirds (a relative of mockingbirds) found that where there are high densities of owned cats that are allowed outdoors, cats were responsible for 79% of the deaths of nestlings and juveniles. Still, stray and feral cats are responsible for most of the harm that cats do to wildlife. The upshot: while owned cats are certainly responsible for killing wild animals, stray and feral cats are doing most of the damage. So while it still matters what cat owners do, we shouldn't hold *owned* cats responsible for any more than their fair share of the deaths, and probably shouldn't blame them for things like species extinctions at all.

Second, there are different degrees of confinement, ranging from permanent confinement indoors to more modest options, which might involve "catios" (an escape-proof backyard enclosure to which cats have free access) or being walked on a leash. Obviously, cats don't pose much of a threat to wildlife when outside in these controlled ways. For present purposes, then, being "permanently confined indoors" really means "not being allowed to roam freely." Moreover, it's important to recall that there are degrees of free-roaming. It's one thing to allow your cat unlimited access to the outdoors, day or night (by, say, installing a cat door that remains open at all times). It's another thing only to allow your cat outdoors during the daytime, or only for limited portion of the day, or only in a fenced area. The more limited your cat's access to the outdoors, the less of a threat she poses to other animals. So, while we're going to park as though there are only two options—permanent confinement and free-roaming—this is a simplification. Thoughtful cat owners can look for intermediate options that mitigate risk to wild animals while providing some benefits to cats. As we'll soon see, however, it's likely that all the intermediate options will involve some nontrivial welfare compromises for many cats.

On this point, and third, it's easy to underestimate the impact of confinement on cats. As two veterinarians note, "keeping cats indoors can provoke frustration, unwanted behavioral challenges and lead to unavoidable sources of stress and compromised health, particularly if the home has multiple cats" (Yeates and Yeates 2017, 193). This might be surprising, given that cats are safer indoors (they aren't at risk of being killed by cars or coyotes), have regular access to food, and often have toys with which to play. However, C. E. Abbate argues that confinement denies cats the opportunity to engage in ethological behaviors, which are especially important for well-being. Ethological behaviors are adaptive behaviors that "involve active engagement, cognitive challenge, and control" (2019, 12). Unlike feeding or having sex, which are bodily pleasures, ethological behaviors produce flow pleasures, which are particularly rich and satisfying experiences that come from being absorbed in challenging activities that require a corresponding level of skill. Abbate contends that hunting and patrolling are ethological behaviors for cats—behaviors for which there are no indoor substitutes. So, to deny cats the freedom to roam outdoors is to harm them by denying them especially pleasurable pleasures—a phrase that, while accurate, hides the significance of these positive experiences. The idea here is *not* that being denied these pleasures is, essentially, being denied certain "mountaintop" highs. Rather, the idea is that lives without ethological behaviors are experienced as relatively empty and meaningless. Ethological behaviors are what make animals—humans included—feel alert and alive. Without them, our lives are colorless.

Granted, there are many groups, such as PAWS (the Progressive Animal Welfare Society), that are in favor of keeping cats indoors and provide advice about how to keep cats happy in such circumstances: "As your cat makes the transition to the great indoors, you can transform your living quarters into a veritable cat paradise. The more you give your cat to do, the happier she will be inside" ("Keeping Your Cat"). However, there isn't much research on this issue, and the little that's available isn't so optimistic. A survey of Danish cat owners, for instance, revealed that confined cats had significantly more behavioral problems than free-roaming cats. Insofar as those problems are evidence of boredom and stress, it looks like we should be skeptical of the idea that confinement can be costless for cats.[2] And insofar as we think that Abbate is correct about the significance of ethological behaviors, we should think that confinement is highly costly.

Fourth, let's recall that many animals suffer in the wild, and all animals are going to die from some cause or other (see Chapter 8). So, it matters whether cats cause more suffering than wild animals would otherwise experience, as well as whether cats are making their lives much shorter than they would otherwise be. It's unlikely that cats generally cause *more* suffering than wild animals would otherwise experience in their final moments, though they certainly cause some. For instance, cats often don't kill quickly. Another study using kitty cams revealed that cats often "play" with prey animals: catching them, releasing them, and recapturing them several times, or batting them around for a while before killing them.[3] However, as we've discussed, it isn't obvious that this is any worse than the other ways that wild animals die. Moreover, there is some evidence that owned cats generally kill emaciated and/or diseased animals. One UK study revealed that, across species, birds killed by cats were in significantly poorer condition than those killed by other means, such as being hit by cars or flying into windows. This suggests that at least some significant portion of these deaths are "compensatory" rather than "additive"—that is, they are deaths that would happen soon anyway, rather than death that wouldn't happen for a relatively long time. When we combine these considerations, it isn't obvious that cats are causing more suffering than wild animals would otherwise experience, nor is it clear whether cats are making their lives much shorter than they would otherwise be.

Fifth and finally, caring for companion animals involves being invested in their well-being, even if that exposes others to risk. We don't stop our children from learning to drive simply because they pose a mortal risk to others when they get behind the wheel. Instead, we respect their autonomy and simply try to minimize the chance of an accident. Likewise, while there's certainly reason to try to reduce the risks to other animals—say, by making cats wear anti-predation collars to warn prey animals of their approach—there's a presumption in favor of allowing them to do what enhances their well-being. And for many cats, that seems to involve roaming outdoors. Of course, this presumption can be overridden, but the point is just that it *needs* to be overridden: from the perspective of the person caring for a cat, the burden of proof is on the one advocating for permanent confinement, not on the person inclined to allow her cat to roam.

When we put all this together, we seem to have grounds to challenge the consensus about keeping cats inside. First, the vast majority of wildlife deaths shouldn't be attributed to owned cats, and of the deaths that remain, we know that just over half of owned cats are responsible for them—which means that just under half of owned cats are off the hook. This alone suggests that there's a kind of "missing the forest for the trees" mistake when we focus on the choices of individual cat owners, ignoring the larger and more important issue of managing large stray and feral cat populations. Second, there are lots of ways of giving cats limited access to the outdoors as opposed to confining them entirely. Third, there are good reasons to think that confinement is very bad for cats. Fourth, there are reasons to doubt that cats are, in general, making wildlife worse off, all things considered. When we combine these points with the fifth one, about there being a presumption that cat owners should let cats do what's good for them, it's a lot less clear that cats should be permanently confined. We might think that the conversation should be about the appropriate level of risk to which to expose wildlife rather than a simple "confine or not" debate.

Two Standard Approaches

So that's it? We should we let our cats roam? No, not exactly. The points we've made don't establish that much. Instead, they just serve to challenge the idea that this issue is as simple as it seemed to be at the beginning. To make further progress, it would be helpful to consult some of the major theoretical perspectives to see whether they agree. If they do, that might settle the question of what we ought to do, all things considered. So, let's think through the issues from a utilitarian perspective; then, we'll turn to a rights-based one.

A Utilitarian Perspective

From a utilitarian perspective, the main question is about total well-being. If we confine cats, will there be more or less well-being on balance? Here's a way of making that question sharper. Suppose that we can estimate the average amount of well-being lost by a cat who's kept indoors. Then, suppose we can estimate the aggregate well-being that would be lost by the wild animals whose lives would be shortened by that cat if she were allowed to roam. Which loss is greater? Is there good evidence one way or another?

No one has ever tried to quantify the amount of well-being lost by cats when they are permanently confined; similarly, no has tried to quantify the amount of well-being that wild animals lose when they are killed by cats. So, the best we can do is stipulate some numbers that seem reasonable and see what falls out. Let's suppose, then, that we can represent the daily well-being of animals on 100-unit scale: 50 units represents maximal well-being and –50 units represents the worst possible well-being. On this scale, a positive number indicates that the animal's life is worth living; a negative number indicates that it isn't. Now let's follow Abbate and say that not being allowed to free-roam reduces a cat's well-being significantly, say, by 20 units on that 100-unit scale.[4] By contrast, being killed robs an animal of all its well-being. We might stipulate that, on average, the animals that cats kill would have lived a week longer had free-roaming cats not found them. Then, even if the base level of well-being for wild animals is relatively low, but still positive—say, 10, due to the burdens of disease, injury, and other stressors—that means a loss of 70 units of well-being per wild animal. So, one kill is equivalent to 3.5 days of lowered feline well-being. If, on average, free-roaming cats kill more than two wild animals per week, then cats ought to be kept indoors.

On average, how many wild animals *do* free-roaming cats kill? Remember that study that according to which "free-ranging domestic cats kill 1.3–4.0 billion birds and 6.3–22.3 billion mammals annually" in the United States? As we've seen, not all of those deaths are due to owned cats (vs. unowned ones, which that study defines "to include farm/barn cats, strays that are fed by humans but not granted access to habitations, cats in subsidized colonies and cats that are completely feral") (Loyd et al. 2013, 2). Their median estimates by species are:

Birds: 744 million
Mammals 1.353 billion
Reptiles 52.58 million
Amphibians 19.03 million[5]
Total: 2.168 billion

If they're correct that there are roughly 84 million owned cats in the contiguous United States, then we get an estimate of 25.8 animals killed by free-roaming cats per year—or roughly one animal every two weeks.

Of course, we've assumed something we know to be false: namely, that *all* owned cats are part of the problem. Plainly, many people keep their cats indoors all the time, so the number of deaths we attribute to each owned cat *who's allowed to free-roam* should really be higher. One study found that roughly half the people in their study kept their cats indoors, and if that's true generally (at least in the United States), then we should double our kill estimate to one animal per week. But that might not be high enough either. Cat owners report, on average, 3.5 kills per month, and research indicates that of all the animals they kill, cats bring less than a quarter of them back to their residences. So, what people see is a long way from the total, which suggests an average rate of just over three kills per week.

Given all this, we can figure out what the utilitarian should say about permanently confining cats. Suppose that the well-being lost by each wild animal is equivalent to half a week of lowered feline well-being. Suppose further that cats kill, on average, three wild animals every week. Then, the deaths of those wild animals are worse, in terms of the total amount of well-being lost, than cats being confined. So, cats ought to be confined.

Of course, the devil's in the details, and there are lots of ways to contest the numbers we've used. For instance, it's possible that being kept inside reduces a cat's well-being far more than 20 units, especially if Abbate is correct about the significance of ethological pleasures.[6] It's also possible that the animals cats kill wouldn't live a full week without feline predation; recall the hypothesis that cats generally kill emaciated or diseased animals. Finally, we might think that the baseline levels of well-being for wild animals are negative, both for the reason just mentioned and because of general evidence to the effect that most wild animals have net negative lives. Each of these revisions—and particularly the last one—would shift the assessment decisively in favor of allowing cats to roam freely.

Granted, there is considerable uncertainty here. But for what it's worth, my guess is that utilitarian reasoning favors allowing cats to roam. If the wild animals on whom cats prey are better off dead—and as we've seen, there are two plausible lines of argument in favor of that view—then allowing cats unsupervised outdoor access is good for them and good for their prey. Well-being goes up all around. So, it would be a mistake to permanently confine cats.

A Rights-Based Perspective

Do we get the same conclusion from a rights-based perspective?

Let's remind ourselves of the basics of the rights view. That view, you'll recall, says that animals have inherent worth, that they are valuable in and of themselves.[7] As a result, they have a right to be treated with respect, which means they have the right not to be treated as mere resources. Moreover, although we should minimize the number of rights violations, not all rights violations are equal. More fundamental rights should be protected first, and only after that should we worry about others. So, for instance, while individuals have rights to both life and bodily integrity, the former is more fundamental than the latter. So if we have to choose between someone dying and 1,000 people suffering broken arms, we shouldn't just look at the numbers and say "1,000 against one, so the one should die." Instead, we should recognize that protecting the life of the one is more important than protecting the bodily integrity of 1,000.

Here's a simple way of applying the rights view to the question of whether to permanently confine cats. Either we violate the rights of cats or the rights of wildlife (via
the cats). But there are fewer cats than there are wild animals, and even if that were
the case, the cats are being harmed less severely than the wild animals. (Ethological
pleasures matter, but they're less fundamental than life.) So, cats should be confined.

One wrinkle with this simple version of the argument is that according to standard versions of the rights view, only moral agents—that is, beings who can be held
accountable for their actions—can violate rights. So if Abner shoots and kills Bill,
then Abner has violated Bill's right to life; if, however, Bill has been killed by a
virus, then while he's suffered the same loss (his life), he hasn't had any of his rights
violated. The traditional view is that very few nonhuman animals, if any, are moral
agents. So if we assume that cats aren't moral agents, then we don't actually have a
case where all parties are having their rights violated. Instead, we have a case where
we are violating the rights of cats by confining them, but cats aren't violating anyone's rights, since that's not a thing cats can do. So, let the cats roam.

But look more carefully at the simple version of the argument: it doesn't say that
cats are violating anyone's rights. Instead, the argument says that if we don't confine cats, then *we* are violating the rights of wild animals *via* the cats. When we let
cats roam, we release a threat into the spaces occupied by wild animals, and we are
responsible for what they do.[8]

We'll need to think a bit more about this, and we'll come back to it shortly. For now,
though, let's just note that even if this reply works, the simple rights-based argument
for confining cats is vulnerable to a different and more serious objection. Recalling
the conversation from the previous section, even if ethological pleasures aren't more
important than life *in general*, they might be more important *than the particular lives
being lost to feline predation*. This is because (a) it isn't clear how bad death is for
nonhuman animals generally; (b) death may not be bad for most wild animals due to
the many sources of suffering in the wild; and (c) death may not be bad for the wild
animals on whom cats prey, as they may tend to be ill or injured already.

If that's right—that is, if the loss of ethological pleasures for felines is significantly worse than death is for the wild animals cats kill—then the rights view implies
that cats should be allowed to roam. After all, the rights view says that we shouldn't
impose significant harms on a relatively small number of individuals to prevent relatively insignificant harms to a larger number of individuals. In other words, don't use
the few to benefit the many; don't let a handful of individuals bear huge costs just to
spare small costs to a larger number of others. Utilitarians are willing to accept those
kinds of trade-offs because they can result in utility being maximized; rights theorists
aren't, since they regard that as exploiting the smaller group. So, given that cats are
harmed more by being denied ethological pleasures than wild animals are harmed by
being killed, we shouldn't keep our cats indoors.

Where does this leave us? With respect to both utilitarianism and the rights view, it
looks like quite a bit turns on what we say about the relative costs to cats and wildlife.
And that, of course, turns on a mix of philosophical and empirical questions that are
difficult to sort out, but our provisional assessment seems to suggest that the costs
to cats are more severe.

A Defense of the Consensus Position?

So is there nothing to be said in favor of the consensus that we outlined earlier? Are all those organizations simply mistaken? On one level, that wouldn't be very surprising. Arguably, most of those organizations were not thinking about wild animals as individuals when they came out in favor of permanently confining cats. Rather, they were thinking about wild animals at the population or species level. If you are mostly concerned with preventing species from going extinct, then it makes sense for you to argue that we should prevent novel and abundant predators—which is what cats are from an ecological perspective—from decimating prey populations. But if you are mostly concerned with ensuring that well-being is maximized or that rights are respected, then it's no surprise if you get a different result.

However, we can't assume that *all* those organizations were just thinking about wild animals at the population or species level. Remember that PETA is on board with the consensus position too! So, even if confining cats doesn't get much support from utilitarianism and the rights view, let's pause to consider whether there's anything that can be said for keeping cats indoors. If not, then that will just be further confirmation that the consensus position is wrong. But if so, then we'll need to sort out our commitments, trying to decide which moral approach we find most compelling.

Consider an analogy. You have a teenager with a significant cognitive disability. His disability is such that he doesn't grasp the significance of hazards; moreover, he doesn't appreciate his own strength. This is challenging enough at home, where you've carefully adapted the environment to his needs. When he heads outside, it's far more complicated.

Unfortunately, your son *adores* being outside. And not only that, but nothing else satisfies him. When you keep him indoors, he sits at the window, clearly disappointed that he can't go out. He can be distracted by TV and puzzles for a while, but it doesn't last long. He wants to roam.

Unfortunately, he isn't content to explore just when you're able to accompany him. If you accidentally leave the front door unlocked, he'll slip out and wander the neighborhood. As a result, there have been some close calls. He walks into the street without regard for passing cars, so drivers have had to screech to a halt to avoid him. There have also been some "incidents." You wince, for instance, when you recall the time he hit your elderly neighbor—not because he was angry, but because he thought they were playing a game. Your son left him with a black eye.

It's obvious that your son's well-being depends in some large part on being able to explore the outdoors. It brings him enormous pleasure. It's also obvious—at least to me—that you shouldn't let him leave the house unsupervised. If he were my son, I'd think I ought to minimize the risks he poses to himself and others.

We might think that something similar is true when it comes to cats. Despite the importance of roaming outdoors to your son's well-being, it seems wrong to expose your neighbors to the risk that he creates. It doesn't matter if there are other threats to your neighbors (that is, other ways in which they might be harmed). It doesn't matter if, in fact, your neighbors' lives are far less good than they should be, or even if their lives involve significant suffering—as is plausibly the case for the many wild animals. Still, you ought to minimize the risks that your son poses to others: their well-being isn't his to jeopardize, even if there isn't much well-being to jeopardize in the first place. And since you're partially responsible for what he does, we should note that their well-being isn't *yours* to jeopardize either. You would be acting irresponsibly if you were to let him wander to his heart's content. Finally, it seems irresponsible to expose *your son* to the risk of serious injury or death, even at the cost of an important contributor to his well-being. Moral caution isn't solely for the sake of your neighbors, but for your son himself. Let's call this the Teenage Son Analogy.

Admittedly, there are some important differences between this case and the one we've been considering. For instance, you know that your son is a threat to others, but you might not know that about your cat. After all, 44% of owned cats don't hunt! But this seems like a reason to be more critical of cat owners, not a reason to give them more latitude. People could, in principle, purchase kitty cams and find out what their cats do when unsupervised. But, of course, almost no one makes such efforts. That wouldn't be so bad if there were other ways of getting a good sense of your cat's activities. However, the easy-to-acquire evidence is misleading. Many people probably judge whether their cats are hunters based on whether they bring bodies home. But as mentioned earlier, cats bring back less than one-quarter of what they kill. So, what people see on their doorsteps doesn't represent the total. Hence, a precautionary approach seems like the right one, unless you have good reason to think that your cat doesn't hunt. In other words, unless you have evidence that your cat isn't a hunter, confinement is the way to go, at least according to the Teenage Son Analogy.

Here's another difference that someone might use to challenge the analogy. There's an evolutionary sense in which patrolling territory and hunting are "natural" for cats—that behavior was selected for—but there's no similar evolutionary sense in which the teenage son's actions are natural. So, it's more important for cats to roam than it is for your son to be outside. But while there is something appealing about this thought, it's hard to see how evolutionary considerations are morally relevant here. Suppose that patrolling territory and hunting *hadn't* been selected for, that it was an evolutionary accident that these behaviors contribute significantly to feline well-being. Or suppose, more radically, that an evil scientist found some way to reprogram cats who hadn't wanted to patrol or hunt such that they now *do* want to do these things. Either way, it would still matter that these behaviors are now, in fact, important for well-being, and their unnaturalness would be irrelevant. These cases show that the origin only matters for *evidential* reasons. The evolutionary story *increases our confidence* that these behaviors are important for felines. But the evolutionary story doesn't matter for *moral* reasons. So, while there's a sense in which it's true that patrolling territory and hunting are natural for cats (these are adaptive behaviors for cats) and free-roaming isn't natural for the teenage son (there is no similar evolutionary story to tell), that difference doesn't seem to be important.

Again, the basic idea behind the Teenage Son Analogy is that the well-being of wild animals isn't ours to jeopardize. So, since you are partially responsible for what your cat does, you should prevent your cat from jeopardizing the well-being of wild animals. Obviously, if you can do that without permanently confining your cat, that's ideal. But if you can't—and let's be honest, you probably can't—then you should permanently confine your cat.

Someone might object, however, that the Teenage Son Analogy proves too much. It doesn't only show that cats should be kept indoors, but that we should seriously limit the freedom of human beings. For instance, perhaps we should ban the consumption of animal products from intensive systems, given the harm for which the average American meat-eater is responsible, which is far greater than that caused by the average cat. If we ought to violate the autonomy of individuals when they pose a deadly risk to others, then we ought to violate the autonomy of a great many human beings.

In truth, though, I'm not sure that this is much of an objection. Obviously, banning the consumption of animal products from intensive systems is a political nonstarter. But if the United States' animal protection legislation covered agricultural animals— that is, if the Animal Welfare Act weren't objectionably arbitrary (see Chapters 9 and 11)—many standard practices in the industry would be illegal, and intensive systems would probably disappear. That seems like a good outcome to me, even though it violates the autonomy of individuals who would prefer to be able to kill an extraordinary number of nonhuman animals for food.

Yet another objection: the analogy misconstrues the relationship between cats and cat owners. We might think that there is a crucial difference between the teenage son and a cat: namely, that your cat isn't dependent on you in the way that your teenage son is. In principle, your cat could live without you, finding food, avoiding predators, and generally living the feline life. Your teenage son, by contrast, simply couldn't; he needs you, and he wouldn't be able to fend for himself if left to his own devices. As a result, perhaps we ought to change the way we think about what it means to "have" a cat. Perhaps having a cat is a bit more like having a roommate than it's like having a child. In general, we don't have the right to restrict the liberties of our roommates in the way that we can restrict the liberties of our children. Even if you disagree with your roommate's choices, you're generally not entitled to lock him in his bedroom to keep him from making them.

I'm not sure what to think of this objection. To my mind, one of the hardest parts of animal ethics involves trying to think clearly about how best to characterize the relationship we have with nonhuman animals. In part, this is because it's so difficult to recognize and understand the implications of their similarities to and differences from human beings. I also doubt that it's true that your cat could live just fine without you: if life in the wild is as bad as all that, then while your cat may be able to *survive* without human assistance, at least for a while, her life might be quite poor in those circumstances. But the main problem with this objection is that, typically, you don't have to choose between physically restraining your roommate, on the one hand, and respecting his choice to go out and kill, on the other. If your roommate dates people who are bad for him, that's one thing; shake your head and respect his choices. If your roommate is homicidal, that's another, and physical restraint would probably be justified. So even if we reframe the human/feline relationship, I don't think it follows that cats ought to be allowed to roam.

There is, however, one final objection that's harder to resist. Recall that the idea behind the Teenage Son Analogy is that the well-being of wild animals isn't ours to jeopardize. Based on concerns about wild animal suffering, someone might object that you *aren't* jeopardizing the well-being of wild animals, since they don't have lives worth living. You are jeopardizing their *lives*, of course, but—the objection goes—it isn't wrong to jeopardize lives that aren't worth living.

I tend to think that this is right, even though—as in Chapter 8—it isn't a conclusion with which I'm comfortable. I worry, both here and there, that we aren't giving sufficient weight to the desires of wild animals. I find it intuitive that there's a strong presumption against jeopardizing the life of anyone who wants to live, however bad their life may be. At the same time, though, I think it's clear that there are cases in which human beings ought to make life and death choices for nonhuman animals— as when we make judgment calls about when to euthanize our companion animals, knowing full well that they may still want to live. So, even if my intuitions point in a different direction, I'm inclined to think that the arguments we've canvassed support the view that cats should be allowed to roam freely.

Conclusion

This chapter has been a deep dive into one particular puzzle in companion animal ethics. Should we confine our cats for the sake of wildlife, or should we let them roam? (Or, to put the question more pointedly in light of what we've covered, should we let them roam *for the sake of wildlife*?) We've seen, yet again, that the debate turns on a mix of philosophical and empirical questions. How bad are things for wild animals generally? For prey animals specifically? How much do various goods contribute to animals' well-being? How many wild animals do cats kill?

At the same time, the "cat wars" draw our attention to the much larger questions that I mentioned earlier on. How should we understand our relationships with the animals with whom we live? Are they more like our children, our roommates, or something else entirely? What burdens can we impose on them? Can we deny them a significant source of satisfaction if, in fact, that's the best way to protect the well-being of vulnerable others? Finally, should we be keeping these animals in the first place? Is it okay to live with obligate carnivores like cats—animals to whom we feed other animals and who sometimes kill other animals themselves?

This last question is the one that really troubles me. In the wake of all the moral complexities raised by comparing animals, I sometimes find myself thinking that we shouldn't have them at all. It seems to me that we have too much power and too little moral knowledge. We're in the unenviable position of having to make high-stakes decisions with woefully inadequate information.

Of course, the same worries apply to having children. My relationship with my kids is incredibly precious and, for that reason, profoundly morally difficult, since it matters so much to me that I get things right. I feel this acutely when I face questions about the limits of partiality, the degree to which it's acceptable to privilege the near and dear. I love my children and would do almost anything for them. Does that make it okay for me to promote their well-being at the expense of others? If so, when? Other people love their cats and would do almost anything for *them*. Does that love make it okay for them to promote the good for their cats at the expense of others? If so, what are the limits? Perhaps we don't need to be able to offer general answers to such questions; that might be asking too much. Still, it wouldn't hurt to try.

Further Reading

Bradshaw, J. 2013. *Cat Senses*. New York: Basic Books.

Du Toit, Jessica. 2016. "Is Having Pets Morally Permissible?" *Journal of Applied Philosophy* 33(3): 327–343.

Grier, Katherine C. 2020. "Pets." In *The Routledge Handbook of Animal Ethics*, edited by Bob Fischer, 291–301. New York: Routledge.

Marra, Peter P., and Chris Santella. 2016. *Cat Wars: The Devastating Consequences of a Cuddly Killer*. Princeton: Princeton University Press.

Milburn, Josh. 2015. "Not Only Humans Eat Meat: Companions, Sentience and Vegan Politics." *Journal of Social Philosophy* 46(4): 449–462.

Overall, Christine. 2017. *Pets and People: The Ethics of Our Relationships with Companion Animals*. New York: Oxford University Press.

Pierce, Jessica. 2012. *The Last Walk: Reflections on Our Pets at the Ends of Their Lives*. Chicago: Chicago University Press.

Pierce, Jessica. 2016. *Run, Spot, Run: The Ethics of Keeping Pets*. Chicago: Chicago University Press.

Sandoe, Peter, Sandra Corr, and Clare Palmer. 2015. *Companion Animal Ethics*. Hoboken: Wiley Blackwell.

Yeates, James. 2019. *Companion Animal Care and Welfare: The UFAW Companion Animal Handbook*. Hoboken: Wiley Blackwell.

Notes

1. It's interesting to consider whether these groups also agree about the answers to some of the questions we raised earlier. We might think that they are all assuming that we shouldn't systematically declaw cats, since that would make it harder (though not impossible) for them to catch prey; that we shouldn't simply discourage people from owning carnivorous animals; and that we shouldn't try to genetically modify cats in some way that makes them less of a threat to wild animals. Alternatively, these organizations may simply think that confinement is the best strategy for saving wildlife, quite independently of their stances on these questions.

2. Still, it doesn't follow that confinement has a negative effect on feline well-being overall, given that indoor environments protect cats from various threats. Lots of cats are killed by cars, and if we assume that we should count their lost future pleasures when calculating their overall well-being, then it might be worth some boredom to have a much longer life. Likewise, cats are more vulnerable to disease and injury from other animals (including, of course, other cats) when allowed to roam, and again, it would take some work to show that the overall cost/benefit analysis turns out one way or another.

3. The claim here is not that cats are malicious. There are many reasons why cats might appear to play with prey without it actually being play behavior. One hypothesis is that many owned cats simply aren't that skilled, and so struggle to kill the animals they've caught. Another is that cats are tiring out their prey, trying to ensure that their prey can't injure them when they go in for the fatal bite. For our purposes here, however, even if cats did delight in torturing wild animals, it might not make any difference. We might be more concerned with how much the wild animals suffer, not why they suffer.

4. To be clear, the claim here is *not* that cats confined indoors have 30/50 possible units of well-being. Rather, it's that *relative to their base rates of well-being*, which are determined by a range of environmental and individual factors, confinement reduces feline well-being by another 20 units.

5. I generated the numbers for reptiles and amphibians by assuming that we can attribute 89% of the total estimate to unowned cats, which is the percentage of mammalian deaths that they attribute to unowned cats (vs. the 69% of avian deaths that they attribute to unowned cats). This only helps Abbate, but it doesn't make much difference, as those numbers are relatively small to start.

6. That being said, I find it hard to believe that cats' lives aren't worth living indoors, so I doubt that confinement reduces their well-being below zero on the scale that we're employing. But I could be wrong. "Live free or die," as they say in New Hampshire.

7. Not all animals! Only the ones that are experiencing subjects-of-lives. But of course, that's very many nonhuman animals, and arguably all the ones who are relevant to this discussion.

8. People sometimes talk about "anthropogenic predation" in a conservation context, which is a similar notion. Usually, though, those are cases where people want predators to kill prey animals, so the killing is, in some sense, intentional. This certainly happens with cats, as some people have cats to control rodent populations. However, let's assume that most people don't want their cats to kill the animals in question, which means the deaths would be foreseeable but not intended.

References

"14 Billion." *PeTA*. www.peta.org/features/keep-cats-inside/.

Abbate, C.E. 2019. "A Defense of Free-Roaming Cats from a Hedonist Account of Feline Well-Being." *Acta Analytica*. https://doi.org/10.1007/s12136-019-00408-x.

"Cats Indoors." *American Bird Conservancy*. https://abcbirds.org/program/cats-indoors/.

"Cats Inside!" *Texas Parks & Wildlife*. https://tpwd.texas.gov/education/resources/texas-junior-naturalists/watching-wildlife/cats-inside.

"Common Ground for Cats & Wildlife." *The Humane Society of the United States*. www.humanesociety.org/resources/common-ground-cats-wildlife.

"Keeping Your Cats Happy Indoors." *Paws*. www.paws.org/resources/keeping-your-cat-happy-indoors/.

Loss, S.R., T. Will, and P.P. Marra. 2013. "The Impact of Free-ranging Domestic Cats on Wildlife of the United States." *Nature Communications* 4: 1–7.

Loyd, K.A.T., S.M. Hernandez, J.P. Carroll, K.J. Abernathy, and G.J. Marshall. 2013 "Quantifying Free-roaming Domestic Cat Predation Using Animal-borne Video Cameras." *Biological Conservation* 160: 183–189.

Radbil, Sam 2016. "Pets Over Everything." *Abodo*, July 25. www.abodo.com/blog/pets-over-everything/.

Routledge, Clay. 2018. "Are Americans Too Attached to their Pets?" *National Review*, May 21. www.nationalreview.com/2018/05/americans-pets-too-attached/.

Yeates, J., and D. Yeates. 2017. "Staying in or Going Out? The Dilemma for Cat Welfare." *Veterinary Record* 180: 193–194.

14 Activism

OVERVIEW

If animals matter, then given all the harm people cause them, there are probably going to be situations in which we need to advocate for animals. This chapter provides an overview of several ethical questions facing animal activists. What kinds of tactics are permissible? What's across the line? If we're going to help, which causes should we prioritize? It is okay to help however you want, or should you do the most good you can? How should we think about the ethics of trying to reform existing institutions, knowing full well that they are going to continue exploiting animals—and may even use small reforms as proof that they're the good guys?

If you want to take the Liberation Pledge, then all you need to do is:

1. Publicly refuse to eat animals—live vegan
2. Publicly refuse to sit where animals are being eaten
3. Encourage others to take the pledge

("Liberation Pledge")

To show others that you've taken the pledge, you can wear a bracelet that you can make yourself; just bend a fork so that it can be worn around your wrist. The idea is that you are turning the fork "into a symbol of nonviolence," thereby reclaiming the "tool most responsible for the immense suffering and unimaginable deaths animals endure." In so doing, you "beat swords into plowshares"—a quote from Isaiah, a book in the Hebrew Bible. In other words, you are turning an implement of war into an implement of peace ("Liberation Pledge").

The rationale for the Liberation Pledge is simple:

Animal rights groups have investigated some of the most celebrated farms in the world, certified humane suppliers of animals' bodies, and found unimaginable cruelty. While animal agriculture has attempted to justify using animals as humane, we know the truth: using animals is inherently violent. To show this truth to the world, however, we have to make a public stand and create social norms around the idea that animals are not ours to use. Refusing to sit where the bodies of victims lie, and publicly displaying your commitment with a fork bracelet, is a powerful way to do this.

("Liberation Pledge")

As one Liberation Pledge-taker puts it:

My social crowd all challenge sexism, homophobia and other isms, so for me to be consistent as an anti-speciesist and do the same as I do with other -isms I had to challenge speciesism, and that meant asking those around me not to eat animals in my company.

(Lockwood 2019)

Those who take the pledge disagree about how, exactly, to interpret the second part of the pledge: "Publicly refuse to sit where animals are being eaten." The weakest interpretation says: only dine with people who are willing to eat vegetarian. It's fine to spend time with people who eat meat in other contexts, but when you're at the table, no one should be consuming animal flesh. On this reading of the pledge, you're willing to tolerate people consuming eggs and dairy, but you aren't going tolerate them feasting on the corpses of animals—that is, meat. A more demanding interpretation says: only dine with people who are willing to eat *vegan*, which is motivated by the thought that the story behind eggs and dairy is just as bad, if not worse, than the story behind meat itself; moreover, these stories are intertwined, as egg-laying hens and dairy cows are eventually slaughtered too (see Chapter 6). So the most demanding interpretation says: only dine in vegan homes and restaurants. After all, it might be the case that everyone at the table's eating vegan but the folks at the table next to you are digging into pork chops. To avoid that scenario, you limit yourself to places where you know that animal products will be absent.

This chapter is devoted to animal activism, with the Liberation Pledge being one of many forms that activism can take. Here are some others:

- Tabling and leafleting might be the most familiar forms of activism: people stand at tables on university campuses—or on street corners, or anywhere else—and hand out pamphlets with information. Now, of course, much of this happens online, and leafleting has largely taken a backseat to posting on social media, targeted ads, lifestyle influencers, and the like.
- Protests take many forms, and if you've heard about an advocacy group on the news, this may be why. Members of a group called Direct Action Everywhere—DxE—have been known to occupy grocery stores and restaurants while carrying signs that say, "It's not food, it's violence." Members of People for the Ethical Treatment of Animals (PETA) have covered themselves in fake blood and packaged themselves as though they were chicken breasts. Members of

Mercy for Animals once made a 12-foot-high inflatable gestation crate with a fake injured sow inside, placing it outside a Walmart to protest their pork supplier.

- Various groups engage in legal advocacy for animals. This can involve things like challenging ag-gag laws, which were designed by industry groups and impose harsh penalties on those who record footage of abuses on farms. There are also legal firms that sue for false advertising. Consider the Organic Consumers Association, which sued Smithfield Foods "for falsely advertising Smithfield pork products as the 'safest' US pork products . . . [even though] the USDA has notified Smithfield slaughter plants on multiple occasions that their pork was more likely to be contaminated with salmonella than similar products in slaughter plants of the same size" (Flynn 2020).

- Corporate campaigns typically involve trying to encourage individual companies to swap out animal products for plant-based products or to pressure their suppliers to improve animal welfare. For instance, the Humane Society of the United States (HSUS) was the first organization to convince a major grocer, Costco, to sell cage-free eggs exclusively, and they've long been involved in attempts to improve the welfare of broiler chickens—promoting the use of slow-growth breeds, increases to the amount of room that the birds have available to them, better enrichment, and the switch to more reliable slaughter methods.

- Political lobbying can involve trying to convince legislators to reform laws that affect animals, or where it's possible, to launch ballot initiatives to change the law directly. One of the more widely known examples of this is Proposition 12 in California, which was approved in 2018, the aim of which was to "establish minimum space requirements based on square feet for calves raised for veal, breeding pigs, and egg-laying hens and ban the sale of (a) veal from calves, (b) pork from breeding pigs, and (c) eggs from hens when the animals are confined to areas below minimum square-feet requirements" ("Proposition 12" 2018).

- Finally, entrepreneurs are trying to change the landscape for animals by developing and selling plant-based animal product alternatives and cultured animal products. The Beyond Burger, for instance, is a plant-based burger patty that has been adopted by many restaurant chains, including Burger King and Dunkin' Donuts; a company called "Just" produces a product called "Just Egg," made from mung beans, which is designed to scramble just like the product we get from chickens. And eventually, companies like Memphis Meats and Finless Foods hope to produce true animal products without animals, growing meat in labs rather than inside animals.

In my experience, anyway, when lots of people think about activists, they seem to think about slightly crazed individuals who shout in other people's faces. But as this quick survey reveals, there are activists who are fitness influencers, activists who wear suits in courtrooms, activists who do research in labs, and activists who give slideshows in corporate boardrooms. These people are united by their desire to change the status quo—not by their methods.

Animal activism raises several intriguing moral questions. For instance, we might wonder about its limits. What methods, if any, should be off the table? We might wonder whether most people *ought* to be engaged in activism—that is, whether it's simply one good project that you might pursue, or whether it would be a moral failure not to get involved. In a different vein, we could consider how activists should set their priorities. Should animal causes be privileged over human ones? And either way, of the animal causes, which one is most important? Finally, to what degree should activists compromise with the industries and institutions they want to change? Should they simply seek their abolition, or should they try to reform them in the meantime? This chapter takes up these questions, and in each case, we'll see links between the ethics of activism and a range of other issues that we've explored throughout the book.

The Limits of Activism

Let's turn to questions about the limits of activism. We'll begin with the Liberation Pledge, but we'll quickly move on to yet more radical activities.

Are There Limits to Activism?

Even if we opt for the weakest interpretation, the pledge might still seem to be extreme. Isn't it *rude* to refuse to eat with someone simply because she isn't a vegetarian? Would you really skip a family dinner just because you and your mom don't see eye to eye about animals? Can you imagine saying to a date, "I thought we could have dinner together, but it turns out we can't"?

As natural as these thoughts are, we should be careful not to give them too much weight in our assessment. When people are described as activists in the media, there is often a subtext that these individuals are too partisan to be trusted, that they are fringe enough that their ideas aren't worth taking seriously. And that may be true in some cases. However, it's a dangerous policy to dismiss non-mainstream perspectives simply because they aren't mainstream. History is chock full of examples of widely accepted practices that we now regard as morally bankrupt, as well as widely condemned activist strategies that we now regard as morally exemplary. So, we should be charitable to activists as we consider their reasoning.

In the case of the Liberation Pledge, the *point* is to be extreme relative to widely accepted social norms. We live in a society that says: choices about eating are personal, not moral. People shouldn't criticize each other for what they decide to consume. Friendship and family matter more than your dietary preferences. The animal activists behind the Liberation Pledge disagree with all those claims; those are exactly the social norms that the activists want to change. On their view, choices about eating are moral choices. We should indeed criticize people for what they consume, at least if they're consuming a product with a history of enormous suffering. And while friendship and family matter, going vegan isn't just a dietary preference—it's a moral mandate. And just as other moral mandates can interfere with our close connections—we draw lots of lines about the behavior we won't tolerate, even when it comes to the people we hold near and dear—you shouldn't just go along to get along when it comes to the way people treat animals.

Although the origins of the Liberation Pledge are bit difficult to discern, it's often associated with one of its main backers—DxE. However, DxE is actually more famous, and considered more extreme, for its open rescues, during which activists enter farms to liberate animals. Here's how one activist describes the way these rescues proceed:

> First, we find a way inside, without breaking anything. We don't break down doors. We don't break down windows. We are peaceful and practice nonviolence. We go inside, and then if the decision has been made that it's a lockdown [where the aim is to remain locked inside the facility until the media comes to film the conditions in which the animals live], we quickly lock ourselves down in case workers come upon us. . . . We also take in carriers, so we have an open rescue opportunity as well. We have walkie-talkies with us. We have biosecurity gear, which is one of the most important elements. We have received advice on using good foot coverings. We have thick masks to cover our faces in case any of us struggle with the air, which is generally full of ammonia. And we have gloves on, as always. This is a very tight team of people that is willing to risk their personal safety. . . . We have training beforehand, and we advise anyone on our team about the risks inherent to this kind of action. And we make sure that we don't have anyone whose citizenship is in doubt. We are very careful with the people who we bring in. We know them. We train everyone in nonviolence and biosecurity and we provide all the supplies.

This particular activist was involved in a rescue operation at a duck farm:

> It's fascinating to me that our team saw the ducks struggling on the ground, trapped in the wire mesh, their backs getting covered in the slippery feces—and yet, the looks on the ducks' faces is one of contentment. And this is where the problem lies. Animals who are being abused, such as these ducks, have happy looks on their faces. The industry can take pictures of them, and the public is not hearing the machinery or smelling the ammonia. There are no windows in these places. The air hurts your lungs. You're coughing. It's a nightmare. It's like going inside hell, it really is.
>
> The operation was lockdown, rescue, filming, getting more adult [ducks], then negotiating with the police and the workers, and asking for the media to come inside. Sometimes, situations will change. We arrived and found that a worker was on-site in one of the other sheds. We decided to do a major rescue of the babies, so we managed to get 26 of them, and by then, we knew that the police were there. Twelve police cars came, but they didn't seem to want to come to speak to us inside. A decision was made at the time to end the lockdown and exit without walking in front of the police. We had an alternate exit that we used. [. . . Now, the] ducks are doing amazing. They really are. They are in safe homes.
>
> (Harris 2020)

In this particular case, no one was arrested. However, DxE activists often end up spending time in jail, which, in DxE's view, is an important part of their advocacy work. DxE insists that activists be willing to take legal responsibility for their actions as a form of civil disobedience—that's what they mean when they say that the rescues are "open." They take the stance because one of their objectives is to demonstrate that laws preventing rescue are unjust. The idea is that it's essential to reveal both exactly what's happening to animals in these facilities and that it's illegal to try to save animals from suffering in such extraordinary ways. As DxE's founder, Wayne Hsiung, frequently puts it, these rescues are supposed to demonstrate "the injustice of a system that would lock up those who are doing what any child would recognize as the right thing to do" (Klein 2019).

Obviously, these activists were breaking the law. They didn't have permission to enter that farm; they didn't have permission to remove any of the animals. They were trespassing and stealing. Was that wrong? In asking that question, we're brushing up against the much larger one that we mentioned earlier: What, if anything, should be off the table when it comes to trying to change the society in which you live? However, rather than try to answer that question in the abstract, let's simply focus on when it's okay to break the law for the sake of a cause.

The civil rights movement makes it almost impossible to say that it's *never* permissible to break the law: it seems completely obvious that it wasn't just *okay* to break various unjust laws; it was morally important for those protesters to do exactly what they did. When society is deeply unjust, and that injustice is codified in law, those laws don't deserve our respect. Indeed, they seem to deserve our disrespect.

It seems equally clear that there have got to be some limits. Imagine someone opposed to the construction of a new natural gas pipeline and whose strategy for preventing it involves summarily executing all the executives of the corporation that's going to build it. Presumably, no one wants to defend this behavior. So, we know that the extreme positions are off the table—the "never break the law" and "anything goes" options—and the challenge is to draw a line somewhere between them.

It would be incredibly surprising if the location of the line didn't depend on the stakes. That is, it's one thing to be concerned about a lack of environmental regulations on commercially zoned properties in your city and to consider what kinds of activism might be justified to put those regulations in place. It's another to be concerned about whether members of marginalized groups have the same basic rights as those in nonmarginalized groups. You probably can't use violence in the former case. In the latter, it's more complicated. Maybe you shouldn't do it, but there's probably a conversation to be had before you reach that conclusion. The upshot is that we will need to think about specific objectives and the specific contexts—political, social, and historical—in which people are trying to achieve those objectives.

So let's think a bit more carefully about the practice of open rescues. How would we decide whether that's justified? Well, we might ask: Is it morally permissible to trespass on someone's property and then steal something they own—which is the way the law frames the actions of these activists? Of course, the activists themselves reject that framing. On their view, what's happening is that people are unjustly imprisoning individuals with rights, treating them terribly, and then killing them. If we frame things the way the law does, then the activists are criminals who are brazenly violating property rights. If we frame things the way the activists do, then they seem like heroes.

Given the Limits, Now What?

There are two ways the conversation can go at this point. On the one hand, we can ask: Who's right? If we ask that question, then we will be right back into familiar debates about the moral status of animals, the merits of the rights view, etc. (Call this the Who's Right approach.) On the other hand, though, we can ask whether there are any *neutral* standards that we can apply in this context—standards that don't rely on answering all those other moral questions. This would be helpful. After all, activism is often controversial precisely because of deep disagreements about what matters and how people ought to live. Maybe we need an ethics for activism that says: "Here are the ground rules for living in society together, and when you want to change something, you need to play by those rules." (Call this the "Ground Rules" approach.) Of course, saying this doesn't tell us what the rules are. In principle, we could still accept theft as a morally legitimate way of trying to advance your moral agenda. We can imagine a society where the rule is: "don't steal, unless stealing is the only way to achieve some morally important social change." However, the odds are good that if we go the Ground Rules route, then there's going to be a strong presumption in favor of obeying the law. Civil disobedience will still be justified in some circumstances, but not many.

Moreover, there seems to be a weighty objection to the Who's Right approach: namely, that it leads to chaos. Sure, it seems very plausible that what's justified when it comes to open rescues depends on who, in fact, is correct about animals. But if we say that, then the risk is that people will think their acts are justified based on what they *believe* to be correct, not on what's *actually* correct. Of course, we can be careful to say that people should be very suspicious of their views when those views imply that it's okay to violate the rights of others. But I, for one, don't feel terribly optimistic about that warning being heard.[1] So, given the advantage of the Ground Rules approach and the problem with the Who's Right approach, it might seem like we should be critical of open rescues.

However, the worry about the Ground Rules approach is that it's so concessive to the status quo. When is it ever the case that the problems in society are completely independent of the institutions and laws that compose it? Basically never. So if there's always a very strong presumption in favor of following the laws (or being civil, or conforming to any other aspect of society), then it will be tremendously hard to change society's unjust features. Essentially, this approach stacks the deck in a way that makes sense if your society is basically good and you want to preserve that goodness. But it's a disaster if your society is basically unjust and you desperately need reform. And again, this is a case where differences in perspective become obvious. From the perspective of many activists, our society is basically unjust, as it treats animals so stunningly badly. Unsurprisingly, farmers—and many consumers—disagree. Those who benefit from the status quo will be happy with the Ground Rules approach; those opposed to the status quo will have reason to complain about it.

After working through some of these complexities, we might want to restart the conversation. Maybe we aren't sure what to say about the relative costs and benefits of the Who's Right and Ground Rules approaches. Is there any other way that we might make progress on the ethics of open rescues?

If we are sympathetic to the plight of animals, then here's one thesis on which we're likely to agree: no one should do open rescues *if they are bad for animals on balance*. That is, we might grant that a particular open rescue is good for those 26 ducks who were removed from the farm, but we might worry that rescuing ducks makes animal activists seem extreme and not worth trusting, and thus that people will be less likely to listen to animal activists in the future. If that happens, then while it might have benefited 26 individuals, it's bad for many more, since activists can't make any progress for animals if they are being ignored. So, we will end up with more of the status quo.

At this juncture, though, we run up against one of the hardest problems in animal advocacy: namely, making predictions about the long-term impacts of particular advocacy strategies. It seems totally reasonable to worry about whether open rescues are bad for animals on balance. But a reasonable worry is just that: a concern that's worth taking seriously about the merits of a given approach. It is not, however, a decisive objection to employing that approach. After all, on the opposite side of things, we might point out that while there will always be people who are turned off by this or that activist strategy, the goal, at least in the short run, may not be to change everyone's views. Instead, the goal may be to inspire other would-be activists to take up the cause. The thought here is that social change is *not* necessarily achieved by converting people *en masse* to a particular perspective. Rather, it's sometimes achieved by creating a critical mass of highly devoted individuals. Those folks can then achieve significant social and political reforms in virtue of having reached some tipping point of influence. In other words, while we might assume that activism is about changing most everyone's mind, it might turn out that—at least in the short run—activists are simply trying to make more activists. And radical methods may be the right way to do that.

It's an empirical question whether open rescues are an effective way of achieving social change, and we haven't resolved that question here. As a result, we haven't settled how to assess open rescues; we've just laid out some of the issues that are relevant. Even doing that, however, should be enough to set aside any knee-jerk condemnation of open rescues: the issues are too complicated for that. We could, of course, forge ahead here, trying to resolve some of the new questions we've raised. But for the sake of space, let's turn our attention to some of the other questions that we can ask about activism.

Are We Obligated to Be Activists?

The next question that we'll consider, if only for a minute, concerns whether we *ought* to engage in animal activism, whether we're obligated to be activists. I suspect that most people think not. They think of activism as a kind of passion project—something that some people love and in which they find meaning—but not something that most people need to do. However, if some standard arguments for veganism succeed, then I suspect that many people ought to be activists. Let's see why.

To begin, let's consider some of the charges that have been leveled against those who eat animals. Alastair Norcross (2004), for instance, compares meat eaters to someone who, essentially, tortures puppies for pleasure. Gary Francione (2007) says that those who eat animals are like Michael Vick, the football player who was convicted of a federal felony for running "Bad Newz Kennels," an elaborate dogfighting operation. Mylan Engel draws a parallel between animal consumption and torturing a Labrador before slaughtering him for food; unsurprisingly, Engel describes the practice as "morally abominable" (2016, 4). Breaking the streak of canine-focused accusations, J. M. Coetzee (2003) claims that meat eaters are like the German citizens who were complicit in the Holocaust; David Sztybel (2006) does the same. Michael Huemer (2019) says that meat eaters are like the soldiers who participated in the My Lai Massacre. In every case, the gist of the argument is: "There is no morally relevant different between [*insert horrible action here*] and eating animal products. So, if [*insert horrible action here*] is wrong, then so is eating animal products. And if it's wrong to eat animals products, then, by definition, we ought to be vegans."

A brief aside. There's much to be said about comparing the plight of animals to the Holocaust, as well as comparing animals to slaves (as someone will later in this chapter). I've generally avoided these analogies, as they are often criticized for being anti-Semitic and racist. Typically, the charge is that these analogies dehumanize the victims of both the Holocaust and various regimes of slavery, and in so doing, trivialize the distinct human tragedies that Jewish and black people (among others) suffered in these contexts. For what it's worth, I think it's safe to say that those who use these analogies have no intention of being anti-Semitic or racist. However, it's also safe to say that the potential *effects* of these analogies may have nothing to do with the intentions of those who deploy them, and when it comes to anti-Semitism and racism, effects often matter far more than intentions. So, while we will need to grapple with arguments that make such parallels, we should also be sensitive to objections to them.

I could give many other examples of people arguing not just that it's *wrong* to purchase and consume animal products, but that it's *very seriously* wrong to purchase and consume them. Indeed, if there really aren't any morally important differences between, say, torturing a Labrador and what we do in purchasing and consuming animal products, then purchasing and consuming animal products is probably the worst thing that average people do. (If there really are no morally important differences, then what would be worse?) And it seems very plausible that if something is morally atrocious—if, on top of that, it's the worst thing that's done by anyone around you—*and* you have the ability to discourage people from doing that thing, then you really ought to try. Maybe you don't have to do it all the time; maybe you don't have to let this cause take over your life. But it doesn't seem like a big step from "don't be like someone who tortures a Labrador yourself" to "discourage others from being like someone who tortures a Labrador." So, if these arguments against eating animals succeed, then they probably imply that you should be trying to get others to stop as well.

Of course, I haven't said anything about how, exactly, you ought to try to get others to stop eating animals. It's one thing to say: you ought to be willing to have conversations with close friends and family about their food choices. It's another thing to say: you ought to start participating in open rescues. I don't think these analogical arguments get you all the way to activism of the latter kind. But they probably do imply that you ought to do more than tell Mom that farmers aren't so nice to chickens these days. And they might imply that you ought to do something like take the Liberation Pledge.

To see why, let me say just a bit more about the analogy that Alastair Norcross uses. I said earlier that in Norcross's example, the person tortures puppies for pleasure. That's true, but the full story is a bit more complicated. The puppy torturer's name is Fred. It turns out that although Fred is condemned as a sadist, he doesn't think of himself that way. As a result of a tragic accident, Fred can no longer taste chocolate. He learns, however, that he can taste it again if he takes a supplement they can only be made from a hormone that puppies produce when severely stressed—that is, tortured—a hormone that can't be secured any other way. He sincerely regrets that this is the only method, and certainly wouldn't torture puppies if there were another option. But puppies are just animals, after all, and he feels that his life would be "unacceptably impoverished" without the pleasures of chocolate (Norcross 2004, 230).

Now imagine being Fred's neighbor and knowing about his little basement operation prior to his arrest. Imagine further that you're on fairly good terms and he invites you to join him at his favorite restaurant, which he loves because of its remarkable chocolate mousse. So you know that if you go, he'll be using his puppy-derived supplement. Would you feel comfortable having dinner with him? Would you think it was fine to do that? If not, then maybe there is something to the Liberation Pledge; perhaps we ought to try to make a statement to people by refusing to share a table with them when animals' bodies will be on it.

The point here is *not* that we all ought to take the Liberation Pledge. There may be a problem with Norcross's argument for veganism; if so, then there's going to be a problem with the extension of that argument to activism. Rather, the point is just that *if* that argument works—or any of the others that I mentioned earlier—then they probably imply more than that we ought to be vegans. Additionally, they probably imply that we ought to engage in some forms of activism. In making this observation, I'm not criticizing those arguments. I'm not saying, "Because certain arguments might imply that we should be activists, there must be something wrong with them." Instead, I'm calling our attention to the fact that these issues are linked. What we say about consumer and dietary ethics will have ramifications elsewhere.

What Should Activists Prioritize?

Let's now turn to a third philosophical question concerning activism: namely, how to decide what to try to change. How should we prioritize all the causes that we might take up? There are, after all, so many different ways you might try to make a difference in the world. Even once you narrow things down to animal-oriented issues, there are so many possible ways to help. What should you do?

A very common answer is: whatever you care about most. This makes cause prioritization a personal affair. So if you've always loved Irish Terriers and you have the opportunity to support an Irish Terrier rescue organization by, say, volunteering some hours at their kennel, then go for it. Or if you've always been into wildlife and there's a proposition on the ballot that would improve protections for habitats in your state, then maybe you should make some calls on its behalf. On this sort of view, you might have a moral obligation *to do something or other* for animals, but no obligation to do any particular thing.

An alternative view says you should do whatever does the most good. The argument for it is simple. Your time and money are scarce resources that have to be allocated. Some of the causes to which you can devote your energies are really significant, and you could make a big difference; some of them are relatively trivial, and you couldn't do much anyway. So, devote your scarce resources where you can make a big difference.

As support for this second view, imagine being a medic in a war zone, and you chose to help a person with a small cut on his arm when you could instead help someone whose leg has been blown off by an improvised explosive device (IED). That would be wrong. And, you might think, we live in a world that's very much like a war zone, full of both enormously important and relatively unimportant causes, and the way you allocate your resources determines whether a few individuals are helped a little or many individuals are helped a lot. Sure, it sounds nice to help the handful of Irish Terriers in your local kennel, but their lives will be basically the same either way. However, if you were to devote the same amount of time to leafleting, letting people know about the many problems with intensive animal agriculture, you might change someone's behavior. And as we discussed in Chapter 7, many philosophers think that even a small behavior change can make a big difference in terms of the number of animals who suffer. So, that's what you should do (assuming you have no even better option).

Someone might object to this argument by saying, "But we aren't in a war zone, and in any case, I'm not a medic. I'm just a regular person, living my life in ordinary circumstances." However, I'm not sure that these differences are as important as they may initially seem to be. Let's begin with the bit about your not being a medic. That's probably true, of course, but in the context of the analogy, it doesn't really matter. Imagine that you aren't a medic on the battlefield, but you're just an ordinary civilian who happens to come across wounded soldiers after a battle has occurred. Some of them are suffering intensely, and you realize that you can help. But then, instead of helping someone who needs you to apply pressure so he doesn't bleed out (which, let's suppose, you're able and not too squeamish to do), you decide to focus on the guy with a sprained ankle. In such circumstances, you don't get a gold star just for being willing to do anything at all. Instead, your action is *worse* than not doing anything at all, as it demonstrates that a soldier's life really could have been saved—there really was someone there with the capacity to help who chose not to.

As for the war zone part, someone might think that war is an extraordinary circumstance, where the stakes are so high that people have an obligation to be careful about how and what they prioritize. In daily life, on the other hand, we don't have that obligation since the stakes are much lower. But of course, the stakes *are* just as high in ordinary life. Though we rarely recognize it, it's nevertheless true that so many seemingly mundane choices have significant consequences for someone, somewhere. If we decide to volunteer in a way that makes us feel good, as opposed to one that maximizes our impact, then some lives will go significantly worse than they otherwise would. Again, then, we've got reason to think that if we're going to do anything, then we ought to do whatever produces the most good.[2]

We began this section by asking how we ought to prioritize the various causes before us. There is something appealing about the idea that this is, ultimately, a deeply personal decision. Perhaps surprisingly, that idea turns out to be somewhat difficult to defend. So while there are other moves to make in this exchange, let's just suppose that we ought to prioritize causes based on our ability to do the most good. What issues come up next?

Here's one pressing issue. If we want to do the most good we can for animals, we find ourselves asking hard questions about the trade-offs we should be willing to accept. We've considered some trade-offs already when we discussed open rescues; in that case, we were thinking about the importance of following the law (as well as long-term reputational concerns for animal activists) versus the importance of helping individual animals. But there are plenty of examples that don't involve breaking the law. Consider one of PETA's more famous campaigns. From 1990 to 2020, PETA recruited attractive women to pose naked behind a sign saying, "I'd rather go naked than wear fur," running these photos as ads in popular magazines, on billboards, and later on the Internet. Over the years, PETA was regularly criticized for them. Maneesha Deckha offers one version of the objection:

> [Many of these ads] are problematic from a feminist intersectional ethic. This is because the images are evocative of the soft pornographic images that appear in publications such as *Playboy* and *Penthouse* in their reproduction of nude white female bodies to be consumed by a male, heteronormative gaze. . . . The images, and the popularity of long, nimble, blond, and able-bodied white model bodies that appear in them (Pamela Anderson, Dominique Swain, Alicia Silverstone, etc.), also engage and perpetuate a racialized, gendered, and ableist discourse of beauty and their attendant practices of self-presentation to achieve impossible standards of attractiveness to heterosexual men.
>
> (2008, 50)

On Deckha's view, while it's important to advocate for animals, we shouldn't do it in a way that, among other things, sets back the interests of black women (by promoting a racialized conception of beauty) and disabled women (by presenting an ableist conception of beauty). The trade-off isn't worth it.

We might ask, of course, whether Deckha is correct. Are these women actually being presented "to be consumed by a male, heteronormative gaze"? Is it actually bad for women of color to have white women depicted in these ways? (Does it matter that PETA ran other ads that depicted women of color in the same ways?) How important is it that these women are being presented as having a moral agenda, very much unlike the women in pornography?

However, suppose that we're sympathetic to Deckha's critique. That doesn't necessarily settle the question of whether the ads should be created and disseminated. After all, it could turn out that the plight of animals is so bad that it's worth doing whatever it takes to raise awareness about animal causes. In other words, if the price of ending the fur trade is making a marginal contribution to the objectification of women, then maybe the price is right.

To be clear, I'm not saying that the price *is* right. Instead, I'm just pointing out that once we accept that we ought to do the most good, it's an open question whether we ought to make some sacrifices with respect to some important causes in order to make progress on more significant ones. Someone might insist, of course, that it's generally counterproductive to ignore some causes for the sake of others—that in the long run, movements are most successful when they don't marginalize anyone, and so develop the broadest possible coalitions for change. I'll just note, though, that I'm not sure history supports this view. The major successes of the civil rights movement and the gay rights movement were driven by single-issue activism. What's more, those successes preceded general sympathy for black and gay causes; neither group had public opinion on its side when it won the most crucial court battles. We might see this as some evidence for saying: don't worry about broad coalitions; just get a sizable minority on your side and then press like hell for legal reform.

Here too, then, there are important historical and empirical questions that are beyond the scope of this chapter. But before we move on to the final philosophical question that will occupy us, which is closely related, let's just note that our answers to questions about acceptable trade-offs will reveal a great deal about our views on the relative importance of various animal and human causes, as well as the degree to which we see forms of oppression as entangled with one another. Do we think that we can make significant progress on racism without addressing classism? Do we think that we can make significant progress on speciesism without tackling sexism? If so, then it becomes much easier to defend a narrower, single-issue focus—and there will be many more trade-offs with which to be concerned.

Abolition or Reform?

In the final section of this chapter, let's turn to an issue that's closely linked to the conversation we've been having about cause prioritization and acceptable trade-offs, though that isn't the way it's normally framed. Instead, it's usually framed as a debate between people who are more sympathetic to the rights view (the abolition-ists) versus those more sympathetic to consequentialism (the welfarists). So under-stood, the debate becomes about whether activists ought to try to improve existing systems—say, by arguing for larger cages for chickens, or more time on pasture for cattle—versus trying to abolish systems that are based on the idea that animals are resources for our use.

The thing is, though, that nearly all the consequentialists—that is, the welfarists—also want to abolish systems that are based on the idea that animals are resources for our use. On one level, then, nearly everyone in animal advocacy circles is an abolitionist, and in that sense, there's very little disagreement in the animal advocacy community about the long-term objective. Still, there remains a deep moral dispute. The question is whether it's okay to tolerate the idea that animals are our resources—an idea sometimes called "the resource paradigm"—as we work for change. If you think we shouldn't, then you're a radical abolitionist; if you think we may, then you're a pragmatic abolitionist.

Jason Wyckoff gives a powerful argument for radical abolitionism over pragmatic abolitionism, which he sums up this way:

> It does not matter from the point of view of justice how particular people treat particular slaves (though this is important from the ethical point of view), and so institutional reforms that provide for improved treatment of slaves, while leaving their status as slaves intact, do not address the underly-ing injustice. Likewise, from the point of view of justice it does not matter how particular humans treat particular animals, and so reforms that require better treatment for animals without challenging the current paradigm do little to address the injustices of animal commodification and the collective understanding that animals are the resources of humans. To that end, we should commit ourselves explicitly to a withdrawal of support for the resource paradigm; this entails a commitment to veganism and vegan activism.
>
> (2014, 551)

The basic idea here is simple. Let's think about ethics as focused on the way individ-uals ought to act, and justice as focused on the way that societies ought to be struc-tured. Moreover, let's assume that everyone's interests deserve equal consideration, whether human or nonhuman. Now, let's note that if animals have an interest in not being categorized as mere resources, it's wrong to treat them as though they didn't have this interest—just as it would be wrong to try to improve the treatment of slaves while leaving their status as slaves intact. In numerous lectures and essays, another radical abolitionist, Gary Francione, says that pragmatic abolitionists are people who see someone being waterboarded and argue that there ought to be a bit more padding on the board. They aren't attacking what really needs to be attacked—the idea that it's okay to waterboard someone in the first place. So, animal advocates ought to be trying to undermine the resource paradigm, not just trying to improve the welfare of animals within industries and institutions that view them as resources.

If this view is correct, then it has big implications for contemporary animal advocacy, much of which is devoted to improving the welfare of farmed animals. What
should we say about it?

To begin, it might be helpful to think a bit more about the context in which we
are trying to achieve various reforms. Just how bad is the situation? We might
think that in truly disastrous situations, we should just do whatever helps the
greatest number in the short run—saving lives and relieving suffering however
we can. We might think of contemporary animal agriculture as a burning house.
Around the house there are many problems to fix—the third-rate safety codes that
made the fire possible in the first place and the poor funding model for the fire
department, which explains why the firefighters are stretched too thin and can't
respond rapidly to all the calls they receive. In the midst of the fire, though, it's
hard to imagine saying that we should focus on these structural problems. When
disaster strikes, it seems like we're dealing with rule fetishism when we fail to
do the most good we can. So, *contra* Francione, it seems like we ought to support
pragmatic abolitionist reforms. Taking this pragmatic approach isn't the same
thing as putting some extra padding underneath the person being waterboarded.
Instead, it's more like giving a sip of water to someone who, on the way to his
execution, is suffering from terrible thirst.

In principle, someone could defend radical abolitionism against this objection by
denying that we're in the midst of a disaster. But this isn't a very promising maneuver. Untold billions of animals being killed per year is a disaster. Moreover, disasters needn't be relatively brief affairs (example: droughts), they needn't be natural
(example: genocides), the causes of the disaster can be due to institutional structures
(example: slavery), and disasters don't need to *feel* like disasters, since people can
be wrong about whether we're facing one (example: climate change).

So, rather than challenge the idea that we're in the midst of a disaster, someone
who wants to defend the radical abolitionist perspective should make a different
move. They should say that if we ought to tolerate the resource paradigm when it
comes to animals, then it follows that we should have tolerated it when it came to
human slavery, as all the same considerations apply there. However, the reply goes,
it's clear that we ought to have been radical abolitionists about slavery.

This is a compelling objection, and it's unclear whether the pragmatic approach
can answer it. Perhaps the best move for the pragmatic approach, however, is to try
to put things in historical perspective. Maybe there was a time when, in the context
of American slavery, pragmatic abolitionism was the right way to resist. In 1700,
for instance, perhaps the best you could do was try to make marginal improvements
for the victims of a terribly unjust system. (Imagine a closeted Southern abolitionist
who knows that if her views were discovered, she'd lose the few chances she has to
provide aid to the slaves in her town.) And maybe there was a later time when radical abolitionism was the right way to resist human slavery. In 1850, perhaps the best
you could do was actually better. It had become possible to challenge the resource
paradigm itself, as opposed to simply improving the conditions of individual slaves.
(By then, maybe it would have been a mistake to be a closeted Southern abolitionist.
It was worth being vocal about your abolitionism, agitating for change.) Likewise,

pragmatic abolitionism with respect to the resource paradigm might be a viable moral position now but not in a hundred years.

Of course, this is perfectly compatible with saying that justice required the abolition of slavery all along, and similarly, that justice requires the abolition of practices and institutions that subordinate animals. Again, the debate here isn't about whether animal agriculture (or anything else) ought to be abolished; it's about whether it's okay to work within the system in the interim.

Let's consider one last way that someone might defend the radical abolitionist view. The thought goes like this: welfare reforms will slow the absolute end of animal agriculture, the realization of a fully vegan world, as they will make people more comfortable with systems that exploit animals. Once animal agriculture isn't so horrifying—or once animal research isn't so horrifying, or any other manifestation of the resource paradigm—most people will say, "Well, we're actually treating animals pretty well, and the benefits to human beings are significant, so there's no reason to dismantle these practices and institutions." So, if you're really an abolitionist, then you should be a radical abolitionist, as you shouldn't be willing to risk doing what might, in the long term, prop up the very practices and institutions that you're trying to dismantle.

Recall that the radical abolitionist thinks that we should be focused on trying to undermine the resource paradigm, the idea that animals are there for our use. As a result, the radical abolitionist rejects ways of helping animals that don't call that paradigm into question; even if you might make some marginal gains for animals in the short run, the trade-off isn't worth it. We should prioritize trying to undermine the view of animals that leads to their exploitation, not particular instances of exploitation.

There is something attractive about this position. My guess, though, is that no one really knows whether a pragmatic approach will prolong the resource paradigm. It could just as well work out that as people spend more time reflecting on why it's worth reforming animal agriculture, research, and much else, they will become much more sympathetic to animals, coming to see them as the kinds of beings who shouldn't be resources in the first place. (This, it seems, is exactly what has happened over the last several decades, as attitudes toward animals have shifted dramatically, even if behavior has lagged behind.) And if we regard these possibilities as equally likely, being unsure of how the future will develop, it seems reasonable to prioritize the beings we know we can help now—namely, all the animals currently on farms, in labs, and elsewhere.

Granted, that may involve some risk of prolonging the resource paradigm, which certainly seems objectionable. But there's something strange about taking animals so seriously without being willing to take risks to benefit them. Imagine a debate between two suffragists at the end of the 19th century, with one of them saying that it would be a mistake to try to get women the right to vote in one state, as it might create a backlash that would set back the national cause. You can understand the point, but it's hard not to think that the appropriate response is, "Don't forget all the women it would help! It's worth the gamble!" Likewise, if animals are important enough to reorganize much of human society for animals' sake, they are important enough to make it worth gambling on what seems like the best way to help them.

Conclusion

This brings us full circle. It is, as we've already noted, enormously difficult to know how to predict what will happen if we pursue different advocacy strategies. We are therefore taking risks whatever we do. It may seem extreme to refuse to eat with those who are eating animals or to enter farms to liberate animals. But we also take risks when we eat with those who are eating animals and respect the laws that represent animals as property. We risk communicating that it's acceptable to eat animals, that it isn't the kind of thing that's worth complicating a relationship over. Similarly, we risk communicating that the law is more important than the lives of sentient beings. If we should be activists, we will have to decide which risks to take.

I tend to be risk-averse. I'm a "bird in the hand is worth two in the bush" sort of guy—except for the killing birds part. So I favor more pragmatic approaches, as I would rather see some change now rather than hold out for larger changes later. I'm wary of damaging relationships for the sake of a cause, not least because it's so hard to regain lines of communication—and so influence—once they're lost. I'm disinclined to break the law, not because I think it's sacrosanct, but because being law-abiding matters in the circles where I think I can have influence.

Others come down on the opposite side of each issue, and I sometimes wonder whether these debates bottom out in differences in temperament. But while that's bad for consensus, perhaps it's good for the overall effectiveness of animal advocacy. Maybe we need a mix of pragmatists and radicals—the former to make incremental change, and the latter to shift the Overton window, making it possible for the society at large to imagine entirely new ways of relating to nonhuman animals. I don't know whether this conciliatory vision is true, but I hope it is.

Further Reading

Abbate, C.E. 2020. "How to Help When It Hurts: ACT Individually (and in Groups)." *Animal Studies Journal* 9(1): 170–200.

Brueck, Julia Feliz. 2017. *Veganism in an Oppressive World: A Vegans-of-Color Community Project*. Sanctuary Publishers.

Francione, Gary, and Robert Garner. 2010. *The Animal Rights Debate: Abolition or Regulation?* New York: Columbia University Press.

Hadley, John. 2009. "Animal Rights Extremism and the Terrorism Question." *Journal of Social Philosophy* 40(3): 363–378.

Hadley, John. 2017. "Religiosity and Public Reason: The Case of Direct Action Animal Rights Advocacy." *Res Publica* 23(3): 299–312.

Jamison, Wesley V., Caspar Wenk, and James V. Parker. 2000. "Every Sparrow That Falls: Understanding Animal Rights Activism as Functional Religion." *Society and Animals* 8(3): 305–330.

Kemmerer, Lisa. 2006. "Verbal Activism: 'Anymal'." *Society and Animals* 14(1): 9–14.

Leenaert, Tobias. 2017. *How to Create a Vegan World: A Pragmatic Approach*. Brooklyn: Lantern Publishing & Media.

MacAskill, William. 2015. *Doing Good Better*. New York: Oxford University Press.

Sebo, Jeff. 2020. "Effective Animal Advocacy." In *The Routledge Handbook of Animal Ethics*, edited by Bob Fischer. New York: Routledge.

Notes

1. Some ethical theories are *self-effacing*, which is to say, very roughly, that if they're true, not everyone should *believe* that they're true. Usually, people present utilitarianism as a self-effacing moral theory. The principle of utility—the idea that you ought to do whatever maximizes utility—is billed as the criterion of right action; it's what specifies the conditions under which actions are morally obligatory. However, it isn't billed as a decision procedure; it isn't the thing that you consult every time you are trying to decide what to do. So maybe we should teach people simple moral rules, like "don't steal" and "don't murder," and those should be their guides. Or maybe we should encourage people to cultivate the virtues and let them act out of charity or courage or what have you. In any case, if you are comfortable with a self-effacing moral theory, then there is a sense in which you don't really have the problem that I'm talking about here. You can say: "Yes, who's right determines the kind of activism that are justified, but of course we shouldn't tell people that, because then they'll do crazy things. So, we should promote some other account of the ethics of activism—one that isn't specified directly by the facts about who's right in any particular debate." Fair enough; that dodges the problem as I've sketched it. But it still leaves you with the task of developing that other account of the ethics of activism, and all I'm suggesting is that it's a tricky thing to do, with unpleasant costs whichever way you go.

2. There may be ways of resisting this conclusion, but let's suppose we're willing to accept it. How do we decide what does the most good? A standard answer from the effective altruism community—people who are committed to doing the most good they can—is that you ought to consider three factors: scope, neglectedness, and tractability. The scope of the problem is just the size and intensity of it. How many individuals are affected, and how severely? The neglectedness of a problem is essentially the degree to which others aren't doing anything about it. This matters because it means that, all else equal, you can make a larger difference, since you won't simply be crowding out others who might have done the same work anyway, but now won't have to because you've done it. Tractability concerns the degree to which you can actually do something about the problem. Some problems are very important but very hard to tackle, such as the threat of nuclear war, and it isn't clear that the average civilian can do anything about it. So, nuclear warfare scores very low on tractability. Other problems, however, are more manageable: we know how to make a difference it comes to reducing animal product consumption—say, by encouraging school cafeterias to include more plant-based options. By comparison, this cause scores very high on tractability. Of course, this proposal isn't the only one out there for trying to maximize effectiveness, but it's probably the most prominent in philosophical circles.

References

2018. "California Proposition 12, Farm Animal Confinement Initiative (2018)." *Ballotpedia.* https://ballotpedia.org/California_Proposition_12,_Farm_Animal_Confinement_ Initiative_(2018).

Coetzee, John Maxwell. 2003. *Elizabeth Costello.* London: Harvill Secker.

Dechka, Maneesha. 2008. "Disturbing Images: Peta and the Feminist Ethics of Animal Advocacy." *Ethics and the Environment* 13(2): 35–76.

Engel, Mylan. 2016. "The Commonsense Case for Ethical Vegetarianism." *Between the Species* 19(1): 3–31.

Flynn, Dan. 2020. "Food Safety Claims Land Smithfield Foods Inc. in D.C. Court." *Food Safety News*, May 26. www.foodsafetynews.com/2020/05/food-safety-claims-land-smithfield-foods-inc-in-d-c-court/.

Francione, Gary. 2007. "We're all Michael Vick." *Philadelphia Daily News*, August 22. www.abolitionistapproach.com/media/pdf/philadelphia-daily-news-20070822.pdf.

Harris, Jesse. 2020. "King Cole Duck Rescue: Interview with Activist Jenny McQueen." *Sentient Media*, February 28. https://sentientmedia.org/king-cole-duck-rescue-interview-activist-jenny-mcqueen/.

Huemer, Michael. 2019. *Dialogues on Ethical Vegetarianism*. New York: Routledge.

Klein, Ezra. 2019. "When Doing the Right Thing Makes You a Criminal." *Vox*, December 5. www.vox.com/podcasts/2019/12/5/20995117/wayne-hsiung-animal-rights-the-ezra-klein-show.

"The Liberation Pledge." *The Liberation Pledge*. www.liberationpledge.com/.

Lockwood, Alex. 2019. "Liberation Pledgers Won't Eat at a Table Serving Meat: I'm Vegan, but Can't Do It." *PBN*, March 20. www.plantbasednews.org/opinion/liberation-pledgers-refuse-eat-table-serving-meat-vegan-cant-do-it.

Norcross, Alastair. 2004. "Puppies, Pigs, and People: Eating Meat and Marginal Cases." *Philosophical Perspectives* 18: 229–245. https://doi.org/10.1111/j.1520-8583.2004.00027.x.

Sztybel, David. 2006. "Can the Treatment of Animals be Compared to the Holocaust?" *Ethics & The Environment* 11(1): 97–132.

Wyckoff, Jason. 2014. "Toward Justice for Animals." *Journal of Social Philosophy* 45(4): 539–553. https://doi.org/10.1111/josp.12077.

15 Conclusion

OVERVIEW

What's next for animal ethics? To answer this question, this chapter considers the idea that animals should be granted legal personhood. Two lessons emerge. First, animal ethics can make progress by putting familiar ideas to work in new contexts—as seen, for instance, in the way that the Nonhuman Rights Project has tried to advance the legal rights of animals. Second, animal ethics can make progress by being more self-critical—as seen, for instance, in an objection that this chapter sketches to one of the arguments on which the Nonhuman Rights Project relies.

Dave Sabo used to run Sabo's Chimps—a company that, among other things, leased primates to film production companies. Toward the end of his life, through various twists of fate, he and some of his chimps wound up living outside of Gloversville, New York, on the property of a trailer rental business. When Sabo died in 2008, the owner of the property, Patrick Lavery, came to own the animals.

Since then, Lavery has kept one of these chimps—Tommy, who played "Goliath" in the 1987 film, *Project X*—caged in a small shed. The walls are painted to look like a jungle, but that's about the only effort to make the space akin to a chimpanzee's natural habitat. Tommy has a TV to watch and a radio to which to listen, and he's sometimes allowed into a separate enclosure with a little jungle gym. It's a lonely life. Still, this arrangement doesn't violate any of New York's animal welfare laws (as you might expect, given the discussion in Chapter 11). Someone who "deprives any animal of necessary sustenance, food or drink, or neglects or refuses to furnish it such sustenance or drink . . . is guilty of a class A misdemeanor," according to Chapter 69 of the Consolidated Laws of the State of New York (Article 25-B, Chapter 40, Part Three, Title H, Article 130, § 353). But Lavery hasn't done any of those things. The law forbids denying animals what they need to survive; it doesn't require people to provide the kind of enrichment that allows them to flourish.

Steven Wise, the founder and president of the Nonhuman Rights Project, thinks it's wrong to keep Tommy in such conditions. Indeed, he thinks it ought to be illegal. And so, in 2013, the Nonhuman Rights Project filed a petition for a common law writ of habeas corpus. In other words, the Nonhuman Rights Project asked the court to consider arguments to the effect that Tommy was being unjustly detained. In particular, this petition asked the court to "issue a writ recognizing that Tommy is not a legal thing to be possessed by [Lavery], but rather is a cognitively complex autonomous legal person with the fundamental legal right not to be imprisoned" ("Nonhuman Rights," 2).

As we come to the end of the book, I want us to reflect on the efforts that the Nonhuman Rights Project is making on Tommy's behalf. What glimpses does it give us into the future of animal ethics? How should the conversation proceed? As you'll see, I hope that we follow in Wise's footsteps, applying standard arguments in new contexts. At the same time, I hope that we'll stay true to the ideals of philosophical ethics, which means, in part, that we'll be willing to challenge the very arguments we develop.

Legal Personhood

Let's begin with this. If Tommy is a "cognitively complex autonomous legal person," then he probably has a legal right not to be imprisoned. His cognitive complexity and autonomy ground his fundamental interest in liberty, and if he's a legal person, then that fundamental interest grounds a right to liberty. That right could be overridden, at least in principle, but there's no cause for that: he hasn't committed a crime; he poses no danger to himself or others. So, there is no reason to deny him his freedom. The question, then, is whether the law should recognize a chimpanzee as a legal person.

Why think it should? The argument has two parts. First, the Nonhuman Rights Project has amassed an enormous amount of evidence for Tommy's mental sophistication. Second, they've argued that the court has no good reason to deny Tommy standing as a legal person. Basically, he counts as a legal person by any plausible standard of legal personhood, and we should reject the other standards for independent reasons.

I'm not going to review all the evidence for Tommy's mental sophistication.[1] Instead, let's focus on the standards of legal personhood. There are four ways to deny Tommy that status.

Way #1. "Tommy isn't human! Only humans can be legal persons!"

In 2014, this is exactly how one court responded. It pointed out that writs of habeas corpus have only been granted to members of our species, so there's no precedent for extending such protections to nonhuman animals. But why, exactly, does a biological category matter so much? Without an answer to this question, the appeal to species membership seems entirely arbitrary. Moreover, there are reasons to think that no good answer is waiting in the wings. There are familiar reasons for this, which we discussed at length in Chapter 2. The upshot of that conversation was that species just aren't equipped to do much in the way of normative work. There's no particular trait that an individual must have to be a member of a species; there's no single trait that makes an individual a member of a species; and species are constantly changing, so there's no trait that invariably identifies a species over time. This means that we probably aren't going to find a property such that (a) all and only human beings have it and (b) it explains why all and only human beings deserve legal personhood. So, species membership seems like a bad reason to deny Tommy the status that would guarantee his freedom.

Way #2: "Tommy isn't *really* autonomous, so he isn't a person!"

The idea here is that you can't be a person unless you are autonomous *in the right way*. It isn't enough to make plans, act for reasons, and so on. As always, the challenge is going to be to give a plausible account of "autonomy" that doesn't exclude humans who lack the relevant traits and yet which manages to rule out chimps. But given the cognitive sophistication of chimpanzees and the relative simplicity of many human beings, it seems quite clear that there isn't going to be any such account of autonomy. So, since we shouldn't exclude those humans, we shouldn't exclude Tommy.

Way #3: "Tommy is a member of the wrong community! Human communities are *person-creating* communities, and he isn't one of us!"

The claim here isn't that human communities make babies, though that's true. (Questions? Ask a friend.) Instead, the claim is that there's something about participating in the human community that *makes* you a person. However, I have no idea why that would be true. And even if we were to accept it, it doesn't show that Tommy isn't a person. First, why would human communities be the only ones that can make individuals into persons? Why couldn't communities of chimpanzees—or dolphins, or wolves—do the same thing? Second, why think that you have to be a human being to be a member of "our" community? It seems pretty clear that many people treat their companion animals as members of the human community, and in virtue of the way that Tommy has been socialized into—and made dependent on—human communities, he seems to have some claim to be a person even by this standard.

Way #4: "Legal personhood should be restricted to beings who can make contracts!"

Contractors, you'll recall, are rational beings who can make agreements with others about how to live together. Tommy isn't one of those, at least on the face of it. But as a standard for legal personhood, this view faces a serious objection. The reason to restrict legal personhood to contractors is that contractors can engage in reciprocal relationships. Not only can they agree to and follow rules, they can also be held accountable for breaking rules. Put differently, contractors don't just get rights out of the contract; they get responsibilities as well. There's a give-and-take here that requires some cognitive sophistication. But you can already see where this is going. It would be a mistake to restrict legal personhood to individuals who can have responsibilities, as that would exclude infants and many other human individuals, all of whom we ought to count as legal persons despite their not being contractors.

Given the problems with all four of these arguments, you might think that there would be at least one court that would grant the petition for a writ of habeas corpus, thereby freeing Tommy. But to date, none has. The Nonhuman Rights Project has been turned back by every judge who's heard their arguments. Presumably, no judge wants to deal with the media firestorm that would ensue were they to decide that chickens are people—which, of course, wouldn't be the upshot of the decision, but it's the way the story would be told on the Internet. So, the Nonhuman Rights Project gives the same arguments, the judges give one of the same replies, and each petition eventually gets denied.

This must be enormously discouraging for the lawyers involved in the Nonhuman Rights Project, and I don't envy the way they've been treated by the courts. Still, there's an important sense in which they are revealing what's next for animal ethics. These lawyers are taking standard, run-of-the-mill arguments in the field—the kinds of arguments that we discussed as preliminaries in Chapter 2—and trying them out in new places. And, of course, they can only do that because they know enough about the law to adapt the arguments to that context. You combine some basic philosophical insights with legal expertise, and you get a striking result: Tommy should be a legal person.

In a sense, that's what I've tried to do in parts of this book: I've tried to bring some standard philosophical arguments to bear on issues that haven't gotten much attention. There is nothing particularly fancy, philosophically speaking, about the ethics of running institutional animal care and use committees (IACUCs), pest control, or industrial fishing. Instead, there are a range of empirical details that, once seen in light of some basic observations about membership in the moral community, wild animal suffering, and so on, lead us toward interesting conclusions. One way animal ethics moves forward, then, is just by engaging with previously neglected animals, or previously neglected human–animal relationships, wherever they happen to be found. I've tried to model how this can be done, digging into the complexities that affect how we assess the status quo. We might have thought that if we grant the assumptions that shape how IACUCs assess protocols (proposals to use animals), it would be easy to justify using animals in the classroom. Not so. Likewise, we might have thought that, given the sheer number of fish we haul out of the ocean, it would be straightforward to show that industrial fishing is a moral catastrophe. It might be just that, of course, but the issue is more complicated than it initially seems.

I hope that as animal ethics proceeds, we see much more of this. In my view, people haven't spent enough time thinking about all sorts of animals in all sorts of contexts: feral hog management; the use of dogs in therapy; extracting blood from horseshoe crabs to create vaccines; living with predators in cities (from foxes to big cats); farmed animals other than chickens, pigs, and cattle (such as goats, sheep, and llamas); the rise of fish as research models; and much else. In every case, there are philosophical and empirical issues to explore, and with some luck, people will give them the attention they deserve.

Unpleasant Work

At the same time, I hope there's a different future for animal ethics, one that's less comfortable for people who want to see things improve for animals—myself included.

Some animal ethics is tantamount to animal advocacy, and that's all well and good. I've done some advocating in this book. But animal ethics is also a subfield of philosophy, and as such, we're interested in the merits of arguments, which we try to assess as impartially as possible. In particular, this means being charitable to our conversation partners by helping them improve their arguments, even when we want them to be wrong. This is called "steelmanning": trying to come up with the strongest version of an argument that, ultimately, you reject. (The contrast here is with "strawmanning," the mistake of presenting a weak version of your opponent's argument.) That's what I was trying to do when I raised objections to arguments against consuming products from intensive animal agriculture; it's what I was doing when I tried to complicate the case against industrial fishing. Philosophical integrity requires that we don't simply say what we want to be true, but what we can defend. And to give a claim a real defense, we have to level the best objections to it—even if we have to generate some of them.

Of course, "what we can defend" (here, today) isn't the same as "what can be defended." There are plenty of very smart philosophers who would disagree with me about one or another of the conclusions we've reached in this book. So the point is not that the arguments here represent the final word. I'm only human; I'm sure I've made mistakes. Rather, the point is that doing philosophy honestly often involves pointing out problems with arguments whose conclusions we support. Likewise, it involves coming up with good arguments for conclusions we reject. After all, as I said in Chapter 1, ethics is something we do in conversation with others, where the endgame is rational persuasion. We aren't trying to win; we're trying to find conclusions that survive careful scrutiny in hopes that we'll all be convinced of their truth. That would provide some confirmation that we aren't just doubling down on our biases, preconceptions, and preferences. Steelmanning can be unpleasant work, but it's work that needs doing.

Legal Advocacy Revisited

All this applies to the legal advocacy work that we've been considering here. I'm excited by the prospect that nonhuman animals might be counted as legal persons. This would radically change the odds of being able to improve their lives. It would, in my view, be an enormous moral victory. At the same time, I worry that there's a problem with the case for Tommy's legal personhood. While those judges may well be rejecting the Nonhuman Rights Project's petitions for the wrong reasons, there may actually be a good reason available to them. Let's try to do some steel-manning on their behalf.

Here's a quick sketch of what I have in mind. Remember the idea that you have to be a contractor to be a legal person? We quickly set that aside, as it runs into a familiar problem. To make that view work, you have to say that contractors need to have responsibilities as well as rights—otherwise, Tommy could be a contractor too. But if you say that contractors need to have responsibilities as well as rights, then human infants are out, since they don't have any responsibilities. Since we shouldn't say that human infants are out, we shouldn't say that legal persons need to be contractors (understood as beings who can be held accountable for their actions).

Put differently, this challenge to Tommy's being a legal person is based on the idea that rights require duties. Now, the idea that rights *require* duties makes reciprocity a necessary condition for the possession of rights; no one counts as a rights holder, and so a legal person, unless she's the kind of being who can have responsibilities too. However, we don't have to frame things that way. Instead, we could see having responsibilities as a *practical constraint* on the number of rights-bearing beings who aren't able to engage in reciprocal relationships. In other words, though it isn't the case that every rights-bearer needs to be able to engage in reciprocal relationships with other rights-bearers—not everyone needs to be blamable for not following the rules—most rights-bearers do. Otherwise, the burdens on rights-bearers could become crushing. They could find themselves living in a world that is full of beings who are owed things, without owing anything in return; beings who require accommodation, but never accommodate. And if animals should be legal persons, that would be exactly the way things are. There would be countless individuals with legal rights—every nonhuman animal who meets the relevant threshold for cognitive complexity—none of whom could be asked to do anything at all.

This worry about reciprocity makes sense of so many judges' resistance to the efforts of the Nonhuman Rights Project. The precedent would indeed have consequences. It may just be chimps today, but it's going to be chickens tomorrow—or next year, or the decade after. And if that were to happen, human society would have to change dramatically, given how many of our ordinary practices assume that we may treat the interests of animals differently than the interests of human beings. On this picture, there's a kind of background assumption about rights being in place to protect a certain kind of life and its associated liberties. The reciprocity constraint is there to ensure that people don't have to be fully devoted to sustaining moral patients. They can instead pursue their own projects.

To be fair, "things would have to change if animals were to be legal persons" is not, in and of itself, much of a reason to deny rights to anyone. I'm not impressed by this as a piece of moral reasoning. This is the kind of argument that slave owners could have made in response to calls for black liberation. Still, I think that those responsible for upholding the law could argue that the cases are importantly different. Liberated slaves can join society; they can be integrated into the life of a community that once excluded them. Granted, the process isn't seamless. The society is bound to discover, over time, that seemingly just laws are, in fact, radically unfair to former slaves and/or their descendants. The legal and institutional structures of a society can appear neutral when they aren't. In the grand scheme of things, however, it's *relatively* easy to make the law less discriminatory toward groups of human beings. Things won't be so easy in the case of nonhuman animals. When it comes to human beings, we can suss out the necessary changes in the tax code or revise the list of criminalized substances. But it's quite another thing, in hopes of advancing the cause of animals, to abandon the idea that getting usually requires giving—that is, the thought that if you're going to benefit from society, you're going to have some responsibilities in return.

This idea—that getting usually requires giving—doesn't necessarily mean contributing financially or via your labor, though that's certainly desirable. Minimally, it's just important that you be able to follow the rules of the society, that you not injure others unnecessarily or steal their belongings. You can "give back" by respecting the side constraints that the society places on normal interactions. More robustly, you can give back by doing the sorts of things that enrich the society, economically or otherwise. Law-abiding consumers, for instance, provide a way for others to make a living.

Granted, as Sue Donaldson and Will Kymlicka (2011, 120) point out, we don't know how many animals are such that they can be integrated into human communities. We just haven't tried. Many animals may be able to live quite peaceably with us, assuming that we are willing to think hard about how they might fit into society. But while we could probably do better, even Donaldson and Kymlicka acknowledge that most animals can't be trusted to follow the rules of human societies. Big cats regard people as prey. Elephants sometimes stampede through villages, crushing whatever's in their way. Monkeys steal from vendors at outdoor markets. Squirrels refuse to respect property rights, damaging power lines at a stunning rate. With a lot of effort, you can teach an entire generation of young humans not to fear one another, and so not to lash out against one another. However, you simply can't do that with snakes. By and large, animals don't understand—and have no incentive to follow—human laws and customs.

One response to this observation is to say that there are plenty of human beings who don't follow human laws. But in many cases, we blame them for not following the law, whereas it would be silly to blame animals for the same offense. They can't be faulted when they have no grasp of the rules. And where the same is true of human beings—that is, where human beings can't be blamed for not following the law— they're generally (a) children, and so we expect they will learn to follow the law eventually, or (b) relatively few in number (such as those with severe cognitive disabilities), and so managing their behavior places a relatively small burden on society.

The upshot: to grant animals legal personhood is to grant political rights to an enormous number of beings with no real prospect of having them align themselves with the norms of human communities. It would massively increase the burdens on humans—who would need to accommodate and care for all these legal persons— with no reciprocation on their part. That might be too much to ask of current legal persons (namely, humans). Granted, then, it's somewhat arbitrary to deny legal personhood to Tommy. Nothing about the "the burdens are too great" story explains why *Tommy specifically* shouldn't be a legal person. But lines have to be drawn somewhere, and it doesn't seem unreasonable to say that the species boundary is at least as good, if not better, a place as any alternative. This position may even be appealing as long as we can address Tommy's needs via some mechanism or other—say, by improving animal welfare laws. We can understand why judges might take it to be the most sensible option.

To be clear, I have no idea whether the judges who have considered petitions from the Nonhuman Rights Project have had these thoughts. If so, they haven't said it explicitly. But concerns of this kind may be in the background, and they aren't clearly ridiculous. Judges might see themselves, in this instance, as needing to preserve a societal order that's based on a certain way of balancing privileges against obligations. Maybe we can fault them for calling it a just order. But perhaps we can't fault them for thinking that relative to their roles as stewards of that legal framework, they shouldn't disrupt that framework in the way that the Nonhuman Rights Project wants them to.

Care and Conclusions

There's much more to be said here; there are many objections and replies to consider. And I am not trying to say that this sounds the death knell for the argument that the Nonhuman Rights Project has been making. Rather, I'm trying to illustrate that animal ethics is not just—or even primarily—animal advocacy. Animal ethics involves doing ethics, and that means being transparent with the people we want to convince. If we can see a better way for them to defend their view, we should lay it out, partially out of respect for them, but also out of a concern to check our own biases. That's what we were doing in the last section. I want a better world for animals, so I'm disposed to accept arguments for conclusions that say we should be helping animals in one way or another. But as I said in the introduction, this isn't a game. There's much at stake. The lives of trillions of animals are in human hands, and our societies are built on the assumption that our interests trump theirs. (Can you even imagine communities rebuilt to respect animals? The changes would be staggering.) For their sake and ours, we need to be careful.

I also said, and still believe, that we need to draw some conclusions, even if only provisional ones. We can't hide behind our carefulness, always deferring until we've considered yet another round of objections and replies. At some point, we've done enough to establish that, whatever the costs, change is in order—whether those changes are in us or in the wider world. And I do think we can draw some conclusions from everything we've explored in this book. Among them, species membership isn't morally important (even if it's legally significant). Animals are being treated wrongly in intensive agriculture. While some animal use may be justified in research contexts, it's harder to justify that use in educational contexts. The standard defenses of zoos are weak. Wild animal suffering makes many issues more complicated. We should be wary of condemning activist strategies that seem extreme to us. And so on.

These may seem like modest results. They aren't. A world that took them seriously would be a far cry from what we see around us. And in any case, as I said before, these results don't mark the end of the discussion. Instead, they are a start on your journey into this field of inquiry. I hope that having read this far, you'll spend more time on the topics we've explored, coming to your own conclusions after further reflection. I hope you'll think about the many animals we couldn't discuss in this book, all of whom are worthy of attention. And though I want you to push hard for animals, I also want you to turn around and question the arguments you've made. For what it's worth, though, my guess is that many arguments against the status quo will survive scrutiny. Its problems are real.

Further Reading

Andrews, Kristin, Gary Comstock, G.K.D. Crozier, Sue Donaldson, Andrew Fenton, Tyler John, L. Syd M. Johnson, Robert Jones, Will Kymlicka, Letitia Meynell, Nathan Nobis, David M. Pena-Guzman, and Jeff Sebo. 2018. *Chimpanzee Rights: The Philosophers' Brief.* London: Routledge

Cupp, R.L. 2015. "Human Responsibility, Not Legal Personhood, for Nonhuman Animals." *Engage* 16(2).

Kittay, Eva Feder. 2005. "At the Margins of Moral Personhood." *Ethics*, 116(1): 100–131.

Wise, Steven M. 2010. "Legal Personhood and the Nonhuman Rights Project." *Animal Law* 17(1).

Note

1. But see: www.nonhumanrights.org/content/uploads/Petition-re-Tommy-Case-Fulton-Cty-NY.pdf

References

Donaldson, Sue, and Will Kymlicka. 2011. *Zoopolis: A Political Theory of Animal Rights.* New York: Oxford University Press.

"The Nonhuman Rights Project, Inc. on behalf of Tommy." *Nonhuman Rights.org.* www.nonhumanrights.org/content/uploads/Petition-re-Tommy-Case-Fulton-Cty-NY.pdf.

Index